Producing Power

Kevin A. Yelvington

PRODUCING POWER

Ethnicity, Gender, and Class in a Caribbean Workplace

TEMPLE UNIVERSITY PRESS | *Philadelphia*

para Bárbara, con amor

Temple University Press, Philadelphia 19122

Published 1995
Printed in the United States of America

♾ The paper used in this book meets the requirements
of the American National Standard for Information Sciences—
Permanence of Paper for Printed Library Materials, ANSI Z39.48-1984

Text design by Arlene Putterman

Library of Congress Cataloging-in-Publication Data
Yelvington, Kevin A., 1960–
Producing power : ethnicity, gender, and class in a Caribbean
workplace / Kevin A. Yelvington.
p. cm.
Includes bibliographical references and index.
ISBN 1-56639-285-3.—ISBN 1-56639-286-1 (pbk.)
1. Power (Social sciences)—Trinidad and Tobago. 2. Women—
Employment—Trinidad and Tobago. 3. Ethnicity—Trinidad and
Tobago. 4. Working class—Trinidad and Tobago. I. Title.
HN246.Z9P69 1995
305.8\00972983—dc20 94-34679

Contents

Tables and Illustrations

TABLES

MAPS

FIGURE

Acknowledgments

THE FIELDWORK on which this book is based (1986–87) was not funded by a grant or fellowship. Like the women workers I write about, I pieced together a little funding here and a little there to help support my work during the long writing stage. I am grateful to the Royal Anthropological Institute for a Radcliffe-Brown award that helped in the writing of an earlier version. In addition, I used part of a grant from the Mellon Foundation and the Latin American and Caribbean Center at Florida International University, which also helped to support another research project of mine, to collect further archival data for this book.

At Florida International University, where I taught from 1990 until 1994, I was assisted by my colleagues in the Department of Sociology and Anthropology and those affiliated with the Latin American and Caribbean Center. I would especially like to thank Stephen M. Fjellman, María Cristina Finlay, Guillermo J. Grenier, Michelle Lamarre, Kathleen Logan, Anthony P. Maingot, Walter Gillis Peacock, René Ramos, John F. Stack, Jr., Richard Tardanico, Mark B. Rosenberg, and John French, who is now at Duke University.

At the University of Sussex, where I was a postgraduate student from 1985 until 1991, I received invaluable assistance and instruction from Richard D. E. Burton, A. L. Epstein, Ralph Grillo, David Harrison, Ann Whitehead, and Donald Wood.

I would also like to acknowledge the assistance given to me by the officials at the Institute for Development Studies library at the University of Sussex. A thank you as well to Calum Turner for all of his encouragement and assistance over the years.

At Temple University Press I have been fortunate to work with Senior Acquisitions Editor Doris B. Braendel, who, besides providing patience and professionalism, has provided good humor and good advice. *Un fuerte abrazo* to Doris. Lots of thanks are also due to Debby Stuart and Henna Remstein for all of their help, and to Jeff Beneke, who copyedited the manuscript with skill and suggested a number of improvements. I would also like to thank anonymous reviewers for the Press. I have tried to incorporate as much as possible of their insightful suggestions. *Gracias* to René Ramos, who prepared the map of the Caribbean, to Maggie Council, who drew the remaining maps and the figure with precision and creativity, to Becky Hembree and Ken Marlewski, who helped produce the figure, to Neill Goslin for his editorial help, and to Richard F. Phillips and the staff of the Latin American Collection of the University of Florida Libraries for their timely assistance with bibliographic materials.

In Trinidad the people to whom I owe gratitude are too numerous to mention. I would like to thank the faculty and officials of the University of the West Indies (UWI) at St. Augustine, including Lloyd Braithwaite, Bridget Brereton, and Patricia Mohammed. I would also like to thank Rabia Ramlogan and Margaret Rouse-Jones of the West Indiana Section of the UWI library for their help and kindness, and I would like to thank the UWI officials for permission to use the library. I would also like to thank Wendy Jones of the United Nations Economic Commission on Latin America and the Caribbean (ECLAC) library.

In Trinidad I also benefited from assistance from Sonia Cuales of ECLAC, Thelma Henderson of the Transport and Industrial Workers Trade Union, Cecil Paul of the Oilfields Workers' Trade Union, Nello Samodee of the Industrial Development Corporation, Marjorie Wilson of the Union of Commercial and Industrial Workers, Clotil Walcott of the National Union of Domestic Employees, and officials of the Industrial Court of Trinidad and Tobago.

I would like to thank Annette Ching for all of her help and advice. Without her and her family—especially Uckleen, Guy, and Mark Chan Poon—my stay in Trinidad and my fieldwork might not have been successful, and it certainly would not have been so pleasant. I would like to thank Roger and Aulrica McFarlane and their lovely family for treating me as one of their own. Thanks for the same reasons are due to Cheryl Ali and Tony Salandy. I would also like to thank the DeGannes family and all the members of Maple Club.

My biggest thanks to those in Trinidad has to be to the workers and owners of the Essential Utensils Ltd. factory, who must remain anonymous, for allowing me to intrude into their public and private lives. I hope some of the results of this research will in some way benefit the workers who are the "subjects" of the study.

Material on the factory appeared earlier in my articles: "Gender and Ethnicity at Work in a Trinidadian Factory," in Janet H. Momsen, ed., *Women and Change in the Caribbean* (Bloomington: Indiana University Press, 1993), pp. 263–77; and "Ethnicity at Work in Trinidad" in Ralph Premdas, ed., *The Enigma of Ethnicity: An Analysis of Race in the Caribbean and the World* (St. Augustine, Trinidad: School of Continuing Studies, University of the West Indies, 1993), pp. 99–122. I am grateful to the publishers for permission to reproduce some of the material here.

Earlier versions of the book were read whole or in part by Ananthakrishnan G. Aiyer, Stephen M. Fjellman, Ralph Grillo, Eric Hanley, David Harrison, Daniel Miller, and Shalini Puri, all of whom suggested ways to improve it. I am grateful for their comments. I would also like to thank John Pulis for pointing out to me important theoretical arguments.

Last, but certainly not least, I would like to thank my wife, Bárbara C. Cruz, for all her loving and emotional and practical support. This book is dedicated to her.

To everyone mentioned here and those I have forgotten, a heartfelt thanks.

Foreword

THE RELEASE of *Producing Power: Ethnicity, Gender, and Class in a Caribbean Workplace* coincides with a significant anniversary: the publication, twenty years ago, of Rayna R. Reiter's edited volume *Toward an Anthropology of Women* (New York: Monthly Review Press, 1975). That book was itself a milestone, a long overdue response to the silence that had previously engulfed women as subjects of research in the social sciences. Reiter's anthology was followed by a rich period of research whose purpose was to uncover the historical and social causes of women's extensive subordination. Feminism infused vitality into the endeavor. At the same time, ideological intensity was often upheld at the expense of theoretical rigor. By the late 1980s, the portrayal of women passively enduring the excesses of patriarchal power was reaching the point of exhaustion. Longings grew for nuanced studies of women as complex participants in the shaping of their own circumstances.

Kevin Yelvington shows how far we have come in our understanding of gender. In this volume, he undertakes an ambitious project: to examine class, race, and gender inequalities as facets of the same unitary structure by contrast to earlier approaches that envisioned capitalism and patriarchy as separate systems. The result is a richly textured analysis which succeeds where others have failed. It would have been easy for the author to depict women as mere victims of patriarchal or capitalist forces operating at the global level but he does nothing of that sort. Instead, he reveals the strains between the intentions of workers and those of employers, between resistance and compliance, between pleasure and alienation. His is a vivid portrayal of women as social agents reconstructing their own feminine identity albeit under the constraints imposed by larger economic and political forces.

Producing Power simultaneously attains three objectives: one is to summarize and combine findings and theoretical knowledge drawn from disparate literatures to create a valuable analytical framework. The reader will find that the first two chapters of this book constitute a superb review of key writings in political economy, neoclassical economics, post-structuralism, and the new international division of labor—to say nothing about feminism. In their own right, those chapters are a precious resource consolidating more than a decade of dense thinking on the subject of gender, class, and race.

The author's second accomplishment is to weave a compelling narrative about women who endure oppression while at the same time reclaiming their dignity. Yelvington contrasts, for example, the experience of older and younger workers in a Trinidadian factory, uncovering a generational cleavage around the concept of reputation. More experienced women constitute self-definitions by contrast to what they perceive to be the flightiness and unreliability of the young. The latter, in turn, seek their own unique identities in counterposition to what they believe to be the superciliousness of older workers. Paradoxically, the constitution of contrasting feminine identities becomes an impediment for collective action on the basis of social class. There are similar and complementary implications with respect to the question of women's solidarity. Class divides gender; gender fragments class. Yelvington's conclusion, that social identities endure because the social relations upon which they are predicated remain unchanged, derives from detailed ethnographic descriptions that underscore the importance of human agency without underrating structural determinants.

The book's third, and perhaps most significant, achievement is to provide a satisfying description of the labor process as a societal institution which becomes a central locus for the creation and contestation of ethnic, class, and gender identities. The author shows how the very definition of women's sexuality interacts with race and social class to shape contradictory practices. Daily life in the factory is formed by transactions between men in positions of comparative power and women in a situation of subordination. Class and gender inequalities, however, are alternatively exposed and concealed through the deployment of metaphors whose meanings are known to both oppressors and oppressed. Workers and bosses alike describe circumstances of pleasure and resentment, trust and suspicion, cooperation and resistance. The affective bonds, finely woven by continuous interaction, between employers and workers are often predicated upon sexual tension, and upon the possibility of intimacy whether real or imagined. The plot thickens as race enters those interactions. Status, respectability, and performance are judged on the basis of the appearance and behavior of workers attempting to resist or manipulate employers at the same time that these seek control over women's productive capacity. What attracts in Yelvington's analysis is his ability to create images of life as it actually happens—with all its drabness, petty rancor, and ambiguity—while at the same time documenting the invisible forces that account for the contradictions.

In the end we come out of the task of reading *Producing Power* with a more profound and less sentimental understanding of working-class women.

Although the setting is the English-speaking Caribbean, the book provides a model for research and analysis whose implications are far reaching.

Studies of gender and development have often been perceived as an endless litany of feminist complaints about the perceived or real abuses of men. This book makes clear, however, that the analysis of gender entails more than that. As Yelvington conducts it, an investigation of gender refines our understanding of economic, political, and ideological phenomena by identifying aspects of the productive system that other concepts are able to explain only in limited ways.

M. Patricia Fernández-Kelly
Research Professor
Department of Sociology
Johns Hopkins University

Producing Power

INTRODUCTION

THE YOUNG WOMAN said, "Nigel coming like a slave driver. And they say slavery days finished. He does say, 'If you stop work today, I have someone else here workin' for me tomorrow.' He knows people want to keep their jobs in these times."

This statement could have come from a historical study of the plantation Caribbean. It could have been said by a recently freed slave, commenting on her overseer's attitude and the harsh conditions that prevailed on the sugar estates after the end of slavery, when many exslaves saw little change in their living conditions to match the change in their legal status. Or it could be from one of the early indentured workers who came to the Caribbean from Asia. Thrown into competition with the exslaves for scarce jobs, they suffered under a system of coerced labor just as cruel and inhuman as plantation slavery.

Yet the statement actually comes from the late 1980s, spoken by a twenty-five-year-old Trinidadian factory worker, the descendent of indentured East Indian workers. Perhaps I took her words more seriously than she intended, but they made me pause, look around the factory, and wonder how much had changed since slavery times. While Trinidad and Tobago is a modern, politically independent nation-state with a parliamentary democracy, it is still possible to see in the factory continuities between that day in 1986 and the defining moments of modern Caribbean history. In the factory, the shop-floor workers are black and East Indian women; during slavery and indenture, women toiled in the sugarcane fields alongside men, performing the same back-breaking manual tasks, while some men (but generally not women) were given occupations plantation owners considered skilled and the workers considered prestigious. In the factory, all the supervisors are men, most of them white, whose authority is established by their formal position within the firm, which is not unrelated to the kinds of authority that "whiteness" commands in society at large. Their authority over the women workers within the factory was exercised by more informal means, including the practice of blatant sexual harassment. During slavery and indenture, white men were employed as overseers on the plantations, many of them using their position to take sexual advantage of women workers. The owners of the factory are white. Nigel and Jane Tiexiera are husband and wife. He is the descendant of Portuguese indentured laborers, while she is part of an elite French Creole family. The factory-floor workers are black and East Indian, and they receive some of the lowest wages in Trinidadian industry. This structure in large part mirrors the ethnic division of labor that prevailed during slavery and indenture. In the factory, the workers earn such poor wages that they are forced to enter what is called the "informal" economic sector to make ends meet, earning money on the side sewing, minding their neighbors' children, and growing fruits and vegetables for their households and for sale. During slavery and indenture, the planters "allowed" their slaves and indentured workers to grow and even sell provisions from their own kitchen gardens. While this gave a certain freedom to slaves and indentured workers, it effectively subsidized the planters, who were thus relieved of some of their obligation to provide for their workers' upkeep.

Because of these historical continuities, this book departs significantly from the many studies of women's work in factories that have taken as their point of departure situations in which women factory workers are introduced suddenly to capitalism's industrial discipline, as capitalistic firms (usually foreign-owned) locate in "underdeveloped" and isolated regions of the Third World, sometimes recruiting women workers from the countryside (for reviews, see Warren and Bourque 1991; Ong 1991; Zavella 1991). In these studies, ethnographers have tied local situations to the effects of changes in the organization of industrial production worldwide, such as the incorporation—and the general exploitation—of women as factory workers (e.g., Bookman 1988; Cavendish 1982; Freeman 1993a; Grenier 1988; Kondo 1990; Lamphere 1987; Ong 1987, 1991; Pollert 1981; Wajcman 1983; Westwood 1984; Zavella 1988). This is part of a process that has seen many multinational enterprises locating their labor-intensive production centers in developing countries in order to cut costs, especially in wages (Elson and Pearson 1980, 1984). Many of these offshore industries are located in export processing zones (EPZs) in developing areas.

By contrast, women have been involved in almost every stage of Caribbean industrial production, from the very first days of European expansion to the present. Thus, the study of women in the Caribbean diverges significantly from conventional approaches to "women in development" because women's involvement in the work force has been central to women's lives since the days of forced migration, slavery, indenture, and the plantation system. As Joycelin Massiah writes, "Women in the Caribbean have always worked" (1986: 177). Women have always been active in a number of occupations (e.g., Mathurin 1974; Reddock 1994), most visibly in trading activities (e.g.,

Durant-González 1976; Katzin 1959, 1960; McKay 1993; Mintz 1971). This has no doubt contributed to their relative economic autonomy from men (cf. Safa 1986). These are the defining historical processes that distinguish the study of women in modern industrialization (e.g., Abraham-van der Mark 1983; Bolles 1983, 1985; Freeman 1993a; Kelly 1986, 1987; Pearson 1993; Safa 1990, 1995; Yelvington 1990a, 1990b, 1993c, 1993d).

María Patricia Fernández-Kelly in her study of the *maquiladoras* of the Mexico-United States border argues, "It is necessary to investigate the meaning of 'cheap labor' in concrete circumstances" (1983:3). This book is about the social relations of female and male factory workers in a factory operated by Essential Utensils Ltd. (EUL) in Trinidad, West Indies. The factory is a small, locally owned firm producing household durable goods for the local market and for export. About 80 percent of the line workers are women. Although the factory contrasts with the general trend in that it is locally owned, it owes its creation to the "industrialization-by-invitation" economic-development strategies devised by the colonial government in the 1950s and continued after independence in 1962. These strategies seek to invite foreign capital to locate manufacturing in Trinidad. Thus, the factory is linked to international capitalism in certain historical ways.

This study is the result of participant-observation fieldwork undertaken from July 1986 to July 1987. It explores the social relations of the factory workers and traces how ethnicity, class, and gender permeate those relations. Using an approach that draws from a number of academic disciplines, I place my subjects within Trinidadian history by specifying a historical context distinguished by the hegemonic forces of a colonial and neocolonial division of labor. Among other factors, I follow the development of the state; the cultural construction of ethnicity, class, and gender; and economic dependency.

In the factory a division of labor exists along gender and ethnic lines as well. The owners are white. Five of the eight line supervisors are white men; the rest are East Indian men. Nearly all the line workers are black and East Indian women, with a few young male line workers.

I argue that gender and ethnicity are integral elements of the class structure, not merely adjuncts to it. This is because ethnicity, class, and gender are determining and determined in the way the production process is ordered. At the same time, the production process becomes a site where the meanings of ethnicity, class, and gender are constructed, contested, and consented to. Here, in accord with the logic of how capitalism reproduces itself, in contests waged to control the production process. In describing the social relations of the owners, managers, and workers in the factory, I try to show how a number of social and economic forces impinge on and affect these relations. As I outline the relationships within the factory itself, I provide data on the workers' extrafactory relations. This allows me to analyze the "survival strategies" of workers in the context of economic marginalization and show that there is an interdependency among workers in the struggle to obtain scarce resources.

My goals in the factory study are to describe the social relations of the workers and to show how ethnicity, class, and gender are implicated in those relationships.[1] It is the main thesis of this book that power and production are intimately bound up with each other and that we cannot understand the creation and contestation of such significant social identities as ethnicity, class, and gender without also understanding the material productive arrangements of the specific context. The process described in this book is best characterized as a dialectical one in which such social identities constitute and determine the nature of the production process—including recruiting certain kinds of workers to strategic places in the process—while, in another historical moment, these identities are themselves complexly determined outcomes of production. I examine how such identities are produced by looking at how power is exercised in the everyday life of the factory workers.

Theoretical Antecedents

While most contemporary anthropologists agree that the social identities of ethnicity, class, and gender are socially and culturally constructed, often they are unable to specify the mechanisms by and through which these constructions take place. In this book, I point to the labor process a primary locus for the creation and contestation of these identities. I see the book arising out of recent developments in anthropology that emphasize an approach to "practice" and "reproduction" theory (Ortner 1984: 144–57), as well as history and political economy (e.g., Roseberry 1988, 1989). I both draw on and significantly depart from the ideas of such thinkers as Karl Marx, Michel Foucault, Pierre Bourdieu, Anthony Giddens, and Eric R. Wolf.

While my theoretical approach derives from and is in many ways similar to Bourdieu's "theory of practice" (1977) and Giddens's "theory of structuration" (1984), there are nevertheless important areas of difference in our approaches. Giddens and Bourdieu begin with a criticism of theories that explain behavior with reference to face-to-face interaction without taking into consideration the constraining power of social structures. At the same time, they are critical of theories that attribute causation to the workings of "structure" or "culture" without reference to the intentional, conscious agency of humans. For instance, in explicating his theory of structuration, Giddens refers to the "duality of structure": "Structuration, as the reproduction of practices, refers abstractly to the dynamic process whereby structures come into being. By the 'duality of structures' I mean that social structures are both constituted 'by' human agency, and yet at the same time are the very 'medium' of this constitution" (1979:121).[2] This view has been criticized, however, by the philosopher Roy Bhaskar, among others: "It is because the social structure is always a *given*, from the perspective of intentional human agency, that I prefer to talk of reproduction and transformation rather than of structuration as Giddens does (although I believe our concepts are very close). For me 'structuration' still retains voluntaristic connotations—social practice is always, so to speak, *restructuration*. . . . I am inclined to give structures (conceived as transfactually efficacious) a stronger ontological grounding and to place more emphasis on the *pre*-existence of social forms" (Bhaskar 1983:84, 85).

Indeed, the theories of Giddens and Bourdieu have been criticized for a tendency toward "static reproductionism" (e.g., Gose 1988) and "behavioralistic conditioning" (e.g., Gell 1985) and toward precluding the possibility of historical change because they conflate ideational and material aspects of culture and social structure. This "central conflation," as Margaret S. Archer (1982, 1985, 1988) puts it, leads to theories that downplay the prior, historical existence of social structure and culture. Underemphasized in these theories is the role of human agency in creating human history. As R. W. Connell writes, "Reproduction analysis, to put it in the most general way, is based methodologically on a bracketing of history which, unless the most strenuous efforts are made to prevent it, must suppress the agency of people in creating history, in creating the very structures whose reproduction is being examined" (1983:148). Further, Connell suggests: "Dualist models, then, need an opening toward history. The crucial point is that practice, while presupposing structure in much the sense Bourdieu and Giddens explain, is always responding to a *situation*. . . . Practice is the transformation of that situation in a particular direction. To describe structure is to specify what it is in the situation that constrains the play of practice. Since the consequence of practice is a transformed situation which is the object of new practice, 'structure' specifies the way practice (over time) constrains practice" (1987:95).

In order not to reproduce these errors, I develop an approach that unites history, culture, structure and agency. First, I conceptualize relations between the ethnographic context and the larger structures that affect the subjects of the ethnography, especially in terms of the causal mechanisms that underlie the subjects' relative power. Second, I conceive of the activities that take place inside the factory in terms of structure and agency and the transformation of historical situations. Thus, the subjects are not reduced to "bearers" of the properties of the structures within which they operate. The historical evidence will allow us to understand these wider processes as they relate to the ethnography. I want to look at one causal mechanism as a key determining force—the production process and the way in which it is culturally and structurally organized.

To show how this process works out in the factory, I refer to the wider historical context. In depicting social identities, I concentrate on what the workers and other Trinidadians seem to regard as the relevant and most encompassing social identities, and the ways they define the nature of those identities. Yet I go beyond "folk models" that tend to be too ensconced in interested social action to offer adequate explanatory purchase. For me, the interpretive privilege of the anthropologist must be retained, despite what seems to be the threat posed to this position by the recent trend of "postmodern" anthropology. Those identified with postmodern anthropology have rightfully drawn our attention to the power differentials involved in depicting the cultural "other" and to the need to present multivocal texts. But in so doing, they are in danger of reducing the anthropological narrative to the anthropologist's personal confessional. It is not elitist to tilt against such a stance. For if it gains predominance, the politically aware anthropological project is dead.

In this book I am concerned with the culture of domination in the factory, and in Trinidadian society in general, and how cultural features and attributes are used in the exercise of power and resistance to it. The domination I describe is for the most part insidious, hidden, and contorted, and the actors are not necessarily consciously aware of the full extent of its workings. Thus an anthropology based solely on the subjective views of the actors—especially in the context of domination based on ethnicity, gender, and class—might actually serve to perpetuate and reinforce that domination.

Doing Fieldwork

This book arises out of a doctoral thesis in social anthropology at the University of Sussex (Yelvington 1990a). When I went to Trinidad I spent time looking for a suitable factory in which to carry out my fieldwork. Through personal contacts, I visited a couple of factories. One was unsuitable for my purposes, and the officials of the other factory did not think it would be a good idea if I carried out a year-long study in theirs. Then, through a friend who works for a government-owned firm with connections in the private sector, I arranged to meet Nigel Tiexiera, the owner of Essential Utensils Ltd.

Our first meeting was held in a conference room at his factory. I had prepared a short research summary and had dropped it off for him to read. He had not read it. He asked me what I wanted to do and for how long I wanted to do it. Then he asked me some sharp questions in a very brusque manner. "What are your personal politics like?" he wanted to know, "because I tell yuh, when I was in college I was very liberal, but now, I'm very conservative." I told him that while I vote Democratic in U.S. elections, I do not consider myself to be "on the left" (which is not true—my personal politics are of "the left").

He then asked me, gruffly, "Do you want to know what my workers think, or do you want to tell them what to think?" I assured him that I was interested only in what the workers think, and throughout the fieldwork I maintained this promise. However, I was also honest with the workers to the extent that I told them of my promise to Tiexiera, and I always answered their questions honestly regarding what I thought about conditions in the factory and wages and about other general topics of conversation. It was a tightrope I was walking, and I believe I did so fairly well.

In the meeting with Tiexiera, I told him that for methodological reasons I wanted to work alongside the workers and that I did not expect any pay. It is possible that the prospect of having two free hands around the factory clinched it, because when I phoned back the next day Tiexiera gave me permission to do my fieldwork there. I still feel fortunate and am very grateful to him.

My next hurdle was winning the confidence of the workers. At first they thought I was a new supervisor. Although somewhat younger (I was twenty-five years old when the fieldwork began) than the other supervisors, I suppose they thought that I, as a white male, resembled most of the other supervisors. They even thought I was some sort of "spy" for Tiexiera, who has a bad temper and whom they believed capable of all sorts of tricks. The following is from my field notes two weeks into the study: "The workers are suspicious of me. It seems unfortunate that I have arrived at a time when Tiexiera is out of the country—they may think that I'm minding them until he gets back. They think him capable of all sorts of things." But this is why anthropologists spend long periods doing participant observation fieldwork—not only so that they can know their subjects better but so that their subjects can know them better.

In the first two weeks I spent my time working alongside the workers and introducing myself to them during break times. I told them exactly what I was doing: that I was a student from the United States at a university in England, that I was interested in the situation of female workers in the Caribbean, that I was interested in Trinidadian culture. I told them that I was going to work in the factory for a year without being paid in order to do research for my doctoral thesis. I told them I wanted to know what they thought about all sorts of things. I told them that I was going to use pseudonyms for them (which I let them choose) and for the factory when I wrote about them. In this book, I have tried to be true to their thoughts and words to the extent that statements are recorded verbatim, as close as possible to Trinidadian dialect.

During the fieldwork, I tried to immerse myself in the factory and extrafactory lives of the workers. I was invited by some workers to weddings, to a Spiritual Baptist church, to Carnival, to Hosein celebrations, to Hindu and Orisha "prayers," to christenings, to cricket matches, to Christmas celebrations, to parties and to beach *limes*,[3] to mention a few extrafactory events. And I occasionally invited some of the workers to come over to the room I was renting to "*lime* by me."

That I earned the workers' trust is evidenced by some of their comments in the ethnography and in some private information that they shared with me that I have not written down, including topics ranging from birth control to family squabbles. I still correspond with some of them.

About This Book

The data and the arguments are arranged as follows. In Chapter 1, I outline my theoretical approach to the ethnography and develop my "resource theory of power," which conceives of power in its relational, structural, definitional, historical, and cultural manifestations. I then relate power to the construction of social identities with my "practice theory of social identities." Concentrating on ethnicity, class, and gender, I propose ways in which these phenomena arise from and inform the production process in the context of capitalism and its reproduction. I regard these two theoretical moves to be the major original anthropological contributions of the book. Chapters 2 and 3 situate the factory historically and in the orbit of local and international divisions of labor. I provide data on the kinds of wider forces that influence the daily lives of the workers, supervisors, and owners. Chapter 2 contains a discussion of the history of women workers in Trinidad, the role of the state in promulgating development plans, and the nature of the local and international economies. The ethnography begins in Chapter 3, where I describe the point of production, the work force, and the daily routine of work in the factory.

The main body of the ethnography is contained in Chapters 4, 5, and 6, which disaggregate the roles that ethnicity, class, and gender play at work in the factory. The book concludes with a discussion of how we might conceive of the relations between ethnicity, class, and gender and how these identities articulate with power. The ethnography shows that social action occurs under the conscious "banners" of ethnicity, class, and gender, and "as concrete social relations, they are enmeshed in each other and the particular intersections involved produce specific effects" (Anthias and Yuval-Davis 1983:63). Ethnicity, class, and gender are socially constructed in relation to each other. However, they are not, as some theorists imply, separate but equal variables that modify each other with equal weight. Thus the relation between these constructs occurs in specific ways.

In many ways, this book arises from the Marxian tradition. I take a dialectical approach to the construction of forms of power and forms of identity. I also endeavor to show how culture is historically "made," and how it entails forms of consciousness and identity that both presuppose a given mode of production and are the product of that mode of production.

Chapter 1

ETHNICITY, GENDER, CLASS, AND THE POLITICS OF POWER

There are many ways of looking at the world, there are many ways of exploring reality. Anybody who believes that he holds the truth, and the whole truth, about any given reality, or because he has a bundle of statistics in his hand, that he knows more than a poet, a novelist, a visionary who does not hold the statistics, is a fool.
—Carlos Fuentes

THIS PARTICULAR Thursday appears to be a day like any other in the factory. The Caribbean sun beats down on the corrugated *galvanize* metal roof and the din of the many small and large electric fans used to catch any breeze blowing through the open windows almost drowns out the whirring and screeching of the many machines that drive the production process. The movement of hot air caused by the fans almost makes working in the heat bearable; it almost, but not quite, dries the sweat on our bodies. Perhaps, I think, if the workers placed the fans in one direction, in a coordinated movement, the hot air would be expelled and we could find relief. Other times I think that the oppressive heat will prevail no matter what the workers do.

In the hot, stifling air inside the factory, smells become more acute and suffocating. In one part of the factory, there are large machines that produce plastic parts from pellets made of resin. When these are in operation, the odor of freshly molded plastic floods the factory, overpowering the smells that prevail in other departments of the production process. In one department, solder is a prevalent scent, punctuated by the smell of burned flesh or hair when one of the workers accidentally touches the hot soldering irons. In another department, glue is the prevailing smell; in another, grease.

Inside the factory, the styles of fashion vary somewhat. The younger workers favor a casual, sporty look. Jeans are the normal attire for most young men and women, although on occasion some young women wear skirts. The older women almost without exception wear dresses, often ones they have made at home or have paid a kinswoman, close friend, or fellow factory worker to make. Their dresses are covered by gray, cotton aprons. Many wear their hair in kerchiefs. Vera, an unmarried forty-five-year-old worker, wears nice slacks or dresses to the factory, clearly overdressing, according to the other workers. Her style resembles that of the women office workers in downtown Port-of-Spain. It is rumored by the other workers that she insinuates to her neighbors that she has a more prestigious office job in town, not a factory job. The male supervisors dress in jeans and casual work clothes. A couple of them wear mechanics' overalls.

While the production process at the Essential Utensils Ltd. (EUL) factory does not feature the same sights, sounds, and smells as the sugar production that sustained the Caribbean economy for more than 400 years, it nevertheless has a number of things in common with plantation work. Seasonal variations in production are very important. In the few weeks prior to this Thursday, the factory had been increasing its output of household appliances to meet the demands of the Christmas season.

Another parallel to the plantation regime is that the owners are not above employing coercion to secure increased production. One such technique in the EUL factory is forcing the workers to work overtime. On this particular Thursday, Nigel Tiexiera came out of his air-conditioned office onto the factory floor and announced to some of the supervisors that some of the workers would have to work extra time today in order to meet increased demand. There is little the workers can do when they are forced to work overtime. Tiexiera has on more than one occasion told members of his nonunionized work force that if they do not comply they will be fired. So most of the workers stayed after the normal 4:30 P.M. quitting time. The two workers who said they would not or could not stay were called into the office and warned that they might face dismissal.

At lunchtime the next day, the youngest of the supervisors, thirty-year-old Winston, called the workers around the table in his department, which is on the second floor of the factory and away from most of the noise of the main factory floor. He told them that, because the company had an order for Puerto Rico that had to be shipped the following Wednesday, they would also have to work on Saturday. There were loud complaints from the workers, who had had to work overtime on several occasions during the previous few weeks. In response, Winston, an East Indian with a moustache, dressed in khaki trousers and a Hawaiian print short-sleeved shirt, tried to evoke some sympathy from the workers by observing that Tiexiera was pressuring him too: "Look, I know what you all going to say, but we have no choice and I wish you could help me out."

Susan, a young black woman, exclaimed, "Ha! Tiexiera don't care about we."

Cokie, also young and black, agreed. She wears jeans, and her hair is "Jherri curled" (that is, treated to produce wet, loose curls). She said, "And when it have no work, he the first to jump up and say 'send they home!' "

Winston replied, "But these are difficult times out there."

Then, Denise, a thirty-five-year-old black woman, who is one of the fewer older women to wear jeans regularly and who seems to influence many of the younger women, said, referring to the country's post-oil-boom economic crisis, "He always usin' the excuse of the Recession, but [pointing to an addition to the factory that was being constructed at the time] look out dere—that big buildin' goin' up, the big buildin' he have going up. Like, he ent feel the Recession like the rest of we."

Winston started to appeal to Denise as a sort of "ringleader," but Margarita jumped in: "But Winston, *he send us home* when it have no wuk."

"Look," Winston said, "on Wednesday we didn't have no components and I went ahead and didn't send you home and had you make up parts. Now I'm just askin' for help."

But Cokie objected to his excuses: "You had no right without talking to we."

The workers started mumbling among themselves, but their discussion was cut off when the lunch bell rang. They disbursed slowly, still talking about the developments.

At lunch, Carla, an unmarried twenty-four-year-old East Indian who lives at home with her mother and siblings, went to talk to the workers in some of the production departments downstairs. Many of these are black women in their thirties and forties who have much in common with each other. Many are neighbors and attend the same churches, and almost all have children. Many eat lunch together on the benches in front of the factory. They had also been "asked" to work on Saturday, but for only half a day. They were told that they would receive a flat rate of $12 (Trinidad and Tobago, or TT)—about U.S. $3.35—for two and a half hours of work. This was a slight incentive for many workers, some of whom were paid as little as TT$2.75—about U.S. $0.75—an hour. When they arrived at work the next day, they learned that on Saturday they would receive only "time and a half," based on their regular hourly pay. Thus, workers making TT$2.75 an hour were to earn TT$10.32 for two and a half hours of Saturday work.

Carla began to try to organize collective resistance, emphasizing that Tiexiera "can't fire all de departments." Val, a stocky twenty-nine-year-old black mother of two, who was pregnant with her third child, disagreed loudly, arguing that Carla had to think of people with "responsibilities," that "times are hard," and that this was not the right time for collective action. Val's comments provoked a negative response among the other downstairs workers.

Feeling defeated, Carla went back upstairs and joined Myra, a thirty-three-year-old black woman with two children, who was eating her boxed lunch purchased from a nearby snack bar. When Carla began telling Myra what happened, Myra looked away and kept eating.

Later, Carla said to me, "I went down to talk to dem at lunch and dey still listenin' to dat Val. She still have control over dem. She bawlin' 'Times hard.' " In private, Myra told me that she would work on Saturday. "My husband retrenched," she said, shrugging her shoulders.

In a fury, Carla then went into the office, saying that she was going to get a list of the prices of EUL's products because she wanted to "publish what going on in a letter to the newspaper." She said to me and other workers, "I don't know what hold Val have on they. She hearin' me and she bawl out loud 'Oh Gaaaawd'—one set of nigger chupidness [i.e., stupidness]. She sayin' 'She ent even have one chile yet and she know what best for we' and 'She too young to have responsibility to see about a family' and ting. She have a real big mout. She just bawl the loudest and they listen. It like they don't want to lift theyselves up. They been workin' here for so long. I leaving in July when I married. I don't care."

Carla went back upstairs and read her horoscope in the newspaper. It said "Don't be afraid to look after your own interests." "That's it then," she said, determined. Thinking about the overwhelming alignment of forces against her—the owners, other workers—she tried to justify her efforts to improve conditions for herself and her fellow workers. "But it just that I care what happen. And don't forget, it have my sister workin' here too."

As the workday ends on Friday, the workers file out of the factory and through its gates, where, according to company policy, each of them have their handbags checked by the security guard. They head for the main road, where they will catch route taxis or *maxi taxis* (privately owned minibuses) for the trip home. They discuss the recent developments in hushed tones. Many, like Carla, are frustrated that the workers "just can't seem to come together," as one whispered, to take collective action. In their minds they are quickly reorganizing their schedules for Saturday, wondering how they will do the shopping and cleaning, and what relative or neighbor they can ask to look after their children while they are working. They await the morning with anxiety and trepidation.

Producing Power

This incident typifies the interplay of the forces of power and production at EUL, which I try to capture in the title phrase *Producing Power*. "Producing *power*" refers to working through the intricacies of domination and subordination, autonomy and dependency, causation and stasis. With an emphasis on production and process, this view sees power not as a state to be reached but as something wielded, something exercised. Social identities such as ethnicity, class, and gender are implicated in this process through their symbolization in the factory.

But I also mean "*producing* power," in the sense that power is derived from the formal economic process of producing commodities, where acquiring and wielding control of the production process provides a means of realizing power. Here, although the ethnography concentrates on the relations of production at the factory level, I mean economic production in a wider sense than is usually assumed. By use of not only ethnographic but historical and political-economic data, and by showing how wider cultural, political, and economic forces impinge on the culture of the workplace (and not necessarily the reverse), I take account of a number of activities in what are sometimes referred to as formal sector, informal sector, household labor, and other forms of economic activity as well as noneconomic activities that link up with and are integral to the economic domain.

We cannot discuss the concept of power without referring to the recent work of writers, mainly historians and anthropologists, who have documented the "hidden" struggles of disempowered groups—be they proletarians, peasants, women, or ethnic minorities—in specific historical contexts (e.g., Scott 1985). Besides fundamentally altering our understanding of social life, this work on "resistance" has questioned the assumptions of the "established social order" upon which the staples of social-science theory are based. By highlighting hierarchy and domination, the rejection of top-imposed cultural orthodoxy and hegemony, and the development of viable alternative "cultures" by the disenfranchised, these scholars have challenged traditional theoretical schools and injected a potentially progressive political mission into scholarship. This book in many ways fits into that literature and is inspired by it, but here I also seek to specify the contingencies of historical situations that serve to circumscribe uses of power and the resistance to it. In other words, in addition to depicting struggle and resistance on the part of disempowered groups and individuals, I feel the need to point to the processes and structures that tend to maintain the advantages of the powerful.

Before we return to the factory floor, however, I need to define what I mean by power. I have learned a great deal about conceptualizing power from the philosophical discussions of Jeffrey Isaac (1987), Henry Krips (1990), and Thomas E. Wartenberg (1990), as well as from sociologists such as Giddens (1984) and Steven Lukes (1974). While my project has anthropological antecedents (e.g., Adams 1970, 1975; Fogelson and Adams 1977), I begin my discussion with the ideas of Foucault (1978, 1979, 1982) because many anthropologists have recently incorporated his work into their own ways of thinking about power and resistance (for distinct views, see, e.g., Abu-Lughod 1990; Cowan 1990).

Foucault is concerned with the acts of power behind the establishment and enforcement of certain social and cultural categories. Locating power in this way is one of the most important concerns of this book. For Foucault, power and the resistance to it are seen in reciprocal relation. By the same token, resistance, like power, is transparent, intended, and local, while at the same time it is dispersed, unintentional, and global. Foucault's analysis of power and resistance, as well as the one I advocate here, begins with a structural—and hence relational—perspective. "Power is exercised, rather than possessed; it is not the 'privilege,' acquired or preserved, of the dominant class, but the overall effect of its strategic positions—an effect that is manifested and sometimes extended by the position of those who are dominated" (Foucault 1979:16, quoted in Cowan 1990:15). Besides emphasizing the ubiquity of power (and thus resistance), Foucault suggests that the effects of the exercise of power (and thus resistance) are historically contingent and that similar exercises of power on the part of a dominant group produces different effects in different contexts.

My approach to the anthropology of power builds on Foucault but is somewhat different. In his analyses, Foucault tends to take the categories of the subject as givens in that he concentrates on the power involved in establishing categories of the subject and pays relatively little attention to how, once established, these very categories are themselves contested.[1] These differences become more apparent with my definitions of ethnicity, class, and gender below. Here, however, I want to emphasize that an anthropological perspective allows us to see how and under what conditions categories of the subject are reproduced and contested, transformed and held constant, and how this activity is the result of a complex interplay of material conditions and ideational forces.

This leads me to the second difference between my approach and Foucault's, which has to do with the *basis* upon which an individual or group is able to exercise power in a certain domain against others. I argue that we need to specify by what means the subjectors are able to establish their subjections. Whereas Foucault is little concerned with the means by which subjects are inserted into particular places within a given social setting and the material consequences of this placement, I specify the ways in which, and the degrees to which, the exercise of power—including the power to "subject," in Foucault's sense—in the factory is determined by one's labor and one's relation to the means of production. In other words, I want to establish, where Foucault does not, the relationships between the control over productive arrangements, which are culturally defined, and the control over cultural categories that constitute these arrangements and presuppose them.

The corrective to Foucault's formulation begins with an emphasis on the contingent nature of power. Thus, what is required "is a sustained discussion of the nature of, and conditions for, autonomy (and its relation to social determination)" (Lukes 1974:34). However, the concept of resources as "the media whereby power is employed" (Giddens 1982:38) not only implies that all social actors have capacities to dominate and resist but also allows us to analyze the effects of power and the *means by which* power is exercised, which, again, are themselves contingent. David Harvey argues that "those who define the material practices, forms, and meanings of money, time, or space fix certain basic rules of the social game" (1989:226). Here, money, time, and space become resources in the sense in which I use the term. In addition, this concept also forces us to tie certain abilities (and liabilities) to certain structural arrangements and, in an anthropological sense, to certain human beings and their location within certain social structures. As Dorinne K. Kondo writes, based on her study of gender relations in a Japanese factory, "Within the factory, meaning and power are coextensive; this intertwining of meaning and power creates sets of institutions and disciplinary practices: from the structure of the company, to the designation of the people who work there as different kinds of selves—*shachō*, artisans, part-timers, to everyday interactions. . . . Power/meaning *creates* selves at the workplace, and consequently, no one can be 'without' power" (1990:221). Kondo means " 'without' power" in two senses: in the sense of "lacking," as in nobody lacks power, and in the sense of being outside of, for the workers, managers, and owners in the Satō factory "can never escape to a romantic place beyond power" (1990:224). Hence, the creation of "selves" out of the intertwining of meaning and power suggests that "resources" such as ethnic, class, and gender identity come to be constructed in just this way.

Here I want to propose an anthropological definition of power, which, as such, entails material and ideational aspects of culture and is grounded in particular productive and historical relations. Specifying the latter insures that we will not see power as some universal object for, as Peter Rigby argues, power is "an essentially historical phenomenon and hence cannot be the basis of any general theory of transformation" (1992:38). What is needed is a conception of power that is general enough to encompass personal and institutional power, as well as a conception of power that is specific enough to encompass the local causes, effects, and forms of power. I claim that power is a determined causal property achieved through means of resources that are hierararchically distributed. More specifically, my resource theory of power is one that allows us to see power in the following dimensions, which, while interrelated, are not of the same kind: Power is relational, structural, definitional, historical, and cultural.

The Dimensions of Power

By *relational*, I mean that power is relative to complementary entities, where increments in power in one entity may tend to decrease power in others affected by the first. At the same time, still others may or may not be affected by the increases or decreases in relative power flowing to, or away from, those in question. Thus, power is manifested in relationships of power, not as an abstract entity. All actors, then, have certain capacities to act, which are relative to the capacities of others. What needs specification are the kinds of entities and their properties, be they gendered individuals or national economies in the world economic system.

In the factory, as we will see, there is a constant tug-of-war over issues relative to the successful wielding of power. As seen in the ethnographic vignette at the beginning of this chapter, one tug-of-war is over production. The theme is familiar—owners and management try to increase employee output, which workers resist. In Marxian terms, this represents the attempt by the capitalist to increase the rate of surplus value. Let's take a hypothetical outcome based on the situation described above. If the workers were to achieve their ends, they would reduce the power of the owners in more than one respect. Most profoundly, by diminishing the amount of products the owners have available to sell, the amount of profit accruing to the owners would be diminished (because the owners' wage bill would remain the same), and, given the affinities between control over economic resources and power, the owners' power would tend to be diminished in the long run because their control partially rests on their ability to expropriate profits in the form of surplus value—a power that is backed up by the legal apparatus of the state.

If the workers were successful, there would be implications. Limiting output without a rise in wages might not directly increase the power of, say, the families of the workers, except that many would now have a mother that was slightly less tired when she arrived home from the factory at the end of the day. If the workers continued to be successful at diminishing the economic power of the owners in this way, the result might be the closing of the factory, which may or may not further the ends of the workers.

The larger point is that power is relational in two senses. First, in that power is derived from scarce resources (e.g., time, money, commodities) where the control over these resources by a social entity (an individual, a group, a class) is based on relations between the entity and the resources. Second, power is relational in that it exists in relationships (of power) between such social entities.

Closely linked to the relational dimension of power is the *structural* one. By structure I mean the historical pattern of ongoing social relationships and the hierarchy associated with it. Structure is the result of human activity, but it stands partially independent from the individuals and from the activity it constrains and governs. Thus, structure is the precondition for the reproduction or transformation of structures themselves. Further, structure is the very condition for intentional acts of human agency. Power, then, is structural in the sense that it derives from humans who occupy positions in the social structure, although it is exercised through the media of social resources. This principle reminds us that power and relations of power are not only the result of intentional action but that nonintentional activity also tends to reproduce power relations. This perspective grounds the factory workers, managers, and owners in relationally situated positions within the factory production process and accounts for the effects of the structure that assigns different kinds of people to different occupational statuses.

But this perspective also emphasizes the wider network of structures that locate the various statuses in the factory in Trinidadian society and beyond. With this last point in mind, it is possible to see how the social structure of the wider society buttresses for some, and undercuts for others, the ability to exercise power within the factory. The owners, for example, count on a whole economic, ideological, and state apparatus to shore up their power over the workers by defining their role in the productive process. This apparatus is one that is derived from the colonial "industrialization-by-invitation" development strategy. This strategy, which is discussed in detail in Chapter 2, was designed primarily to provide incentives to attract and protect foreign companies. Even though they are locally based, the EUL owners are able to take full advantage of the incentives offered by this program, including tax holidays and duty-free importation of most raw materials and inputs, as well as government-built factory structures for which they are charged at low costs. Further, Trinidadian history has shown the state's willingness to impose limitations on the rights and mobility of organized labor, from the passage of the 1965 Industrial Stabilisation Act (see Parris 1976), to the passage of the 1972 Industrial Relations Act (see Okpaluba 1975), to the removal, during my fieldwork, of a number of rights and benefits from employees in the large state sector (see Yelvington 1987, 1991b).

Differing significantly from Foucault, this structural perspective of power maintains that power is implicated in the ways in which structures are created in the first place. In addition, it suggests an investigation that ties individuals' relations to the production process to the kinds of power they are able to utilize through the media of social resources. By "production process," here I mean the process responsible for the production of resources, be it the production of commodities under capitalism or the production of religious knowledge in a noncapitalist social order.

Power is determined by who actually occupies certain structural positions, but power is also involved in who may occupy these positions in the first place. Thus, power is *definitional*. It is so in two ways. One is in the ways in which institutional rules are explicitly set and codified. This is definitional power in an explicit mode. It is exemplified in the workings of bureaucracy where hierarchy is specified, as are the channels through which power is designed to flow. In the factory, power is exercised by the owners to set, institutionalize, and legitimize the formal rules of the work and the employer-worker relationship, including the time and duration of the working day, the amount of time for lunch and breaks, hourly wages, forms of payment, maternity leave, vacation time, punitive action for absences and indiscipline, and so on. Of course, in the context of the Trinidad and Tobago state, the owners are not completely free to set these rules. However, they have some success at flouting the law, which, depending on the influence of the owners and the disposition of state authorities, is not always genuinely enforced.

The imposition of formal rules by the owners is contested by the workers in practices that, while called "informal," nevertheless become routinized and institutionalized. As in the incident reported above, workers can resist attempts to impose a new set of formal rules—those having to do with the number and length of working days and payment. The workers resisted by referring to other formal rules, either those that exist in the factory or that exist in the country's labor laws. They referred to what they claim are universal "rights" for workers and for women, and, in some cases, actively resisted by withdrawing their labor or purposely working slower and thus producing less. Power and resistance, then, revolve around the definitions of what constitutes the formal and the informal.

Power is manifested by the effects of specific attempts at domination and by exercises that define the social situation, that erect the "taken for grantedness" of cultural meanings that is present in all social situations. Power is definitional in this sense too. This notion of "taken for grantedness" is the essence of Bourdieu's concept of *doxa*, which is the whole complex of undiscussed social and cultural practices (1977:164–71). *Doxa* is always, however, contested. What emerges from *doxa* is a complex of discourse and practices that aim at becoming "defended orthodoxy or confrontational heterodoxy" (Weismantel 1988:17). In the factory, the everyday life proceeds with a number of notions of the meanings of ethnic, class, and gender identity that are at one level undiscussed but at another re-made and contested in certain situations.

One way in which definitional power is manifested is control over context, which enables the construction of a "taken for grantedness." While this might appear to occur in a setting like a factory, control over context is achieved by ruling groups in wider contexts. In his important interpretive analysis of Walt Disney World and its place in American culture, Stephen M. Fjellman identifies a process he calls "decontextualization" that he uses to analyze the way in which "Distory," or the world and history according to the Disney Corporation, is asserted at the amusement park: "If the meaning of things is found in their relations to contexts, then one way to gain control over these meanings is to capture the contexts. By doing so one can sever meanings from their previous environments and leave them hanging or separate, or one can reinsert them into new contexts. To manage either of these pieces of sleight of hand is to change the conceptual resources available to people" (1992:31).

Besides power struggles over the meanings associated with the factory context, there are struggles over the meanings of the factory contents; that is, the content of the identities of the owners, supervisors, and workers, where, in a dialectial process, these definitions create and enable relations of power. The ethnic and gendered division of labor in the factory is partially the result of certain meanings attributed to "black," "white," and "East Indian" identity in Trinidad, as well as meanings attributed to "man" and "woman" and "poor" and "rich." The meanings of these identities and their differential relationship to labor and the production process are historically a key site of discursive conflict. Yet the factory owners and workers often refer to colonially derived stereotypes to "make sense" of their world. Definitional power is manifest in the factory by and through the processes of inventing and establishing the "taken for grantedness" of these identities and how they, in turn, distribute power.

Power is *historical* because relations of power are always dynamic and grounded in specific contexts. Even supposed transhistorical entities such as capitalism and relations of economic dependency on the part of the Third World need to be grounded in historical relations. This is not to reduce theory to historical particularism. It is precisely a call to understand the relations between relatively continuous and relatively specific factors that limit the claims of our social theories. A theory of power is no exception. Thus, the temporal dimension of power is crucial for understanding power as part of a process.

A whole host of historical trajectories situate the wielding of power in the factory context. These will be analyzed in the next chapter. Foremost among them are the structural relations between local and international economies and thc position of the factory within this nexus. These contemporary relations, of course, are built on the historical structures established during the colonial era due to the dictates of colonial labor schemes, first slavery and then indentured labor. Implicated in these processes are the historical forces that account for the construction of categories of identity. Relations between capital and labor, between men and women, between ethnic identities, and between sectors of the local and world economies and the nature of Caribbean capitalism are the relations of real people located in real historical currents and locales. As Nicholas Thomas (1989) suggests, anthropology must integrate history on a par with culture and structure into its theorizing. Power relations, like culture and structure, are reproduced, but only as the result of individuals and groups responding to some prior state of affairs.

Perhaps this is to say that power is *cultural*. That is, relations of power are not only signified in certain ways but, as Wolf argues, relations of power are internal to symbolization and signification (1990:593). People experience the exercise of power—and the exercise of power against them—in cultural terms. That is, if culture is defined by routinized practices and a system of symbols and meanings, then the exercise of power is "felt" by and through its effects on practices, symbols, and meanings.

Arguing that power is cultural entails a perspective that locates but does not equate power within a whole cultural field. This perspective locates power in people's conceptions of it. It takes seriously the power of discourse and it identifies the actors, their interests, their ideology, and their systems of meanings behind the establishment of discourses. Further, a cultural perspective on power entails attention to practice that is based on emotion, which is also culturally coded, as Lisa Douglass argues in her study of the role of "sentiment" among the Jamaican family elite (1992:267). All of this is to say, then, that a cultural perspective on power insists that systems of signification and meaning are *made*, and, thus, that culture is historical (cf. Gose 1988:118). Systems of signification and meaning are modified through practice, and practice, in turn, incorporates relations of power.

Identities, and the meanings associated with them, are constructed in the context of power relations. Elsewhere I refer to a "symbolic universe," which refers to the complex system of signs, their referents, and meanings that become established to connote identity. In the process of establishing and then elaborating or limiting a given symbolic universe, symbols of identity become the contested terrain of intergroup struggle, and more powerful groups find it easier to establish their own representations of themselves and of competing others: "Symbols are available to be interpreted: however, not just any symbol and not just any interpretation. The availability of certain symbols and of a certain symbolic universe is determined (though not in any simple or complete way) by the groups who hold political-economic power and those who are able to legitimate this power and the prestige that accompanies it (usually—but not always—these groups are one and the same) and it is contested by the subordinate groups. This is the conjunction of political-economic and symbolic resources" (Yelvington 1993b:10). In other words, through struggles over a certain symbolic universe, power relations are contested and reproduced. Identities become reified and objectified in this process. These power struggles are organized around questions of meaning.

This process occurs in the context of "struggle," which is not to say that dominant cultural orders are always and everywhere contested by the dominated. This situation is the result of the effects and effectiveness of cultural power, in which, in erecting a "taken for grantedness" (which is never complete), alternatives are denied, ignored, or go unnoticed. Further, and as a result, subordinate groups often are seen to uphold the very systems that subordinate them. Often, though, resistance is effected through the disempowered's making use of subordination, as we will see later.

The theory of power elaborated here is an attempt to articulate for anthropology Raymond Williams's (1977) ideas of hegemony (see, e.g., Roseberry 1989:45–49; Weismantel 1988:34–37n.13), although I place "hegemonic power" in more of a structural context than Williams would allow. For Williams, "A lived hegemony is always a process. It is not, except analytically, a system or a structure. It is a realized complex of experiences, relationships, and activities, with specific and changing pressures and limits. . . . [It is] a whole body of practices and expectations over the whole of living, the shaping perceptions of ourselves and our world . . . [which] does not just passively exist as a form of dominance. It has continually to be renewed, recreated, defended and modified. It is also continually resisted, limited, altered, challenged by pressures not all its own" (1977:110). Hegemony, according to Williams, is necessarily incomplete. It must be constantly reasserted and it is constantly resisted. It is also not expressed or expressible in "directly political forms" or as "direct or effective coercion," but rather as a "complex interlocking of political forms." Thus, hegemonic power is not "naked" power, but encompasses cultural relations. But despite the ubiquity of power, its effects are never total nor complete. If, as Kondo argues in her study of gender relations in a Japanese factory, "Multiplicities, tensions, and layerings of meaning undercut simple resistance at every turn," and the act of resistance itself "is riven with ironies and contradictions," this is because the "matrices of power and meaning are open-ended, with room for play, subversion, and change" (1990:221, 224).

The concept of hegemony exhibits Williams's insistence on the "indissoluble unity" of material reality and consciousness (Merrill 1978–1979) and a complex web of determination, where "Determination of [a] whole kind—a complex and interrelated process of limits and pressures—is in the whole social process itself and nowhere else: not in an abstracted 'mode of production' nor in an abstracted 'psychology.' " The concept of hegemony as formulated by Williams implies the workings of macro systems of "not only the conscious system of ideas and beliefs but the whole lived social process as practically organized by specific and dominant meanings and values" (1977:87, 109)

Some anthropologists, such as William Roseberry (1989), have employed the concept of hegemony in describing wider historical and political porcesses, while others, such as Aiwha Ong (1987) and Jane K. Cowan (1990), use hegemony specifically to characterize gender and class relations. As John D. Kelly argues, though, we should not equate "hegemony" with "culture" (1990:55–56). My use of the concept of hegemony in the factory context encompasses multiple determinations of ethnicity, class, and gender similar to M. J. Weismantel's (1988) discussion of the culture of domination in relation to these relations of power in the Ecuadorian Andes. Rather than conceive of hegemony as an already established state of affairs, I analyze the rise and imposition of hegemonic forces—achieved through culture—and the rise and resistance of counterhegemonic forces, which are also achieved through culture. Thus, the concept of hegemony has utility for the factory study because it will be necessary to analyze the ways in which ethnicity, class, and gender interrelate with power and are constructed and contested with reference to material as well as ideational processes, within the factory and beyond.

Producing Identities

Power is exercised by people—and against others—in the name of identity, and thus difference. This is not to equate difference with power, nor to argue that the establishment of power follows from the establishment of difference. It is to argue, in contrast, that difference, and the meanings associated with it, is established in the context of power relations. I am suggesting, in other words, that we look at the ability to establish difference and, once established, at how these constructions of identity inform power relations by becoming a site for the contestation of power. In order to account for how the social identities of ethnicity, class, and gender are created and contested in the context of power relations in the factory, I elaborate my practice theory of social identity.

My definitions of ethnicity, class, and gender arise from the ethnography and my reading of Trinidadian history, as well as from comparative anthropology. Ethnicity, class, and gender are social phenomena that have a number of attributes, including emotional, conscious, behavioral, and structural referents. In this book, I will emphasize the conscious aspect of ethnic, class, and gender "identity." But identity cannot be seen as divorced from the network of social relations. Further, identities of all sorts are constructed in relation to the constructions of others (see Thomas 1992). Thus, I shall be emphasizing "social identities," constitutive by and constitutive of practice.

Trindad's historical development justifies the analysis and definition of ethnicity, class, and gender because the society has been stratified along ethnic, class, and gender lines. I focus on ethnicity, class, and gender because they are totalizing identities. By this I mean that in Trinidad it is conceived that everyone must "have" an ethnicity, a class, and a gender, even though, from an anthropological perspective, the exact meanings of these social identities are relatively open to change and reinterpretation according to the situation. In the definitions of the terms and concepts that follow, I employ an approach that first utilizes emic terms and concepts. But I analyze how these emic terms are used and I analyze their functions in the logic of Trinidadian society generally and the factory setting specifically. Emic terms thus lead to etic definitions. For example, in the case of Trinidad it might be argued that one's sense of class identity is not as overt and pronounced as in industrial countries, but is refracted through other aspects of identity, most notably through ethnicity. This, however, does not diminish the salience of class in the objective or subjective senses. We are forced to look at local languages and conceptualizations of class in local terms.

Ethnicity, class, and gender are oppositional identities as well. By this I mean that one type of identity cannot exist without the existence of a counterpart identity that itself cannot be equated with the first one. In the course of social action, these properties act in complex interaction, but it is further useful to separate them for purposes of analysis. As Douglass writes regarding the nexus of color, class, and gender in the Jamaican social order, "As analytic categories, the hierarchies of gender, color, and class may be separated for heuristic purposes, but in social practice they operate in concert" (1992:11).

I will analyze ethnicity, class, and gender in their manifestations as "social identities." These phenomena are also "cultural identities," because they derive from the workings of cultural practice and meanings. Thus, they do not acquire the same meanings in every cultural system. "Identity" is a complex process involving "inner" *and* "social" manifestations. There exists a dynamic and dialectical process between the formation and patrolling of boundaries between identities, on the one hand, and what can be called the content of those identities on the other. I emphasize the concept of social identities here to underscore their social origins.

In his psychological studies of identity, Erik H. Erikson emphasizes the importance of the ontological security provided by routinized activities in early childhood for identity formation, Routinized, predictable practices provide "a rudimentary sense of ego identity which depends . . . on the recognition that there is an inner population of remembered and anticipated sensations and images which are firmly correlated with the outer population of familiar and predictable things and people" (1964:247).

The "outer population of familiar and predictable things" in this sense can include both other social identities and the social identities of others. While the social informs the personal, the personal cannot be seen without the social. A similar view is offered by Joan W. Scott, who advocates a strategy of historicizing identity and, in so doing, decentering it and calling for an analysis of its production. This strategy "calls into question the autonomy and stability of any particular identity as it claims to define and interpret a subject's existence" (1992:16) which, counterintuitively, allows us to see identities (and thus difference) as intertwined, relational, and hierarchical. This leads us to the understanding that "identities are historically conferred, that this conferral is ambiguous (though it works precisely and necessarily by imposing a false clarity), that subjects are produced through multiple identifications, some of which become politically salient for a time in certain contexts" (1992:19).

In elaborating a similar theory of social identities, I begin with Gerard Duveen's and Barbara B. Lloyd's (1986) use of Emile Durkheim's notion of social representations to explain social identities. For Durkheim, *représentations collectives* expresses the way a particular group conceives itself in its relations with the things that affect it (Lukes 1973:6). Social representations are related to social identity in that "social identities reflect individuals' efforts to situate themselves in their societies in relation to the social representations of their societies" (Duveen and Lloyd 1986:220).

Social identities represent real constraints and enablement for individuals. These identities are social in that individuals are "related to society through their participation in soical groups defined by gender, age, social class, etc., and within the social representations of these systems particular 'individual-society interfaces' are defined" (Duveen and Lloyd 1986:221). This approach is suited to an analysis of relations of ethnicity, class, and gender in that individual identity cannot be thought of as independent of the social context. Through interaction and communication with others, by the use of symbols, an individual acquires an identity or conception of the self. But that identity is incomprehensible apart from the particular context that gave rise to it and by which it is maintained. As Duveen and Lloyd state, "Membership in particular social categories provides individuals with both a social location and a value relative to other social categorized individuals. These are among the basic prerequisites for participation in social life, and can be described as social identities" (1986:221). The concept of social identities, therefore, places these identities squarely within the nexus of practices, systems of meaning, and power relations.

In my writings on ethnicity in Trinidad elsewhere (e.g., Yelvington 1990a, 1990b, 1993b, 1993c, 1993d; see also the contributors to Yelvington 1993a), I have defined ethnicity as a particular "involuntary" social identity seen in relation to a socially constructed ultimate ancestral link between an individual and a named group, which has presumed to have shared ancestors and a common culture. By "involuntary" I mean that ethnicity in emic terms is taken to be fixed and immutable (see Ching 1985), even though emphasis or deemphasis of one's ethnic identity is seen as possible. This belief in common ancestry obtains because of a socialization process (albeit an incomplete one) that takes place within group parameters. Ethnicity is characterized by cultural processes that mark boundaries between distinct groups. This boundary-making processs is a dual one, with an "internal" boundary established by intragroup activities such as socialization and an "external" boundary becoming established through the process of intergroup relations (Isajiw 1974). Both processes act on each other and account for social change. The subjective identification ethnicity entails is not arbitrary nor purely imaginary. It is characterized by what Annette M. T. Ching (1985), writing on Trinidad, called the "social construction of primordiality." This social construction can be seen as an "invented tradition" (Hobsbawm 1983; Hobsbawm and Ranger 1983; Sollors 1989). The kinds of symbols associated with ethnicity tend to euphemize sameness of birth through metaphors of blood, heredity, and bodily essence. People of the same ethnic identity see each other, not exactly as kin, but as "possible kin" (Yelvington 1991a:165–68).

As Daniel A. Segal (1993) argues, the concept of ethnicity is played out in Trinidad under the rubric of the colonial term "race," where it is presumed that "races" exist independently of their invention. As he points out, while groupings termed "races" are really contingent, this contingency is precisely what is obscured then they are called "races" and, as such, they are handed down as "facts." Thus, the "discourse of race," promulgated in popular wisdom and perpetrated by academic declarations (see Wade 1993), both organizes social relations and determines our understanding of them (Segal 1993:81). While "race" is referred to in the factory, I prefer the term "ethnicity" as an analytic concept to note that this phenomenon is not some absolute or fixed entity existing independently of the way we act and think about it. Rather, ethnic identity is the result of human activity and systems of meaning. As with all aspects of human culture, communicating ethnicity depends on the use of symbols.[2]

It is clear, though, that in emic terms individuals in many settings can and do make distinctions between "race" and "ethnicity" as well. For example, those identifying themselves as "German Americans" and "Anglo-Americans" in the United States may agree that they share "racial" similarities but argue that they are "ethnically" different (Conzen 1989). The same may hold for "African Americans" and "black" Caribbean migrants in Miami (Stepick 1992:60–69).

People in Trinidad generally use the term "race." "Race," then is, an emic term of description. Some Trinidadians have also begun to use the term "ethnicity," but when they have they have called up the images of immutable biological origin associated with "race." "Ethnicity," then, *as a term*, is both emic and etic. However, because "race" is based not on biological fact but on the construction of reality, and because the notion of ethnicity usually implies this social and cultural construction, I prefer to subsume the notion of "race" under the rubric of ethnicity for purposes of analysis. In this way identity—with all that it entails—can be seen as contingent and changing, depending on culture, history, and relations of power.

Conceptions of gender in the factory revolve around supposed biological "givens" about male and female. Most social scientists have sought to differentiate between "sex" and "gender." Ann Whitehead (1979:10) writes, "In brief, sex is the province of biology while gender is the province of social science. A corollary is that gender relations, as social constructs, are historically specific forms that relations take between women and men in a given society." Whitehead suggests that gender, per se, can only be seen in relation to gender relations, where conflict is often emphasized. As we shall see in the factory ethnography, gender relations are often conflictual and revolve around conceptions of sexuality. Whereas sexuality is conceptually distinct from gender, the focus on sexuality in the factory indicates the cultural ways in which gender identity is attributed to sex, (supposed) reproductive functions, and, thus, located in immutable biological "facts."

Instead of seeing gender as either biological or social in origin, John Archer and Barbara B. Lloyd point out that the "very identification of an individual as male or female depends on a complex attribution process," with attribution—to categories such as male or female, masculine or feminine—being derived from social criteria. Gender, they argue, "is attributed to us on the basis of a variety of behavioral and bodily cues" (1985:17, 18). These "bodily cues," that is, the presumed role played by biology, are cultural, as are notions of the role biology plays in gender differences. As Sherry B. Ortner and Harriet Whitehead note, "some cultures claim than male-female differences are almost entirely biologically grounded, whereas others give biological differences, or supposed biological differences, very little emphasis" (1981:1). An anthropological definition of gender must be one that conceives of gender as a particular identity and cultural construct where social characteristics of individuals and groups of supposed "like" individuals are attributed to assumed biological facts having to do with their role in the reproduction of the species. Here, individuals are assigned to exclusive categories of "male" and "female," and maleness and femaleness are given normative content within which particular individuals are placed on an evaluative scale as to how they approximate these norms in practice.[3]

The people in the EUL factory experience their class position in cultural terms. They refer to their places within the relations of production as workers, supervisors, or owners. But, as we shall see, the workers also refer to themselves as black women, as Indian women, and so on, and express their conceptions of the problematic and contradictory relations between capital and labor in these terms. For the women workers, it is their sense that they are, in fact, incorporated into the labor process with reference to their "need" to work, given their economic status as well as their status and responsibilities as mothers. When asked why the majority of workers at EUL are women, the women workers say that Nigel Tiexiera (their ire is usually directed to him and not his wife and co-owner) realizes that low-wage work and women's employment go hand in hand, that he takes advantage of the fact that, as women with household responsibilities, they will, in desperation, take almost any work that is offered. They further point out that this sense of desperation is heavily conditioned by the "Recession," their term for the post-oil-boom economic "bust," a crisis that saw up to 25 percent unemployment during the year I did fieldwork in (1986–87). Many of the workers' menfolk were among the ranks of the unemployed.

The supervisors, all of whom are men, tend to explain their position as supervisors of an almost all-female work force by indicating the need for "strong" supervision. By this they mean the kind of "guidance" and "discipline" that a man can provide, especially, they argue, in a context where women do not easily submit to the requirements of factory production, typified by a disciplined labor force. They see the younger women especially as needing vigilant control, and, in fact, this "vigilance" is manifested in incidents of sexual harassment that tend to keep the women workers somewhat in check. Ironically, though, the supervisors also complain about their treatment by the owners and do not identify completely with the aims of the owners.

The owners themselves do not see—or look for—just "workers" when they hire labor. Nigel Tiexiera indicated to me on more than one occasion that he preferred to hire women for factory jobs because women are more appropriate for tedious and repetitive tasks due to their "natural" talent and patience with household tasks such as sewing and cooking. This rationalization is widely shared by world-market factory owners that employ women workers. He also indicated that he preferred to hire younger women who would not be absent from work because of familial responsibilities. Jane Tiexiera saw the factory as providing a social service by hiring women. She told me that money in the hands of women would be "well spent" on household goods and on children.

The workers' sense of the ethnic hierarchy is generated from an understanding of colonial history and the privileges and liabilities accruing to different ethnic identities. Black workers frequently refer to the slavery past and East Indian workers sometimes refer to the conditions of indenture to explain why they are forced to sell their labor not just to capitalists but to white capitalists in Trinidad. The Tiexieras definitely sought to incorporate workers differently according to ethnicity. One cannot help but conclude that the arrangement between floor supervisors and workers was purposeful; that the social distance between white and East Indian male supervisors and an almost entirely female work force that is three-quarters black and one-quarter East Indian was part of a strategy carefully cultivated to prevent supervisor-worker collusion and ensure maximum productivity.

Nigel Tiexiera explained that East Indians were preferred as workers over blacks. While this may have accounted for decisions to hire individual East Indian workers over black applicants, the entire work force doesn't reflect this attitude, given the fact that the factory is located in an area where blacks are a majority. Tiexiera's attitude, nonetheless, recapitulates ethnic stereotypes that can be traced to the mid-1800s and planter justifications of the indenture system and the attributes of East Indians as a certain "kind" of people (as ascribed by the planters and colonial officials) who were replacing another kind of people, that is, Africans, who were only a few years earlier thought to be the only kind suited to slavery and sugar plantation labor.

Conceptions of class in Trinidad are often articulated by reference to individual behavior and comportment. Supposed improper behavior and an incomplete command over cultural resources such as literacy and aesthetic taste will often draw the disparaging epithet *low class*, which is defined in *Cote ce Cote la*, a dictionary of Trinidadian dialect words, as "Rowdy, vulgar. Prone to display qualities that show lack of good taste or breeding" (Mendes 1986:90). Even if individuals have a lack of "breeding," they are rewarded for not displaying it. Thus, individuals can mitigate to an extent ascribed attributes with "proper" behavior. By the same token, though, if people do possess "breeding" but do not display proper behavior, they are usually roundly criticized. In the factory, the workers criticize Tiexiera for behavior not befitting someone of his "position" or "kind."

These notions of class are used by the powerful to veil racism. For example, there have been a number of charges of racism leveled at managers of trendy nightclubs and discos, such as Power Station and Genesis, located in two shopping malls in the Port-of-Spain suburbs. Regarding Power Station, an article in a popular working class newspaper reported that "It was alleged that some dark-coloured people were denied entry . . . and ferocious security dogs were almost set on them." The article goes on to quote Andrew Ferreira, the nightclub's manager, saying "It's a blatant lie." The article continues: "Ferreira said the main criteria for entrance into the spanking new club was proper dress. Sneakers and hoods are out, he stressed. 'The only thing that we ask for is a decently behaved crowd, which is required to stick to the dress code,' Ferreira said. 'As far as discrimination goes, that's madness,' he added" (*TnT Mirror*, March 19, 1993, p. 28). The truth of the allegations regarding this incident is almost beside the point. The fact that a popular newspaper would make these charges reveals that such incidents (while no doubt having a basis in empirical fact) register as true or likely to be true for Trinidadians. The wider theoretical point is that, in Trinidad, class is conditioned by personal attributes such as ethnicity, personal conduct, or manners, and these attributes are, in turn, also mitigated by class.

Class, then, is often conceived in terms of individual attributes seen, momentarily at least, as distinct from any *necessary* involvement with the production process. How can we make sense of this process where individuals experience class not only in ethnic and gender terms but with reference to cultural forms, and where ethnicity and gender, among other factors, structure objective class relations? Given the workers' experiences of class, which includes such "cultural" variables as ethnicity, gender, comportment, and command of cultural resources, it is clear that a concept of class such as that of classical Marxism, which identifies one's class position simply as one's "relation to the means of production," is inadequate for empirical or theoretical explanation. Moreover, it does not do justice to the ways in which Trinidadians themselves construct the categories of class.

Frank Parkin (1979) proposes an alternative to the traditional Marxian concept of class in order to take into account historical situations where such factors as ethnicity and gender determine access to economic class and power. I adopt some of Parkin's concepts in an attempt to provide a cultural analysis of class in Trinidadian society. Central to Parkin's notions of class is the concept of closure, "the process by which social collectivities seek to maximize rewards by restricting access to resources and opportunities to a limited scale of individuals" (1979:44). Max Weber used the term closure to refer to a process whereby one group monopolizes advantages by closing opportunities to another group, with "material monopolies" providing the most effective, but not the only, means and motives (Weber 1968:935). Power is central to this concept, since the power of the owners of the means of production allows them to monopolize opportunities in the market. This monopolization may be based on various criteria, such as ethnicity, gender, credentials, language, and religion.

In extending Weber's ideas, Parkin conceives of two reciprocal modes of closure, "exclusion" and "usurpation." Exclusion and usurpation differ in the kinds of closure being affected. Exclusionary closure is in a "downward" direction, as an advantaged group might undertake in order to secure its advantages by closing off avenues of opportunities to subordinate groups. In contrast, usurpationary closure is the exercise of power in an "upward" direction by a subordinate group in order to win some of the resources of the superordinate group. This theoretical move enlarges on the restricted Marxian concept of exploitation to include all exclusion practices through which one group enhances its rewards by closing off opportunities to others, whether the basis of exclusion be property ownership, credentials, or ethnicity, regardless of the official legitimation (see Murphy 1986:23).

The relation of closure to class consciousness may be problematic, but power and symbolization must be separated and the interplay analyzed. The class position of a group can be defined as more than just the group's relation to the means of production. In addition, we must take into account the mode of closure that members of the group practice to maintain or improve their situation in relation to other such defined groups. We must also take into consideration their class social identity, which may be indicated by their restrictive behavior or by their identification with others of the same or similar position. Thus, we have a definition that does not reduce class consciousness, closure, and consumption to economic relations.

The concept of closure seems fitting in the Trinidadian situation, where class is a complex cultural phenomenon. Parkin enlarges the Marxian concept of exploitation to include various kinds of exclusionary practices whereby one group denies opportunities to others based on a number of criteria. The criteria on which groups base their class practices can be distinguished. "Collective exclusion" is exclusion based on a group attribute—often ethnicity or gender, but also behavior and manners—and "individualist exclusion" is based on property and credentials. Using collective criteria, the Caribbean elites are adept at restricting the opportunity of the masses by not only controlling property laws and access to the means of production, but by restricting access to other resources, such as education.

Closure theory can account for the positioning of groups in a society, but there are problems with Parkin's version. These were pointed out in a searching critique by Raymond Murphy (1986). Parkin conceives of two opposite types of closure, exclusion and usurpation, and he maintains that the dominant class uses exclusion and the subordinate class uses usurpation. Murphy shows, however, that instead of being mutually exclusive, exclusion and usurpation—both of which can also involve the withdrawal of capital, labor, and services by either side—can be practiced at the same time by the same group (1986:31). For example, we can conceive of a subordinate group excluding another subordinate group while at the same time trying gain some of the privileges of the dominant group. Further, closure theory can explain how something is done but not *why* it is done. This may be corrected if we keep in mind the social identities of individuals and the noneconomic motivations they often induce.

However, closure theory also needs to be "grounded" in some sort of relation to production or to the relations of production. Parkin's theories are not inimical to an approach that emphasizes the causal power of production, despite his satirical treatment of academic Marxism and his misunderstanding of neo-Marxist approaches (cf. Solomos 1986). Indeed, as one critic has noted, "the usefulness of the notion of social closure lies not in its ability to replace the framework of Political Economy but in the ease with which it can be incorporated by it" (Mackenzie 1980:584).

Yet, these possibilities have been underdeveloped. A first step would be to specify what it is that is capitalistic about closure. Parkin's conception seems to be too general in this regard. But, as the ethnography shows, closure along "cultural" lines is integral to the ways in which capitalism is able to find ways to reproduce itself and appropriate surplus value. At the same time, this tendency is culturally resisted by the workers along "cultural" lines as well.

The problems of incorporating "cultural" and "objective" approaches to class are widespread in anthropology. For example, Edward LiPuma and Sarah Keene Meltzoff argue that Spanish ethnography is characterized by a separation of "cultural" and "objective" (defined as the relation to the means of production) approaches to class, which they relate to "a form of thought shaped by capitalism" (1989:328). "Indeed," as Peter Gose argues, "the separation of 'communicative' from 'instrumental' action in recent cultural theory reflects all too closely the mental/manual division of labor within contemporary capitalist society, and cannot help but take on an ideological tone as a result" (1988:105).

LiPuma and Meltzoff suggest that "anthropology must reconceptualize the relation between class and social structures by finding a way to transcend the opposition between culture and production and examine their intrinsic connection" (1989:317). They locate the connections in the dual character of labor and in the labor process, locating the intrinsic relationships between cultural concepts of class and the process of production. By looking at class in this way, they urge, we can determine the cultural criteria of class membership (such as education or wealth) and the relation to the production process (for example, as landholder or laborer) (1989:318).

In arguing that the relations of class and culture are not exogenous and external but mutually constitutive, LiPuma and Meltzoff (1989:318–19) utilize Bourdieu's (1977, 1984, 1986 [1983], 1991) notions of capital, which extend beyond the purely economic connotations of the term. For Bourdieu, there are four forms of capital: economic capital, or productive property (money and material objects that can be used to produce goods and services); social capital, or positions and relations in groups or social networks; cultural capital, or life-style, tastes, skills, educational qualifications, and linguistic styles; and symbolic capital, or the use of symbols to legitimate the possession of varying levels and configurations of economic, social, and cultural capital (see Jenkins 1992:85). The overall class structure represents the total amount of capital (of all kinds) possessed by various groups, with those that possess relatively more dominating those that possess relatively less. Much class conflict revolves around the marshaling of symbols into ideologies that make a certain congelation of resources (such as capital in its various forms) legitimate. My use of the term "capital"—as opposed to, say, "status"—is justified because I use it to describe the relations of a complex capitalist society.

To adapt this scheme in analyzing the factory context, the concept of social capital must encompass the role of ethnicity and gender in establishing class relationships. For Bourdieu, "Social capital is the aggregate of the actual or potential resources which are linked to possession of a durable network of more or less institutionalized relationships of mutual acquaintance and recognition—or in other words, to membership in a group—which provides each of its members with the backing of the collectively-owned capital, a credential which entitles them to credit, in the various senses of the word" (1986 [1983]:248). Bourdieu has in mind a number of groups, from kinship groups to social clubs, which have criteria for membership and institutionalized rites of incorporation. By contrast, ethnicity and gender are what I call "embodied social capital." I use the term "embodied" because the social capital of ethnicity and gender is marked on the individual's body. This is not to say that embodied social capital is not attributed by virtue of individuals' membership in ethnic groups, for example, or in being "male," a relation of relative similarity to others deemed "males" and dissimilarity to others deemed "females." Embodied social capital is relatively static, fixed, and unchangeable. This contrasts to what I call "generalized social capital," which includes the social networks and kinship groups that Bourdieu has in mind, all of which (including kinship) have incorporation rites. Embodied social capital and generalized social capital are modified by and through other kinds of capital, "although it is relatively irreducible to the economic and cultural capital possessed by a given agent" (Bourdieu 1966 [1983]:249).

Certain configurations of embodied social capital, then, both facilitate and preclude the acquisition of other kinds of capital, including other kinds of social capital, embodied or generalized. This theory, then, does not portray the distinct phenomena of ethnicity and gender as coequal variables but, in contrast, establishes their distinction and their articulation with other forms of capital. It also provides a way to analyze the articulation of capitals as they come into play in a historical situation that gives them life.

LiPuma and Meltzoff propose that we analyze class as the intersections of the forms of capital (economic, cultural, social, and symbolic), the distribution of which determines the nature of class and class structure in a given setting: "The argument is that the class statuses are the product of the way in which a community objectifies patterns of correspondence between economic, social, and cultural capital. . . . From this standpoint, what we call class status is the objectification of these capital forms within the objective structure simultaneously determined by the capitalist production processes and cultural traditions" (1989:323, 322).

This view has important implications for the analysis of historical processes in Trinidad as well as for the factory ethnography. For one thing, this perspective reveals what is "Trinidadian" about class in the factory by incorporating a view encompassing the historical trajectories of the different kinds of capital in the formation of the society's class structure. This leads me to a view of class structure that does not resemble a layer cake with individuals and groups assigned unambiguously to discrete places and identities (perhaps by their relations to the means of production) but instead to a view of class structure that allows for crosscutting alliances, class fractions, and cultural differences within classes.

Class in the factory is experienced, assigned, and determined (and determining) in a number of ways, depending on the amount and configuration of the forms of an individual's capital. Yet these forms are distinct, and their convertability—that is, the convertability of the kinds of capital—on various "markets" is not straightforward and, in fact, much social struggle and contradiction over their convertability in the factory and in Trinidadian society in general revolves around this issue.

For our purposes, then, class can be defined as an identity based on a cultural understanding of one's capital resources and the mode of closure one habitually employs within the objective structure provided by capitalism as a totalizing cultural system. The coalescence of economic capital, social capital (in its generalized and embodied states), cultural capital, and symbolic capital is determinative and determined by closure. Closure both encompasses acts of actual exclusion or usurpation—that is, exploitation—and becomes a principle means of struggling over the convertability of capital and the symbolic moves to legitimate the configuration and value of the capital possessed by various individuals and groups.

Theoretically, the relationship between class and power is contingent. We will see the nature of this relationship below, however, when we look at one definitive element of capitalism, the labor process. The labor process in capitalism locates, defines, utilizes, and reproduces distributions of class. Yet, the category "labor" is not unproblematic. In developing a cultural approach to capitalism, Kelly identifies two basic operations in what he calls the "grammar of capitalism"—"objectification" and "uniscalar valuation." "Capitalism," he writes, "is a world of objects, an ontological field created by agents capable of discerning the discrete and objective character of the most complex, fluid and even immaterial phenomena," where "the objects so discerned in the ontological field of capitalism are measurable against one another on a single, quantifiable scale—uniscalar valuation." The movements involved in objectification and uniscalar valuation are integral to the creation of one of the forms that constitute capitalism, the "commodity." Commodity value, according to Kelly, "enables (and later requires) a particular evaluative perspective toward worldly forms, the object it creates. The grammar of capitalism makes it possible to enquire into the value of any thing. Histories of capitalist practice then make it necessary" (1992:102–3).

Histories of capitalism involve the increasing power of "commoditization" to define the ontological field of capitalism. As Kelly writes: "Historics of commoditization involve the reconfiguration of many substances, events, and relation into things with objective value and then into commodities transacted for their objective value. . . . Most critical to histories of commoditization is commoditization of labor, the creation of objects in a class called labor with a value comparable to other commodity values. These labor commodities are objectifications of human activity, put onto markets, bought, and sold with the same currency used to transact other commodities" (1992:103).

It is possible to take issue with Kelly's argument against Marx and others for seeing labor in all of the activities of human beings, even the activities of those in noncapitalist societies (see 1992:104, 105). Kelly urges us to see the relationship between labor and commoditization not as the commoditization of an already existing form (i.e., labor) but of human activity into different labor forms. But this view is based on the assumption that labor can only be commoditized under capitalism, which is perhaps a historically untenable proposition because labor was commodified throughout human history even in the absence of formal capitalism. But this does not invalidate Kelly's important point that we must not conceive of labor as a universal, and thus ahistorical, human attribute and capacity, but we must historicize its existence and role.

Further, Kelly's use of Georg Simmel (1978) to criticize Marx's labor theory of value as a "money theory of labor" (Kelly 1992:105) may be technically misplaced, as others have sought to reinterpret, rejuvenate, and reestablish the validity of at least some of Marx's ideas in this connection (e.g., Cohen 1979, 1983; Holmstrom 1983; Wartenberg 1985). For example, the reformulation by Herbert Gintis and Samuel Bowles makes the theory "valuable" (pun intended) for our purposes:

> We may characterize the labor theory of value as *the theory of the articulation of practices at the site of capitalist production*. Thus we sharply distinguish ourselves from those who would present the labor theory of value as a theory of price, of exchange, or even of profit, though each of these must be encompassed by any viable theory of value. The labor theory of value, by focussing on the contingent nature of surplus-value, bids us analyse those technical, political, and cultural mechanisms within the site of capitalist production that allow such a surplus to arise and be reproduced. It treats the production process not as purely technical, but a political structure within which the domination of capital is a condition of existence of profits, and as a cultural structure geared toward reproducing the forms of bonding and fragmentation on which the political dominance of capital depends. (1981:4)

While not wanting to discard the labor theory of value, I want to extend the discussion by proposing a way of analyzing the way one commodity—labor—acquires value and is commodified and how this relates to the various kinds of exploitation (see Warren 1993), including the extraction of surplus value, in a capitalist context. The classical Marxian labor theory of value states that the value of a commodity is the quantity of abstract labor socially necessary to produce the commodity (see Wartenberg 1985:257). Yet this says nothing about the value of one special kind of commodity, labor.

Marx argues that the value of a particular commodity is not generated by the labor of a specific individual but that the value of commodities needs to be measured in terms of a social average of production times of individual laborers, that is, a property of the social class of laborers (see Wartenberg 1985:256–69). As Marx writes in volume 1 of *Capital*, "let us remember that commodities possess an objective character as values only in so far as they are all expression of an identical social substance, human labor, that their objective character as values is therefore purely social" (1976 [1867]:138–39, quoted in Wartenberg 1985:257). In developing his notion of "abstract labor" as it applies to capitalism, Marx levels or equalizes the various forms of labor and treats all labor as exchangeable for money and thus interchangeable. Indeed, treating labor as "abstract" (as in "abstracted from") is necessary in Marx's labor theory of value, where the product of labor "has already been transformed in our hands. . . . [It is no] longer the product of the labour of the joiner, the mason or the spinner, or of any other particular kind of productive labour. . . . The different form[s] of concrete labour . . . can no longer be distinguished, but are all together reduced to the same kind of labour, human labour in the abstract" (Marx 1967 [1867]:38, quoted in Gintis and Bowles 1981:8).

On the other hand, one could argue that there are places in Marx's work where he seems to acknowledge differences between workers: "As capital, the *value* of the worker varies according to supply and demand, and his *physical existence*, his *life*, was and is considered as a supply of goods, similar to any other goods. The worker produces capital and capital produces him. Thus he produces himself, and man as a *worker*, as a *commodity*, is the product of the whole process." But in the next breath, he says, "Man is simply a *worker*, and as a worker his human qualities only exist for the sale of capital which is *alien* to him" (1961 [1844]:110).

The notion of abstract labor has made its way into ethnographies, from both the etic (or observer's) and emic (or subject's) perspective. For example, Paul Willis, in his classic study of the "lads," working-class male adolescents in the English industrial Midlands, and their transition from school to workplace, argues that

> It is indeed the case that what is common to all wage-labour work is more important than what divides it. The common denominator of all such work is that labour power yields to capital more in production than it costs to buy. . . . It does not matter what product is made since it is money which is really being made. The labourer will be switched with alacrity from the production of one commodity to another no matter what his skills or current activity when 'market conditions' change. . . .
>
> The inner logic of capitalism is that all concrete forms of labour are standardised in that they all contain the potential for the exploitation of abstract labour—the unique property all labour power shares of producing more than it costs when purchased as a commodity. It is this which links all the different branches of production and forms of labour, and makes the concrete form of labour, and the specific use of its products, contingent upon the central fact of its status as abstract labour.
>
> This commonality may be clear from the point of view of capital and less clear from the point of view of labour. (1981 [1977]:133–34)

Willis sees a tendency toward "de-skilling" and a standardization of manual tasks, both of which make abstract labor a "living principle in real social relations," while the measure of abstract labor becomes time: "As it is, we are approaching the day when filling in standard minutes of the timesheet every day will be, despite their different forms, the most basic reality of the working life of the teacher and social worker as it is now for the plumber and carpenter, and as it always has been for the industrial worker under capitalism" (1981 [1977]:135).

Further, Willis argues that the "lads," through their cultural insights, which he calls "penetrations," come to see accurately that the kinds of manual jobs open to them are basically similar: "This sense of the commonality of labour is in marked contrast to the sense of range and variety in the jobs projected by careers advisory services and teaching" (1981 [1977]:133). However, the theoretical and ethnographic material Willis supplies undercuts his arguments and the "lads' " penetrations. The manual jobs the "lads" eventually find themselves in are constructed as masculine jobs, which Willis thoroughly documents throughout the book, demanding strength and skills that are thought of as being particularly masculine from both the point of view of the "lads" and those employing them.

This view severely impoverishes our theoretical purchase on exploitation by conceiving it as occurring only at the point of production, and it precludes our understanding that when labor is created under capitalism—and thus commodified—it is created in many different forms. These forms are not equal in the estimation of those buying them, but, instead, acquire different values. The labors of the weaver and the tailor, to use two of Marx's favorite examples, are substantially different, not only in terms of their renumeration and the kinds of objects they produce, but in the kinds of qualities they imbue in the objects they produce. To put it another way, if capitalism can invent labor, it can invent different kinds of laborers, each with a different specialization and value. I will show how labor in the EUL factory is commodified in several forms and this process of commodification is dependent on evaluative practices on the parts of the buyers (i.e., owners of economic capital and the kinds of capital that it entails) of noneconomic capital, which nevertheless have an economic effect.

My argument is similar to that of David C. Griffith, who explores the role of what he calls the "nonmarket labor processes" in advanced capitalist labor processes, pointing out that "Labor's cost and availability depend on social, historical, cultural, and political factors that occur beyond the market" and that "employers have developed political and cultural mechanisms to maintain, extend, and legitimate their control over the quantity and quality of labor available for commodity production" (1987:838, 840).

The evaluative nonmarket process is integral to the objectification and commodification of labor and the economic production process in general and, in a larger sense, contradicts traditional Marxian notions of the autonomy (or relative autonomy) of the economic realm. General histories of the transformation to capitalism in Europe, such as Karl Polanyi's *The Great Transformation* (1957 [1944]), trace the way in which productive activities, which had previously been governed by the rules of kinship or community, came to be governed by the autonomous economic realm of the market. This historical process forms the basis for ethnographic discussions of class. For example, Fjellman grounds his discussion of the role of the consumer and consumerism in Walt Disney World in the philosophy of the "possessive individual" that was entailed in the "disembedding" of the economy (1992:42). Similarly, LiPuma and Meltzoff, writing on Spain, show how the category of labor itself arises out of and is objectified in this process "as labor progressively preempts overt social relations such as those based on kin and community, the ascribed class statuses are objectified to constitute classes as historical categories" (1989:323).

However, in the case of Trinidad and the Caribbean in general, labor became created and objectified in precisely the opposite way. While Trinidad became part of Europe's colonial orbit in 1498 with Columbus's third voyage, it remained largely a deserted island until the last years of Spanish colonial rule, when in 1783 French planters and their slaves came and set up plantations based on slave labor. This system expanded when the British captured the island in 1797 and annexed it in 1802. Sidney W. Mintz (e.g., 1989 [1974]) has long argued that the first large-scale capitalist enterprises were not in Europe but in the Caribbean and that, unlike in Europe, peasantries were created *after* industrialization. In Trinidad, African slavery, and later Asian indentureship, meant that labor was objectified and commodified from the very start. There were no communities before labor. Indeed, in the Caribbean in general it could be said that there has been a struggle to create family and community in the face of the commodification of labor and laborers. That is, there have been sustained attempts at "decommodification."[4]

While the specifics of the slavery and indenture experiences will be treated in the next chapter, the point here is that the degree of "embeddedness" of the economy into other social and cultural arrangements is a historical question and, in places like Trinidad, an incomplete process that is itself a site of cultural and class conflict. Writing about the proletarianization process among fishermen in Camurim in northeastern Brazil, Antonius C. G. M. Robben observes that it is often in the interests of the capitalists to portray the economy as separate from society, while it is in the interests of workers to point to the social and moral obligations inherent in the capitalists' positions (e.g., 1989:20–21).

By portraying the economy as a separate domain, the capitalists obscure their reliance on nonmarket labor processes for the exploitation of labor. In Trinidad, slaves were bought. They became objects. They were commodified. They were valuated. Their value rested on the kinds of labor they could provide. At the same time that they *were* capital, they *possessed* capital in all its forms. At the end of slavery in 1838, the kinds of capital possessed by the exslaves took on different meanings as they were suddenly deemed ill-suited for plantation labor. The planters and colonial administrators wanted a docile and compliant labor force to replace the slaves for the continuation of sugar production. They justified the indenture of East Indians beginning in 1845 by referring to the *kinds of people* they were and, therefore, the *kinds of labor* they could provide. The descendants of African slaves and East Indian indentured workers who now inhabit the production line in the EUL factory have "inherited" economic, social, cultural, and symbolic capital from their ancestors. While in many ways they have transformed this capital, in the factory and in the wider society they continue to grapple with the ideologies that have been legated by colonial labor projects. Furthermore, in the factory the owners refer to the supposed "natural" attributes of women that make them suitable for the kinds of labor that are required. This practice is buttressed by a state apparatus that seems intent on using "cheap" female labor to attract foreign investment and thus making Trinidad a platform for export industries, such as those that exist in the Dominican Republic and Jamaica. While these historical trends will be discussed elsewhere in the book, I want to emphasize that, in the process of objectifying and commodifying labor, identities are constructed, objectified, and commodified as well because they have an economic function.

Ethnicity and gender are commodified identities. Conversely, class is constituted by the kinds of labor being sold and the kinds of laborer doing the selling—and class is also constituted by the ways in which labor and laborers are appropriated. The kinds of labor and laborer have to do with the amount and configuration of the laborers' capital. In a dialectical and historical process, identities become constructed by the practice of assigning men and women, blacks and East Indians, the credentialed and noncredentialed, to particular places in the production process based on their economic and noneconomic capital. The resulting amount and configuration of economic capital, in turn, articulates with their noneconomic capital and gives it form, content, and value. The levels and kinds of capital (of all kinds) that can be exploited, which become reified in this process, determine power. In another historical moment, capital (of all kinds) is derivative of power. The kinds of capital and the configurations of capital(s) are indices and determinants of power and, further, become resources for the exercise of power. This is *not* to equate capital with power, but to suggest the ways in which capital and power are related.

Economic capital is derived from wealth, position in the process of production, and ability to control the process of production. In the factory, this "position taking" involves the appropriation of surplus value on the part of the owners. But people sell their labor and it is appropriated based on noneconomic capital as well. Capitalists incorporate labor differentially. Exploitation, then, is "dual," as capitalists push in two directions. They exploit labor by appropriating surplus value at the point of production. They also exploit, in a noneconomic way that pays economic dividends, individuals and groups by inventing identities and incorporating them differentially in the production process. Rather than accept the objectifications that are foisted on them, the workers often respond to this exercise of power by denying the validity of these symbols and images (see Thomas 1992). This second form of exploitation also involves the cultural construction of the subsistence wage, the lowering of which increases the rate of appropriation of surplus value at the point of production. In this second form, exploitation takes place on a number of bases and in a number of ways. The entire process of exploitation is regulated by and defined through modes of closure.

So, for example, a woman is hired to work in the EUL factory at low wages because she is black and a woman (different forms of embodied social capital), because she has not completed secondary school (cultural capital), because she has no alternative but to sell her labor (economic capital), and because she is not connected to any trade union or workers' organization (generalized social capital). Because of these attributes, she is placed in a position in the production process and assigned tasks that are, according to the owners, befitting her kind of labor. She is exploited at the point of production when, as in the incident described at the beginning of this chapter, the owners get her to produce more and more objects without an incremental increase in pay. The power to control the production process (which is complexly determined) enables the owners and others like them to accumulate the kinds of capital necessary for the exercise of power. In this case, because of accumulated amounts of capital (of all kinds) that are given form under capitalism, the owners are able to structure the relations of production and they are able to impose their definitions of the social identities of relatively disempowered groups, which are experienced in cultural terms. While the power of the owners of the factory is not complete, the worker in this example is relatively disempowered and has relatively few resources with which to erect alternative structures, definitions, and identities. When identities such as ethnicity and gender are symbolized in such a way as to make one set of workers different from another, then the owners reap the benefits because the likelihood is reduced that workers will identify with each other and collaborate against the owners.

Therefore, in the process of exploitation under capitalism, identities are invented. This is not to say that the labor process—the ethnic and gendered division of labor, for example—completely determines the content of social identities. Nor is it to say that these identities are at odds with the workers' interests all the time. Being thought of as a "factory girl" may be more liberating than being identified as "unemployed" or "housewife" or "housewife to be." But even in these cases, it is clear that the content of social identities is reproduced in such circumstances as described in the factory. Thus, when we look to the ways in which social identities are created, objectified, commodified, and deployed, we must look at relations of power, which, in turn, are created and recreated in the production process. As the factory ethnography shows, power and identity are forged in the crucible of the labor process under capitalism.

Chapter 2

LOCATING THE ETHNOGRAPHY IN HISTORY, ECONOMY, AND SOCIETY

It must be stressed that the integration of varied forms of labor-extraction within *any component region addresses the way that region, as a totality, fits within the so-called world-system. There was give-and-take between the demands and initiatives originating with the metropolitan centers of the world-system, and the ensemble of labor forms typical of the local zones with which they were enmeshed. . . . The postulation of a world-system forces us frequently to lift our eyes from the particulars of local history, which I would consider salutary. But equally salutary is the constant revisiting of events "on the ground," so that the architecture of the world-system can be laid bare.*

—*Sidney W. Mintz, "The So-Called World-System: Local Initiative and Local Response"*

LIKE THE REST of the Caribbean, Trinidad is not on the margin of the "so-called world system" (Mintz 1977) but, historically, squarely in the system's foundation. Thus, our ethnographic context presupposes a unique historical one and, as such, we must specify not only the ways in which connections exist between historical situations and processes and social and cultural arrangements but also the political and economic relations of causation that distinguish these connections.

My aim in this chapter is to explore the nexus of political and economic power relations on an international scale as they have operated in Trinidad, as well as the local political and economic context within which the factory and its workers are located. In terms of theory, I want to establish the historical trajectories, with reference to ethnicity, class, and gender, that come to constitute the culture and structural relations of the workers, supervisors, and managers of the EUL factory. Theorizing about the macro-micro relations of work and economics in a Caribbean setting is crucial given the unique way the Caribbean "fits" into the "world system" and the related controversies of definition and description.[1] This is especially relevant in Trinidad, with so much history that is distinct from the rest of the Caribbean, a history that saw African slavery buttressed by peasant-like groups, slavery giving way to Indian indenture, which was also sustained by peasantries and other indentured laborers, and then a transition to "free" labor.

I begin the chapter with a discussion of the advent of European colonialism in Trinidad and the production of sugar that entailed African slavery and indentured labor schemes. I lay out the parameters of colonial control, the development of an ethnic/class social structure, and the ideas about ethnicity that inform present-day notions of ethnic identity. I also analyze women's work in these systems of forced labor, focusing on the colonial state's and the planters' control over women's reproduction and how this control was designed to maintain these labor schemes.

Moving to the twentieth century, I discuss women's role in industrialization. In general, working women have been employed in menial occupations, suffering with relatively onerous working conditions, while receiving less pay than male workers. Women's participation in the labor force has been historically affected by a number of demographic, cultural, and legal factors. I discuss the role of these factors in women's employment history.

I also discuss women's participation in the "industrialization-by-invitation" development strategies that have been pursued by Caribbean governments. In Trinidad, this strategy was formulated under colonial rule in the 1950s. The EUL factory was established under this legislation. I locate these developments in local economic and political contexts, especially emphasizing the role of the state in ethnic, class, and gender relations in Trinidad. My treatment of the data is roughly chronological, ending in the late 1980s when I did fieldwork. I do not claim that this chapter is a complete history of capitalism in Trinidad (for an additional view, see Sebastien 1978) or a history of the working class (e.g., Ramdin 1982; Reddock 1994). But I hope this work as a whole contributes to these histories.

Women's Labor Under Slavery and Indenture

The distinguishing features of Trinidadian history have been the ways ethnicity and gender have ordered access to the society's colonial and postcolonial productive arrangements. Trinidadian history is full of cleavages and fault lines running across class distinctions and, especially, ethnic, cultural, religious, sexual, and national boundaries. This history is one of competition and features constant battles for group ascendancy and, often, epic struggles for mere survival.

Social historians have investigated how the aboriginal population was virtually wiped out after contact with Spanish explorers who came after Columbus's voyage in 1498, how the Spanish colonists granted land to French slave owners in 1783, and how Britain captured the island in 1797. They have also investigated African slavery and abolition under British rule and the immigration of indentured Portuguese, Chinese, and, in large

MAP 1
The Caribbean Area

numbers, Asian Indians for work in the sugar industry.[2] What has preoccupied the historians, not to mention the sociologists and anthropologists, are the ethnic and class antagonisms and the associated ethnic-class occupational and status hierarchies. African slaves and their descendants were brought to the island by the plantation owners of French and British ancestry. After slavery and the apprenticeship system finally ended in 1838, Asian Indians were imported from 1845 until 1917 to work as indentured sugar workers, as were the smaller numbers of Chinese from the Cantonese ports of Whampoa and Namoa and Portuguese from Madeira. At the same time, there developed a sexual division of labor that also typified plantation society. Yet, historians and other social scientists have only relatively recently considered the historical development of the sexual division of labor in Trinidad and the differences between how women and how men were incorporated in the plantation system.[3] The slavery experience is important for the understanding of contemporary Trinidadian society. Two of its defining features—the ethnic and sexual divisions of labor—are ontological arrangements that are fundamental to this ethnographic study.

The slavery experience in Trinidad was unique among the Caribbean islands. The slave period lasted little more than fifty years (beginning in earnest in the 1780s and ending in 1838) and there were not vast numbers of slaves toiling on the plantations: By 1812, only 1.8 percent of the land was cultivated (Sheridan 1985:8) and, on the eve of abolition, in 1833 only 1 percent of owners had more than one hundred slaves and 80 percent had fewer than ten (Williams 1964:85). But the system in Trinidad was just as harsh as in other slave systems. Because of severe malnutrition Trinidadian slaves were among the shortest in height in the entire Caribbean (Kiple 1984:69) and they were more susceptible to pneumonia than whites (1984:144). George W. Roberts (1952:243) calculates the average age of a West Indian slave at less than twenty-three years at the end of slavery. This high mortality "presag[ed] the labor shortage which was to plague some West Indian colonies by the nineteenth century and [gave] rise to indentured immigration."

Although there was no significant incidence of *marronnage* (slaves running away, often to form their own communities), Trinidadian slaves proved just as determined and cunning as their Caribbean counterparts. In 1805, a network of secret societies among the slaves was discovered. They were organized into regiments had elected "kings," "queens," and "princes," and had planned attacks on plantations. The conspirators were dealt with harshly.

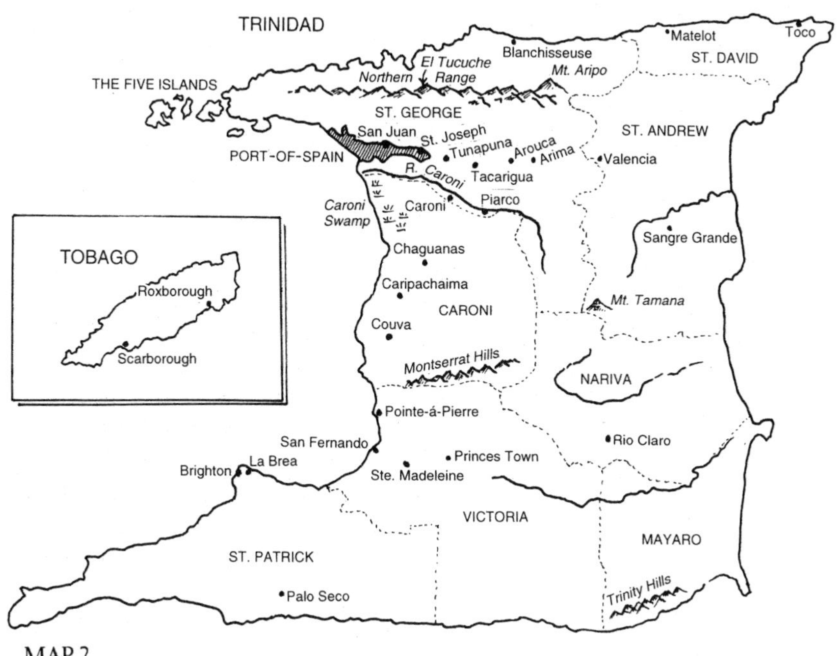

MAP 2
Trinidad and Tobago

Later, Trinidad's East Indian indentures struggled just as heroically against a different, but equally as harsh, system of coerced labor (cf. Haraksingh 1988; Samaroo 1987).

It is not that male slaves worked while females did not. Regarding the sexual division of labor, what is remarkable about the slave period is that: "slavery on Caribbean plantations gave effective quality to women and men; its levelling effect minimised gender differences. Except for the last years of British West Indian slavery, enslaved women were valued primarily as agricultural workers and only secondarily as reproducers. . . . Production took priority over reproduction and gender distinctions mattered relatively little in the day to day operation of the slave plantations" (Brereton 1988: 122).

In contrast to African slaves, East Indian women who came to Trinidad came as free agents; that is, they were adults who had chosen to undertake the terms of indenture just as had Indian men. For many, emigration from (mainly) North India provided the chance to escape from the dislocations caused by expanding British capitalism and colonialism, as well as the especially oppressive conditions suffered by higher-caste widows, deserted wives, and those women who chose to make a life of their own, on their own. "For such women," writes Bridget Brereton, "indentured immigration to the Caribbean, despite the coercive nature of this labor system, could indeed offer an escape route" (1988:125). East Indian women negotiated their own way into the indenture contracts, worked on the estates and earned their own wages. Both black and East Indian women were productive workers who worked alongside their male counterparts on the plantations, although, unlike a select few of their male counterparts, they were not employed in high-status supervisory and skilled occupations.

The planters also sought to control the reproduction of slave labor power (see Reddock 1984, 1985a, 1988, 1994). To the planters, the slaves were factors in their economic equations and to be considered of value in respect to their productive and reproductive functions. Slavery historians have remarked at the low fertility rates among female slaves in the eighteenth-century Caribbean. This was due to overwork, disease, malnutrition, and psychological factors. Yet the initial opposition of the planters to high birthrates came down to economics: A pregnant slave could do less work—it was calculated at approximately half—during the last three months of pregnancy and fifteen months of breast-feeding. Added to this was the cost, borne by the planter, of raising a newborn slave. Male adult slaves were bought instead. From the planters point of view, this practice was cheaper.

Toward the end of the eighteenth century, however, planters realized that the supply of Africans would dry up: The slave trade was indeed abolished in 1807. Pronatalist policies were introduced and inducements offered with amelioration measures (see Reddock 1985a:69–74), but often the slave woman went on "birth strikes" and practiced infanticide rather than bear children into slavery (Patterson 1967:107).

As mechanization on the estates increased, so did occupational specialization. Women remained in manual occupations—mainly field labor—and they were required to work longer in the fields than the men. At the same time, male slaves were trained in more skilled work. Far from being less efficient than men, women field laborers produced just as much as men (Reddock 1988:108–9). In addition, during the "seasoning" period—one of acclimatization to the rigors of plantation life and labor—female mortality was much lower than male mortality. One overseer remarked that, during this process, "three men died to one woman" (Patterson 1967:99).

Men were chosen for training in occupations deemed as "skilled," to the near exclusion of women. Men, therefore, came to monopolize the specialized and prestigious occupations in the sugar factories, as boilermen and distillers, and in the fields, as watchmen and drivers. Women's specialized occupations were as nurses and midwives. Black slave women were employed as domestics only when "colored" (i.e., mulatto) female slaves could not be found. So, while the majority of all slaves were field laborers, a significant proportion of males and females were channeled into specific occupations, as Barry W. Higman's evidence attests (1984:600–660). Orlando Patterson argues that this division of labor came about simply because of the physical requirements of the jobs (1967:256). But, given that women's performance in the fields was at least equal to that of men's, this really indicates the planters's conceptions of "men's" work and "women's" work.

From the age of about four, slave girls began to work on the plantations alongside boys in the "vine gang," doing small tasks like collecting vines for the animals and light weeding and hoeing. These were the only gangs with female drivers. Where females were employed as domestics, they were almost always under the authority of male domestic slaves (Reddock 1984:129). Some slaves were contracted out by their owners to other plantations or to urban enterprises. Since many women did not possess industrial skills, many were hired out in urban areas as domestics and some were forced to become prostitutes, handing over their earnings to their owners. Other women, including manumitted slaves, became hucksters, selling food and dry goods from estate to estate and in the towns. Indeed, in Trinidad women slaves dominated the growing urban areas (see Higman 1979, 1984).

Of all manumitted slaves in Trinidad in 1811, nearly 57 percent were female (Knight 1978:107). Rhoda E. Reddock notes that this higher rate has been attributed by historians to the promise of a return of sexual favors, but she points out that women's entrepreneurial activities and relatively independent economic base meant that many could afford to purchase their manumission outright (1984:137).

Caribbean anthropology of the 1950s and 1960s was preoccupied with the supposed "deviant," "matriarchal," female-headed black family and the supposed "independent," "strong," black "matriarch."[4] This phenomenon was attributed either to the strength of African "cultural retentions" or traced to the effects of the plantation system (for a discussion of this literature, see Mohammed 1988b; Higman 1975, 1979). While this is not the place to enter into the debate, I do want to point out that neither of these factors ("African culture" or the plantation system) was a static entity, as the majority of the debaters have assumed. It is clear that the slave "family" changed over the course of slavery. When buying Africans rather than "breeding" slaves made economic sense for planters, the formation of slave nuclear families was discouraged. However, toward the end of slavery, the planters began to try to impose the European nuclear family model (for some slaves at least) to encourage procreation and the slaves' production of their own food (Reddock 1988:131).

One of the measures of the 1800 Slave Ordinance, promulgated by Governor Picton, was for slaves to be allocated plots for "provision grounds," and this was done on an individual basis. The food produced from the provision grounds was meant to augment the planters' rations, and therefore reduce operating costs and allow the slaves more freedom. The slaves were able to sell their excess at the Sunday markets and, in the process, erode some of the planters' economic control. Women were said to be particularly adept in this activity. But most of the decisions regarding the provision grounds were made by the male slaves, which was one indicator of the power wielded by slave men over slave women. As Michael Craton writes,

> It seems clear that the plots were allocated to heads of household and that these were predominantly male. The working of the grounds (and the smaller garden plots around the houses) was normally a family, almost proto-peasant, activity. Men, women, and children worked together as a household unit, under minimal supervision, during the one or one and one-half days allotted by law and whatever the other time could be squeezed from the plantation's demanding routine. But in the division of labor the men decided what should be grown and did most of the planting and reaping, the children carried and weeded, and the women tended the house plot and domestic animals, cooking the provisions and carrying the surplus to market on Sundays. (1982:50)

At the end of slavery the planters sought to keep the exslaves as paid plantation laborers. When they worked on estates, women continued to be employed in the fields, while many men continued to be employed in the more prestigious and (now) higher-paying jobs. Yet, even when they were employed in the same position, men received more pay than women. Reddock writes on the significance of this development: "This differentiation in wages might be seen as a change equally as important as the introduction of the wage itself. It concretized differences within the newly emerging agricultural working class. Its effects as far as men and women were concerned must also have been important, for the status of the male as the official breadwinner must have been strengthened by the differential wages and access to skilled positions" (1985a:75).

When recruitment of East Indian labor began, planters were interested in obtaining males, as they considered the financial risks of childbearing too great. Consequently, more men than women were recruited. This imbalance (for a discussion of the sex-ratio imbalance in British Guiana, see Mangru 1987) caused much difficulty in the barracks on the estates and a number of "chop" murders of women occurred as men not only fought over women but turned on "their" women with cutlasses (machetes) when they tried to show sexual or other kinds of autonomy. Between 1859 and 1863, twenty-seven wives or mistresses were murdered (Wood 1968:154), and between 1872 and 1900, eighty-seven wives or mistresses were murdered (Brereton 1979:182).[5] At the end of the 1880s, officials made calls to increase the ratio in the migratory stream to forty women to one hundred men, and by the turn of the century economic incentives were being offered to recruiting agents in India to recruit females. It was not until the turn of the century that the ratio exceeded fifty women to one hundred men (Reddock 1994:41–42).

There were parallels to the situation of women under slavery. Each Indian women on the estates found themselves—as had black slave women before them—subject to a system in which white overseers had sexual advantage over them (see Singh 1985:38). A division of labor along gender lines was also established among the indentures as it had been under slavery, and it too was rooted in the planters' conception of "men's" and "women's" work. Here again, men were given the heavy tasks and women were relegated to light work. The skilled positions on the estates were occupied by black men. Women did mainly weeding and manuring, the lowest paying jobs, while male labor was utilized in cane cutting, truck loading, forking, and work in the mill and factory (Reddock 1984:176). However, this pattern was not constant and contemporary commentators noted the incidence of women in heavy tasks, such as loading the cane into trucks.

For East Indian workers in 1908, the average wage, per day, per year was 13.56 cents for men and 5.31 for women. Women's pay was well below the 12 cents stipulated as the minimum for men (Reddock 1994:38). Because of this situation, women's economic dependence on men increased, and what some have seen as a form of the patriarchal Hindu Indian family was revived. Ironically, the "patriarchal" form of the Indian family in Trinidad (see, e.g., Angrosino 1976; Klass 1961) has been attributed to, as with the black family, either "ancestral culture" or the effects of the local plantation system.

The emerging structure of the East Indian family was due to a combination of factors. Given the context of what planters felt was a labor shortage, the planters wanted to encourage a stable work force, tied to the estates. To this end, the East Indians were given land in lieu of a return passage back to India when their indenture contracts were completed. The indentured Indians would not have been allowed to have the kinds of family forms they had (which were themselves conditioned by British colonialism in India) if the planters had not seen it as in their own interests.

Some scholars argue that, when their indenture period ended, wives were often withdrawn from wage labor by their husbands so that they could devote time to household chores, childrearing, cane farming, and the family's provision grounds. Adherents of this view further argue that the government and churches acted to reinforce the policies of East Indian men (see the debate between Reddock 1985b and Jain 1986).

It is true that the "possession" of a wife on the plantations was a crucial element of a husband's self-esteem and status (Brereton 1979:182). But, as Brereton argues, it is important to consider intentionality as a factor explaining the phenomenon of East Indian women's withdrawal from the labor force in the last part of the nineteeth century (1988:125–26). She points out that most jobs women did on the estates were physically taxing, poorly paid, and difficult to reconcile with childrearing. Under the circumstances, withdrawal from full-time wage work to raise children was largely a rational decision. In any event, the establishment of what came to be seen as the typical male-headed, extended Indian family was not a foregone conclusion, even given the planters' economic interests.

Ethnicity and Class: Nineteenth-Century Foundations

By the end of the nineteenth century, as Brereton (1993) shows, there existed a "four-tier" ethnic-class system, with "whites" (of differing national affiliation) at the top; "coloreds" (the offspring of black-white sexual unions) below them in middle-class occupations, along with small-scale "Chinese," "Portuguese," and later "Syrian/Lebanese" capitalists; the "black" masses forming the third tier; and "East Indians" comprising the bottom tier.[6] This was concomitant with an ethnic division of labor that saw the whites as owners of capital and colonial administrators; coloreds in professions; Chinese, Portuguese, and Syrian/Lebanese as owners of small grocery and dry-goods shops and as petty merchants; blacks as skilled artisans; and East Indians as agricultural laborers. Power and prestige were distributed in such a way that more of both accrued to those whose mannerisms, phenotypes, and culture approximated the Europeans. This segmentation was also expressed geographically. Many whites and coloreds were in urban areas, as were Portuguese and Chinese (although many were village shopkeepers). Blacks, while they formed a large peasantry, began to migrate to the urban areas, especially around Port-of-Spain and San Fernando, and East Indians continued to be predominate in the central and southern sugar-growing areas. The ethnic division of labor and occupational structure has tended to break down unevenly since the nineteenth century, but the vestiges remain to inform contemporary power relations (Yelvington 1985).

The relative isolation of the ethnic groups of nineteenth-century Trinidad did not prevent serious conflict between them. Antagonisms and negative stereotypes between blacks and East Indians were cultivated by planters (Brereton 1974, 1979, 1981; LaGuerre 1974; Wood 1968; for Guyana see Williams 1991). Even though planters during slavery had claimed that African slaves were ideally suited to plantation labor, after slavery blacks were regarded by planters—and later by East Indians—as being lazy, irresponsible, and profligate. East Indians—almost without regard to Hindu-Muslim religious divisions among them—were seen as a whole by blacks and others as being miserly, clannish, acquiescent to authority, prone to domestic violence, and "heathen" for not adopting "Western" ways. "Indianness" became associated with labor in the sugar industry (Ching 1985).

Given these and other negative images generated by and sustaining colonial labor relations, blacks and East Indians did not mate with and marry each other. Brereton quotes the protector of immigrants who, in 1871, wrote "there is not probably at this moment a single instance of an indentured immigrant . . . who cohabits with one of the negro race," and she reports that by 1900 there were no known cases of legal marriage between blacks and East Indians (1979:183). This does not mean, however, that there was no interethnic sexual contact.

The overall trend continued through the twentieth century, although the incidence of intermating increased only slightly. According to data compiled by Patricia Mohammed from the 1946 census, in 1911 there were 1.47 "mixed" East Indians per 100 "unmixed" East Indians; in 1921 the incidence increased to 1.87; and by 1946, 4.29. There was a much higher rate in the urban areas, however. By 1946, there were 21.37 "mixed" East Indians per 100 "unmixed" East Indians in Port-of-Spain (Mohammed 1988a:388).

Despite small increases in the rate of intermating, as Colin G. Clarke's work on intermarriage (1971, 1986, 1993) shows, the low incidence of intermating and intermarriage continues. One cause, according to Mintz, was that the content of the ethnicity of various groups who migrated to the Caribbean after slavery (e.g., East Indians, Chinese, Portuguese) was dictated by the paucity of female migrants, where "the absence of culturally familiar partners of the opposite sex . . . gave any motive for the perpetuation of ethnicity a particular and distinctive pathos" (1987:54–55).

Marianne Ramesar (1976) outlines the pattern of regional settlement and economic activity for Trinidad from the middle until the end of the nineteenth century. She shows that during this time the estate labor force increased because of the arrival of the Indians and an increase in Creole participation. In the 1860s, the sugar industry had been aided to recovery because of increased production. Cocoa production boomed and French Creoles and peasant "contractors" joined in its production. The prosperity in cocoa was responsible for the resurgence of the French Creoles, many of whom lost their sugar estates to British merchants. In 1897, 10 percent of the population was engaged in cocoa production. The depression in the sugar industry in the 1880s meant an increased reliance on cane farmers. This gave blacks and East Indians a degree of independence and was economically important for the sugar industry as well: By 1928, 40 percent of the cane provided for estates' factories was provided by cane farmers. Food production started on a small scale, but tropical staples like yams, sweet potatoes, and plantains were imported for the wage-earning urban population.

By the end of the nineteenth century, the most difficult struggle of the laboring poor was for existence. The East Indians struggled under onerous conditions in rural areas, many in the barracks of the sugar estates. The urban areas were dominated by Creoles. Brereton describes the lot of the poor blacks who inhabited the "Barrack Yard" (1979:chap. 6). Barrack ranges were situated behind the frontage of city streets and were nothing more than sheds divided into ten or more rooms of ten square feet each. The rooms were separated by wooden partitions that did not reach the ceiling. There was one water tap for each range and there was a communal cess pit covered by a dilapidated wooden hut. The severely overcrowded barracks were unsanitary and their residents were unemployed or had turned to prostitution and theft. They were subject to a range of diseases, including yellow fever, malaria, and dysentery. "The result," writes Brereton "was epidemics, deaths, and a mass of human misery" (1979:118).

The sugar industry was reeling from another setback as Trinidad entered the twentieth century, with yet another decline in world prices. Cocoa, which had surpassed sugar as the island's number one export crop, suffered almost irrevocable damage by 1905, with almost all of the island's cocoa crop destroyed by witches'-broom disease. In 1912, though, the Royal Navy started to switch from coal to fuel oil, and this began a long-term trend that saw agriculture decline and the oil sector gain in importance for the island's economy.

From the beginning of the twentieth century the economy became more diversified. Employment in the service and industrial sectors became more and more important. Blacks were the first employed as oil-field workers, but they were soon joined by smaller numbers of East Indians. By the late 1930s, Trinidad was supplying 40 percent of the empire's requirements, and local employment in the industry went from 4,202 in 1931 to 14,311 in 1946. East Indians began to take advantage of educational facilities. In 1911, of the 50,585 Trinidadians born in India, 1,365 could read and write English. In 1931, the literacy rate for the non-Christian population, which was 28.3

percent of Trinidad's total population (80.5 percent Hindu and 18.2 percent Muslim) was 15.3 percent. For the Christian population, the literacy rate was nearly 70 percent. In the 1931 census, the "official and professional" category included 440 teachers, 69 public officials, 9 lawyers, and 6 doctors who were East Indian. The "commercial" classification included 1,841 proprietors and 127 merchants. By 1936, East Indians received about 13 percent of the new appointments to the civil service (Baksh 1978).

The twentieth century started with mass criticism of the crown-colony form of government, which gave full political power to the governor and the local elite. There were renewed calls for popular representation and the appeals became more radical. The Trinidad Workingmen's Association was formed in 1897, and it petitioned the government for working-class issues. In 1902, the Ratepayers Association was formed as a pressure group and "watchdog" organization that sought to supervise public expenditure. When the government decided to meter water usage, the middle-class leaders of the organization whipped up support among the lower classes, capitalizing on antigovernment feeling, and the crisis culminated in the "Water Riot" of 1903 (Magid 1988; Reddock 1994).

The democratizing ideals of the First World War had effects on Trinidad's rising black and colored professionals, middle class, and bourgeoisie. Political agitation became more and more acute. In 1917, when the indenture system ended, Trinidad's East Indians were forced to come to terms with their society. The reenculturating effects that were achieved with the constant introduction of further immigrants from the subcontinent ended. For those in Trinidad there was no longer the possibility of return. Urban Creole radicals were joined by a small cadre of East Indian intellectuals.

The 1930s experienced labor unrest, capped in 1937 with violent strikes (Basdeo 1985; Thomas 1987). The local effects of the worldwide depression were widespread unemployment, rising prices, and low wages, although during this time sugar remained profitable (Williams 1964:231). Living conditions continued to be appalling for the working class. In this era, Trinidadian fiction came to the fore, and the barrack yard became the setting for novels like C.L.R. James's *Minty Alley* (1971 [1936]) and Alfred Mendes's *Black Fauns* (1984 [1935]), where the working class was portrayed as noble despite its base environment (Sander 1978, 1988).

Part of the wave of labor unrest that swept the Caribbean in the late 1930s, the violent labor strikes in Trinidad were led by T.U.B. "Buzz" Butler, a black Grenadian immigrant oil-field worker who used a messianic oratory to rally the workers. Principle among the workers' complaints was ethnic discrimination in the workplace, exacerbated by the fact that white South Africans were being employed as managers with the oil companies. For a time, the black and East Indian workers formed an alliance based on class; the predominantly black oil-field unions elected an Indian, Adrian Cola

Rienzi, as leader after Butler was forced into hiding and troops were called in. The disturbances of the 1930s had far-reaching consequences, including the advent of the trade-union movement. As a direct result of the recommendations of the Moyne Commission, which had been sent to the West Indies to investigate the strikes, in 1946 universal adult suffrage was achieved and property qualifications were rescinded. The Barbadian novelist George Lamming (1985) argues strongly that the labor movement in the West Indies has been the region's most powerful democratizing force.

The events of World War II were extremely important for Trinidad (Anthony 1983), although the effects were contradictory. On the one hand, the construction of the U.S. bases at Chaguaramas and Wallerfield meant a boom on the island. Work was available at much better wages than usual, resulting in an exodus out of agriculture—so much so that, in 1943, the Benham Commission was sent to Trinidad to investigate yet another labor crisis in sugar. There was for a time a situation of almost full employment and, as Lloyd Braithwaite (1975 [1953]) notes, this situation was instrumental for a society-wide feeling of pride. The technology that the "Yankees" brought with them influenced Trinidadians: They saw bulldozers performing tasks in minutes that would have taken days for work gangs to accomplish. It was the first time Trinidadians had seen white men performing manual labor, which tended to break down the image of superiority shown them. The Americans, with their free-spending behavior, demonstrated affluence and initiated the "Rum and Coca-Cola" era (see Ralph de Boissiere's 1956 novel of the same name). There was an acute rise in prostitution and gambling as a result of the presence of the troops. And instead of the more subtle racism of the British, Trinidadians were subject to the overt American "Jim Crow" variety.

The direct economic effects of the construction of the bases were extremely important. At the peak of construction activity, 30,000 workers were employed. This represented about 20 percent of the total work force. People left the cane fields to work on the bases. Employment in sugar fell from 30,000 at reaping time in 1939 to 18,000 in 1943, rising again to 21,000 in 1944, when the base construction was finished. Sugar acreage fell from 31,000 in 1937 to 20,000 in 1943. Work on the bases was attractive because it represented somewhat "cleaner" work in general and the wages were higher than could be earned in sugar or in government works.

The war had important economic effects on the colony (see Carrington 1971:122–28), and Trinidad became more involved in the economic orbit of the United States and less involved in Britain's. For example, in 1936–39, an average of 37 percent of imports came from the United Kingdom, compared to 34 percent from North America. By 1944, the United Kingdom and North America provided 11 and 59 percent, respectively. Because of the German U-boat threat, seaborne supplies became unreliable and government bodies were set up to regulate food imports and encourage the local growing of food. Producers were offered guaranteed prices and sugar cultivators were compelled to devote large areas to vegetable cultivation. As a result, by the end of the war the total acreage under food production was around two-and-a-half times the 1939 figure. The island's foreign cultural influences, too, were firmly redirected to the United States. As the late Gordon K. Lewis wrote in 1968, "The natural anarchism of the colonial society was thus reinforced by the disruptive influence of Americanization. In the end-result contemporary Trinidad, twenty years later, has become a roughly-hewn combination of British snobbery and American vulgarity" (1968:212).

Women's Role in Early Industrialization, 1900–1950

Whereas most of the male and female labor force was employed in agriculture at the end of the nineteenth century, industrial production increased in the early decades of the twentieth century. During this period the amount of women's work began to be curtailed, part of a process Reddock sees as "housewifeization," that is, attempts at imposing the nuclear-family norm by the ruling elites (1994:chap. 2). Although the gainful-worker rate declined throughout the first part of the century for both sexes, mainly women were affected (Table 1).

The total employed in agriculture for Trinidad and Tobago in 1931 was 87,022, of whom 64,750 were male and 22,272 were female. Agricultural occupations represented 50.3 percent of male employment and 34.9 percent of female employment. By 1946, there were 46,799 males and 10,070 females working in agriculture. Agricultural occupations were 29.8 percent of all male employment and 20.5 percent of all female employment (Harewood 1963:74). Between 1946 and 1960, more significant changes took place along these lines. The most significant was the relative decline in the types of jobs that provided low incomes and the relative increase in occupations that provided a higher income (Harewood 1963:71). By 1960, 22.8 percent of the male working population and 16.5 percent of the female working population were employed in agriculture. Employment for males in the "mining and quarrying" industrial group went from 4.2 percent in 1946 to 6.5 percent of the male working population in 1960. In "commerce," the proportion increased from 8.0 to 12.1 percent during the same period. In 1957, of males employed in agriculture, only 26.3 percent earned TT$600 or more a year. On the other hand, the proportion of males earning TT$600 or more a year in mining and quarrying was 94.6 percent and in commerce, 68.3 percent. For the colony as a whole, the proportion earning TT$600 or more per year was 63.7 percent for males and 26.0 percent for females.

It is likely that there are a number of simultaneous trends that explain the

TABLE 1
Labor-Force Participation, 1891–1958

Gainfully Occupied Population					
				% of All Persons ≥10 Years Old	
Year	Males	Females	Total	Males	Females
1891	79,931	56,716	136,647	87.4	73.9
1901	94,583	65,814	160,397	85.0	67.6
1911	115,378	77,210	192,588	85.8	64.6
1921	123,014	85,565	208,579	85.4	62.7
1931	128,492	63,570	192,242	81.1	40.5
1946	160,137	52,956	213,093	78.6	26.0

Labor Force					
				% of All Persons ≥15 Years Old	
Year	Males	Females	Total	Males	Females
1946	161,742	54,111	215,853	92.0	31.0
1955[a]	186,200	84,000	270,200	90.0	39.0
1958			295,000[b]		

SOURCE: Trinidad and Tobago 1959:42.
NOTE: The difference between "gainfully occupied population" and "labor force" is definitional. For a discussion, see Reddock 1994:70.
[a]November.
[b]Estimated.

apparent lowering of the rate of women's participation in the labor force. One is that, during times of recession, the marginal activities in the service sector that women occupy would be rationalized. In a later stage of industrial development, it could be that men are marginalized from industrial production and their places taken by women, who are almost always paid less. By contrast, in times of relative prosperity, women may choose to withdraw themselves from the labor force to pursue culturally valued domestic activities, legitimated by "official" capitalist ideology. The presence of a "housewife" was a sign of a family's status. But what these statistics on the formal labor force may not take account of is women's increased participation in the informal sector. This is a plausible explanation when we remember the role of black women in petty trading in urban areas during and after slavery. At the same time, East Indian women were withdrawing from the labor force—or being withdrawn—for the reasons discussed above.

The period 1921–46 was one of rapid decline in female participation in the labor force, but it was halted thereafter. Between 1946 and 1960 there was a large population growth, 2.8 percent per year, and this took place in a context of a labor surplus. The working population increased 21.8 percent for males (1.4 percent per year) and 31.1 percent for females (2 percent per year). When the level of school attendance is allowed for, there was a slight increase in female labor-force participation rates, while at the same time there was lower participation by older and younger males.

Female labor in agriculture declined until the sugar revival after World War I. In the 1920s, the rate dropped again as mechanization was introduced to the fields. Almost the only women engaged in agriculture were East Indians. The "independent" black women dominated in the towns (women were 56.7 percent of the population of Port-of-Spain in 1931), where they were engaged as domestic servants, seamstresses, hucksters, factory workers, cooks, and in a range of illegal activities. By 1931, 89 percent of all domestics were female, and this category represented 34 percent of all female employment. At this time, about 14 percent of the female work force was self-employed as dressmakers. In factory employment, women were found in textile production and the emerging garment industry, which began to recruit them into poorly paid jobs. Women were also employed as shop assistants. In 1938, though, male shop assistants were paid TT$28 per month, while women of similar age and experience received $18 to $19.

Clerical occupations, which required office skills, were filled predominantly by males in the first part of the century, with women gaining increasing access as they received education and training in these areas. For middle-class women, most employment was found in teaching, as nurses, and in the lower rungs of the civil service. In almost all cases, when women did the same jobs as men, they were paid less than men. However, following the 1946 equal-pay report in Britain, in 1949 the wages of women and men in the same posts in the civil service were equalized (Reddock 1984:525). In 1950, women comprised 26.8 percent of civil servants. While women in the civil service may not have enjoyed the same promotion opportunities in these days, by the early 1970s there was little disparity in the public sector between men's and women's income. The private sector, however, was another matter (see Table 2).

The presence of the U.S. bases during the war affected female employment and speeded up the exodus of women from agriculture. In addition, the garment industry received a boost from the wartime economy as demand for local production of uniforms grew and imports were not available. This was a boost for garment factories, and, as a consequence, dressmaking, as an individual occupation, declined. Because the garment manufacturers have been the traditional employers of women in industrial settings, much of my discussion and comparisons are based on their experience (Reddock 1990, 1993). Whereas there were 8,917 individual dressmakers in 1946, by 1960

TABLE 2
Monthly Income, Public and Private Sectors, 1971 (in TT$)

Sector	*Both Sexes*	*Males*	*Females*
All sectors	154.50	167.50	93.50
Government	184.50	186.00	179.60
Nongovernment	133.00	155.00	72.50

SOURCE: Compiled from Trinidad and Tobago 1972:1.

there were 4,600. In 1953 there were thirty-eight garment manufacturing establishments and together they employed 1,366 people.

In 1957, there were 357 female and 317 male manual laborers in garment manufacturing industries. Men, though, earned an average of TT$839 per year while women earned an average of $384. Women were also employed in the manufacture of such products as rum, beverages, cigarettes, and food. But they earned an average 20 to 60 percent less than men. Most of the new industrial jobs created under the Pioneer Industries Ordinance (discussed below) were immediately for men, and women's share in manufacturing actually decreased from 1946 to 1960. The disparity in rates of pay during this time was dramatic (see Table 3). In 1957, for example, there were 68,138

TABLE 3
Working Population, by Industry Group, 1946–1960, Showing the Proportion Earning More than TT$600 in 1957

	Employed in 1946		*Employed in 1960*		*Employed in 1957 and Earning TT$600+ per Year*	
Industry	Males	Females	Males	Females	Males	Females
Agriculture, forestry, fishing, and hunting	29.8%	22.8%	20.5%	16.5%	26.3%	4.7%
Mining and quarrying	4.2	6.5	0.2	0.5	94.6	—
Manufacturing	18.2	18.6	21.7	14.3	70.4	25.9
Construction	14.4	15.0	0.8	1.5	81.7	54.0
Commerce	8.0	12.1	11.9	16.7	68.3	49.3
Transportation, communication, and storage	7.7	7.8	1.3	1.6	86.2	—
Services	17.7	17.2	43.6	48.9	80.7	28.7

SOURCE: Harewood 1963:75.

male and 10,801 female manual workers in industry. The average man in this category earned $1,115 per year while the average woman earned $564.

Industrialization and Politics, 1950–1990

With the granting of universal adult suffrage in 1946, the political topography of Trinidad would be distinguished by ethnic voting and a lack of a formal alignment of trade unions and political parties. At the same time the colonial state set about establishing a formal industrialization policy. In 1950 the Aid to Pioneer Industries Ordinance was passed. The pioneer industries were supposed to bring foreign capital, technology, and connections to foreign markets as well as providing local employment, generating local income, earning foreign exchange, and utilizing local inputs. In return, the industrialists were granted a period free from income tax, duty rebates on imports of raw materials and machinery, accelerated depreciation allowances, and subsidized industrial sites. The considerable growth the country experienced during the 1950s was partly attributable to the growth in manufacturing. The manufacturing sector exclusive of oil, asphalt, and sugar production registered an average annual rate of growth of 9.4 percent between 1951 and 1961 (Rampersad [1963?]: 31).

The absence of a formal alignment of trade unions and political parties gave rise to a pragmatic politician named Dr. Eric Williams, a former university lecturer and an Oxford-educated historian who started the People's National Movement (PNM) in 1955 along with a close-knit group of colored and black urban, middle-class intellectuals and professionals. "The Doc" alone defined policy, and the party demonstrated personal loyalty and deference to him (Boodhoo 1986; Oxaal 1968; Sutton 1984; Ryan 1972, 1981). He became a legend, a charismatic and Messianic figure. As Oxaal writes: "the image of Williams as a racial messiah was not limited to the black lower class, although it was strongest there, but could be found in the Creole middle class as well. Among members of the latter, however, the belief in personal and collective salvation through Dr. Williams often shaded over into a more secular variant of the True Believer in which the *rationality* and *honesty* of the Doctor were so fervently espoused as to occasion the willing surrender of independent judgment and will, associated with an intense hostility to any form of criticism, direct or implied, of the Political Leader" (1968:101).

Black Trinidadians, as Keith Q. Warner writes, "saw in this new black leader someone who could, and would, do for them what an insensitive white colonial regime never did." He quotes a calypso by the Mighty Striker (1993:278):

Annabelle stocking want patching
She want de doctah help she wid dat
Johnson trousers falling
He want de doctah help he wid dat
....
Now Dorothy lose she man
She want to complain to Doctah Williams

Williams maintained that the PNM was a multiethnic party, but its interests were soon identified with blacks. The PNM held power from 1956—taking the country to independence in 1962—until 1986. Its perpetual opposition were parties identified as "Indian," given their leaders and followers, such as the Democratic Labour Party (DLP) during the 1960s and the United Labour Front (ULF) during the 1970s.[7] Entrenched colonial ideologies of "race" became used in zero-sum electoral politics that would determine who would be the inheritors of colonial power.

With the coming of independence, symbols of the state and "nation" became identified with what was taken to be Afro-Trinidadian "culture," such as Carnival, the steel band, and calypso. Cultural practices seen to deviate from this norm, such as "East Indian culture," were labeled as unpatriotic and even racist.[8] Trinidad and Tobago was depicted as a melting pot, where races "mixed" (sexually as well as socially)—and those that did not were somehow less than Trinidadian. The national motto became "Together we aspire, together we achieve." The national anthem features the linc, "Where every creed and race find an equal place," which, for emphasis, is sung twice.[9] As Brackette F. Williams (1989, 1990, 1991) argues, ethnicity becomes essential in New World nationalism when there is cultural contestation over which group has historically contributed the most to "the nation," which therefore is constructed as "belonging" to that group (see also Khan 1994; Munasinghe 1992; Segal 1987).

Thus, the relationship between ethnicity and nationalism in Trinidad and Tobago has been characterized by two opposing but related processes. On the one hand, there is the conflation of nation/state/ethnicity to construct a "non-ethnicity," in which there are "Trinidadians" and "others," that is, "ethnics." On the other hand, there is the construction of ethnic and cultural differences to prove and justify contribution, authenticity, and citizenship.

Besides very successfully achieving an identification with the state, nation, culture, and ethnicity, the PNM maintained dominance through a patronage network targeted at (especially urban) blacks (Craig 1974, 1985). One method was the establishment of the government's Development and Environment Works Division (DEWD), which employed workers on road construction and maintenance. Almost every DEWD project was aimed at black areas and hired black workers. Many people acknowledged that these jobs were make-work projects and alleged that in many cases workers worked only two hours each day but were paid for a forty-hour work week. While patronage was accomplished most effectively through the state sector, as Percy C. Hintzen (1989) and Steven Vertovec (1992) argue, the PNM's industrial strategy was also aimed at urban blacks, at the expense of agriculture, the livelihood of many rural East Indians.

Despite attempts to distance themselves from Albert Gomes's quasi-ministerial regime, which preceded them, the PNM continued development plans that were already in place, the path of "modernization" (Parris 1983:314). These programs were influenced by W. Arthur Lewis (1950) and were modeled consciously on the Puerto Rican Operation Bootstrap development strategy (see Premdas and St. Cyr 1991).

Import-substitution strategies and the protection of local producers that they entail may have been designed to cut into the power of the whites, as many were involved in the importation of goods as "commission agents," and to provide an opportunity to establish nontraditional members of the bourgeoisie. However, with the move toward import substitution, the traditional elite was able to parlay their advantages and set up manufacturing and assemblying ventures, making "the same products that they previously imported as final goods" (Henry 1988a:479).

A system of import restrictions to protect local manufacturers was established. This system remained in effect during my fieldwork, under the purview of the Industrial Development Corporation (IDC), the government department responsible for the administration of industrial-development policy. From 1966, by amendment of the trade ordinance, goods that were manufactured locally were put on the "negative list," and thus importation was prohibited without a license. Although an emphasis on manufacturing can be an important economic and political priority, it is also a difficult goal to attain because of limitations faced by local and foreign investors. As Terisa Turner writes: "As regards the expansion of manufacturing, the major obstacle has been limited profitability for both national and multinational firms, due mainly to relatively high labor costs as well as to government policies of protecting high-cost local production by placing tariffs on a large number of imports on the 'negative list' "(1982:2-1).

Given the direction of these policies, it is ironic that Williams chastised the white elite in 1961 for rejecting the PNM's conciliations to their interests after 1956 with his famous "Massa Day Done" campaign platform (Williams 1961; Ryan 1972:270–82). Rather than undercut their interests, the industrialization-by-invitation policy tended to facilitate the continued economic (and social) dominance of the commercial elite.

Trinidad's industrialization development strategy, like Operation Bootstrap in Puerto Rico, has been widely criticized. Some argue that the local elite is in fact reinforced and that benefits do not accrue widely to others in the society. Others argue that foreign companies enjoy too many benefits in locating production in Trinidad. In an incisive article looking at the effects of the first two decades of the industrialization policy, Edwin Carrington argues that in all of the areas where benefits were supposed to accrue, there was instead disappointment. He points out that, although the contribution of the Pioneer Industries to GDP was important, these industries fell far short of the cited goals (1971:144–49).

Carrington argues that these industries placed a severe burden on government finances and increased dependence on foreign capital. But directly pertinent to our study were the particularly disappointing performances in the area of employment creation and foreign-exchange earnings. Between 1950 and 1963, the labor force increased about 100,000, but the Pioneer Industries were able to absorb only 7,000. Seven thousand jobs were created from an investment of TT$257.8 million because of the capital-intensive nature of the venture. Unit labor costs were kept low and, therefore, advantages to labor were minimized. Further, the manufacturing industries used more foreign exchange in the purchase of intermediate goods than they earned in export sales. This is partly because only about 40 percent of the raw materials utilized by these industries during this time were local in origin. Therefore, they stimulated little growth in local sectors because they created few backward linkages with those sectors.

Even though Carrington's analysis is somewhat dated—an up-to-date assessment is, in my view, urgently needed—from his analysis we can get an idea of the severe limitations of the development strategy chosen by the country as well as the investment climate and its effects on the EUL factory.[10] Ramesh Ramsaran writes:

> The industrial policies adopted became essentially an import substitution strategy centered around the local packaging or assembly of goods previously imported. This strategy has had serious limitations, not only with respect to employment, but also with respect to exports and growth. The framework offered was used by traditional suppliers operating with local business cliques to capture the local market, and the kind of dynamic expected did not emerge. Exports was not a major objective and the small markets contributed to high cost of production, while the creation of local monopolies protected from imports removed the element of competition that would have encouraged higher quality, lower priced products. A high propensity to remit profits abroad rather than reinvest also served to limit the rate of expansion of the capitalist sector. (1992:104–5)

By the late 1960s, the limitations of the Puerto Rican model were apparent. Widespread labor unrest resulted in the Industrial Stabilisation Act (ISA), which limited strike action (Parris 1976). In 1972, the unemployment rate was more than 13 percent, underemployment was a serious problem, and income distribution was more unequal than in 1957–58. Industrial action was curbed further by the Industrial Relations Act (IRA), which replaced the ISA. The foreign-reserve situation became critical as the country retained only enough for a few months worth of imports. From 1969 to 1973, public debt increased by 59.4 percent, from a gross debt of U.S.$370.4 million to $625.9 million. There was escalating inflation. This situation led to the first political challenge to the PNM, the Black Power "revolution" (Nicholls 1971; Oxaal 1971; Sutton 1983; Bennett 1989) of the early 1970s in which, somewhat ironically, urban blacks complained about high unemployment, which they blamed on continued multinational and local white domination of the local economy. While they suffered as well, East Indians were excluded—and excluded themselves—from the movement and its symbols related to "blackness," that is, putative African ancestry. There was evidence of continued ethnic discrimination in state and private-sector employment (Camejo 1971; Harewood 1971).

The industrialization strategy's goal of employment creation may have been impossible because the strategy was ill-suited to provide employment in what the late Dudley Seers called an "open petroleum economy." Seers argued that one could not understand an economy like Trinidad and Tobago's by means of traditional economic models of industrialized countries (1964:237). In an open petroleum economy, revenue is determined by exports, and when the wage rates become high in the petroleum sector and in other sectors that have benefited from a healthy petroleum sector, there arises an increased demand for imports, particularly consumer durables. Rising wages result in cutbacks by foreign firms, thus contributing heavily to unemployment.

Further, the industrialization program suffered from a lack of an economy of scale. Trinidad's economy was never fully integrated into a regional economic union. In 1968, the Caribbean Free Trade Association (CARIFTA) was formed and most tariff barriers between territories were lowered. In 1973, CARIFTA evolved into the Caribbean Community and Common Market (CARICOM). CARICOM's goals were to establish a common market, expand functional cooperation, and formulate common foreign policy (Payne 1980). Trinidad, the richest member, granted loans to poorer states like Guyana and Jamaica during the oil boom (see below). But CARICOM, like the ill-fated Federation of the West Indies before it, has been plagued by territorialism. Relations, strained in the mid-1970s, came to a head in a trade war in 1983. As Lewis describes it, Jamaica set up a two-tiered exchange rate for its currency and Barbados retaliated by allowing its dollar to float against the Jamaican one. Trinidad and Tobago, in turn, moved to protect its manufacturers by placing all CARICOM imports under license (Lewis 1985:244–45). In a more recent row between Trinidad and Tobago and Antigua and Barbuda over air-traffic rights, the first thing both countries did to retaliate was to place each other's goods under trade license (*Caribbean Insight*, March 1988, p. 1).

In Trinidad there is significant foreign participation in the nonpetroleum economy—although not to the extent of some of its Caribbean neighbors—and there is a heavy dependence on external sources of finance in the oil sector. According to Turner (1982:3-3, table 3), in 1976, around 41 percent of the total assets in the twelve sectors she analyzed were owned by foreigners, but one presumes that this number diminished in the 1980s as the government bought out a number of companies, including oil companies, with its petrodollars.

It is instructive to compare locally owned and foreign-owned firms in the "assembly and related" sector, as EUL is a locally owned firm that comes under this classification. According to Turner (1982:3-1), in 1977 multinationals employed 47 percent of the workers in this sector, with the remaining 53 percent being employed by locally owned firms. However, the average number of workers employed by multinationals was 241, which was larger than for local firms (176). Foreign firms were more capital intensive, with a capital-labor ratio of about TT$30,000 per worker in 1977. This compares to a ratio of around TT$22,000 per worker for local firms. Turner's data, however, does not allow for the comparison of wages and productivity for foreign versus local firms.

The PNM was able to survive the crisis punctuated by the Black Power movement only when action by the Organization of Petroleum Exporting Countries (OPEC) drove up worldwide oil prices in 1973. When the resulting oil boom hit Trinidad there was enough foreign exchange to pay for about two months of imports. Between 1963 and 1973, the total revenue from oil was TT$786 million. In 1975 alone it was more than TT$1.2 billion. In all, between 1974 and 1985 the government earned TT$28.8 billion from the oil industry. The series of formal five-year development plans were abandoned. Money became, in Eric Williams's words, "no problem."

The effects of the oil boom in Trinidad were massive, economically (Sandoval 1983) and culturally. As Vertovec writes: "Within a short time, the island society quickly became absorbed in an 'easy money,' free-spending, consumption-dominated ethos which one popular calypso at the time described as 'Capitalism Gone Mad.' The number of cars in the small country increased by 65 percent between 1974 and 1980, and the number of televisions trebled over the decade. Electricity became more readily available throughout the island, and refrigerators, stereos, TVs and video recorders became universal possessions" (1992:138; see also 143–55).

The oil windfall of 1973–80 allowed the government to expand employment as it nationalized a number of industries, creating jobs especially for the black, urban working classes, the backbone of the PNM's support. The government began to entrench a policy of state capitalism. There was an increase in anti-imperialist rhetoric, and increased restrictions were put on foreign ownership in the economy. Williams felt that since Trinidad had shed its "cloak of poverty" (*Miami Herald*, April 14, 1974, p. 14G) the country could thumb its nose at the sharks of foreign capital. Oil reached its high point in 1980 when it accounted for 42 percent of GDP, directly provided 65 percent of government revenues, and accounted for TT$9.17 billion of the country's total export earnings of TT$9.72 billion. The country became one of the richest in South America, reaching a per capita GNP of more than U.S.$7,000 per year.

Yet, the seeds for a disaster were being sown as the country started a consumption binge that relied heavily on foreign goods, especially food, that undermined local production: "Per capita food production in 1975 was almost half of what it was in 1965. Meanwhile, as the income from food exports increased negligibly from TT$87 million to TT$125 million during 1973–82, the value of food imports to the island soared from TT$161 million to TT$904 million over the same period" (Vertovec 1992:140).

When OPEC began to cut the prices of its oil in the early 1980s, there was a rapid decline in revenues accruing to the government, whose financial situation was, by many accounts, worsened considerably by massive government waste, corruption, mismanagement, and ill-advised investment, including the establishment of a steel mill that had no market (Yelvington 1991b). At the onset of the oil price "bust," the PNM government still sought to maintain the level of state employment and salaries. In 1985, wages and subsidies accounted for 87 percent of recurrent expenditure. Wages and salaries outstripped oil revenue by about TT$20 million in 1986, in contrast to 1981 when oil revenue was four times the expenditure on wages. The trade-union movement, which had achieved success in bargaining during the boom, was now being blamed for the crisis. Foreign reserves were drained: In 1982 the country had U.S.$3.2 billion, in 1983 $2.04 billion, in 1984 $1.18 billion, and by mid-1985 only $875 million. Trinidad and Tobago's economy contracted 7.4 percent in 1984 and 5.2 percent in 1985. Oil's contribution to GDP fell from around 42 percent in 1980 to around 24 percent in 1984.

During the boom period, the government sector's role in employment doubled, and by 1980 40 percent of the entire work force was employed by the government, including 36 percent of all agricultural workers. In the second half of the 1980s, however, the government was not able to create jobs at the same rate. Measured unemployment was 11.1 percent in mid-1983, 12.8 percent in mid-1984, and 17 percent by the end of 1986. Unofficial estimates put the figure at 20 percent or more (Farrell 1978, 1980), and underemployment is considered chronic.

In 1985, strict corrective measures were announced by Prime Minister George Chambers (who replaced Williams after the latter's death in 1981) to correct the bleeding of foreign exchange. There were, for example, new port duties, some increased by more than 100 percent. The balance of trade situation improved from a deficit of U.S.$708 million in 1984 to a surplus of almost $300 million in 1985, while at the same time inflation was cut from 18 to 9 percent. To further stabilize the situation Chambers devalued the Trinidad and Tobago dollar against the U.S. dollar from TT$2.42 to TT$3.63. The government was the biggest winner in the devaluation as it enjoyed a 50 percent increase in oil revenues, which are paid in U.S. dollars. By the mid-1980s, foreign reserves were dwindling at the rate of TT$35 million per month. The country was 20 percent poorer in 1986 than in 1982. In 1986, the year my fieldwork began, the economy contracted by 6.2 percent in the fourth consecutive year of decline.

But the maintenance of wages has meant the maintenance of import consumption as Trinidadians have acquired expensive tastes for foreign goods and many Trinidadians are still used to the oil-boom days of easy money when shopping trips to Miami were the norm for a rapidly created middle class. Trinidadians also became more familiar with "American culture," especially African American cultural styles in fashion and music.

With the end of the oil boom, Trinidadians began to try and face the realization that prosperous times were over. The following period is termed the "Recession," and the notion of the Recession has become contested ideological terrain. The fact that the period is called the Recession, which indicates some hope that the effects will be temporary, may indicate that Trinidadians continue to place hopes in a return to prosperity, which leads to an avoidance of dealing with the new paradigm of diminished wealth. In any event, the Recession has created much soul-searching throughout society.

In the Aftermath of the Oil Boom

The PNM's concessions to capitalists ensured that the traditional elite remained in place and with power. Carl Parris (1985:105) in his study of interlocking directorates of the large and powerful companies in Trinidad shows that of the directors of the twenty-eight companies on the stock exchange in 1982, twenty-three were members of more than one board and twelve of them were white, five East Indian, four black, and two Chinese. Further, Hintzen (1985:148) argues, "A white-dominated local commercial and manufacturing group has been the primary local beneficiaries of international capitalist penetration." For Hintzen, the advent of transnational corporations directly and indirectly affected government policy and strengthened the role of whites and other emerging capitalists, such as East Indian and Syrian/Lebanese merchants. In the context of economic development, Hintzen argues that there has been unity in the upper and middle classes despite ethnic differences, but heightened disunity between working class blacks and East Indians (1985, 1989).

A well-publicized example of this convergence of interests, as well as the direction of "ethnic business succession," occurred during my fieldwork when, in December 1986, the ANSA Group, headed by Anthony N. Sabga, a prominent member of the Syrian/Lebanese elite, invested TT$30 million in the McEnearney-Alstons Group, previously controlled by the white elite (*Trinidad Guardian*, December 6, 1986, p. 1). Soon afterward, Conrad O'Brien, the white chairman and chief executive of the McEnearney-Alstons Group, resigned "in order to make way for younger executives" (*Trinidad Guardian*, February 4, 1987, p. 1).

While the PNM's state capitalism and state patronage strategies no doubt opened up opportunities for blacks, East Indians also benefited, even if indirectly and in large part unintentionally (Reddock 1991; Ryan 1991a). The traditional view was that East Indians were the ethnic group with the lowest income, as a result of agricultural employment and low education levels. However, the more recent argument is that, because blacks were able to depend on government employment and related patronage, East Indians moved out of agriculture and were compelled to specialize in entrepreneurial activities. Thus, as the oil money ran dry and the subsidies were removed, the argument goes, blacks suffered and East Indians gained the advantage. While many East Indian capitalists have indeed become wealthy and influential, Winston Dookeran argues that the high visibility of the retail sector belies its generally low income, thus giving the false impression of East Indian economic strength (1985:72–73).

That traditional elites and East Indians enjoyed gains under the PNM seems to be supported by the data of Jack Harewood and Ralph Henry (1985:65). They note that the difference in income between blacks and East Indians is not significant and that the differential between blacks and East Indians as a group and the rest of the population remains wide, although the differential has declined. Income distribution during the crisis years of the early 1970s was actually worse than in the late 1950s, when the colonial economy was fairly buoyant. In more recent work, Henry (1988a:486–91, 1989, 1993) shows that, by the early 1980s, there was a decline—albeit slight—in the income disparity between blacks and "others" (whites, Chinese, Syrian/Lebanese, and mixed), between East Indians and "others," and between blacks and East Indians. Empirical evidence indicates that by the early 1980s, blacks and East Indians had become level in group income, but that income was more widely distributed among East Indians than among blacks (see Tables 4–7). When the economic situation improved in the late 1970s, income distribution also improved, although at a rate that was, as Henry writes, "somewhat disappointing" (1993:74). Therefore, we can expect

TABLE 4

Trinidad and Tobago Population, by Ethnic Group, 1980

Ethnic Group	*% of the Population*
Black	40.8
East Indian	40.7
Mixed	16.3
White	1.0
Chinese	0.5
Syrian/ Lebanese	0.1
Other/not stated	0.6
Total	100.0

SOURCE: Trinidad and Tobago 1987a.

TABLE 5

Income Distribution, by Ethnic Group, 1971–1976

	Average Monthly Income (TT$)		*Gini Coefficient*	
Ethnic Group	1971/72	1975/76	1971/72	1975/76
Black	279	412	.48	.46
East Indian	240	454	.49	.44
Other	442	630	.56	.47

SOURCE: Adapted from Harewood and Henry 1985:64–65.

TABLE 6

Disparity Ratios for Trinidad and Tobago, 1971–1982

Year	*Black/Indian*	*Black/Other*	*Other/Indian*
1971/72	1.16	1.58	1.84
1975/76	0.91	1.53	1.39
1981/82	1.00	1.21	1.21

SOURCE: Henry 1988a:487.

TABLE 7
Gini Ratios for Trinidad and Tobago, 1957/58–1981/82

Ethnic Group	1957/58	1971/72	1975/76	1981/82
Black	NA	0.48	0.44	0.47
East Indian	NA	0.49	0.46	0.43
Other	NA	0.56	0.47	0.48
Overall	0.43	0.51	0.46	0.45

SOURCE: Adapted from Henry 1993:74, table 3.1.

that if the present economic crisis continues, income distribution will get worse again.

According to Henry,

> The data show that the Indian community was a major beneficiary of the boom period and that the mix of socio-political and economic factors had brought about a convergence in the level of incomes of blacks and Indians in contradiction of prognostications drawn from earlier analyses. . . . All groups shared in the wealth, but relative to their earlier position, the East Indian community made the greatest advance in correcting any negative status they had *vis-à-vis* other groups. What is also interesting is that this improvement in the relative distribution and in the equality between Indians and Africans was achieved with a consistent decline in inequality within the Indian community, which suggests that the lowest income groups among the Indian community benefited considerably in the economic changes that took place in the 1970s and early 1980s. (1993:74–75)

In 1993, a 414-page research report by the Centre for Ethnic Studies of the University of the West Indies on employment practices in the public and private sectors was published and presented to the government. Regarding the public sector, the report stated that there was a tendency for East Indians to be underrepresented in the higher reaches of the public sector, especially the Central Public Services. Further, East Indians were underrepresented on the boards of public enterprises, and "race" was identified as a factor influencing promotion in some of the public companies surveyed.

At lower levels of the public service, such as the police force and nursing assistants, recruitment practices continually generate controversy. Summarizing its findings, the report stated:

> Many of the alleged cases of racial discrimination could not be substantiated with the available evidence; but the perceptions of discrimination do exist, are strongly felt, and materially affect the dedication and productivity of a number of officers from both major ethnic groups though Indians appear more aggrieved than Afro-Trinidadians. It was found that in a number of cases, what was

> perceived as "racial discrimination" was in fact the end result of a number of factors such as patronage, family network or membership of a clique. It became clear too that in situations where the criteria on which promotions or acting appointments were made were ambiguous, there was a tendency towards speculation that glided easily into charges and counter-charges of discrimination.
>
> It was also striking that certain sections of the Public Services were regarded as the preserves of one group or the other. Competition for such preserves and for what were regarded as lucrative or strategic sections of the Public Services often degenerated into ethnic rivalries. (Centre for Ethnic Studies 1993, vol. 1, p. viii)

The project surveyed more than 500 firms of all sizes. Of these firms, 39.4 percent were owned by East Indians, 24.8 percent by blacks, 19 percent by "mixed" persons, 5 percent by whites, 2.7 percent by Chinese, and 2.2 percent by Syrian/Lebanese. The report argues that employees of a particular ethnic group tended to be overrepresented within firms owned by members of that same group. The survey revealed that no blacks were employed in 21 percent of the firms studied, and that no East Indians were employed in 18 percent of the surveyed firms. The report found ethnic concentration particularly high at the managerial and professional levels. No blacks were represented at the senior level in 88.2 percent of firms owned by East Indians, in 92.9 percent of Chinese-owned, and 81.8 percent of the mixed and Syrian/Lebanese–owned firms. Firms owned by whites excluded blacks from senior positions in 76.9 percent of the cases. East Indians were also excluded from senior levels in firms owned by non-Indians. This was the case in 78.7 percent of firms owned by blacks, 64.3 percent of firms owned by Chinese, and over 75 percent of the firms owned by others (vol. 1, pp. xiii–xiv). Very similar patterns obtained with professionals. Regarding the occupational status of all employees within firms, the report states that:

> Indo-Trinidadians by far occupied senior management positions, in keeping with their dominance as owners of business-firms. There were 700 Indo-Trinidadian senior managers, 504 of mixed races and 390 Afro-Trinidadians. The number of white managers was quite high in relation to their numbers in the survey. More than half—57 percent—of the whites encountered in business establishments were in managerial positions. On the basis of this representation of managerial status by ethnic origin, it is instructive to note that: 80.4% of the Syrian/Lebanese surveyed were in managerial positions; 57.2% of whites; 39.6% of the Chinese; 17.8% of mixed races; 13.3% Indians and 7% Africans. (vol. 2, p. 324)

The report also attempted to balance some of the public perception and stereotypes regarding firm ownership and ethnicity with some of the results of the project's investigation:

> The popular notion that ethnic concentration obtains only in firms owned by Indo-Trinidadians is a function of the fact that there are many more of these than there are firms belonging to members of other ethnic groups. Many of them also tend to be larger than those owned by persons of African descent or of mixed ancestry. Moreover, firms owned by Indo-Trinidadians are highly concentrated in certain towns and along main thoroughfares and are thus a great deal more visible. The ethnic concentration which they display thus strikes the observer more sharply than is the case with firms owned by other ethnic groups.
>
> Ethnic concentration in firms owned by the latter are more to be found at the level of board and management. In part, this is due to the historical circumstances in which the firms began their life. Most began as family companies which grew and became transformed into private or public liability companies. At the level of operations, many of these firms have become ethnically integrated in part because there simply were not enough co-ethnics to employ. This is particularly true of firms owned by the Syrian/Lebanese, the Chinese and the Portuguese. In the case of firms owned by persons of African descent or persons of mixed ancestry, ethnic concentration also exists at the management level but was less in evidence at the operational level than is the case with firms owned by Indo-Trinidadians. (vol. 1, pp. xiv–xv)

A "who gets what, when" ethos dominated the 1986 general elections, which were held during my fieldwork (see Chapter 4; Clarke 1991; Premdas 1993; Ryan 1990; Yelvington 1987). The PNM was defeated by the ostensibly multiethnic National Alliance for Reconstruction (NAR), a new party including the ULF, other parties comprised largely of PNM defectors, and a substantial core from the business elite. The NAR featured a black party leader and a number of East Indians in the upper echelons. The NAR's landslide victory, capturing thirty-three out of thirty-six seats, seemed to signal the end of ethnic voting, and certainly many Trinidadians and Tobagonians felt that this was a positive result of the election. In fact, however, voting patterns did not change all that much. The PNM tallied only 31 percent of the national vote, but it still commanded 41 percent of the vote along the East-West Corridor—the predominantly black urban and suburban sprawl stretching from Port-of-Spain westward to Arima—where it had always been dominant. Crucial was the NAR support by middle and upper-class voters, some of whom had traditionally, if uneasily, sided with the PNM. Selwyn Ryan writes, "While it is true that Indians, mixed and minority elements voted in substantially larger numbers for the NAR and against the PNM, this had invariably been the case in elections between 1956 and 1981. The major difference in the 1986 election was the fact that the black community split its vote about 45–55 percent in favor of the NAR with larger proportions voting NAR as one went up the social class scale. The middle and upper middle class, mixed and black elements supported the NAR, while the bulk of the black underclass stuck with the PNM" (1988a:140).

Despite the country-wide feeling of goodwill and optimism in the first few months after the change in government, the fledgling NAR began to experience problems, most of which were attributable to the deepening economic recession. Faced with an empty treasury, in his first budget speech new prime minister A.N.R. Robinson warned of the consequences if the country was forced to turn to the International Monetary Fund (IMF), saying "We must at all cost escape the debt trap and dependence on the IMF" (Trinidad and Tobago 1987d:5). He then announced his "budget of sacrifices," which, on the face of it, seemed to be in keeping with the ideas of a party that tried to combine the interests of several different ethnic and economic groups. For the very poor, the budget exempted from tax those individuals earning less than TT$12,000 per year and increased taxes for high individual incomes. It was also announced that government ministers would take a small cut in salary.

However, Robinson abolished the cost-of-living allowance (COLA) for government workers, which business-oriented groups like the Employers' Consultative Association and the Trinidad and Tobago Chamber of Industry and Commerce had already called for regarding private-sector workers (*Trinidad Guardian*, October, 10, 1986, p. 1; October 15, 1986, p. 1).[11] This was widely seen as pandering to big business and caused a number of trade-union-led demonstrations, inspired by the fear that the removal of the COLA was the first step of a plan to take away workers' hard-won salaries and benefits (see, e.g., the reaction of the Public Servants' Association president Kenrick Rennie in *Trinidad and Tobago Review*, March 1, 1987, p. 6).

Working class Trinidadians continued to struggle daily with unemployment, not only because the state cut back its workforce, but also because a number of large firms went out of business, including the national discount department store chain Kirpalani's (see "Country too Small for Firms like Kirpalani's," *Sunday Guardian*, September 7, 1986, p. 6). The working class also suffered wage cuts and rising costs of living. The overall cost of food during my fieldwork was twice what it had been in the early 1980s. In February 1987, subsidies were withdrawn from certain food imports with the abolition of the preferential exchange rate that applied to these items. There followed two rounds of price increases at the end of March 1987, affecting government-controlled basic food items, including evaporated milk (which had a price increase of 41 percent), powdered baby milk (up 29 percent), cheese (up 32 percent), potatoes, onions, garlic, and canned sardines. The national Hi-Lo supermarket chain predicted in early 1987 that its prices would rise about 20 percent by the end of that year. And the Economist Intelligence Unit predicted inflation to run between 20 and 30 percent during 1987 (1987–1988:11).

Urban dwellers also witnessed an increasing number of "vagrants," as homeless people are called in Trinidad, indicating for some both an increase in poverty and a decline in values brought about by "modernity" (for example, see an editorial in the *Trinidad Guardian*, September 14, 1986, p. 3). In 1993, there were 300 estimated vagrants in Port-of-Spain, with 84 percent between the ages of twenty-four and fifty (*Express*, March 22, 1993, p. 3).[12]

By 1987, the country was firmly in the grips of the Recession. The popular calypso of the time by Iwer George summed up the situation:

> Times, they gettin' hard right here in Trinidad
> Money runnin' low, low, low here in Trinago [Trinidad and Tobago]
> A dollar ain't what a dollar used to be
> Somebody pumping the country
> Money runnin' low, low, low, right here in Trinago.

Despite these conditions, new industry minister Ken Gordon, who became part of the cabinet as an appointed senator, was allowed almost free reign to implement basically Thatcherite policies designed to attract foreign investment, privatize government-owned industries, and pursue more business-oriented policies, including tax concessions. This strategy was severely criticized within and outside of the government and the NAR as the country was trying to define the new direction it would take politically and economically. It was clear that the NAR would not or could not challenge elite interests.

The idea that the Recession, and all that it entailed, and not the oil boom, and all that it entailed, might be the normal state of affairs, led to open ideological and cultural conflict. People sought to place blame on different economic and ethnic groups for the society's woes. During the period of my fieldwork, both major daily newspapers, the *Trinidad Guardian* and the *Express*, openly sided with the NAR during the election campaign and, in general, with causes of the elite, which used the papers as vehicles for what really amounted to propaganda. Their interests were advanced in editorials and uncritical news articles. For example, immediately after the 1986 election, in a front-page article entitled "Businessmen See Hope for Recovery," Wilfred Espinet, vice president in charge of exports at the Trinidad and Tobago Manufacturers Association, argued that import substitution and protection of local manufacturers were valid means of conserving foreign exchange. He also said that manufacturers should continue their nascent export thrust in order to earn foreign exchange. Ernie Murray, vice president of the Employers' Consultative Association, added that "he hoped that employees would adopt a more productive approach to their jobs and that employers pay more attention to management demands and encourage more dialogue with employees. He also hoped that trade unions would make realistic demands, take into account the harsh economic climate, and that tripartite [government, private industry, and labor] talks not be bogged down by sectoral interests" (*Trinidad Guardian*, December 31, 1986, p. 1).

In Trinidad, when businesspeople talk of wanting to cooperate with workers, they mean that they want the workers to acquiesce to the demands of capitalists. During the oil boom, trade unions were very successful, in some cases winning 100 percent increases in salary from one year to the next. In the Recession, trade unions and their leaders were widely blamed for low worker productivity and high wages that combined to cripple industry. Many union leaders have been accused of corruption, often by the very businesspeople who may have bribed them or tried to bribe them to accept a wage and benefit package that would be less expensive for the owners. Newspaper columnists and businesspeople often blamed the unions for being "agitators" during the Recession, arguing that they should be quiet and make concessions so that the businesses could continue in business. Often the attacks were directed at George Weekes, the highly visible leader of perhaps the most powerful union, the Oilfields Workers' Trade Union (OWTU), which was born out of the riots and strikes of 1937: "In the boom years the oil bonanza was able to cushion the worst cases of corruption, mismanagement, featherbedding, inefficiency and even plain old trade union 'ignorancy.' But, today it's a new ball game. Wishful thinking, impossible dreams, false assumptions and the mumbo jumbo and absurd antics of the likes of Mr Weekes have come to terms with stark economic realities. . . . One of the unfortunate legacies of the boom period is the fact that we are, by and large, high-cost and inefficient producers. While our trade unions are not exclusively responsible for this, they must bear a large part of the blame for it" (*Trinidad Guardian*, September 9, 1986, p. 8).

Employers denied that they were to blame for the Recession, preferring to blame the labor unions. The president of the Employers' Consultative Association, W.A. Hilton-Clarke, said employers should not be blamed for the Recession. In a speech to the Rotary Club two months before the general election, he said "Labour and government must stop trying to blame employers for the country's present position which is really the accumulated failures by all of us over the past several years." He added that, contrary to rumors, employers were not laying off employees out of spite and that every other means of reducing costs were resorted to before retrenchment (*Trinidad Guardian*, October 15, 1986, p. 1).

Workers were asked to temper their demands, and even to take pay cuts. One *Trinidad Guardian* article reported glowingly that workers at Trinidad Aggregate Products Ltd. agreed to a cut in pay and benefits enshrined in their union contract in order for the company to receive a contract for export to the United States (*Trinidad Guardian*, January 10, 1987, p. 3).

However, not all firms suffered unduly during the Recession. The Trinidadian company Neal and Massy Holdings Ltd., which at the time owned more than fifteen companies operating in Trinidad and Tobago, was doing very well. Neal and Massy is probably the biggest conglomerate in the

Caribbean. The parent company includes several groups and over sixty affiliated companies throughout the Caribbean, and its direct subsidaries employ about 4,400 people. For the fiscal year 1991, it grossed TT$1.1 billion (just under U.S.$260 million) and made U.S.$14 million in profit (*Caribbean Action* 7, no. 1, October 1991, p. 13).

Neal and Massy attributed its post-boom successes to the merging of some companies within the group and a new emphasis on manufacturing rather than distribution and retailing. Neal and Massy announced that it would seek to give priority to manufacturing exportable products, given the gloomy prospects for the domestic market (*Trinidad and Tobago Review*, February 1, 1987, p. 19).

To address what the business elite claims are low levels of worker productivity, the government tested ideas for improving the situation. Speaking at a conference on management, then minister of planning and reconstruction, Winston Dookeran, a former University of the West Indies (UWI) economist, said that workers should be included in business decisions and conceived of as an essential part of management philosophy and as one of the foundations on which "economic democracy" was built (*Trinidad Guardian*, March 25, 1987, p. 14). In addition, the government-run Management Development Centre (MDC) came up with a "value-added formula" with which workers could share in the "surplus" profits by the company. In this formula, the cost incurred in manufacturing the product is subtracted from the total sales revenue earned from it. This figure is then divided by the number of employees engaged in the manufacturing process to come up with a "productivity factor" per employee. Any "excess profit" the company makes after its budgeted profit margin would then be shared based on this productivity factor per employee. The MDC director, Neave Beckles, noted that the formula was being used widely in Japan. He also pointed out that one local company began to use it in January 1987 and by May of that year had already made four payments to its employees (*Trinidad Guardian*, May 6, 1987, p. 4). The idea of employee participation has not had widespread acceptance. Also, as Guillermo J. Grenier shows in his study of workers at the Johnson & Johnson plant in Albuquerque, New Mexico (1988), "employee participation" is often a tool in antiunion strategies. Further, the notion of "excess profits" leaves a wide margin for interpretation.

Under Gordon, given the foreign-exchange situation, there was a renewed emphasis on manufacturing, especially for export. It was announced that the IDC was going to set up a One-Stop Shop for local and foreign investors, designed to deal expeditiously with applications for investments (*Express*, March 23, 1987, p. 40). There was also an expressed need for self-sufficiency in food production. Yet, both of these measures challenge the interests of the business elite. The idea that Trinidad should increase its food production runs against the businesses that make large profits as commission agents importing food. Businessman Deen Saidwan, the former president of the South Chamber of Industry and Commerce, told an agribusiness seminar that the Caribbean's large food-import lobby could block regional countries' plans to become self-sufficient in agriculture. "The food import lobby is more powerful than our local food producers. The importers have access to the media and they have all the mass merchandising and mass advertising. . . . Watch the food import lobby in Trinidad and Tobago because they are powerful" (*Trinidad Guardian*, May 6, 1987, p. 1).

The new thrust in manufacturing for export meant that firms that had been protected by the "negative list" and subsidies had to compete in a world market against firms from elsewhere that produce at lower costs and with better quality. They also faced a lack of foreign exchange. In the past, these firms did almost no exporting and relied on foreign exchange earned by the petroleum sector for their own imported inputs. Economists Loyd Best said that the country's economic crisis was caused by the fact that the society has been transformed by a type of industrialization that compounded a problem inherited from the colonial past: "The country is hooked on a high level of spending," said Best, adding that the levels of income and spending could no longer be obtained. He said industrial activity in the country now accounted for a great amount of waste of precious foreign reserves, and he noted that much ongoing industrial production was unnecessary to the country's needs:

> Nearly all of the ventures which we have started in recent years are unable to function unless considerable amounts of foreign exchange are made available to procure equipment, spare parts and supplies and services from abroad.
>
> But these businesses scarcely export. So they cannot furnish themselves with sufficient foreign exchange without the help of the petroleum sector or the old agricultural staples of cocoa and sugar.
>
> What this means is that not only is there a problem of scale. There is also the problem of the orientation of our productive capacity. For want of foreign exchange, we cannot return to the old level of spending simply [by the] expansion of home supply. (*Express*, March 23, 1987, p. 6)

Indeed, a number of manufacturers complained that they could not get enough foreign exchange for production inputs. Joan Vieira, a director of Appliance Manufacturers Ltd. (AML), which manufactures electric blenders, ice-cream freezers, and electric fans, complained that her company could not get enough foreign exchange to import resin to make plastic parts for appliances, steel in coils, and magnet wire for winding motors, switches, and cords. AML is located in the same industrial estate as Essential Utensils Ltd., and their operations seem very similar. According to Vieira, AML was exporting 80 percent of what it manufactured and earned more foreign exchange than it used. The company, according to Vieira, was surviving because it manufactured three products, but she said the company would not be able to do so much longer. She said workers would work on one product when there were no raw materials for the other two. At Thomas Peake and Co., an official said the government's cutting down on the so-called EC-O applications for foreign currency hit the company hard. The company imports components to assemble air-conditioning units. It also imports spare parts and industrial air-conditioning units (*Express*, April 23, 1987, p. 3).

The onset of the Recession saw not only economic groups engaged in ideological battle, as described above, but also the further development of a discourse on the different economic contributions of Trinidad's ethnic groups to both the boom and the bust. For the most part, it is a discourse that harkens back to the planters' and colonial administrators justifications for labor schemes, and the associated objectification of black and East Indian identity. As discussed earlier, during slavery blacks were seen as ideally suited to plantation labor, but during the indenture period planters talked of East Indians as "saving" the economy and depicted blacks as lazy and unwilling to work. A present-day version of the theme is the discourse of the "Carnival Mentality," which is used to explain poor productivity and has received widespread attention in official circles: "This idea that when the master is not around we don't need to work is still rampant. In other words, the worker will not on his own volition—unsupervised rigidly and unsupervised with strong discipline— . . . really give his best" (Percy Cezair, quoted in Button 1981:9).

In the wake of the Recession, the Carnival mentality, symbolized by the DEWD program, is seen as hampering the country's prospects of recovery and providing a major obstacle for adjusting to challenges brought by trade liberalization policies, the need to export competitively, and the need to adjust to the new trends in the global economy.

There have been numerous seminars and meetings and government and academic inquiries into productivity, with no clear-cut solutions emerging (e.g., Nunes 1987; Ryan 1982; Williams 1987). Some scholars, however, have recently started to look critically at management practices as contributing to this phenomenon. Economist "Regis Matson" (a pseudonym) argues:

> The charge that people are lazy here has been overplayed, although there may be some historical truth to it. People are assigned to and paid for certain kinds of work they are reluctant to perform. If people have to work and are properly supervised, they will perform quite well. First, I think that the extent of malingering is exaggerated. Second, I believe that much of it is the result of a lack of supervision. Beginning at the managerial level, things have fallen down; people who are paid are supposed to be at work between eight and twelve and again between one and five, and if they are not there someone should be held responsible for checking on such behavior. (Quoted in London 1991:57; see also 143–44 for the comments of teacher-calypsonian "Hasley Lincoln")

As a response to what some scholars call the "driver style" of supervision, which is seen as a legacy of slavery, it is argued that workers adopt the "Quashie" personality of the slavery period, that is, feigning ignorance, being overly sycophantic to the boss, and avoiding work whenever possible. (cf. Patterson 1967). At the same time, members of the elite attribute apparent East Indian success in entrepreneurial endeavors—often run with unpaid family labor—to qualities inherent in "East Indian culture." Often, East Indians pick up on the argument, asserting that during the boom, when blacks spent, East Indians saved.[13] In an editorial on the "Essence of Divali," the *Trinidad Guardian* tied the focus of the Hindu "festival of lights" and homage to the goddess Lakshimi to the notion that East Indians' supposed frugality was saving "the nation" from the profligacy of Creoles:

> The last two weeks have seen an explosion of Divali celebrations unprecedented in this country. There have been literally dozens of functions marking Divali with the lighting of deyas [small clay lamps] and cultural shows, as it moves rapidly towards becoming a truly national event.
>
> One particular aspect of this festival is of special importance in today's economic circumstances. As festivals go, Divali is strong in the spiritual sphere and very light on the pocket.
>
> It costs very little to celebrate Divali beyond deeyas [*sic*] and oil. The rest is fasting, abstinence and avoidance of alcohol and meat, and a focus on prayer and family unity.
>
> To a great extent, this represents the essence of the East Indian presence in this country and a strong point of the many Hindus in the land.
>
> They have always emphasized thrift, hard work, sacrifice, family life and an attachment to the land, as opposed to the conspicuous consumption and pleasure seeking which characterises so much of our western dominated society.
>
> Such attitudes have been of tremendous benefit to the country, and have made the East Indians one of the economic assets we [i.e., Trinidadians] can count.
>
> If all those who are celebrating Divali this year can take up the spirit of thrift and optimism, it could be a meaningful step towards battling the present recession. (*Trinidad Guardian*, October 31, 1986, p. 8)

The editorial reveals a number of components to this paradoxical ideology. First, it clearly distinguishes East Indians as separate from other segments of the society and "one of the economic assets we can count." Second, the editorial contrasts this "asset" to those groups—*the* group, really—characterized by "conspicuous consumption and pleasure seeking." And third, the editorial indicates that Divali is moving "rapidly towards becoming a truly national event," a view characteristic of the nationalist sentiment (or hope) that each distinct cultural strain and practice is becoming assimilated and thus "Trinidadian." This last point contradicts the notion that a distinct "East Indian culture," with its ethic of thrift, can battle the Recession.

The prevalence of the Carnival-mentality discourse often causes blacks to agree with the depictions of themselves and to question what it is about "black culture" that prevents black solidarity and prevents blacks from achieving successes similar to those achieved by other groups.

There are some who take issue with the notion that the Carnival mentality is bad, pointing out that during preparations for Carnival costume makers and organizers display tremendous amounts of productivity and creativity. "Cletus Boyd" (pseudonym), a management-level officer in the Ministry of Agriculture, said:

> If there is Carnival, people will work, but I think what is at issue here is the question of organization, in which management plays a very, very vital role. It is my firm belief that if management is practiced in all work situations and organizational processes are actualized, the work situation would be very much enhanced, and the old saying, that Trinidadians and Tobagonians are lazy people, might totally disappear. It is an extension of the management devotion, the organizing devotion, from the carnival situation into other normal aspects of life. If that extension is made, I believe the stereotype that Trinidadians and Tobagonians are lazy and don't like to work can be removed. If you go to a calypso camp or mas' camp—and these two are closely related—you will observe the high degree of management that is exercised: planning, carrying out of orders, and product outcome, all reflected in cooperation among people working together. (quoted in London 1991:166)

The Recession has also made Trinidadians question the country's cultural direction. During 1986 and 1987, many of these arguments revolved around foreign versus local TV programs. At the time, the only television station was state-run Trinidad and Tobago Television (TTT), but by the early 1990s, two private stations were in operation as well. Many wealthy Trinidadians, though, had satellite dishes mounted at their homes. In addition to its fare of local news, a few locally produced programs and repeats of American soap operas (see Miller 1992) and situation comedies, TTT bergan to broadcast American channels via satellite for hours each day. Viewers received Cable News Network and broadcast network programming, complete with commercials.

While most Trinidadians could not get enough of foreign television programs, there were some dissenting voices. Immediately after being elected, then-Minister in the Office of the Prime Minister Brinsley Samaroo, a UWI historian, criticized the "Americanization" of society through foreign media content. His statements caused considerable controversy—so much so that he was soon removed to other responsibilities within the government. The public, it seemed, came to regard luxuries such as American television programs as a right.

"Culture" was political in other ways. Shortly after the NAR victory, there were claims that constituencies dominated by East Indians—who now felt they had some tangible political clout—were not receiving political patronage in the form of DEWD-type jobs and public-works projects, which black-dominated constituencies continued to receive. In February 1988, fearing that a caucus within the party was planning his removal, Robinson fired three cabinet ministers, all East Indian and all former members of the ULF. These included Basdeo Panday, the deputy prime minister, who was also a deputy party leader and a powerful leader among the East Indian sugar workers union (Premdas 1993; Ryan 1990; Yelvington 1991b). Panday had accused Robinson and others of operating like the PNM, favoring the interests of blacks at the expense of East Indians, and Gordon of trying to "sell out" the country to the business conglomerate Neal and Massy (*Caribbean Insight,*, March 1988, p. 1). In Trinidad, the "selling out" accusation could also be taken to refer to "selling out" to whites, because the top Neal and Massy executives are from elite local white families. Both the Robinson camp and the Panday camp attributed racist motives to the other side.

When the 1988 budget was presented, in the context of the political turmoil discussed above, there were widespread protests that it was both ill-defined and designed to help the rich. This forced Robinson to announce changes, including further tax relief for low wage earners. Meanwhile, the foreign-exchange reserves continued to be drained. Reserves fell from TT$1,202.2 million at the end of 1986 to TT$376.8 million at the end of 1987, the lowest figure since 1973, At their peak in 1981, reserves equaled TT$7,687.2 million. In August 1988, the government announced that the TT dollar would be devalued to TT$4.25 to U.S.$1 and that further foreign exchange controls would be implemented. It was also announced that the government would be seeking to bring in the International Monetary Fund (IMF), a bitter pill indeed for a country that was once place among the World Bank's upper-middle income category with the likes of Israel, Singapore, and Hong Kong (*Financial Times*, August 19, 1988, p. 8).

After seeing its popularity decline drastically, the low point being an attempted coup in 1990 (Premdas 1993; Ryan 1991b), the NAR was soundly defeated by the PNM in 1991. The PNM continued with a program of privatizing state industries and following the structural adjustments offered by the IMF (*TnT Mirror*, March 12, 1993, p. 29). Members of the business elite felt threatened because many of the trade-liberalization conditions attached to IMF loans require the elimination of protective measures for local producers and even importers (see "Living without the Negative List," *Trinidad Guardian*, March 17, 1993, p. 8).

During this period, the Caribbean region as a whole did not receive meaningful assistance from the region's developed countries. It would have been logical that the United States' Caribbean Basin Initiative (CBI) would play an important part in export-production planning. The oft-criticized

CBI, established by Ronald Reagan in 1983, provided for twelve-year duty-free access to the U.S. market for a wide range of Caribbean exports, as well as numerous tax concessions for U.S. investors in the region. Certain articles, however, were specifically excluded, including textile and apparel articles and footwear (two areas in which Caribbean manufacturers have demonstrated competence), handbags, luggage, tuna, petroleum and byproducts, and watches.[14]

As Karl Bennett (1987) points out, the Caribbean offers certain comparative disadvantages from the point of view of international investors. Labor costs of the countries in Southeast Asia are far lower than even low-wage Caribbean countries, there is the possibility of protectionist lobbies in the United States that would work to prevent entry of Caribbean products, and the region's history of export processing has shown that these industries become enclave operations, with little beneficial spread effects. Thus, even by its own standards, Trinidad's manufacturing policies have been and continue to be failures. As Francisco E. Thoumi writes:

> The boom-and-bust cycle has affected . . . manufacturing branches and has complicated policy-making further. The capital-intensive nature of the sectors in which the country has a comparative advantage led the government to promote the establishment of an assembly sector, designed to serve the domestic market, in order to generate employment in manufacturing. This decision was made when high labor costs prevented the country from developing export-assembly plants. The assembly sector is made up of (mostly inefficient) plants which assemble motor vehicles, electric appliances and other products. These plants received high protection during the oil-gas boom but became very depressed when the price of energy plunged; several closed down during the 1980s. (1989:156–57)

Women's Work, Women's Lives

A number of forces affect the lives of working women. These include an apparent reversal in the long-term employment trends, whereby employment opportunities are expanding in some areas; the persistence of low wages; the state's use of gender as a development strategy; and changing patterns of fertility and family structure. While women were being paid much less than men, they were also being marginalized from waged employment. This is part of a regional historical process. Taken together, the proportion of gainfully occupied women in Barbados, British Guiana, Jamaica, and Trinidad and Tobago declined form 76.2 percent in 1891 to 32.6 percent in 1946 (Harewood 1975:134), which, as discussed above, may indicate women's entry into employment in the informal sector. W. Arthur Lewis saw this regional decline as a problem, whereas the same process would be desirable if it occurred in Britain, for example, because of Britain's relative wealth.

Writing on the "retirement" of women from production to the home, Lewis argued: "Actually we can see from the Census that much of this female retirement from industry is not voluntary but compulsory, for the Census shows that 25% of women in the age group 15–24 wanted a job but had never been able to find one in their lives (37% were at work, 7% unemployed, and 31% not desiring a gainful occupation). What has happened in the islands is that, as the population has grown, the number of jobs has failed to keep pace with it, and women have been forced to retire from industry in favor of men" (1950:4).

Lewis decried women's unemployment and relegation to "nonproductive" jobs in the services and in petty trading. The implication is that, unlike his contemporaries, he felt that women confined to such occupations as those found in the domestic service should be a "target" group for development plans.

Female employment during the 1960s to the mid-1970s remained fairly stable, although the participation rate was still high compared to many developing countries, and, in general, the position of women in the occupational structure went through only slight modifications during that period. But throughout the 1970s and to the early 1990s, there has been increased participation by females, although the number of employed males remained two and a half times higher than the number of females in 1980. It has been calculated that between 1970 and 1984 female labor-force participation increased 3.5 percent, while there was a 1 percent decrease for men in the same period. By the late 1980s, female labor-force participation had increased to almost half that of men's.

As shown by evidence from the 1980 census, women workers are especially engaged in occupations in the service, sales, and commercial sectors (see Table 8). Many are likely to be younger workers, for there are higher proportions of females employed in each of the age categories from twenty through thirty-four, after which the reverse trend is evidenced. This should be taken as further evidence that women are increasingly seeking to enter the labor market, and their entry should be seen as a result of the oil boom and the resulting expansion of government employment, where they are employed under a common pay scale that minimizes disparities in salary. Indeed, the production of labor-saving household items, such as those produced by EUL, shows the demand for such items by middle-class working women. The fact that one class of women (the EUL workers) produces these items for another class of women (white-collar women workers) shows emerging class differentials among women quite different from those on the plantations during the nineteenth century. Women's share in wages increased only slightly during the period from 1960 to the mid-1970s, and they continued to be paid at a rate of about two-thirds of men's salary by the late 1970s. What this illustrates is the extent to which government employment

TABLE 8
Working Population, by Occupational Group, 1980

Occupational Group	*Males*	*Females*
Professional, technical and related; architects and related technicians	2.33%	0.34%
Medical, dental, veterinary, and related	0.69	3.80
Other professional, technical, and related	4.98	12.69
Administrative and managerial	2.05	0.85
Clerical and related	8.25	29.44
Sales workers	6.20	12.24
Service workers	8.81	18.83
Agriculture: animal husbandry; forestry; fishing and hunting	9.73	4.56
Crafts and trades	6.90	6.23
Construction workers	9.08	0.16
Transport and equipment operators	7.32	0.15
Other production and related workers, including laborers	31.88	9.20
Not stated, not elsewhere classified	1.78	1.51
Total	100.00	100.00

SOURCE: Compiled from the 1980 census report.

is generally more lucrative for most women than the private sector, and that the income disparity in that sector is much lower than in the private sector (see Tables 9 and 10). In addition, it is important to note the wage rates for garment workers and those in the service and commercial sectors, where the bulk of women's employment is to be found, are very low.

Overall, women's median monthly income was 73.5 percent of men's in 1979, which was an improvement over 1971 when it was 55 percent of men's and from 1965 when it was only 50 percent (Turner 1982:4-2). In 1977 female service workers earned 35 percent of what males in service occupations earned (Hyacinth 1979:17). At the end of the 1970s, women earned 84 percent of what men earned in clerical occupations. This class of occupations was one of the fastest growing between 1965 and 1977. During this time, women's participation in these kinds of occupations doubled. The income differential between men and women was relatively small because much of the expansion in such jobs came with the expansion of the public sector, where established pay scales and occupational grades tend to mean relative equality in terms of pay (Turner 1982:4-3). By the 1980s, 61.6 percent of females in sales occupations and 54.7 percent of females in service occupations earned less than TT$500 per month. Yet women generally have higher educational levels than men (see Tables 11 and 12).

At the advent of the oil boom, the construction sector assumed massive

TABLE 9
Median Monthly Income of All Paid Employees, by Occupation, 1977 (in TT$)

	Median Monthly Income					
	Total		Government		Non-government	
Occupational Classification	Males	Females	Males	Females	Males	Females
All occupations	449.00	293.00	489.50	466.50	399.50	194.50
Professional, technical, and related worker	862.00	726.50	868.00	750.00	843.00	533.50
Administrative and managerial worker	1,625.50	899.00	1,701.00	899.00	1,551.00	—
Clerical and related worker	486.50	411.00	483.50	461.50	490.50	364.50
Commercial, financial, insurance worker	323.50	176.00	182.50	—	329.50	176.00
Farmer, fisher, hunter, logger and forest worker	284.50	226.50	402.00	296.00	194.00	125.00
Craftsperson, production, process worker, and laborer[a]	529.50	200.00	614.50	399.00	466.00	196.00
Worker in food, tobacco, and beverages	386.50	250.00	525.00	—	336.00	250.00
Worker in garment industry	283.50	161.50	—	145.00	283.50	161.50
Worker in transport and communication	436.50	333.00	456.00	350.00	415.50	282.50
Construction worker	398.50	380.00	408.00	384.00	378.50	199.00
Service worker	455.50	160.00	546.00	382.50	303.50	131.00
Not stated	699.00	—	699.00	—	699.00	—

SOURCE: Compiled from Hyacinth 1979:37.
[a]Not elsewhere classified, including worker in mining and quarrying.

TABLE 10
Working Population, by Income Group, 1980

Income Group	*Both Sexes*	*Males*	*Females*
Over $4,000 per month	4.35%	5.08%	2.54%
$2,500–$3,999	2.35	2.85	1.10
$1,700–$2,499	5.93	6.15	5.37
$900–$1,699	25.35	27.15	17.23
$500–$899	33.40	35.21	28.87
Under $500	20.70	14.77	35.58
Not stated	8.92	8.79	9.23
Total	101.00	100.00	99.92

SOURCE: 1980 census report, vol. 8, p. viii.
NOTE: Percentages may not total 100 because of rounding.

TABLE 11
Educational Attainment of Persons 15 Years Old and Older, 1980

Level	*Males*	*Females*
No education	3.4%	6.4%
Nursery/kindergarten	—	—
Primary	60.8	56.6
Secondary	31.1	33.8
University	2.9	1.5
Other/not stated	1.8	1.7
Total	100.0	100.0

SOURCE: Compiled from 1980 census report.

TABLE 12
Working Population, by Educational Attainment, 1980

	Males		*Females*	
Level	No.	%	No.	%
No education	5,754	2.33	3,035	3.08
Primary	160,218	64.80	43,812	44.42
Secondary	70,158	28.37	47,068	47.73
University	7,996	3.23	3,337	3.38
Other	545	0.22	279	0.28
Not stated	2,606	1.05	1,093	1.11
Total	247,277	100.00	98,624	100.00

SOURCE: 1980 census report, vol. 3, pt. 1, p. xii.

importance in the economy in terms of GDP and employment. That women employed in construction in the public sector receive almost twice what women who are similarly employed in the private sector receive reflects the extent that they have also been able to reap the benefits of political patronage.

It is difficult to predict what will happen to female employment in the present economic situation. Two trends might emerge. One is that the government will be forced to invite foreign capital, hence "enhancing" women's opportunities. The second possible trend is that existing commercial enterprises that employ women will be adversely affected and women will be marginalized. The latter scenario seems evident in the fact that unemployment in garment, textile, and footwear production increased from 8 to 25 percent between 1985 and 1986. In 1986, women's unemployment rate was two points higher than men's (see Table 13). In addition, the economic

TABLE 13
Population, Labor Force, and Employment Estimates, 1986

	Both Sexes	*Males*	*Females*
Total population	1,199,200	600,200	599,000
Population under 15 years old	398,500	202,600	195,900
Population 65 years old and older	66,800	30,400	36,400
Dependency ratio	63.0%		
Noninstitutional population	1,195,500	598,000	597,500
Noninstitutional population 15 years old and older	795,200	394,600	400,600
Labor force	471,200	316,300	154,900
Labor force participation rate	59.0%	80.0%	39.0%
Employed	393,200	265,900	127,300
Unemployed	78,000	50,300	27,700
Unemployment rate	16.6%	15.9%	17.9%

SOURCE: Trinidad and Tobago, 1987c: appendix 16.

decline has forced the government—which employs almost half the country's work force—to retrench.

With the advent of the Recession, the state has used women's labor as a development strategy (Henry 1988b; Turner 1982). The state's efforts to attract foreign investment generally guarantees that unions will be not allowed to represent labor forces in these industries, given the state's willingness to cater to the demands of businesses who could choose to locate in another country. What is less understandable is the unions' relative lack of attention to the special work situations facing women workers. And this is despite a long history of women's involvement in the trade-union movement (see Reddock's excellent study 1994) and unions' frequent reliance on women workers for loud and continuous picketing of workplaces during strikes. The OWTU's Donna Coombs-Montrose (n.d.:2) catalogs recent strike actions by women industrial workers represented by the OWTU: There was a worker occupation by almost 500 women in the American computer company Trinidata in 1979, one of the longest strikes in Trinidad's history by mainly women workers at Texstyle in 1981, and the occupation of the Bermudez Biscuit Company by 200 women workers in 1981 and again in 1983 when they faced retrenchment and plant closure.

The NAR government announced plans to establish an export processing zone (EPZ) at the Pt. Lisas Industrial Estate. This finally prompted protests by the more radical trade unions, especially the OWTU (for example, see their publication *Vanguard*, March 26, 1988, pp. 3–4), by the women's movement, and by academics from the UWI. These critics pointed out that the kinds of industries attracted would be "runaway shops" (Safa 1981)—firms with no real stake in the society which could pick and relocate when they so desired—and that these industries superexploited female labor, that EPZs in other countries prevented unionization, that they provided no forward or backward linkages to the economy, and that they tended to depress the country's wages (*TnT Mirror*, February 26, 1988). Despite protest marches, the House of Representatives voted for the proposal to establish the EPZ, and, even though the country's Senate voted against a government proposal a week after the House vote, the chairman-designate reconfirmed the commitment to the EPZ at Pt. Lisas, promising that the country's labor legislation would still apply there (*Caribbean Report*, August 25, 1988, pp. 4–5).

Development planners in the Caribbean, however, at first did not necessarily seek to incorporate women in their industrialization schemes. But industrialists have been attracted to female labor. The prevalence of women in world-market factories, and their working conditions, are documented by a considerable anthropological literature (see Ong 1991). Industrialists, and later the local governmental officials who are trying to woo them, often justify their preference for female workers in terms of their "natural" suitability for a particular kind of production process. Fernández-Kelly quotes a personnel manager of a *maquiladora* in Mexico's border industries: "We hire mostly women because they are more reliable than men; they have finer fingers, smaller muscles and unsurpassed manual dexterity. Also, women don't get tired of repeating the same operation nine hundred times a day" (1983:181).

Similarly, Victoria Durant-González quotes from a promotional brochure prepared by the Malaysian government to advertise its female workers: "The manual dexterity of the Oriental female is famous the world over. Her hands are small and she works fast and with extreme care. . . . Who, therefore, could be better qualified by nature and inheritance, to contribute to the efficiency of a bench assembly production line than the Oriental girl? No need for a zero defects program here! By nature, they 'quality control' themselves" (1987:9).

With reference to the Caribbean, Eve E. Abraham-van der Mark shows how Curaçao authorities emphasized "the availability of a large reservoir of cheap female labor" when they endeavored to attract assembly industry in the late 1960s, and they succeeded in attracting Texas Instruments, Rockwell, and Schlumberger (1983:380).

But questions remain, too, concerning the potential effects of the government's industrialization efforts, which continue to be guided by the Puerto Rican model. Durant-González reports an encounter with a Trinidad and Tobago government official who said that the government would promote foreign investments that generate employment for women in order to prevent a disruption of the social order: "The official explained that unemployed young females are more dangerous to a society than unemployed young males. The reason for this is that unemployed males will only stand around in the streets and admire women and smoke ganja. While the unemployed female will turn to prostitution and this will break down the moral order. He also pointed out that when women work they will use their income to support themselves and their children, while men spend their income among more than one household and in the rum shops. Thus, export processing jobs are a way of maintaining the moral order, and employing women ensures that income is put to proper use" (Durant-González 1983:4).

This sentiment is not surprising in a country where women's lower status often means they have to contend with sexual harassment at the workplace and where almost any female walking down a public street is subject to cat calls, wolf whistles, and explicit, sometimes threatening, sexual references from men. Trinidadian sociologist Patricia Mohammed attributes what she sees as the recent upsurge in sexual violence and sexual abuse to the male backlash against opportunities afforded to women during the oil boom:

> The growing independence and affirmative actions of women in Trinidad bred its own internal contradictions. If the pre-independence years allowed men at least the medium of verbal and some physical assault to keep women subordinated (especially in the context where she was not in an economic position to question this nor socially supported by public opinion in her challenge), then the 70s with their oil boom and opportunities must have undermined the male ego further. The response was likely an increase in sexual violence and sexual abuse. How does one explain the fact that in 1973/74 one felt safe to walk on the streets at night, as a single woman to go out alone at nights and return quite late and by the mid-80s this was no longer possible. I do not know if my Trinidadian colleagues will agree with me, but I have experienced the worst and most obscene and degraded harassment on the streets of Trinidad—worse than in any other country. Newspaper reports and rumours of rapes, incest, wife battering and sexual harassment increased. . . . it is common knowledge that it had become highly unsafe for women where before there was no great fear. (1989:40–41; see also Chapter 5)

As Mohammed reports, there was a flourishing of the women's movement in the late 1980s and several women's groups were established. However, these efforts at formal organization are not always taken seriously. In addition, there exists a genuine concern in some quarters that these organizations are middle-class based and, therefore, cannot adequately represent the interests of working-class women. These concerns are played upon by those who are hostile to the women's movement for political and economic reasons. For example, there is this account of the celebration of International Women's Day:

> While several "champions of women's causes" held a "mass rally" at Woodford Square on Monday, female vendors on Frederick Street did not know it was International Women's Day. . . .

> They were sweating it out in the sugar cane fields, in factories, the markets, as janitors in office buildings and as maids in rich folks' homes.
>
> Some have described them as the true champions of the women's struggle; women who without a man around, have to clothe, feed, educate and discipline their children without much ado. (*Sunday TnT Mirror*, March 14, 1993, p. 31)

The article also evinces the notion of the strong black matriarch, the single head of husehold capable of making her own way and, therefore, not in need of collective organizations to represent her interests. This view is damaging to women because, as Olive Senior argues in her book *Working Miracles*,

> The myth of the dominant black female is perpetuated today in the glib use of concepts such as 'matriarchic society,' and in the reciting of statistics which show an increasing trend towards female household headship as if headship *per se* confers power on women. . . . The myth of the black matriarch is one of the most pervasive in Caribbean societies. But in what does the matriarch's alleged power and dominance inhere? While some younger, upwardly mobile women nowadays voluntarily choose single parenthood and household headship, for older women there is usually no choice; the role is foisted on them by circumstances. Female household heads on the whole are poor, black, uneducated and in the worst-paid and lowest-status job. It is these women who are truly working miracles, in ensuring at least the survival, and sometimes the advancement, of their families. (1991:96, 102)

The myth of the black matriarch has been used by Trinidadian politicians. Women in the PNM were integral from the beginning, through the PNM's Women's League. But it seems they provided necessary labor and were counted on for their reputed organizational skills and for their fierce heckling of opponents. One article recalling their role stated: "Dr. Williams's faith in the women was politically rewarding to both the party and himself. In return, [t]hey loved and idolised 'de Doc' passionately. They were fiercely loyal to him, which led him to have his own way in the party. He operated through a sort of unspoken philosophy that seemed to suggest that 'as long as the women are on your side, you are a sure winner.' His would-be antagonists found it wiser to curb their tongues than risk the wrath of the female loyalists" (*Trinidad Guardian*, September 28, 1986, p. 5).

While some women have run successfully for elected office, an incident about three weeks prior to the 1986 election revealed perhaps a more accurate picture of women in contemporary Trinidadian politics. At a PNM political rally in Sangre Grande, Prime Minister Chambers and three PNM candidates were being heckled by a group of NAR supporters, who wore NAR T-shirts and waved NAR pamphlets. The PNM speakers on the platform had to contend with incessant heckling while some PNM supporters were also involved in exchanging taunts with the NAR crowd. The hecklers shouted things like "corruption" and "we want work."

When it was his turn to speak, Chambers said, "I want to address a few remarks to the 18 people," meaning the hecklers. "Do you mean to tell me that you allow PNM to bring a crowd like this next door to your headquarters and you only have 18 people?" There were cheers from the PNM supporters. He continued, "I am giving free PNM technical advice; if you want to heckle a meeting you must have a FAB. All yuh have a FAB? You don't send 18 men to heckle a meeting. After two minutes they want a beer. You must put women to heckle a meeting" (*Sunday Guardian*, November 30, 1986, p. 18).

"FAB" refers to "Fat Ass Brigade," the PNM's description of their female supporters and party workers, supposedly large, middle-aged black women—the stereotypical matriarch. Many women were outraged and incensed by Chambers's remarks. One woman wrote to the editor:

> Mr Chambers insisted that all parties must have a FAB for the purpose of heckling. We all know and definitely agree that this name is totally degrading for all those involved. It has nothing to do with politics but the plump and well-rounded posterior of the women of the PNM party. The name cannot be complimentary in any way.
>
> The Prime Minister in using this term has shown that he has absolutely no respect for the women of his party. He has left us women of the country nothing to aspire to, politically and otherwise, since obviously we can only be hecklers.
>
> The most destructive thing about this statement is the fine example it offers to our young men. It is already difficult for a lot of them to accept women as equals and the statement does not help them any. These men have probably patted themselves on the[ir] backs . . . and deem that they have been right all along. Women, are of course, solely for confusion [i.e., gossip and slander].
>
> Mr Chambers has made our task as women a million times more difficult. Since the beginning of time, women have tried to get out of the kitchen and bedroom and take their place as equals in the society but Mr Chambers has pushed us right back into that rut. (*Trinidad Guardian*, December 9, 1986, p. 8)

Another woman wrote:

> If ever I had any doubts about the way the ruling party, led by Chambers, feels about women on the whole and PNM women in particular, I have none now.
>
> His advice to the NAR (alleged) hecklers about getting a FAB to do that job gives a clear indication as to where the Government really stands on the role of the women of Trinidad and Tobago.
>
> Based on his comments, it seems that "de only ting all yuh good for is to heckle at Opposition Party meetings and wine dong de place at your own["] [i.e., to express one's sexual availability through sexually provocative dancing, or "wining"; see Miller 1991].

> . . . Personally, I find his comments downright insulting, degrading, in exceptional bad taste and very typical of the many "man patterns" masquerading as men in Government and in Trinidad and Tobago.
>
> It certainly does nothing positive for the status of women. As a woman who faces almost daily harassment on the nation's streets (not because I wear revealing/tight clothing or because I am incredibly attractive, but simply because as a woman I am perceived as easy verbal prey) to have one's leader spewing forth such rhetoric for all and sundry to hear is a giant step backward for us all. (*Trinidad Guardian*, December 10, 1986, p. 8)

Still another commented: "The Prime Minister has grossly insulted the women of Trinidad and Tobago by proposing that their role in politics should be one of heckling under the banner of the F.A.B. We women as mothers and grandmothers must protect our children and grandchildren against such degrading remarks and prove our dignity and self-respect. . . . We should shout from the housetops for an apology" (*Trinidad Guardian*, December 10, 1986, p. 8).

One woman concluded: "I demand a public apology from the Prime Minister . . . for that comments, not only on behalf of the women supporters, but of women generally, as it showed non-recognition of their improving status, which they work so hard to earn, amidst the many problems that would discourage them—discrimination, sexual harassment, and supporting a fatherless family. Chambers, we demand an apology" (*Sunday Guardian*, December 14, 1986, p. 2B). And even the scandal-mongering tabloid the *Bomb* got in on the act, with the screaming headline "Chambers Degrades Our Women" (December 5, 1986, p. 7).

The NAR candidates sought to gain political mileage out of Chambers's remarks during the election campaign, but when they assumed power they indicated that they were operating with the same assumptions. The NAR government set up for the first time a ministry responsible for women's affairs, the Ministry of Health, Welfare, and the Status of Women. However, many women were galled when a man, Emmanuel Hosein, was named as minister. There were complaints that there were not enough women chosen as senators, which are appointed by the ruling party, the official opposition, and the president of the republic. One woman, who signed her letter to the editor "Constructive Critic," expressed her disappointment in this following way:

> As a woman, I must admit that I was most disappointed in the appointment of persons to the Senate. The choice of members makes a mockery of the idea of including in the Ministry of Health the added responsibility of the Status of Women.
>
> Of the 31 persons picked, the names of only four women appeared on the list. The NAR Government, the Opposition and even the President showed very little respect for the women of our country in their choice.

> If the NAR Government was truly serious about including in the Ministry of Heatlh, the responsibility for the Status of Women, they would have shown this in the choice of their Senators. (*Trinidad Guardian*, January 26, 1987, p. 6)

Early in the NAR's regime, well-known women's rights activist Hazel Brown said that the prospects for women under the NAR were "bleak and disastrous," and she blamed the prime minister: "There is a lot of lip service being paid to the idea of the upliftment of women in the society but that is all. Mr. Robinson is the problem because there is a gap between his stated position on issues, including women, and his actions. But the whole change process will not work unless there is proper participation by women" (*Sunday Express*, March 15, 1987, p. 21).

Under the Employment of Women (Nightwork) Act, there are restrictions that prevent women from working between 10 P.M. and 5 A.M. Exceptions are made when women are working in an undertaking that only employs members of the same family, when women are in supervisory roles, or in industries like the packaging of fresh fruit for immediate shipment and other businesses where raw materials would be lost through deterioration (Daly 1982:110). Further, the National Commission on the Status of Women (Trinidad and Tobago 1976:22) points out that, bearing in mind the number of women employed in restaurants, nightclubs, and airports, this law appears to be honored in the breach. One stipulation of the Factories Ordinance (1950) requires owners to provide seating for female workers and to post notices to the effect that the seating is for their use. One might argue that such restrictions actually affect female workers negatively because they make women less flexible than men as potential employees and preclude them from earning overtime payments in some cases. On the other hand, despite the "protection" intended by these laws, women who have miscarriages as the result of an accident at work are not compensated under the present workers' compensation legislation.

Until 1975, Inland Revenue, the tax-collection agency, treated the income of a wife living with her husband as being the income of the husband. This meant that, even though her income was most likely modest, she paid tax at the same rate as her husband. This probably discouraged many married women from working. Fortunately, this has been changed, and married couples now file separate returns. However, as Stephanie Daly (1982:35–36) argues, despite recent positive developments, the tax system still is hostile to women, with paltry deductions allowed for child care and household help.

Women's participation in the labor force does not occur in a social vacuum. Factors such as fertility, marital status, and education all have a bearing on employment and responsibilities both inside and outside the home. These factors have been changing in the past forty years. For example, the divorce rate increased five-fold between 1946 (12.4 per 1,000 marriages registered) and 1970 (63.4 per 1,000 marriages). In 1975, the divorce rate was 67 per 1,000 marriages. This contrasts to the legal marriage rate, which has increased from 11.4 per 1,000 population in 1946 to 12.5 per 1,000 in 1970. This trend may reflect greater economic and educational opportunities for women, lower fertility rates, and a liberalization of the divorce laws. That black and East Indian women have traditionally been involved in differing conjugal relationships is indicated in information from the World Fertility Survey (WFS) undertaken in Trinidad and Tobago in 1977.

The way women's role in the household affects their employment is dependent upon a number of factors that vary cross-culturally (cf. Stichter 1990), including child rearing, opportunities for productive work in the household (such as self-employment), household structure and kin arrangements, household income, and household decision making. Historically, East Indian women have entered into their first sexual union earlier than blacks or women from other ethnic groups (Roberts and Braithwaite 1967), and this has been associated with their higher fertility levels. However, the age of first union for East Indian women has been increasing. Of the youngest women described in Table 14, East Indians have a higher age of first entry than do black women.

Traditionally, Black and East Indian women have also had different patterns of mating (see Tables 15 and 16), which have been related to differing family forms. For East Indian women the pattern has been to begin in a married or common-law relationship and to stay in it. This pattern is less common for black women. Among the non–East Indian respondents in the WFS, most women who were married at the time of the survey had started in visiting relationships, that is, sexual relationships with a non-

TABLE 14
Mean Age at Entry into Initial Union for Women 25 Years Old and Older, Whose Initial Union Was Before Age 25, 1977

	Ethnic Group			
Current Age	Total	Black	East Indian	Other
Total	18.2 years	18.2 years	17.8 years	18.7 years
25–29 years	18.6	18.3	18.7	19.1
30–34 years	18.3	18.3	18.2	18.3
35–39 years	18.1	18.2	17.7	19.2
40–44 years	17.7	18.3	17.0	18.3
45–49 years	17.7	17.9	16.9	18.7

SOURCE: Compiled from World Fertility Survey 1981:34.

TABLE 15
Percentage of All Women Ever in a Union, According to Union History, by Ethnic Origin, Current Age, and Level of Education, 1977

		Pattern of Union History: Initial/Current Union Status						
Characteristic	*No. of Women*	M, CL/M	V/M	M, CL/CL	V/CL	Any/V	M, CL/S	V/S
Total	3,482	29%	24%	6%	10%	20%	3%	7%
Ethnic origin								
African	1,461	9	29	4	15	32	2	10
Indian	1,377	56	17	9	4	7	5	2
Other	644	22	30	3	13	20	2	11
Current age								
< 25 years	961	19	18	4	12	36	1	10
25–34 years	1,264	31	27	6	11	18	1	6
35–44 years	897	37	26	7	5	7	9	8
45–49 years	360	38	27	7	5	7	9	8
Level of education								
Primary < 7 years	1,354	40	19	10	10	12	5	4
7 years	995	25	25	4	13	23	2	10
Secondary	1,133	23	30	2	8	27	2	9

SOURCE: World Fertility Survey 1981:37, table 3.1.C.
NOTE: M = married; CL = common law; V = visiting; S = single.

coresident man, whereas this pattern represented a much smaller percentage for East Indians. In addition, movements from visiting to legal marriage and from visiting to common-law relationships were much more associated with non–East Indians than with East Indians. Among WFS respondents, East Indians have a much higher proportion who are married than do non–East Indians (73 percent compared to 38 percent for blacks and 52 percent for the category "Other"). Among blacks, visiting and married unions occur with almost the same frequency, each accounting for about one-third of all the unions. Among East Indians aged 20–24, around 74 percent were legally married, and this proportion changes only slightly as age increases. On the other hand, only 20 percent of black women aged 20–24 were married, but the proportion increases steadily so that for the 45–49 age group the proportion married is around 60 percent. The WFS data indicate that the proportion of Trinidadian women in visiting relationships thus declines as age increases, but the decline is from 16 percent to 2 percent for East Indians and from 65 percent to 11 percent for blacks.

Mating patterns are related to family form. To say that the family in the Caribbean was the overwhelming focus of anthropological investigations from the 1950s to the 1970s is an understatement (see Mohammed 1988b).

TABLE 16
Percentage of All Women Ever in a Union, According to Union Status, by Ethnic Origin, Level of Education, Place of Residence, and Religion, 1977

Background Variable	*No. of Women*	*Current Union Status*			
		Married	Common Law	Visiting	Single
All Women	3,482	54%	16%	20%	10%
Ethnic origin					
African	1,461	37	19	32	12
Indian	1,377	74	13	7	7
Other	644	52	16	20	13
Level of education					
Primary					
<7 years	1,354	59	20	12	10
7+ years	995	50	17	23	11
Secondary+	1,133	53	10	27	10
Place of Residence					
Urban	2,103	51	16	23	11
Rural	1,379	60	16	15	9
Religion					
Anglican	522	38	18	34	10
Roman Catholic	1,236	42	20	26	11
Hindu	797	75	12	6	7
Muslim	208	80	8	6	6
Other	719	57	12	18	13

SOURCE: World Fertility Survey 1981:41, table 3.1.K.

These investigations directly followed colonial efforts to eradicate supposedly "pathological" Afro-Caribbean family forms, sometimes referred to as "matriarchal" or "matrifocal." East Indian joint families, on the other hand, were termed "patriarchal" for their "patrilocal" residency patterns and authority structure (see Klass 1961; Vertovec 1991). Often, discussion (anthropological as well as popular) of the "traditional" East Indian family and household structure compared it favorably to the supposed "loose" organization of the black family and household structure and associated the latter with all sorts of social ills. However, data from the WFS and a recent ethnographic and survey-based investigation indicate that profound changes are occurring in East Indian families and their household organization, so that there exists less and less variation related to ethnic and cultural differences. Popular discourse, especially East Indians', however, still tends to uphold the positive values of the "traditional" East Indian family.

In his recent study of four communities in Trinidad—"Newtown," "Ford," "St Pauls," and "The Meadows" (pseudonyms)—Daniel Miller cites

Norma Abdulah's more recent work on mating patterns: "There has been a dramatic change in mating patterns; for among younger women it is now the non-Indians who enter their first union at an earlier age. Moreover, more women of both ethnic groups are now entering a visiting union as their initial relationship; and young women, particularly the better educated ones, are increasingly tending to remain in a visiting union rather than shift to a more stable relationship as was formerly the more common practice" (Abdulah 1988:461). As Miller comments, "Despite the fact that an ideology which equates a powerful concept of family with one ethnic group is used to objectify a powerful set of values within Trinidadian culture, this may not impinge very much on the remaining practices of that group. . . . The ideology of the Indian family as the bastion of certain Trinidadian values has arisen during the same period when actual ethnic distinctions in familial practice have drastically reduced" (1994:142–43).

Miller surveyed 181 households in the four communities. With extended households disaggregated, his data indicate the following patterns: of the 86 East Indian households surveyed, 62 (72 percent) were married (with or without children); 12 (14 percent) were in common-law relationships (with or without children); 11 (13 percent) were female adults (with or without children); and 1 (about 1 percent) was a male adult only (with or without children). For the 67 black households surveyed, 34 (51 percent) were married; 14 (21 percent) were in common-law relationships, 18 (27 percent) were female adult headed, and 1 (about 1 percent) male only. Among the 28 "mixed" or "others," 16 (57 percent) were married, 8 (28 percent) were in common-law relationships, and 4 (14 percent) were female adult headed. "Visiting unions" were not enumerated because Miller's informants felt the concept did not appropriately describe contemporary life, even though the practice that the term describes may continue (Miller 1994:156–57, table 4.3).

Further, Miller points to a number of caveats in the data. In The Meadows, an upscale community, there is only one case of a common-law relationship, the result of class-based "dominant ideologies" that "attempt to construct a consistent moral interpretation of mating relationships" (1994:158). With regard to ethnicity,

> The evidence from St Pauls illustrates the problem of an over-emphasis on ethnicity. With one exception, all the cases of common-law or female-headed households are Indian, even though these are a minority of ten as against thirty-seven households based on legal marriage. This confirms the evidence from Ford that there is increasing empathy among Indians for the refusal of formal marriage, with a growing proportion of families corresponding to the more transient forms associated with the African population. In Ford only a minority of Indian families are in legal marriage, and this is true for the larger joint families as well as for nuclear families. . . . The traditions of South Asian

> family structure have been replaced by a general ideology of the close family. Specific role relations have also been reduced to a general sense of the proper position of at least parent-child, marital, sibling and generalised cousin relations. The older precision of Hindi kinship terminology is replaced by a set of generalising English terms and a general sense of the "appropriate" forms of behaviour. The result is once again much closer than hitherto to the stress on the importance of "aunties" and "uncles" in the African family. (1994:158, 159)

Richard W. Stoffle (1977) in his study of the impact of industrialization on mating patterns in Barbados argues that the entry of women into industrial employment would actually "speed up" the mating process, whereby one passes through the "stages" of visiting, common-law, and legally sanctioned unions. (This does not mean, however, that the West Indian mating pattern is "serial"; see M.G. Smith 1962). We need, then, to consider the articulation of women's fertility strategies with their employment histories and opportunities.

Dorian L. Powell (1976:237) in her study of fertility and labor-force participation among Jamaican women found participation rates higher for childless women than for those with children, with the greatest differential falling between ages 25 and 29. Of these women, 73 percent without children had jobs, while only about half with children had jobs. In the Caribbean these roles are not always mutually exclusive. Constance R. Sutton and Susan Makiesky-Barrow write of Barbadian women: "A job or career for a woman is never spoken of as an alternative to marriage or maternity. Although it is realized that a woman's household and child-care responsibilities might necessitate her withdrawal from work for short periods, the "dual career" conflict experienced by women in industrial societies is not marked. This reflects not only different expectations and assumptions about a woman's economic and social roles but also the presence of a family and kinship system that acts as a support for women of all ages" (1977:306).

It seems that in Trinidad working women are choosing to limit their reproductive activities (see Table 17). There are significant differences in fertility according to a woman's history of economic activity. Women who are currently employed have the lowest level of fertility, followed by those who are not currently working and those who have never worked. Among women who are presently working, the fertility of those who did not work before they had their first child is more than twice the fertility rate of those who were engaged in employment before they bore their first child. This suggests a correlation between low fertility and employment experience. Perhaps women who are working utilize pregnancy planning more than those who do not work, and those women who do not utilize pregnancy planning find access to employment more difficult because of their more numerous domestic responsibilities. When data from the 1980 census are compared to the 1977 WFS, there seems to be a trend of increasing childlessness among

TABLE 17

Mean Number of Children Born to All Women Ever in a Union, by Number of Years Since First Union and by Work History, 1977

	Mean Number of Children				
		Number of Years Since First Union			
Work History	All Unions	<10	10–19	≥20	*Total Women*
All women	3.1	1.2	3.1	5.9	3,482
Currently working	2.6	0.9	2.8	5.3	1,277
Worked before first birth[a]	1.8	0.7	2.3	4.6	879
Did not work before first birth	4.2	1.9	3.8	6.0	398
Not currently working	3.3	1.4	3.8	6.1	1,042
Worked before and after first birth[a]	2.6	0.8	3.5	5.5	430
Worked only after first birth	4.4	2.1	4.1	6.7	317
Worked only before first birth	3.1	1.8	3.8	6.2[b]	295
Never worked	3.7	1.5	4.2	6.3	1,163

SOURCE: World Fertility Survey 1981:55, table 3.2.R.
[a]Includes 0-birth women.
[b]Mean was calculated on a base of fewer than 50, but at least 20, cases.

younger women. This corresponds to Powell's findings of lower levels of fertility among younger working women in Jamaica (1976:254).

Because of lowering birthrates, increasingly higher levels of education, the economic recession, and the needs of foreign capital, women are ready and prepared to enter the labor force in ever-increasing numbers. We can expect that black and East Indian women will be increasingly affected in similar ways as a result of industrialization because of their increasingly similar mating and cultural family experiences. Powell (1976:254) sees female labor-force participation in Jamaica as greatest by those in visiting unions, somewhat less by those in common-law unions, and less still by married women. The evidence seems to suggest that East Indian women are waiting longer to become legally married and engaging in mating relationships that are more conducive to formal labor-force participation. If this is so, it might represent a significant factor in further increased female labor-force participation for the country as a whole.

Since the late 1950s, family planning has been advocated in Trinidad by the PNM government, and as an indicator of the success of these policies, the fertility level of Trinidad and Tobago should be comparable to the levels in North America by the end of the century (Harewood and Abdulah 1972). Thus, Lewis's (1950:1) claim that "the case for rapid industrialisation in the West Indies rests chiefly on over-population" is increasingly irrelevant. I mention this, not because I believe that with the population problem coming under control there is no longer a case for industrialization, but to point out how the model is based on limited and out-of-date assumptions.

In this chapter I have situated the ethnography by examining the historical context of colonialism, neocolonialism, and economic dependency and the ethnic and gendered division of labor. In addition, I have examined some of the historical, demographic, and cultural factors that affect female participation in the labor force. However ironic, women's and men's employment during slavery and indenture was in many ways more equal than it has been in subsequent years. With the advent of industrialization on the island, women have been marginalized from the productive sectors until the recent demand for more female labor. Men's occupations have been renumerated at a far better rate than women's, even when women and men work within the same industry. This situation cannot be justified in terms of men possessing more skill or being naturally more valuable employees.

Rather than provide a backdrop to the ethnography, I have endeavored in this chapter to provide empirical evidence for a theoretical understanding of the ontological bases of hegemony in Trinidadian society. The concept of hegemony entails a complex of meanings based on relations of domination. This perspective implies interaction between the ideational and material levels of culture and the pressures and parameters of social action. While the focus of this book is on relationships of ethnicity, class, and gender and how the meanings associated with these social identities are involved in production, the evidence in this chapter suggests multiple determinations of the dimensions of power in Trinidadian society. In the following chapters, we will see how these social forces impinge upon social relations in the factory.

Chapter 3

THE SITE OF PRODUCTION: A TRINIDADIAN FACTORY

At least the world system has begun recently to be the object of theoretical attention. But this is not the case, as it should be, at the other end of the scale with the elusive but apparently ubiquitous entity known loosely as "forms" of production, "relations of exploitation," "at the point of production," "on farm/in firm" relations, etc. . . . Acknowledging that, in the complex social formations of the Third World, "appearance" and "reality" may be even further apart than usual, [some authors] are naturally reluctant to identify these almost infinitely multiplex and variable relations as being the sort of thing Marx was really referring to in a famous passage: "It is always the direct relationship of the owners of the conditions of production to the direct producers . . . which reveals the innermost secret, the hidden basis of the entire social structure"
—Aidan Foster-Carter, "The Modes of Production Controversy"

OBSERVING TRINIDADIAN CULTURE in the early 1960s V. S. Naipaul wrote: "To be modern is to ignore local products and to use those advertised in American magazines. . . . In the stores the quality of the unbranded goods is not high, the prices extravagant; the mark-up is fifty or a hundred percent, and on some goods, like Japanese knick-knacks, as much as three hundred percent: Trinidadians will not buy what they think is cheap. In December 1959, after the civil servants had received another of their pay rises, Port of Spain was sold out of refrigerators" (1981 [1962]:48, 52–53).

This describes a historical condition of "commodity fetishism," where most Trinidadians put a high value on the latest gadgets, particularly stereos and labor-saving home appliances. Trinidadians are well aware of the status attached to certain foreign brand names, of which they are discerning consumers, and the wealth from the oil boom meant the proliferation of these items (see Miller 1992, 1993).

Before the 1950s, nearly all household durable goods were imported, and this business was controlled by commission agents, who were almost entirely members of the white elite. Commission agencies specialized in the importation of goods, making a profit on their markup for wholesale and retail customers. In the 1960s, with the advent of local manufacturing firms, industrialization-by-invitation plans were modified from an emphasis on production for export to import-substitution, where tariff protection helped the new firms producing for the domestic market.

Although the Tiexieras indicated that EUL's product range was dictated by what they saw as a gap in the market, they were certainly limited by conventional wisdom, or what was thought to be appropriate for Caribbean manufacturers to produce. W. Arthur Lewis commented on the sorts of items he thought would be favorable to produce in the West Indies: "It is also desirable to enter the field of light engineering, and to make such things as bicycles, sewing machines, vacuum cleaners, fractional horse power electric motors, gramophones, refrigerators, and the simpler machine tools; and the field of assembly—e.g., assembling imported parts into radio sets" (Lewis 1950:29).

Assembling imported parts is the essential feature of the so-called screw-driver industries, where items are assembled with components imported from abroad. Most of these industries at present employ women, and they have become a Caribbean-wide phenomenon.[1] The EUL factory arose out of this process. With the Recession, however, the company began to concentrate on exporting its products and thus deviates somewhat from the traditional import-substitution manufacturing model. At the time of my study, company officials estimated they exported more than two-thirds of what they made.

This chapter provides a history of the factory and a description of its geographical and social setting in a Port-of-Spain suburb. I present data on the characteristics of the work force, including the floor workers and their supervisors, showing how people of a certain gender and ethnic identity become channeled into specific functions in the factory. I then examine wages comparatively and show how the factory workers are marginalized economically.

Several factors shape social relations in the factory: the formal organization of production; the informal patterns of behavior; and ideational factors, that is the assumptions, injunctions, and values that workers bring with them and the relationships of which they are a part. Age, ethnicity, gender, work groups, friendship, kinship, and patronage are very important in this regard, as is the structural and historical framework within which the workers are ensconced.

Locales

In 1972, the Essential Utensils Ltd. company was formed by Nigel Tiexiera, a white Portuguese Creole who has a master's degree from a Canadian university, and his wife, Jane Tiexiera (née Deschampsneufs, a well-known and wealthy French Creole family). Jane explained to me how the factory was started: "We were going to get money from my family when we got married, and Nigel said: 'We can either spend it on a big house or invest it in something that will make us money in the long run . . . and in the meantime we would have to do without. And we will have to work at it.' I said, 'Sure, why not. That's no problem.' "

When they decided to establish their firm, the Tiexieras applied to the IDC for a factory building and were allocated one in an industrial estate in Diego Martin. Initially, they imported small household durable goods. In the mid-1970s they expanded the business: They contracted with a U.S. multinational producer of household durable goods to produce under license two items bearing the multinational's brand name. A new factory was built with IDC credit in a different location in the same industrial estate. The Tiexieras own the new factory building and lease the land from the IDC. The multinational brought in its own equipment and machinery, more workers were hired, and the products were sold on the local market and exported to CARICOM countries and the United States.

In the late 1970s, officials of the multinational decided to stop producing the two items EUL was making because they faced increased competition at home and it was calculated that the considerable investments and design updating required to become competitive would not be cost effective. An official of the multinational informed Nigel Tiexiera of this impending decision and indicated that the equipment could be bought from the multinational at what Tiexiera called "a good price." EUL began producing the items under its own brand name in 1980, and at that time was one of the few locally owned firms that was exporting. EUL did so well that the company won the prime minister's Export Award in the early 1980s. EUL expanded its export markets into Central and South America throughout the 1980s and, during the course of my fieldwork, a *Trinidad Guardian* article indicated that 1986 was the firm's best year for exports and that they were now exporting to more than twenty-four countries. In mid-1986, immediately before my fieldwork began, EUL started producing a third item, with some cooperation from a firm in Taiwan. Increasingly, Taiwan has replaced the United States as the major supplier of inputs for EUL's products. By the time my fieldwork ended one year later, the sales of the new product had surpassed the other two.

While the factory gives the impression of being a "screwdriver" operation, Nigel Tiexiera maintains that EUL is involved in "manufacturing, not just assembling." He bases this assertion on the fact that, prior to my fieldwork, the factory began producing the plastic casings for the products. Prior to this, some of the plastic parts had to be imported from suppliers in the United States, while others were supplied, irregularly and inefficiently according to Tiexiera, by a Trinidadian company. To remedy this situation, EUL bought and imported machines that make plastic parts. These four large machines, each nearly the size of a school bus, make screaming noises as they mold grains of dry plastic resin into plastic parts. The resin for the production of the plastic parts is imported from Austria. In fact, 100 percent of the component parts that comprise the three products are imported.

EUL does have some linkages with the wider economy. Exports are shipped out by sea, and occasionally by air, and local container and shipping companies are utilized. Rush orders by air are sent via Caricargo, an air-freight service owned by British West Indian Airlines (BWIA), the state airline of Trinidad and Tobago. Another linkage is in the procurement of boxes, which are provided by Caribbean Packaging Industries (CPI). Nigel Tiexiera often complains about the poor quality of CPI's product and about unreliable delivery. He says that he would like to purchase boxes made in a factory on the island of St. Vincent, which he claims are cheaper and of better quality, but he is precluded from doing this because cardboard boxes are on the negative list and can be imported only with a license.

Therefore, EUL is fairly typical of export-oriented "screwdriver" industries in that its components are imported and it has few linkages with the domestic economy. Where it is different from other export-oriented industries, such as those in the EPZs found in the rest of the region, is that it also produces a considerable amount for the local market and its products are protected from local competition under negative-list stipulations.

The social characteristics of the factory and the work force must be seen in the context of the physical setting of the factory, especially since most of the workers are drawn from the local area. Studies of the social and spatial organization of the country's capital, Port-of-Spain (Conway 1989; Goodenough 1978), have shown the prevalence of traditional ethnic- and status-based residential separation. However, it has been suggested that these have given way to residency patterns based on occupation, income, and education (Goodenough 1978:43). In his anthropological study of Port-of-Spain, Michael Lieber writes: "Some Port-of-Spain neighborhoods have evolved in such a way that social relations among the very different kinds of people inside them are extensive and harmonious. Often interpersonal and intergroup relations extend across classes but not across ethnic lines, while sometimes the opposite is true. In Diego Martin class-based commitments and styles bring together a bourgeoisie of many different shades. In St. James 'Indianness' counts much more than class position in establishing rapport and acceptance. Such diverse arrangements have different implications for the manner in which social relations within and across ethnic segments are conducted" (Lieber 1981:30–31).

Diego Martin, a twenty-minute drive from Port-of-Spain, is a ward of the county of St. George and its boundaries extend from a line just east of St. James to the north coast, encompassing the entire northwest peninsula.

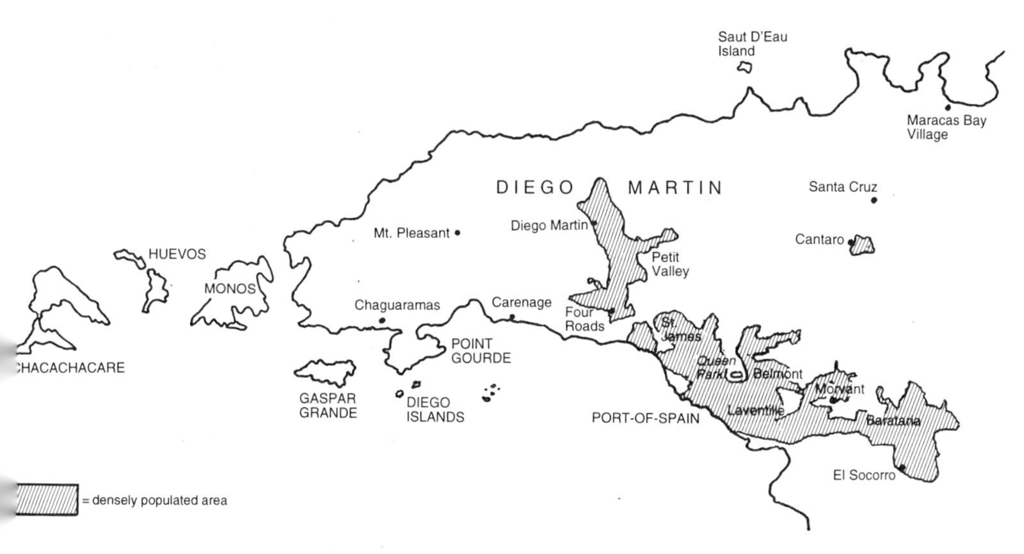

MAP 3
The Northwest Peninsula

However, when Trinidadians think of Diego Martin, they think of an area with boundaries extending from Four Roads to the north coast (see Map 3). According to local legend, the area took its name from Diego de Martín, an early Spanish settler. At one time almost the entire valley area, which is ringed on three sides by green mountains, was under sugar cultivation (de Verteuil 1987). Today, the area can be considered a suburb of Port-of-Spain: Every working day commuters into "town" must leave by 6:30 A.M. to avoid the rush-hour traffic jam, which is reminiscent of major North American cities. Diego (most people shorten the name, which is pronounced DAY-go) is made up of rich and poor neighborhoods, and homes range from modern, multistory air-conditioned houses with high fences, guard dogs, and satellite dishes, to "board houses," which are made mostly of plywood, two-by-fours, and pine planks and built on wooden stilts. There are several "housing estates," including some built by the government, which consist of rows of identical concrete block houses with flat, corrugated-iron roofs. Many residents have migrated from other parts of Trinidad as part of the rural to urban migratory flow (cf. Simpson 1973).

For Trinidadians, and foreign visitors alike, Diego Martin evokes the images of American suburbia. Lieber provides an accurate picture: "Diego Martin is a sprawling, amorphous stretch of scattered and newly developed suburban pockets. It is very much the suburb to move to for the upwardly mobile middle-classes of Port-of-Spain, foremost among them civil servants.

Some sections, such as Diamond Vale, are larage tract developments of endlessly replicated identical houses and streets arranged in a neat, orderly, sterile pattern. Other enclaves are distinguished from each other in various ways—by residents' income levels, ethnicity, architectural style" (Lieber 1981:28).

A similar picture emerges in a scene from the Trinidadian novelist Earl Lovelace's *The Dragon Can't Dance* (1979). In the novel, the calypsonian Philo moves from Calvary Hill, an East Port-of-Spain ghetto, to Diego Martin, a move that represents upward social mobility. In one scene, Philo sits on the veranda of his house, looks across the lawn,

> and for the first time since coming here to live, he was struck by the newness and sameness of everything. . . .
> Watching now, *seeing* now, and overtaken by a king of horror, he felt a calypso on the edge of his brain:
>
> The new people so new, you know, nobody
> Don't know who is who
> They all the same, all of them carry
> The same kinda name
> Same kinda dog, same kinda wife, all of them living
> The same kinda life
>
> Mr John and Mr Harry coming home drunk
> Went to sleep in each other's house
> Live for years and nobody complain
> Until one night drunk again
> The two fellars make back the exchange.
> (1979:213–14)

Carla, a twenty-four-year-old East Indian worker at EUL, put the rural-urban differences in Trinidad in another way. She related the story of a recent *gayap*[2] that she knew about happening in the predominantly East Indian town of Chaguanas in central Trinidad. She told me of how a man she knew bought the materials and his neighbors helped him build most of his house. "That wouldn't happen down here," she said.

But the image of Trinidad suburbia tends to belie the lack of uniformity and the incidence of poverty in and among the middle-class Trinidadian suburban belt. A Caribbean Conference of Churches report identified what it described as "pockets of poverty" in the Diego Martin area (1986:81). Lieber points out:

> Interspersed among all the middle-class housing are squatter pockets. This whole region was very much a squatter area before the developers moved in, and while the developers have been thorough and efficient in altering the face of the Diego Martin region, many squatters remain, tenaciously sticking with their little holdings and coolly resisting the frustrated attempts to evict them

quickly and smoothly. This is one of the juxtapositions of modern Trinidad: squeezing in among what otherwise would be (much to the dismay of the city's respectable escapees) a uniformly bourgeois preserve, live clusters of squatters who grow their crops on tiny tracts of unpopulated land, usually a few miles from where they reside—modern and traditional Trinidad living cheek by jowl. (Lieber 1981:28)

A comparison of the building material of 15,145 separate houses, out of the 20,000 total dwelling units in the area, gives some evidence of the economic disparity in Diego Martin (see Table 18). Here, we can see that the second-largest percentage indicates dwellings made entirely of wood, which indicates to Trinidadians an inferior kind of house, usually associated with poverty. However, not all squatters and impoverished households would be in this category. There are many Diego Martin residents who reside in concrete brick or concrete walled houses that are on the margins of severe poverty.

Ethnically, the area is predominantly Creole, but the number of East Indians seems to be increasing somewhat. The percentage of East Indians in Diego Martin decreased between 1946 and 1980 even though their numbers increased, probably due to the entry of the newly emergent Creole middle classes. The development of Diego Martin has occurred concomitant with the rise of the black, brown, and, to an extent, East Indian middle class (see Table 19 for the distribution of ethnic groups in 1980). In suburban Trinidad, "social change is not expressed in the invasion of elite areas by other groups, and the old high status areas remains intact. In contrast, the more regulated villa-type developments of the middle-class estates are situated in the Diego Martin Valley and along the Eastern Main Road" (Goodenough 1978:33).

TABLE 18
Houses in Diego Martin, by Material of Outer Walls, 1980

Building Material	*Number*	*Percentage*
Brick	9,993	66
Wood	2,233	15
Concrete	1,892	13
Wood and concrete	459	—
Wood and brick	304	—
Wattle/adobe/tapia	127	—
Other	44	—
Not stated	153	—

SOURCE: Compiled from 1980 census report.
NOTE: Negligible percentages are not indicated.

TABLE 19
Ethnic Breakdown for Diego Martin and Trinidad and Tobago, 1980

Ethnic Group	*Diego Martin*	*Trinidad and Tobago*
Black	53.0%	40.8%
East Indian	11.6	40.7
Mixed	27.5	16.3
White	4.5	1.0
Chinese	1.4	0.5
"Other"/not stated	1.6	0.6
Syrian/Lebanese	0.4	0.1
Total	100.0	100.0

SOURCE: Compiled from 1980 census report.

Studies by Colin Clarke (1986, 1993), Dennis Conway, Stephanie Goodenough, Lieber, and others suggest that, while in rural Trinidad blacks and East Indians live apart, in urban areas they live side by side, although sometimes in ethnic "pockets." The East Indians of Diego Martin are somewhat anomalous with respect to the historical patterns of settlement in Trinidad. As most of East Indians in Diego Martin are Christians, many have attended parochial schools and church with Creole children. East Indians in the factory see themselves as being different from Indians "in South," but also see themselves distinct from the factory's Creoles. This rural-urban difference in East Indian ethnicity is also reported by Steven Vertovec (1992), who conducted anthropological fieldwork in East Indian villages in southern Trinidad.[3]

In urban Trinidad, however, there is a notion of the "creolized" East Indian. To both East Indians and Creoles this means an East Indian who is probably a Christian, an urban dweller, and who enjoys Creole cuisine, Carnival, and calypso. East Indians in St. James and Tunapuna, sections of Port-of-Spain's urban sprawl, are contrasted to East Indians in Caroni, which is supposed to be the bastion of "Indianness." One factory worker, Carla a twenty-four-year-old East Indian, expressed this in stark terms "People in Chaguanas real different from people up here in Diego Martin. They learn from and understand Negroes up here but down there they live with other Indians like themselves. They know where I'm from and they look at me like I Negro. One of he [her finacé's] friends say 'Nigger people moving out to Chaguanas. We go need to find a new place for ourselves.' And I say 'Negro sounds better than nigger.' He say 'You is a nigger too, livin' among dem.' "

Diego Martin is religiously heterogeneous as well (see Table 20), with churches of various denominations, including Spiritual Baptist and Orisha

TABLE 20
Religious Composition of Diego Martin and Trinidad and Tobago, 1980

Religion	*Diego Martin*	*Trinidad and Tobago*
Anglican	19.7%	14.7%
Baptist (Orthodox)	2.0	2.4
Hindu (Sanatanist)	3.1	24.5
Other Hindu	—[a]	0.4
Jehovah Witness	1.1	0.7
Methodist	1.6	1.4
Muslim (A.S.J.A.)	1.7	5.8
Other Muslim	—[a]	0.2
Pentecostal	3.3	3.5
Presbyterian	1.0	3.8
Roman Catholic	55.7	33.0
Seventh Day Adventist	2.5	2.5
None	2.5	1.0
Others	3.5	5.1
Not stated	2.3	1.0

SOURCE: Compiled from 1980 census report.
NOTE: Percentages may not total 100 because of rounding.
[a]Negligible

places of worship, one or two mosques, and a Hindu temple. Many East Indians in Diego Martin are Christians. This compares with their rural counterparts, who are in the main Hindu or Muslim. The exception is the area around San Fernando, where Canadian Presbyterian missionaries converted many East Indians during the last century.

In fact, the proportion of Hindus has declined during the first half of this century when compared to the rest of the population. This is especially interesting when it is considered that during this period East Indians have had a much higher natural rate of population increase than have other ethnic groups.

The industrial estate is the site of Diego's only industrial production, although there are a number of small car-repair establishments, often located below private dwellings. Modern supermarkets exist alongside rum shops, market stalls—which sell anything from fish to vegetables to newspapers—fast-food outlets, hardware stores, and roti shops. (Roti is an East Indian curried snack food that is popular among all ethnic groups in the island.) The industrial estate includes factories manufacturing car batteries, nylon stockings, kitchen and household appliances, plastic signs, and ice-cream cones. In addition, there are three garment manufacturers. The factories are similar to EUL in that most of the work force is female. Most of EUL's workers live nearby and take short taxi or maxi rides to work every morning.

The Work Force

Trinidad has had a long history of an ethnic division of labor, although this structure has broken down gradually since the turn of the century, despite notable exceptions, as discussed in Chapter 2. The ethnic composition of the work force at EUL is anachronistic. The owners are white; most of the office workers are white, Chinese, or "high brown"; the accountant is East Indian; most of the floor supervisors are white men; and all of the line workers are black and East Indian women.

The majority of EUL's line workers are female. Of the sixty-three line workers, fifty-two, or 82.5 percent, are female, and their ages range from the late teens to the midforties. The remainder are young men in their late teens and early twenties. There is a thirty-five-year-old male toolmaker, and his assistant is a twenty-year old male. Both are East Indian. The line supervisors are males, from their early thirties to their early fifties. Of the female workers, 71 percent are black and 25 percent are East Indian. There are five East Indian and six black male line workers (see Table 21). Five of the eight line supervisors are white, the other three are East Indian. One supervisor is Dutch and one is a white Jamaican, the rest were born in Trinidad. The majority of the line workers come from urban working-class origins, but differ in their "life situations" and individual backgrounds (see the Appendix). Although few supervisors have received formal technical training, they are expected by Tiexiera not only to supervise production, but also to maintain the machines in their department.

For instance, the supervisor Ruud trained as an engineer in the Dutch

TABLE 21
Age, Sex, and Ethnicity of the Factory Line Workers

	Ethnic Group			
Age Group	Black	East Indian	Mixed	Total
16–25				
Males	6	4	0	10
Females	17	9	2	28
26–35				
Males	0	1	0	1
Females	5	2	0	7
36–50				
Males	0	0	0	0
Females	15	2	0	17
Total				
Males	6	5	0	11
Females	37	13	2	52

navy, and he is responsible for keeping complex machinery in working order. Vishnu, the toolmaker, is a highly skilled worker, responsible for manufacturing and repairing parts for various machines within the factory. Often his skills are essential in keeping the factory operating normally. The rest of the supervisors seem only to have acquired a general mechanical knowledge from working on automobiles that they apply to some of the less complex, relatively antiquated machinery in the factory.

With one exception, all of the male line workers live in households that include at least one of their parents and some extended kinfolk. These young men have all completed some secondary school, but only Terry, a twenty-year-old, has any "O levels," that is, secondary school leaving exams in the British-derived educational system. A few, including Ben, the nineteen-year-old assistant toolmaker, are attending night courses at the John Donaldson technical training college in Port-of-Spain.

The women, on the other hand possess different education and skill backgrounds. Only two of the female workers over twenty-six years old have any secondary-school education. None have any technical training as such, but several have completed courses in crafts like dress making, catering, and cake icing, which are offered for a nominal fee at the Diego Martin Community Centre. Some of the more experienced female workers, however, are expected to know how to maintain and repair their machines, and they are often more skilled at this than the supervisors.

More than half of the women under 25 years old have some secondary-school education, and the general higher education levels of the younger workers is a testament to the effectiveness of the country's improving education program. There are a few younger women who have also taken crafts courses, but others are undertaking technical and commercial training. For example, during my fieldwork, Imogene, nineteen, was finishing an electrician's course at Servol, a Catholic organization in Laventille that seems to be successful at giving youths from extremely underprivileged backgrounds a "second chance" with vocational training. Often, the fact that the young women are wage earners is an improvement on the position of their mothers, many of whom were or are domestic workers. Because they are in continuous employment, some of the young women at EUL have also improved on the position of their fathers in the corresponding period of their fathers' lives.

In terms of domestic arrangements, most women over thirty are in "live-in" mating relationships, that is, consensual cohabitation or legal marriage. Several of the younger women are in "visiting" relationships, and about 95 percent of all female workers over age twenty-five have children. Often, the female workers in live-in relationships are the main breadwinners in their households, with their menfolk having been "retrenched" because of the Recession. The pattern is for the younger women who are not in domestic unions to live in the same household with their elder kin, even if they have children of their own. In some cases, the woman, her mate, and her children live under the roof of one of the couple's parents.

To understand why this particular work force is employed we need to look not only at structural factors, but also at the typical worker's options. In 1986, total unemployment was estimated at 16.6 percent, while female unemployment, at 18 percent, was two points higher than male unemployment. Unemployment of young women is the highest of any group. A young woman who has finished school without educational qualifications has few employment options, and employment in a factory that "favors" young women as employees is relatively attractive. For most workers, marriage is not an alternative to wage labor.

Ethnicity and Gender in the Production Process

The owners' efforts to establish hegemony over the work force extends to their efforts to recruit certain kinds of workers and to control production. These efforts can be explained by looking at a combination of "market" and "nonmarket" labor processes, as we will see.

New workers are often the kin of people already working in the factory, but almost all have heard about a possible vacancy from a friend on the inside. In both cases, the sponsoring employee will enquire about vacancies with the personnel manager and recommend the kinsperson or friend. Nigel Tiexiera said he preferred to hire younger workers because "The older girls with families aren't as dependable. They're late, they're always having babies, they have to take time off when their children are sick. Nah. I definitely prefer to hire young girls."

There are several contradictions in this statement, besides the obviously objectionable way he refers to women as "girls." Just because the "older girls" have familial responsibilities, and therefore depend on their salaries not just for their own survival but for that of their children, they might be considered more valuable to the firm. And because they receive prestige for acting "respectable" at work, the older workers do not engage in the horseplay and flirting that the younger ones engage in (see Chapter 5). Yet the fact that women predominate as workers indicates Tiexiera's adherence to the nearly universal "nimble fingers" theory that holds that women are naturally suited for assembly-line work. Tiexiera seemingly has internalized this almost universal rationalization about female workers being more suitable than men for repetitive production tasks. What is somewhat different in his case is that he claimed men's nature prevented them from being suitable candidates. He said to me, "Boys would get bored with the monotonous work."

The work groups are differentiated on the basis of age. The older line workers are found in the Motor-Assembly and in the Upstairs Final-Assembly

I and Final-Assembly II departments, where the firm's original two products are made. Younger line workers have generally filled the new openings and younger workers were hired to work on the Downstairs Final-Assembly line, which was set up to make EUL's newest product. These two groups—the older and the younger workers—differ in their rates of turnover, with the older workers being much more stable than the younger ones. As we will see, each group is supervised by the male supervisors very differently.

Often, personal relationships develop among members of the same work group. There is a feeling expressed by some workers that workers in the two upstairs assembly departments are "different" from the rest of the factory's employees and socially "closer" (their terms) to other upstairs workers. That is, these workers feel that these departments are characterized by more affective, personal relationships than the workers in the Motor-Assembly and Downstairs Final-Assembly departments.

The social distance along gender and ethnic lines between the supervisors and the work force seems to be actively cultivated by Tiexiera in order to further the economic interests of the firm and to encourage production. He once told me that "there was a time when . . . race was important in hiring, but not anymore." He indicated that race was an important consideration in hiring supervisors. When I asked him if this also impacted on the hiring of workers, he indicated that East Indians were preferred for line workers. As discussed in Chapter 2, this attitude conforms to the colonial Trinidadian stereotype that holds that blacks "don't care about tomorrow" and are only concerned about "feting" (i.e., partying), while East Indians are considered more industrious and serious at work (see also Chapter 4). Tiexiera claimed that he had abandoned his thinking: "Everyone is lazy now," he told me. However, during my fieldwork he replaced a fired Portuguese Creole male supervisor with a French Creole man and then, when that man died, with an East Indian man.

Veteran workers told me of a black male supervisor who, they said, "stood up" to Tiexiera and argued for more money and better conditions for the line workers. Eventually, I was told, this supervisor became disillusioned and quit his job. Some workers felt that this supervisor agitated for better wages and conditions for the mostly black line workers because he was black.

Jobs within the factory are also allocated by gender. The women are involved in soldering, testing electrical components, gluing labels, and other tedious tasks that require patience and concentration. They are machine operators, they are sedentary. The male line workers, on the hand, are given jobs that require and allow time for mobility within the factory. In fact, they seem to take much pleasure in taking the risks associated with leaving their posts and walking around the factory. Some operate mahines, but they are responsible for assisting the supervisors by moving boxes of finished products and retrieving materials from the storeroom. On the whole, they are not in jobs that demand extraordinary physical strength. The workers themselves have formed ideas about "normal" women's and men's jobs within the factory. One day, Jeremy was ordered by a supervisor to work at a machine all day, taking over for an absent female worker. When Vishnu saw this, he teased Jeremy, saying, "I didn't know it didn't have enough *girls* to work here."

Whereas the Tiexieras almost without embarrassment explained to me how their recruitment strategies were based on "nonmarket" estimations of particular laborers and kinds of labor, they explained their wages policies to me and the workers on the basis of the supposed operation of economic forces in the wider society, which, they claimed, constrain them just as severely as the workers. While trade unions in Trinidad were successful during the oil boom, no union represents the workers at EUL. Nigel Tiexiera constantly said that if a union came he would be forced to close the factory down because "I could not afford to pay my workers." According to a number of workers who related the story to me in hushed tones, two years before my fieldwork began Tiexiera fired more than twenty workers who were secretly trying to get union recognition (see Chapter 6). On numerous occasions I witnessed Tiexiera pointing out the country's economic crisis to the workers as a way of exhorting the workers to produce more. He stated rather plainly to the workers that, given the rate of unemployment, they were quite lucky to be employed at all. And he warned them that they had better be concerned with the performance, because "there's a thousand more out there who would love to have this job." But Cheryl's comment when Tiexiera was out of earshot was fairly indicative of the workers' attitudes: "He using this Recession as ah *excuse*," she said and then *steupsed*.[4]

In the EUL factory, female labor is generally paid less than male labor. Winston, the youngest, least experienced (three years' service), and poorest paid supervisor earns a gross salary of TT$450 per week. This is more than double the weekly pay of a female line worker with similar service. Some of the male workers are paid at a higher rate than all female workers. For example, Brian is twenty-one, a stores attendant. He receives a weekly wage of TT$250, which is $6.25 an hour. From this is deducted $6.45 for the National Insurance Scheme, $8.25 for the Health Charge, and $25 for the Pay As You Earn income-tax scheme. This leaves a take home pay of $210.30 a week. At the time of my fieldwork, Brian had been working at EUL for more than three years. His job involves retrieving boxes and parcels of parts for the various departments with a hand trolley, but it is not a job where physical strength is a primary criterion. But when compared with the wages of the line workers, Brian is paid at a much higher rate. This is further evidence of rates of pay being determined by gender and not "skill." The exception to this rule are the young male line workers. They are paid at the same hourly rate as the female line workers. However, they differ in their job requirements. While they are at times called upon to perform the same tasks as the women, performing repetitive tasks with a machine or with a soldering iron, for the most part they are assigned jobs that are somewhat distinctive. For example, they are called upon to retrieve parts from the storeroom (women never are), or they are put in charge of loading finished products on pallets. Unlike every woman's job, the men's require that they move around within the factory.

According to the workers themselves, the low wages offered by EUL attract female labor because women will readily accept almost any wage work because of their familial responsibilities. Low-wage work for women in Trinidad as a whole is the norm, whether it is because employers rationalize paying "pin money," the supposed "second wage" for a family that therefore does not have to be sufficient to fully meet the worker's financial needs, or because unions do not take up the cause of women workers, or because women's very "responsibilities" mean that there will be greater competition for scarce jobs, thus making for a very good market for those who purchase female labor.

Candace, the personnel manager, told me that in 1977 the weekly wages for "temporary" workers were TT$40 a week, $60 a week for "permanent" workers, and $80 a week for those with one year's experience. These can be compared to the wages paid at EUL during my fieldwork period, 1986–1987 (see Table 22).

While EUL workers have enjoyed some increase in their wages over the course of a decade, they are at the mercy of the owners as to the amount, duration, and permanency of raises. The last wage increase was in 1985, amounting to about TT$20 a week. But in October 1985 this wage was "reviewed," according to Candace, and cut back to the 1983 rate. This was done, Tiexiera said, in order to prevent further retrenchments, like those that occurred at EUL in 1983. But retrenchment can also be expensive for a firm, if they abide by Trinidad and Tobago law. The country's severance-payment formula required the company to pay two week's pay for every year completed for workers with one to five years' service and three weeks' pay for every year completed for those workers with more than five years' service.

Factories represented by unions often secure much more favorable retrenchment and severance pay. For example, Sunshine Snacks Ltd., which is represented by the All Trinidad Sugar and General Workers' Trade Union (ATS&GWTU), must pay three weeks' pay for each year of service for workers with one to four years' service; four weeks' pay for each year of service for workers with five to nine years' service; and five weeks' pay for each year of service for those working ten years or more (Employers' Consultative Association 1987:7).

On the whole, wages at EUL are much lower than in comparable

TABLE 22
Examples of Wages for EUL Line Workers, 1986–1987 (in TT$)

	"Temporary"	1 Year's Service
Weekly Wage	110.00 (2.75 hr.)	160.00 (4.00 hr.)
N.I.S.[a] deduction	3.50	4.50
Health charge deduction	8.25	8.25
Take home pay	98.25	147.25
	"Permanent"	2 Years' Service
Weekly Wage	130.00 (3.25 hr.)	180.00 (4.50 hr.)
N.I.S. deduction	3.50	5.75
Health charge deduction	8.25	8.25
P.A.Y.E.[b] deduction	N/A	3.00
Take home pay	118.25	163.00

NOTE: At the time of the fieldwork, the exchange rate was as follows: TT$3.60 = US$1.00; TT$5.28 = £1.00.
[a]National Insurance scheme.
[b]Pay As You Earn income tax scheme.

manufacturing industries in Trinidad. According to statistics compiled by the Central Statistical Office in November 1986, the average minimum wages nationwide for occupations comparable to most of those at EUL were much higher. For example, the average minimum wage for an assembler was TT$10.34 per hour, a machine operator was paid TT$7.99 per hour, and a laborer received TT$9.72 per hour (Trinidad and Tobago 1987b:35). The differences between these rates of pay and those of EUL can be explained partly by the fact that EUL is nonunionized, whereas many work forces in the "screwdriver" industries of Trinidad are represented by successful unions.

The wages at EUL are more comparable to those in the garment industry, which, as I have indicated, has traditionally been a major employer of female industrial workers in Trinidad (Reddock 1990, 1993, 1994). In November 1986, stitchers and machine operators made an average minimum wage of TT$5.71 per our; general workers, helpers, and laborers, $5.34 per hour; and draftsmen, draftswomen, and pattern makers, $9.54 per hour. The average wage was TT$214.82 per week in the garment industry (Trinidad and Tobago 1987b:33, 41).

In 1976, the government passed the Minimum Wages Act, which provides for a board to set minimum wage rates for various occpations and empowers representatives to inspect workplaces and employers' records. During my fieldwork, however, the minimum wages for these kinds of occupations were "under review," according to officials of the Industrial Court, and therefore I was unable to ascertain if EUL workers were paid below the legal limit. A comparison of their pay to the national averages suggests, however, that this might be the case.

Table 23 provides examples of wages for workers at National Canners Ltd., who are represented by the ATS&GWTU. The agreement between the employers and the union stipulated that, from January 15, 1985, each worker would receive TT$35 on top of his or her weekly salary, increasing in succeeding years by TT$10. Female general workers at National Canners Ltd. make around TT$360 per week and machine operators make TT$445. At the same time, a worker at EUL with two years' experience, earned $180 per week before payroll deductions.

In addition, male and female workers are categorized differently, with women receiving lower rates of pay. Trade unions may be forced to operate within this traditional structure by employers, while at the same time increasing female factory workers' share of wages in absolute terms. How far the unions are willing accomplices in defining women's work as less valuable than men's is not clear, but it seems that, in general, trade unions have not been willing to address these and other issues pertinent to women's labor in Trinidad.

There are important differences among the workers that may appear "cultural" but that nonetheless effect the formal structure of the factory. As we shall see, the differences between, in Tiexiera's words, "older girls" and "young girls," occur in ways in which Tiexiera does not articulate. The older workers, for the most part, experience relatively little turnover. The younger workers, by contrast, form a high turnover group that is constantly being "policed" by the Tiexieras and the supervisors (see Chapter 5). The designation of a high-turnover work force at EUL is facilitated by the technology

TABLE 23
Wage Agreements for Selected Weekly Paid Employees at National Canners Ltd. (in TT$)

Occupational Class	*Jan. 15, 1985*	*Jan. 15, 1986*	*Jan. 15, 1987*
General worker (female)	343.78	353.78	360.78
General worker (male)	384.30	394.30	401.30
Loader/general worker (male)	408.62	418.62	425.62
Maintenance helper	408.62	418.62	425.62
Office maid	428.88	438.88	445.88
Warehouse assistant	428.88	438.88	445.88
Machine operator	428.88	438.88	445.88
Office boy/van driver	465.36	475.36	482.36
Boiler room attendant	560.62	570.62	577.62

SOURCE: Compiled from Employers' Consultative Association 1987: 8.

(albeit low-level) of the production process itself. In some ways, it may not benefit the Tiexieras to introduce more advanced technology because this would necessitate an altogether more stable, and hence higher-paid, work force.

New workers are categorized as "temporary" and are required to go through a six-month probationary period, during which they can be fired without warning and paid at a lower rate. This cannot justifiably be called a training period, because almost all of the jobs can be learned in less than half an hour, and a new worker with average ability can be as productive as an experienced one in a matter of days. After the probationary period, depending upon performance, workers are made "permanent" and are given a small pay increase. Sometimes this is withheld as a disciplinary procedure. However, after they are made "permanent," the workers at least enjoy some protection under the country's industrial laws. The company is required to provide at least three written warnings before an employee can be dismissed and if this is not done the employer can be taken before the Industrial Court, which is designed to be the arbiter in organized labor-management and employee-employer disputes.

The Organization of the Production Process

Figure 1 shows the layout of the factory, with the position of the various workers. These positions are approximate in that often workers are required to fill in at another post because of absence or a technical fault with their machine. At other times, one department's workers may be sent to work in another department because a shipment of components has not arrived or because the supplies of components were not ordered at all.*

The factory is a two-story structure, constructed with cinder blocks and with "breeze blocks" (ventilated cinder blocks) at the top of the walls. The roof is made of corrugated iron, and windows are covered with iron bars, an increasingly common sight in Trinidad. The factory is lit with fluorescent strip lighting and is ventilated by a number of household room fans manufactured by AML, a Trinidadian company located on the same industrial estate.

The Motor-Assembly, Upstairs Final-Assembly I and II, and the Downstairs Final-Assembly departments are where the main assembly operations take place, and I spent most of my time working at a variety of tasks in these departments. In the Motor-Assembly Department motors are assembled for incorporation into the product that the firm first began producing under license from the multinational. The motors are transported upstairs for final assembly and packing, which is carried out in the Upstairs Final-Assembly I Department.

*The following description of the factory is intentionally vague so that I can preserve the anonymity of the factory, the workers, and the owners.

Workers in the Motor-Assembly Department operate various machines that press, rivet, and cut the parts, some of which are previously processed in the Machinery, Motor-Testing, and Primary-Assembly departments. The rest of the parts are supposed to be delivered by the storeroom attendants. More often than not, Johnny will be called upon to leave his machine and retrieve boxes of components from the storeroom, sometimes using a forklift. In the Motor-Assembly Department, the direction of production is as follows: Parts that are processed by machines operated by Indira, Val, Nicole, and Lori are passed to the workbench where Gloria, Rachel, Helen, and Sheena assemble these parts with parts processed by the rest of the department. The final products at this stage are given to Walcott for testing and, once tested, they are placed in boxes and transported upstairs, where they are collected by Winston, the Upstairs Final-Assembly I Department supervisor.

The Plastics Department consists of four large machines that mold the plastic components utilized in the operations of the Upstairs Final-Assembly I and II and the Downstairs Final-Assembly departments. When these parts are finished, they are placed in boxes by the machine operators and later transported to the storeroom, where they are cataloged and stored.

In the Downstairs Final-Assembly Department, production is organized around the conveyor belt on the top of a workbench. Martha and Elaine remove components from boxes and assemble them using pneumatic power tools. These partially completed items are placed on the conveyor belt, where they are picked up by other workers, who add various parts. Patricia assembles the body and passes it to Connie, who conducts an operating test using an electric tester. At the same time, Rohan tests a sensitive part and makes the necessary adjustments, while Lisette packs the part in a cellophane wrapper. On another workbench, Geneveve and Jenny manually assemble metal parts with screwdrivers. The finished products are then collected by Art, who places them in boxes, which are sealed by machine. He then places the boxes on wooden palates, on which they will be loaded into containers for shipment. The customer will buy the product with final assembly required, which is done with a screwdriver.

When the finished components assembled by the Motor-Assembly Department are taken to the Upstairs Final-Assembly I Department, they are tested and parts are added by three different kinds of machines. These components are then placed on the conveyor belt, where they are installed in plastic outer shells. The completed product is then passed on a conveyor belt to Myra, who tests the product. She then places the approved products back on the conveyor belt for Terry to collect. He packs them, seals the boxes with an air-powered industrial stapler, and places the boxes on wooden palates.

In the Upstairs Final-Assembly II Department there is a very simple production process, in which only one part is machined and plastic parts are assembled manually and tested by Carla.

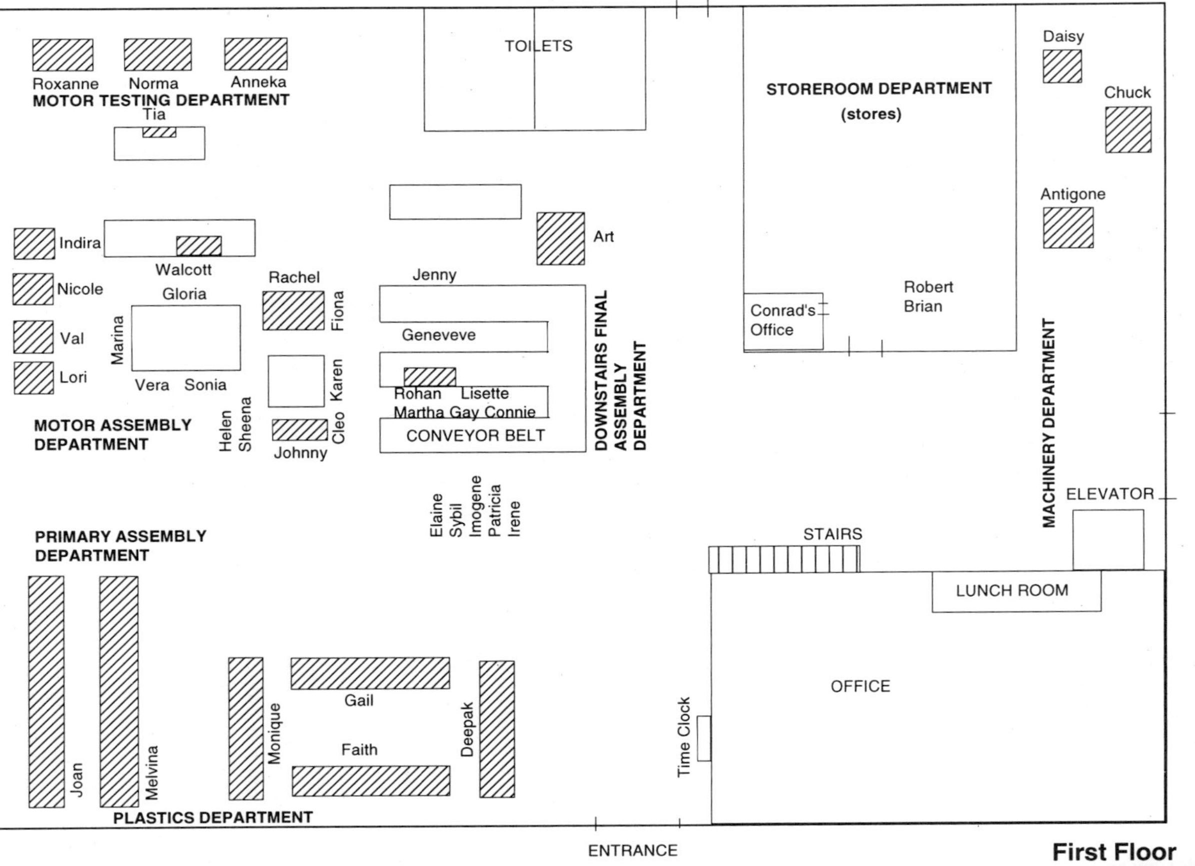

Roxanne
Norma
Anneka
MOTOR TESTING DEPARTMENT
Tia
TOILETS
STOREROOM DEPARTMENT
(stores)
Daisy
Chuck
Antigone
Indira
Walcott
Nicole
Gloria
Marina
Val
Lori
Vera
Sonia
Rachel
Fiona
Karen
Cleo
Johnny
Helen
Sheena
MOTOR ASSEMBLY
DEPARTMENT
Art
Jenny
Geneveve
Rohan
Lisette
Martha Gay Connie
CONVEYOR BELT
DOWNSTAIRS FINAL
ASSEMBLY
DEPARTMENT
Conrad's
Office
Robert
Brian
MACHINERY DEPARTMENT
ELEVATOR
Elaine
Sybil
Imogene
Patricia
Irene
PRIMARY ASSEMBLY
DEPARTMENT
STAIRS
LUNCH ROOM
OFFICE
Time Clock
Joan
Melvina
Monique
Gail
Faith
Deepak
PLASTICS DEPARTMENT
ENTRANCE
First Floor

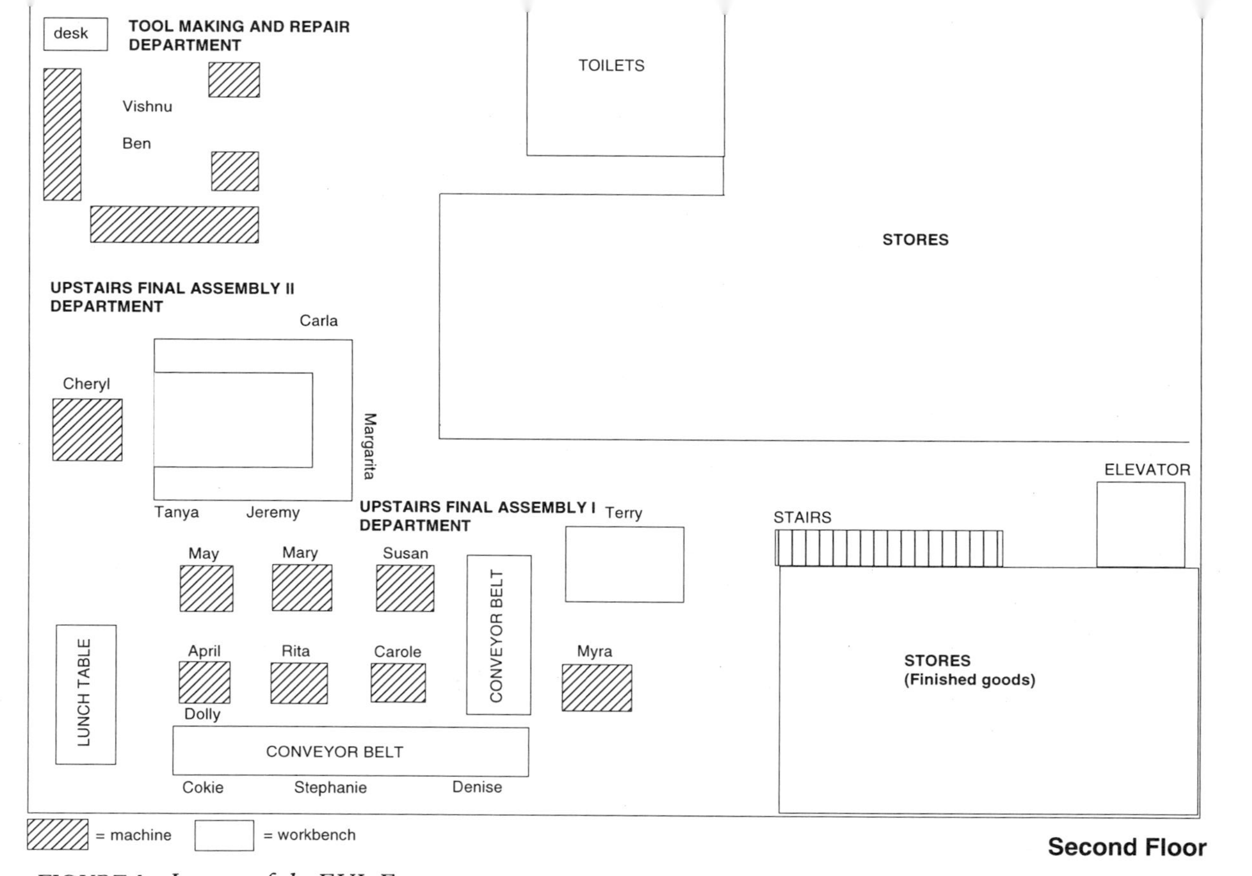

FIGURE 1 *Layout of the EUL Factory*

In the Motor-Assembly, Upstairs Final-Assembly I and II, and the Downstairs Final-Assembly departments the male production workers are differentiated by their formal and informal roles. In each case the males are differentiated from the females in their job description, at no point doing directly comparable tasks on a regular basis. In the Downstairs Final-Assembly Department, for example, Rohan is charged with operating a relatively sophisticated and expensive piece of testing machinery. In all cases, these young men are handed responsibility for retrieving components from the stores by the supervisors, and they often wander around the factory, flirting (see Chapter 5) with the young female workers and engaging in horseplay with the other males.

The "formal" or "supposed" role of the supervisors and their performance is of constant concern to Tiexiera. He constantly "reminds" them by shouting and screaming in cynical terms that they are not doing their jobs properly. This is done within earshot of the workers. What seems to annoy him most is that the supervisors operate machines and assemble parts alongside the workers, while Tiexiera feels they should be organized to a point where all they have to do is to walk around their respective departments checking on production quotas. In addition, the supervisors transport components from the storeroom when a stores attendant cannot be found or is busy with another task. The supervisors argue, although not to Tiexiera's face, that the production quotas are so difficult to achieve that they cannot possibly be met without the supervisors' participation in the production process. Not to meet quotas also incurs the wrath of Tiexiera, who has a volatile temper.

Connections

In their study of the influence of ethnicity and gender on the friendship networks of American white-collar workers, James R. Lincoln and Jon Miller differentiate between "instrumental" ties, that is, "those arising in the course of performing work roles," and "primary" ties, that is, "those informal social relations that have been shown to both enhance and impede the attainment of formal organizational goals." They find that "Race and sex show stronger net associations with friendship proximity than work contact proximity (although the effect of race on instrumental ties is not negligible)" (1979:182, 190).

As at the EUL factory, ethnicity, class, and gender account for the basic nature of "instrumental" ties because, as we have seen, these social identities are used in the recruitment strategies. It is difficult to generalize about the "primary" ties of the workers: a blanket statement would obscure differences based on age, gender, ethnicity, and position within the factory. When the friendship or peer-group relationships of the workers are examined, it is clear that these "primary" ties are anything but informal, if we take informal to mean of a random nature and without structure.

In order to understand how class, age, ethnicity, and gender are implicated in factory social relations, we must first know something about the empirical nature of those relations. In the factory, the supervisors generally spend their break times together and almost never associate with the workers in their free time. Nearly three-quarters of every worker's friendship ties are to people within the same age group. Women aged thirty and over and teenage women especially tend to establish peer-group relationships among those of the same age group as themselves. The teenage-male peer groups are further differentiated by ethnicity. Men are tied to peers of their own ethnic groups far more than are women. There is a pattern relating to gender as well. The older women are more segregated by gender in their friendship groups than are the younger women. But ties among men are reinforced more easily than ties among women, because men are engaged in jobs that allow frequent movement within the factory, and men always seem to find the time to come together and lime in groups that are differentiated according to ethnicity. Within each of five groups—older females, younger females, black males, East Indian males, and supervisors—there are many relationships that cross the workplace boundary. The following case studies demonstrate the kinds of relationships that are formed with different kinds of workers. These are in no way intended to be statistically representative. I provide them as essential ethnographic data for the understanding of subsequent qualitative evidence and theoretical arguments.

> CLEO: Cleo is 36 and a mother of three boys, sixteen, thirteen, and eleven (she was pregnant when I finished my fieldwork and later had another boy). She is now legally married after having been in visiting and consensual relationships with her husband. Her husband has a semipermanent job with the Airport Authority and sometimes goes a week without working. Cleo, therefore, is the main breadwinner in the household, and she earns TT$210 per week. She is a Spiritual Baptist and can often be seen reading a Bible at work. She maintains friendships with women of approximately the same age and who possess similar social attributes. She has a relatively close relationship with her friends Karen and Daisy. The three women can be seen talking with each other during lunch and break times, and they all attend and are active in the same Spiritual Baptist church in Diego Martin. Further, during work all three usually provide assistance to each other that is not required by the exigencies of the production process. Although the younger workers seem to have "easier" friendship relationships, these relationships are not confined to them. Daisy, who is divorced, told of

> how important her friends from work are: "When I first got married, I made mistakes. I feted. I didn't care. But I really didn't have friends like dem [pointing to Cleo and Karen] to talk to, to confide in." Daisy is the godmother of Karen's new daughter. Although Cleo, Karen, and Daisy belong to the same Spiritual Baptist church, Karen's husband is Catholic, so the child was christened in a Catholic church (although in Trinidad being Catholic and Spiritual Baptist are not thought of as being mutually exclusive). Daisy said jokingly about her new role: "Now she [the daughter] get a double *cut-ass* [vicious beating]! One from me and one from Karen," meaning that Daisy feels she has the authority to discipline the daughter in Karen's absence.
>
> Cleo's relationship with Norma is somewhat different. They usually cannot be seen speaking to each other during lunch and break times. The resons for this may have to do with the fact that Norma and Cleo work in different departments and sometimes the workers say they are too exhausted at break times to move about the factory. But perhaps a more likely explanation has to do with the absence of ties between Norma and Karen and Daisy, who are close to Cleo. I do not think there is any hostility between Norma and Karen and Daisy, but there is an important friendship relationship between Cleo and Norma, because both report that Norma provides occasional cash assistance to Cleo.
>
> The relationship Cleo maintains with Fiona is different still. Cleo and Fiona usually work together, with Cleo's job being to prepare the parts for Fiona to place in a machine as part of the production process. They usually talk while they work, and Fiona, although she is the mother of three children, seems to defer to the older woman. Both report that they sometimes see each other outside of work because they are neighbors in Diego Martin, but they have never visited each other at home.

Elsewhere, especially in Chapter 5, I provide evidence about the sexually charged relationships between the supervisors and the young female workers. The absence of such a relationship between Cleo and her supervisor, David, provides one basis of comparison.

> DENISE AND VERA: The example of Cleo's friendship relationships suggests that older women usually have ties to other older women. But there those who do not conform, and they often pay the price of moral sanctions. Denise, who is thirty-five, is an example. She has two teenage children and is divorced. She works upstairs in a department away from the main shop floor and is regarded by most of the workers as someone who spreads gossip. Her network consists almost wholly of younger workers. She often goes to fetes with the younger workers and flirts with the males. "I find for a big woman she fast [i.e., rude or

bold]," said Terry, a young man with whom she does not really flirt. And Norma said of Denise, "For a big woman, she not nice. She like all dem young boys to drink and carry on. I['m] not like that."

Vera is forty-five, has never been married, and has never had a child. She too is regarded by the workers as a person who spreads gossip, and she is ostracized by many older ones. She is also ridiculed behind her back for spending most of her time in conversation with the two youngest women in her department. One twenty-six-year-old worker, the mother of three children, said, "No wonder she crazy. It not *natural* to have no child. If I was she, I'd be crazy too." In Vera's case, I could not tell if she was first isolated and therefore had to resort to associating with younger workers, or if she was ridiculed as a result of her spending time with younger workers. It seems she has little control over not living up to the other workers' expectations. Among the older women in the factory, the ideal of a woman "carrying herself well" is sanctioned. As Cleo said, referring to the behavior of Denise, "It have big women who let dem boys pull dey around. How you supposed to have respect if you carry on so?"

GAY: The example of Gay and her social relations is presented here in somewhat more detail than the other examples because it shows many things about the friendship relations of other workers. It shows the kinds of social ties the younger workers are likely to possess, the importance of those ties in the shop-floor culture of the factory, the overlap between the factory and the outside world, and the importance of relationships developed at work for the general social life of the worker.

The younger female workers often engage in horseplay, and most of these public displays have sex as a submerged or obvious theme. Shop-floor culture reflects the divisions between older and younger female workers. The peer groups of the younger female workers are pervaded by an emphasis on romance: They brought to work and shared magazines named *Photoromance* and *Kiss*, which were produced in Italy and included photos of glamorous white models, where one could follow the story line by reading the captions above the heads of actors, as in a comic book. Anna Pollert (1981:137) writes about similar behavior among the younger workers in an English factory, which she attributes to their having been cushioned from domestic responsibilities. The workers at EUL, however, are not excluded from domestic duties. Indeed, of the twenty-eight females under twenty-five years of age, twelve have children of their own. The workers' responsibilities include contributing to the household income. Some pass on up to half of their weekly pay to elder kin. Irene, for example, is twenty-four and the mother of twin boys, aged seven. At first, her take home pay was TT$98.25 per week, and after the six-month probationary period she was made "permanent" and her take home pay increased to $118.25. She lives with her mother, stepfather, stepsister, stepbrother, and her two children. She contributes $20 to the household each week and takes care of various chores, mainly in looking after her sons.

Gay is also connected to other young female workers. We can see the effects of these relations in action in the following example of Gay's birthday celebration. Irene, Elaine, Sybil, and Patricia collected money for Gay's birthday present. They decided to buy her a clock: They each contributed $15 and they collected $15 from Jeremy, Art, Lloyd, Conrad, Connie, Lisa, Robert, and me. It is possible that the workers were going to fairly elaborate lengths for Gay because she had invited them all to her wedding.

This is an example of existing but latent ties being activated for a specific purpose, though the contingencies of the situation may have induced the workers to create aspects of ties between themselves that had not existed before.[5]

For Gay's birthday, the workers in the department helped her celebrate at lunchtime. Irene had a card made by a friend who is an amateur artist. On the outside of the card, there was a drawing of a girl, representing Gay, asking, "Gerard [Gay's fiancé], how much have you got?" When the card was opened, there was a baby boy holding a huge erect penis. The card was inscribed:

> Money's short
> Times are hard
> So here's your fucking
> Birthday Card

And it was signed by the workers of the department.

Her "present" was given to her in a gift-wrapped box. The groups gathered around to watch her open the box, and there was loud laughter when the box was opened and shown to contain a cucumber covered by a condom, which had been partially filled with hand cream in order to simulate semen. Gay was embarrassed but appreciated the joke. Later, she was presented with the clock.

This group of young female workers sometimes gathers around Connie and looks over her shoulder and collectively reads the explicit sex scenes of a Jackie Collins– or Sidney Sheldon–style novel, the "juicy bits," as some workers call them. Often, Connie reads the story line in a loud whisper and the whole group laughs in unison (probably from embarrassment) at certain points. Many of the younger workers are probably learning about sex from this activity. But the older workers look at them in dismay when they do this. Elaine and Sybil went to Tobago after Carnival Monday and Tuesday and did not show up for work until the following Monday. They were fired. April and Cleo laughed when they found out, and April said, "Maybe they wouldn't act that way if they had responsibilities." Cleo later said: "Dem dere *skylark* [i.e., engage in horseplay] too much. When I was dere I used to solder fifty a day myself. Now, dey act like chirren. And some have chirren of they own. And it have chirren younger than dey actin' more mature. . . . It never used to have some many coming back [for repair]. It 'cause dey skylarking. They need a supervisor like Ruud. He would fix dey, *oui*."

GAY'S WEDDING: The group of younger female workers celebrated an important *rite de passage* for Gay. She invited many of her friends at the factory to the wedding. I knew that Gerard, who works in another factory, was East Indian, and I asked her if it would be an "Indian wedding." She said no, "It not in the religion." It may be interesting to note here that, at another time, I was speaking to Carla, who is also a Catholic East Indian, and she said she was having an Indian wedding because "is we kind of wedding." The difference may have had to do with the fact that Carla's fiancé is a Hindu who lives in Chaguanas. I asked Walcott what I should expect. "Oh, it ent ah Indian wedding," she said. "Well it Creole then. You should get deejay music then. And plenty drink."

Gay's wedding ceremony was held in a Catholic church in Diego Martin. When the formalities were completed, the Irish priest took time to impart some advice, and he did so using Trinidadian stereotypes. He told Gerard, "You can see other women, but you mustn't *look* at them." He then went on for a while about the dangers of in-laws who, borrowing Trinidadian parlance, "*mash up* [i.e., break up] de marriage." "Keep them at arm's length," he said to Gay and Gerard. "And to the family, I would say support them but don't interfere with them." Later, one of Gay's aunts told me, "He [the priest] used to say 'Let your in-laws be your outlaws.' "

The reception was held in the Woodbrook house of another of Gay's aunts. Of the approximately 150 guests, about half were Creoles and half were East Indians. Present from the factory were Irene, Robert, Imogene, Art, Jeremy, Patricia, Lloyd, and me. Robert and Imogene were dating at this time and they came together, Irene brought her boyfriend, and the supervisor Lloyd and the worker Patricia came together (I discuss their relationship in Chapter 5).

There were huge amounts of Indian food, and, indeed, more than enough liquor and beer. At the start, Gay's uncle made a speech in her behalf and Gerard's boss, a white Trinidadian, was called upon to speak on Gerard's behalf (although Gerard's parents were present). He said, "Gerard is a hard worker who has a great future with the firm. He is also a quite cocky young man." At this point Lloyd blurted out, "Let's hope so!" And there was laughter. The boss continued, "He is a good worker, but I better shut up or he'll ask for a raise."

The calypso and soca music then started and the guests, even the older ones, danced through the night. At one point, while Gerard and Gay danced provocatively (wining down), Irene took several snapshots with her camera.

JOHNNY AND DEEPAK: Johnny's peer group is permeated by the other young black men in the factory. For Johnny's birthday, there was a get-together at Brian's house in San Juan. Brian has a "board house" on a Sou-Sou Lands project in a ravine. Sou-Sou Lands is a project started by local politician John Humphrey that is designed to allow the poor to purchase parcels of land cheaply. Present from the factory were Brian, Johnny, Paul, Richard, Jeremy, Terry, and myself. All workers present were black men, except for Terry, who made roti, channa, and curried mango for the occasion.

The peer groups of the East Indian men are similar, in that the other East Indian men are prominent in them. Every day at lunch time, Deepak, Ram, and Ben pile into Vishnu's car and go home to eat. Vishnu gives the others a lift to their respective homes and then drives to a relative's home, where he sleeps during the week. On the weekends he goes to stay at his mother's house in Princes Town, in the south part of the island. The relative's house is across from where Ben lives with his family. Besides all being East Indian men, they do similar jobs within the factory.

LLOYD: Most of the supervisors tend to stick together and some get together after work to have a few beers in the rum shop. Mainly, they lime together in Conrad's office and identify with each other's problems related to work. This is not to say that they present a unified voice. Some privately indicate that they mollify others because a cordial relationship means that their jobs are easier. Winston said that he does not really like Vishnu—who is not technically a supervisor but is treated as such because of his age and skill—but needs him to help fix the machines: "I need his help for the machines. I went to him the other day for help and he say 'no.' This is after I tell he off for bothering one of the girls and for slowing up production."

Most supervisors have an easy relationship with the male workers and are not overly formal. Even Ruud, who is the informal factory manager and Tiexiera's confidant, gets involved in macho horseplay, as one day he was wrestling with Deepak in front of Vishnu and Ben. And some have been given nicknames: Winston's nickname is "Magnum P.I.," after the American television show, although he is not called this so much anymore. Ben explained, "When they first started showing *Magnum P.I.* down here, he used to wear Hawaiian shirts and ting so we started calling him that." Winston also has a moustache, as does Tom Selleck, the actor who plays Magnum. On the other hand, most of the supervisors' dealings with the younger female workers are characterized by "flirting" and sexual harassment (see Chapter 5). What distinguishes Lloyd's workplace peer ties from those of the other supervisors, however, is his relatively close relationship with Nigel Tiexiera. Lloyd is probably the most skilled supervisor and is in charge of maintaining the large machines in the Machinery Department. When Tiexiera complains loudly to the supervisors about lagging production rates and criticizes their performances, Lloyd is usually immune from such reprimands. He often can be seen talking in a friendly manner to Tiexiera. It is perhaps because of this relationship that he does not regularly spend time with any of the other supervisors outside work.

UPSTAIRS-DOWNSTAIRS: The divisions in the factory are not only based on age, class, sex, and ethnicity. There is also some difference according to work group. Their exists a rivalry of sorts between the workers who work upstairs and those who work downstairs. An upstairs worker, Carole, said, "It have some people downstairs who ain't friendly. See up here? Well, they don't get on like we do upstairs. And some of they racial too. I ain't naming names but it have some who pretend to like you but they real racial inside. I ain't like that. You see me? I does talk to everybody. My husband a dougla, he father Indian."

With these remarks, Carole sums up how most of the EUL workers feel: That there is more solidarity among the upstairs workers than among the downstairs workers, and that each group is naturally disposed against the other. But it is also significant that in the second part of her statement she refers to racism. In Trinidad "ethnic conspiracy theories" are trotted out with willingness and impunity, but Carole is the only one I am aware of who refers to the rivalry in these terms. A downstairs worker blamed "all the Seventh Day Adventists" upstairs. However, the ethnic breakdown upstairs is roughly similar to downstairs, and there is no Seventh Day Adventist working upstairs. It is unclear just why, then, references are made to these issues except somehow to explain and justify other kinds of attachments. In any event, it belies the misunderstanding and the relatively isolated instances of friendship between upstairs and downstairs workers. Indeed, an overwhelming number of workplace friendship relations exist between those workers who work on the same floor in the factory and, especially, within the same department.

In-group feelings according to work group are prevalent. For example, the workers in the Upstairs Final-Assembly I Department, who work in a relatively isolated and quiet department, brag that they are "closer" to each other than are the workers in other departments. It seems much of this feeling can be attributed to age. The workers who said they were "close" were the younger ones, who indeed spend time with each other outside the factory. Many of the workers of the Downstairs Final-Assembly Department formerly worked in the Upstairs Final-Assembly I Department. Many spend their lunch and break times in this department, talking to friends they made while working there.

As evidence of their "closeness," the workers in the Upstairs Final-Assembly I Department point out that they have a system where they exchange birthday presents. In this system, which the workers call the Birthday Club, names and dates are put on a sheet of paper on the wall and when a birthday is approaching $5 is collected from all the names on the list (except the birthday person) and a present is selected, usually by Denise. Two of the workers from the Downstairs Final-Assembly Department joined the Birthday Club. None from the Motor-Assembly Department did. As Denise herself said, many of the younger workers looked upon Denise as an older sister and, as mentioned above, her close friendship ties are to workers younger than herself.

For the Birthday Club, workers go to a known *partner* (i.e., close friend or associate) of the birthday person for advice on what they would like for a gift, and sometimes they put the partner in charge of purchasing the present. However, Denise is usually in charge of the purchasing. Once, she did not return with a receipt for her purchase and there was grumbling that she had used some of the Birthday Club money for herself. The practice of asking the partners shows that workers are aware of the social relations that the other workers are caught up in, and acutely aware of the alliances and distribution of power.

In February 1987 it was Connie's birthday party. She works downstairs, but she is an "honorary" member of the upstairs crew. Although this was a rare situation, the celebration ceremony was typical of other birthdays celebrated by the Birthday Club. For her party, there was a small gathering (Jeremy, Denise, Brian, Cheryl, and Stephanie). Jeremy said, "On behalf of the Birthday Club, I'd like to wish you Happy Birthday," and kissed her on the cheek. She was required to open her presents, which were an address book, perfume, makeup, and a battery-powered reading lamp that were bought with Birthday Club money.

She also received a card signed by all that contained the $6 left over from the $165 collected to buy her presents.

The Birthday Club can be a source of controversy. In 1984, according the Myra, her birthday was the same day as one of the workers who was "in the clique" (workers no longer employed at EUL) that ran the Birthday Club at that time. While a nice gift was bought for the other woman, Myra said she received "a cheap-cheap gift. Everybody saw that play. That wasn't right man. Those people gone from here now. It run fair now. . . . We used to bring in food and have a meal for each other's birthday. What they used to be doing is take from the money for the gift and buy something like a pie and bring it like they bring it from home."

Irene's birthday was on the same day as Connie's. This was celebrated downstairs in not nearly so formal a manner. From her work group, Irene received a gift-wrapped box. When she opened it, she found old wires and a condom. This scene was punctuated by howls of laughter, exclamations of "Oh Gaaaawd," and general ribald behavior, which reached a climax when Irene took the condom out of its wrappings and blew it up like a balloon. She chased Sybil around with it in her hand, and Sybil squealed, "Don't touch me wid *dat*!" When the excitement died down, Conrad gave her a "real" present—a diary purchased by some of the workers in her department.

The claims that the upstairs workers are "closer" to each other do not seem to be verifiable, but the belief persists, perhaps in part because few friendship relationships are maintained between workers from different floors. Further, it may be that the upstairs workers have the opportunity to be "closer" for several reasons. First, the groups there work in an environment more conducive to conversation because of the lack of noise created by machinery. Second, Tiexiera is not likely to check on them because their part of the operation depends on the production of the Motor-Assembly Department. If this department does not provide the inputs, the final products cannot be made. As the supervisor Winston said, "Production by me is dependent on Motor Line production. I can't make the final product if they don't make the parts." In addition, the Upstairs Final-Assembly I Department supervisor, Winston, is constantly required to obtain materials from the storeroom and from the Motor-Assembly Department downstairs, so he is not able to directly supervise the workers much of the time.

Chapter 4

ETHNICITY AT WORK

These people don't care about black people you know, they want you to work and they make their money, they got you as some sort of machine that they plug in and make money for them . . . sometimes they get angry with the girls and so, the things they say to you, especially one day the wife said "she sorry that Hitler or something don't wipe us out," I think that's what she said. Sometimes the girls they even get sick on the job and they really don't show much interest you know, so that is why I say they don't care.

—Caribbean woman factory worker

IN THE BRILLIANT, fast-moving novel by Edgar Mittelholzer A *Morning at the Office* (1974 [1950]), the characters who inhabit the Trinidadian office of a British-owned company during the 1940s find their lives caught up in a complex and unforgiving web of ethnicity, class, and gender—from the colonial society's political and economic conflicts that are played out within the confines of the office, to the characters' position within the firm and their possibilities for advancement, to the fits and starts of office romance and the novel's underlying sexual tension.

Because of an acute awareness of the significance of ethnicity, class, and gender, each character is cognizant of their place within this structure. We are introduced to Horace Xavier, the office boy, who "was a negro nineteen years old, five feet nine and thick-set in build, with broad shoulders" (p. 5). His mother, a cook for a wealthy French Creole family, had always impressed upon him the need for smelling sweet and clean: "When you sweet and clean," she said, "people will respect you, and you will get on in de world, but when you smell sweaty and nasty de *bacra* [an unflattering term for whites] people turn away from you and call you a stink nigger—and you punish and dead bad" (p. 6). At eight, Horace told his mother he wanted to be a doctor. She burst into tears and said, "Ah know you would mek a good doctor, me boy. You got it in you. But dat not for you. Dat not for you, Horace. Your skin black and you poor" (p. 7).

Xavier is infatuated with Mrs. Nanette Hinckson, the chief stenographer and the manager's secretary. Yet he wondered what the point was, because, "It was true that she was charming and attractive—physically as well as in manner—but he should have remembered that he was only a black boy, whereas she was a coloured lady of good family. His complexion was dark brown; hers was a pale olive. His hair was kinky; hers was full of large waves and gleaming. He was a poor boy with hardly any education, the son of a cook; she was well off and of good education and good breeding. He was low-class; she was middle-class" (p. 9).

The social convention that prevented Everard Murrain, the chief accountant and assistant manager, an Englishman, from following through on his sexual attraction to Kathleen Henery was not just the fact that he was already married: "Miss Henery—like Mrs. Hinckson—belonged to the coloured middle-class, and was very conscious of her background of gentility and her social superiority over the negro, East Indian, and Chinese elements which counted, in her estimation, as low-class. The whites debarred her from their society, but—like everyone in her class—she considered herself the equal of the whites in breeding and general culture" (p. 45).

Mr. Murrain is very disturbed by what his "secret, honest parts" are telling him:

> Now and then he considered it absurd, even demeaning, that he should be experiencing any attraction for her at all. He tried to despise himself. Miss Henery was an olive-skinned girl with kinky, negroid hair artifically straightened; her features were more European than negroid, it was true, and she was pretty—but the fact remained that he was a white man, an Englishman. . . . She was a spirited, haughty young woman, and had so often outraged his sense of authority and feeling of Caucasian superiority that he had grown to be unsure how he felt about her. At times he was positive he disliked her; at other times it required a great deal of restraint to prevent himself asking her to lunch with him, or to go for a drive with him one evening. (pp. 45–47)

Miss Henery, for her part, is somewhat amused by Mr. Murrain's evident attraction, but grows impatient with his delay in granting his permission for her annual two weeks' leave, which this year she wants to take earlier than the customary time, July or August, in order to accompany her cousin on a trip to Barbados. She thinks, "Why should she have to go using her wiles on him and taking advantage of his mood to get her leave? She was entitled to two weeks every year, wasn't she? And she had already broached the subject with him. It was his place to give her an answer. Perhaps he was purposely keeping her waiting. These white people were so mean and nasty sometimes—especially the English. . . . And who was Murrain at all! For all she knew, she had much better class than he. Most of these English people who came out to the colonies were dregs. But the instant they arrived they were gods. . . . His white skin was all that made him somebody in Trinidad" (pp. 92–93).

Mr. Murrain's officiousness was just part of a sham. He realizes he is in no way qualified for his position of authority:

> Many times it troubled him that he did so little work yet drew such a big salary—three hundred and sixty dollars a month—when his hard-working

> junior, Jagabir, received only a hundred and twenty. But, on the whole, it did not bother him; not having an excess of energy, he never suffered from boredom.
>
> Often, by a feat of reasoning, which deep down he knew to be specious, he justified his idleness to himself. As one of the heads of the office, he argued, the assistant manager as well as the Chief Accountant (and a white man, at that, among coloured peoples of the tropics), he had every right to be idle. The company had put him here, in reality, to superintend these people—not simply to work among them. They were a subject people, and he was an Englishman in a colony dominated by the British Crown. (p. 37)

Mr. Jagabir, the thirty-eight-year-old East Indian assistant accountant is a scheming sycophant. Yet the deference he shows to his bosses and the wrath he incurs from his coworkers is explainable because his stigmatized "East Indianness" is always in their, and his, consciousness: "He had been brought up to feel that an East Indian's place was in the Fields. . . . An office was meant for white people and good-class coloured people." Yet, "There did occur moments when he realized that this fear of being dispensed with or demoted was an irrational one. Mr. Murrain knew hardly anything about accountancy and never exerted himself to become familiar with the books. Without Mr. Jagabir he would be lost—and Mr. Murrain knew it, as did Mr. Waley the Manager. Still, felt Mr. Jagabir, he was an East Indian, and that made all the difference. He was a coolie; he had worked in the fields for four years after leaving primary school; he had been cursed at and threatened and humiliated by white overseers—once nearly kicked: only his agility had prevented the muddy boot landing in the seat of his pants" (p. 22, 32).

Even in his office job, Mr. Jagabir goes around never knowing "when the white people might decide I'm of no use to them anymore in this office" and it will be "back to the estate to some field job" for him (pp. 32, 91).

If the whites in the office look down on Mr. Jagabir but find him useful, his coworkers barely conceal their dislike for him. Mary Barker sweeps the office in the morning and comes back at three in the afternoon to make tea for the staff. When we meet her, she has come in "groaning, a look of misery on her black face" (p. 14). She has this look because she has been to the police office this morning because her seventeen-year-old son Richard has been arrested for disorderly behavior when his steel band clashed with another at a dance the previous night. Richard's father, Boysie Lamb, lived with Mary for two years and supported her, but left her for another woman. For over six months Barker has been employed at the office and no one, except Mr. Jagabir, has found fault with her. "And Mary was contemptuous of all East Indians (cheap coolies, she called them), so Mr. Jagabir's fault-finding did not count; it was what she should have expected of him, she assured herself" (p. 20).

For Miss Henery, "It was not that she hated East Indians," it was Mr. Jagabir himself "that made her sick in every way." Yet,

> Her upbringing, too, did not help matters. In her social sphere, a child was from an early age made to feel that the East Indians were inferior, contemptible people. They were dirty coolies, you learnt, who had come from India by the shipload to work on the sugar estates. . . .
>
> It was only of recent years that East Indians had begun to get rich and become somebodies. Her grandparents . . . were ladies and gentlemen living in respectable surroundings—educated, well-bred people—when the East Indians had still, in every sense, been coolies labouring in the cane-fields. (p. 55)

Although East Indian herself, Miss Edna Bisnauth, the manager's assistant stenotypist, does not readily identify with Mr. Jagabir: "She was East Indian like himself, but she was educated and moved with well-to-do Indians—Indians educated like herself—and even with good-class coloured people. Her father was a wealthy provision merchant in Henry Street, and she did not need to work in this office; she could stay at home and live in idleness like a lady if she wanted; she regarded him with as much contempt as the others did: to her, too, thought Mr. Jagabir, he was only a dirty coolie" (p. 69).

For Miss Bisnauth, it is not class but ethnicity that stands in the way of her own happiness. For her, Arthur Lamby

> was the best man in existence; the different bloods of which he was composed meant nothing to her. Once he had told her: "But do you realize that I have English, French, German, Chinese and negro blood in me? I'm a regular U.N. Council."
>
> "Then we must have thousands of U.N. Councils in the West Indies," she had laughed. (p. 77)

Even though her parents think well of Lamby, a journalist who, "In features . . . had taken more of the European than of the negro or Chinese" (p. 77), they cannot see him as a son-in-law.

> They were thoroughly Christian and western in outlook, like their parents before them—Hinduism had ceased with their grandparents, the sugar estate coolies—but they were still clannish; it was as though this trait had continued subconsciously in them from the seed of their forebears so that whenever there came a decision that involved a mixing of racial strains it rose to the surface. They had told her that an East Indian should marry an East Indian. They just felt so; they could offer no explanation of the matter.
>
> Several of their friends were coloured, and were invited to the home on such occasions as a birthday party or a Christmas or Easter party. The Bisnauths spoke not one word of Hindustani; they belonged to the India Club, but the India Club is run on western lines. . . .
>
> Yet, they objected to Arthur as a son-in-law because he was not an East Indian. (p. 78)

The way in which Mittelholzer portrays the confluence of identity and power resembles with eery precision the order of things in the EUL factory.

It is not for nothing that Caribbean society has been called "an area where the poet, novelist and, indeed, the song writer, have very often provided the best descriptions of social reality" (Maingot 1983:4).

Ethnicity and Authority in the Factory

When I began fieldwork I was interested in investigating, among other things, the importance of ethnicity in an industrial setting. But, I was worried that there would be no "ethnicity" to report, that factory behavior would not at all be influenced by ethnicity. However, on one of my first days in the factory, I heard Martha singing part of the song "War" by the late reggae singer Bob Marley:

> Until the color of a man's skin
> Is no more significant
> Than the color of his eyes
> All you'll have is war.

"And you know what?" she asked. "You'll *never* see that. It will always have racism." So I realized that I could start by talking to Martha about the subject. When I broached the subject of ethnic relations in the factory with her, she said, "I will move and talk to Indians natural. They may think different, but that OK. But the whites, they have that reputation of being real racial. Karl, though, is the best supervisor. He puts heself in the work, not like the others. He will do things to help out the line."

However, many Trinidadians claim that racism is a fact in others—even of their other ethnic group—but that any ethnocentric impulses do not involve themselves. Terry, who is East Indian, remarked, "Race is important at work, because it have some Indians who don't like Negroes and it have some Negroes who don't like Indians at all. Like Martha, for instance. She say plain-plain that she don't like Indians. I say 'But Martha, how could you say that?' And she say 'It have a few I like, but I really don't study most of they.' I mean, we lime and . . . we friends, but that real hurt me man."

The fact that in the EUL factory there is an ethnic order to formal power and authority is not lost on the workers. As Carole, who is black, said, "Race important in here too. Whoever have straight hair think they higher than us." (Perhaps this is why the very day before she had gone to the beauty shop to have her own hair straightened.)

Regarding the ethnicity of the supervisors, she said, "I ent seen a nigger supervisor yet. They all have straight hair. Now, I don't know if it racialism or if it that they more qualified or what. But it look like racialism to me. . . . I just keep myself to my little gang. If them have a [racial] problem, that they problem." And Norma, a thirty-eight-year-old East Indian who has been working at EUL for ten years, said of Tiexiera, "He don't like blacks at all."

Most of the workers would say that what they saw as selective hiring was not confined to a particular ethnic group. To quote Martha, "Everybody want to push he race to the top. If you go to a Indian place, it only have Indians working there. Negroes, we would do the same. It natural to help you own people."

When he comes out into the factory floor and starts yelling at the workers, Tiexiera's behavior is interpreted as "racial" by some, but others put it down to bad temper and greed. When reflecting on his hiring practices, though, the workers seem to agree that these are ethnically motivated.

Carole used to work for a fabric store in Port-of-Spain that was owned by Syrians. She said, "We couldn't have a little laugh, a little lean-up, like we do here. They serious-serious. And they racial. I might be a little brownskin, but we all niggers to they. They all care about they own people, they own skin color."

By referring to herself as "brownskin," Carole was placing herself outside the "nigger" category and arguing that, as such, she was worthy of better treatment. Her contention was that Syrian bosses are unaware of or unaffected by such distinctions.

Speaking of Tiexiera, Irene said, "Tiexiera is racial the way he carry on and who he hires. He's not the only one. My friend got a job at a security firm where the Negro boss didn't want Negroes working there! Where I used to work the higher staff was like Tiexiera—they were all white or high brown. You could see the difference between the way he treated whites and blacks. *He was Negro*! His wife was high colored."

In the factory, there are charges that some of the East Indian supervisors show favoritism to East Indian workers. Martha used to work under Winston upstairs. She said, "Winston real racial, you know. He *tells* us [blacks] to do things, when he *asks* them [East Indians] to do things. There was real confusion up there. We found that it wasn't fair. He not supposed to do that."

In Winston's case, it could be that he uses his position to flirt with East Indian female workers. As he admitted: "I may be a little racial. They say that I give easier jobs to Indian girls. I don't know." But Lois, who is East Indian, felt that Tiexiera would rather hire white supervisors: "Maybe he feels his own will take care of his property and his business. If Tiexiera were East Indian, I don't think he would hire all Indians. But it would take a very trustworthy Negro to get hired. He would be checked-up on." She said Tiexiera is "real racial. You can see it in he face. I don't know how he is in private, but here he real racial."

She used to work in an East Indian–owned grocery, where the owners made her feel "part of the family." "But I don't think they would have been that way if they was white," she said. And Cheryl, who is black, told me, "Tiexiera don't like black people. He like dem to work for he. But he don't like to mix wid dem."

Here, Lois and Cheryl both claim that not every ethnic group regards ethnic "others." But others are not so sure. Martha said, "See, all Tiexiera want to do is make money." And Brian said, "You see all dem [the white supervisors] get *buff up* [i.e., rebuffed] the same by Tiexiera. So he's not racial."

Most East Indians seem not to feel that Tiexiera is "racial" toward them. "Why should he be?" was the typical reply. This may be due to the fact that, when they look around them in the factory, they see other East Indians in supervisory roles.

The older workers, however, sometimes say they do not see Tiexiera as "racial" but as lacking in manners and "respect."

> Daisy: I wouldn't say Tiexiera racial. No, that I can't say about him. He just studying money. Money, money, money. He don't know how to talk to people.
>
> Cleo: He don't know how to respect his elders.
>
> Daisy: He can't talk to big people the way he do. He have loyal employees who have been here years—me, Walcott, Cleo, Karen. He need to go to school to learn how to talk to people. And he buff up the supervisors too. He can't talk to they like that. They tryin' too.

Later I asked Cleo if she thought David is qualified to be a supervisor. "Me ent know, but he do try to tell we what's wrong wid de machines and we know better than he," she said. Then I asked if David is a supervisor because of his "race." "Well, it look as though to be a supervisor you must have color or hair," she said. "See, *we kind*, especially the men, won't put up wid the foolishness, the way Tiexiera carry on."

Discourses of Ethnicity

The ethnic identities of factory workers are caught up in the social representations of ethnicity in Trinidad, including the Carnival mentality. The Carnival mentality shows how invented traditions are themselves "contested terrain," with groups only partially controlling the invention of "their own" tradition, and it also provides an example as to how ethnicity is defined in relation to economic activity and resource distribution.

Basically, Tiexiera and the supervisors adhere to Douglas McGregor's (1960) "Theory X," which holds that people do not naturally like to work and that they must be pressured to produce. However, when we remember that many of the workers have further occupations, and keep in mind the general desire for material possessions, the Carnival mentality view cannot, of course, be supported. Besides, several studies have attempted to operationalize these ideas emperically and have found little connection between ethnicity and work attitudes.[1]

What comes out of my fieldwork, though, is that one of the workplace norms is not to be seen working hard. In his early studies of the workplace, George Homans (1951) showed that the "informal" aspects of the production process impinges on the "formal" organization and, usually, the "informal" holds sway. This is so at EUL. Workers of all ages are adept at "go-slows" and other usurpationary activities.

It is not at all clear what part ethnicity plays in these acts of resistance. Although many workers, especially black workers, are not only aware but disapprove of the fact that most supervisors are white, there is still an undercurrent of ambiguity on the subject of white supervisors. A survey taken in the mid-1970s shows that both blacks and East Indians would rather work under a white supervisor than for each other (Ryan, Greene, and Harewood 1979:46). In fact, a third of East Indian respondents indicated a white boss as their preference. Blacks, on the other hand, were less partial to whites than to other blacks (see Table 24). These findings reflect the continued salience of colonial notions of ethnicity.

Respondents were asked, "Would you prefer to work for a Negro boss, a white boss, an Indian boss, or does it matter at all?" The responses reflect not so much a belief in the legitimacy of white individuals in supervisory capacity and even a mistrust of the ability of one's own group, but also, more strongly, a feeling among blacks and East Indians that, given the chance, a member of the opposite ethnic group will take undue advantage whenever possible. There is a feeling that historical animosity can be worked out and revenge achieved in these situations. When the same question was posed in a survey taken in 1987, the results were very much the same. Of all respondents, 59 percent expressed no preference for their boss's ethnicity, but 22 percent expressed preference for a white boss. Among blacks and East Indians, both registered 23 percent as preferring a white boss. Again, almost no blacks

TABLE 24
Workers' Preferences Regarding Supervisor's Ethnicity, 1979

Ethnicity Preferred in Supervisor	*Ethnicity of Respondent*		
	African	Indian	Mixed
African	25%	2%	11%
Indian	3	16	1
Chinese	0	2	0
European	12	34	8
No preference	54	37	74
Don't know	6	9	6

SOURCE: Ryan, Greene, and Harewood 1979:46, table 2.16.

surveyed expressed preference for an East Indian boss, while almost no East Indian expressed preference for a black boss. But it is interesting to note that only 15 percent of blacks preferred a black boss and only 9 percent of East Indians preferred an East Indian boss. In the 1987 survey, blue collar and agricultural workers preferred white bosses more than other occupational groups did; the lower down the class scale, the more preference for a white boss (Ryan 1988b:224–25).

There is no reason to think, then, that members of one's own ethnic group, especially in such a competitive society, will not seek to exploit situations and that common ethnic identity makes one immune from suspicion. This is precisely because of the fictive familialism that characterizes ethnicity, where, because they are considered like kin, individuals may have their motives questioned more closely than those deemed as "outsiders." As Martha said; "I would rather lime with Indians. Negroes are trouble when they get together—they're war. I mean, Negroes are my people, man, and that's forever."

What this indicates is that an individual would sometimes prefer to be with individuals of another ethnic identity because they feel that members of their own group expect them to have moral obligations toward them, and they themselves may feel that they will be inclined to honor those expectations. When a supervisor is of the same ethnic identity as a worker the worker may enjoy some favoritism, but this also works in the reverse when the supervisor makes unnecessary demands on the worker based on an appeal to ethnicity.

The following comment from Irene, a twenty-four-year-old black EUL worker, incorporates many assumptions about ethnicity that all Trinidadians seem to share. In fact, she also sums up the major contribution of academic analyses of ethnicity in Trinidad:

> They say Indians will stick together to bring each other up. Negroes don't do that—they're ignorant in that way. At least on a big scale. You know that [East Indian-owned] store Kirpalani's? Well you hardly see Negroes working there. I was there the other day and this Indian woman was chatting to her Indian friend. I asked for assistance but she ignored me. But I didn't take her on [didn't pay her any mind] . . .
>
> They say there's places where Negroes can't go. Places in Central in Felicity [the village where Morton Klass (1961) did his fieldwork] and Chaguanas. . . . Indians from Central are more to themselves, and they haven't adapted the way the ones in town have. They live only among themselves and are real racial. Negroes don't like Indians because Indians don't like Negroes. I've heard them say they ain't going to cow to no Indian. I think the whole thing it ridiculous. Me? I get along with everybody.

She is saying East Indians are clannish and that they take care of each other economically. The implication is that blacks are not so inclined and are "disorganized" in comparison. She is also saying that East Indians from rural "Indian" areas are inclined to retain their "culture"—which included intolerance of other "races"—much more than urbane urban dwellers. One implication for a theory of ethnicity is that the intensity of one's ethnic identity is not absolutely fixed. Blacks, who are more urban than East Indians, are seen to be more "accommodating." Her statement also reflects the rivalry between blacks and East Indians over scarce resources and the mutual fear that a member of the other group will be in a position of authority and thus extract historical revenge. Finally, she exudes, even if sincerely, an attitude that is a byproduct of the official fiction of the multiethnic society, in which "each race finds an equal place": Trinidadians acknowledge the existence of racism, but "Me? I get along with everybody."

These kinds of comments, heard frequently when the workers are philosophizing, indicates the existence of one discourse of ethnicity in the factory. We have seen in previous chapters how ethnicity has influenced access to occupations and resources historically. Earlier, I indicated how recruitment to the factory is made with reference to ethnicity. At the work place, many of the emotional meanings associated with ethnicity coalesced around matters of the economy and business. Ultimately, they relate to the supposed suitability of an individual of a certain ethnic identity for certain economic functions. In addition, there are ethnic conflicts over the country's formal political structure, which has been characterized by institutionalized ethnic voting.

Workers often relate feelings that betray their "sense" of ethnic identity, suggesting that they see ethnicity in terms of a primordial "given," but in varying degrees of strength, depending on the proclivities of the individual. I interpret this to mean that an ethnic social identity is assigned by the society, based on several relevant criteria, but not necessarily resigned to by the individuals in question. One's own sense of self may be, and probably always is, at variance with society's definitions. Ethnic social identity is constructed in an oppositional manner; that is, it is dependent on how other groups, possessing different social trajectories, define themselves and define others. Between these two constructs of an "inner" and "outer" nature, there is "social space" where individuals actively redefine their history through practice, but always in relation to structural constraints. This is evident in the ways Trinidadians regard ethnic economic "types" as an essential part of their culture. Indeed, ethnicity is dependent on an invented history with reference to the position of groups in the occupational structure and their supposed economic suitability. There is an East Indian man who comes around to the factories in the industrial estate selling *doubles*, an Indian curried snack, from the trunk of his car. One morning during break, about twenty workers were crowded around his car trying to buy doubles, which cost $1 each. Johnny tried to take advantage of the confusion and paid the man $3 and asked for three doubles. When the man gave him the third, Johnny said, "I have one more coming, I paid already." The man gave Johnny a fourth. Other workers saw what was going on and one worker, a "mixed" woman, said to Johnny, laughing, "You have a head like ah Indian." She said this twice, because he did not hear her the first time, but when he did he just smiled. Here, she meant that Johnny was a schemer who know how to wrangle people out of their money.

Most of the above comments that deprecate the business sense of blacks come from East Indians. However, I regularly heard the same thing from blacks as well. Martha said, "Look at Indians in Trinidad. They still keep they Hindu, Muslim ting. Know why? Whites molded the Negroes, they took they and took they away from they religion, and wouldn't let they sing and ting. . . . Indians mainly stick to their ways, while Negroes changed. They adopted white man's ways. To me that is all. Each can stick up for their own. Negroes, I wouldn't have a place [be the owner of a business] with they at all—I might go bankrupt!"[2]

Although damaging ethnic stereotypes exist, one wonders about their basis in truth, especially when one finds the members of the group subject to those stereotypes explaining the behavior of other members of the group in stereotypical terms. The following incident between Rohan and Ali may help illustrate just how pervasive certain discourses are in Trinidad.

Once, toward the end of the work day, Rohan was liming with Deepak in Deepak's department. Ruud gave Karl a loud and angry telling off for allowing Rohan to be there. Karl was the Motor-Assembly Department's supervisor at the time. Martha overheard the conversation between Karl and Ruud and came over to Rohan, who had gone back to his post in the Motor-Assembly Department, and said, "See what I tellin' ya. That's your fault. And they will sooner fire you than he [Karl] 'cause he on salary," referring to Karl's supervisor status. Rohan, who is East Indian, told me later, "De Indian fella told on me. *Dey is like dat.*" Here he was referring to Ali, a temporary worker in the Primary-Assembly Department, who was there to start some night work.

I was not able to verify Rohan's claims that it was indeed Ali that had reported his absence to Ruud. Certainly there is circumstantial evidence to support his argument, and Ali may have had a motive. Ali had been an assistant supervisor to Ruud but had been retrenched because, as Ruud said, "Nigel decide he don't need a second supervisor there." At the time of the incident, he had only recently been rehired, but without supervisory authority. So it is possible that Ali was trying to impress Ruud with his usefulness. In any event, the point is that the East Indian Rohan chose to refer to an ethnic stereotype of East Indians when attempting to explain the behavior of Ali, who, like Rohan, is a Muslim.

Soon afterward, Rohan was called into the office and told by Candace that he was going to be suspended. This order was rescinded, and Rohan was then told that he was going to be reinstated and put on the night shift, which was active at that time of year to meet the Christmas demand. But the rumor reached the workers that he had been fired. The workers were of the opinion that he made his mistake not when he left his post, but when he got caught.

> Martha: He didn't know no conduct on the job. He so young. He wasn't no worker. He didn't know how to work. . . . *You don't go messin' around when the boss is right there*!
>
> Terry: If you get fire for something good—like you idling and the man come and talk to you and once he turn he back you still idling—then I can dig it. But not for going to say something to the next fella.
>
> Deepak: I tried talking to him. I've been working three years and I know it's tough now. He's so young.

These workers were in agreement in their condemnation of Ali for allegedly reporting Rohan, especially because, as Terry said, "Jobs hard to come by now."

This example does not support the arguments that East Indians are more industrious and more "respectful" of authority, and thus willing to ingratiate themselves with those in authority. Deepak once described the work habits of the Vishnu and Ben, the East Indian toolmaker and his East Indian assistant: "Dem fellas upstairs? When they does work, dey work. When they don't have not work to, dey does *skylark*. What!?" And once Karl was visibly upset when two East Indian workers in his department were talking at a machine that only takes one person to operate. "And I want production," he said looking toward the sky before going over to tell the workers to get back to work. If East Indians are really "naturally" more inclined to work than blacks, we would not expect them to be skylarking.

The inaccuracy of these racist stereotypes is further evidenced in the examples of black workers like Brian and Myra, who put in extra time in order to cook and sell their food and other goods. Terry an East Indian, said, with reference to Brian: "I find sellin' pies real shit. I wouldn't sell pies. I have my pride." These are not the remarks one would expect if one believed in these stereotypes.

Ethnicity as Fixed and Variable

Referring to Elaine's complexion, Fiona asked Elaine, who is termed "light skinned" but regards herself as a "Negro," what her parents look like:

> Elaine: My mother is pure; she dark-dark.
>
> Fiona: So where you get your color from?
>
> Elaine: From my father. His complexion like mine.

From a basis in "race" and the constraints it entails, the workers believe that race is modified by "color" (see Segal 1993). They also hold that an individual is relatively free to choose to adhere to an ethnic "ideal type." But it should be emphasized that there is only a certain amount of leeway, because there are serious sanctions for pretending to be something that you are not.

There is also the obverse, "ethnic outcasts," who are thought to betray the ethnic group by denying—in deeds or words—their full membership in that group. Vishnu was talking about the "people who don't know where they are," meaning East Indians who are "relaxing" their grip on "traditional" Indian cultural institutions.

Vishnu: [*Motioning to Winston*] See this guy? He don't know where he stand.
Winston: What do you mean?
Vishnu: You ain't a Hindu.
Winston: So? Well, I have traces of Hinduism, but . . .
Vishnu: So? Where is your Hindu name?
Winston: I have my last name.
Vishnu: So? My first name is Vishnu. That's a *real* Hindu name. [*Even more seriously*] You don't know where you stand. You need to get back to your roots.
Winston: [*Trying to defuse the situation, which was causing him visible anxiety*] Hey man, you want me to shoot you, or what?

After Vishnu walked away, Winston admitted: "He a *real* Hindu, you know." Later, I asked Vishnu if he would ever go to India. "I don't think I'd be going. They don't recognize us as Indians there. They ignore us, I understand," he said after commenting that the study of Hinduism should be kept up. He then added, not in a direct response to any question that I asked: "Maybe one in a hundred people in Trinidad are racial now."

Trinidadians, like many in the New World, are in a position of inventing and maintaining beliefs about ethnicity and descent but experience alienation when confronted with the actual "homeland." As Carla said: "My cousin went to India and he say it very different than here. The Hindus there, they keep different prayers and ting. I mean, some de same. But they don't see him as being Indian. They tell him he different than they. He see people shit in de streets and on de train. It disgusting and it have some people so poor dey have to live in de street. It really not like here."

Although it may have not been the case in the recent past, in Trinidad many young people identify strongly with "national" symbols and speak of themselves as "Trinidadian," paradoxical as that identity can sometimes be. I asked several workers if they considered themselves Trinidadian first or "African" or "Indian." Here are some samples:

Martha: I consider myself a Trinidadian, of African descent.
Winston: I consider myself Trinidadian first.
Carla: I consider myself Trinidadian first. I was born here but my ancestors from India. But you learn the ways and customs so you Trinidadian.

Trinidadians are aware of and learn to manipulate the symbols of nationalism and ethnicity. They are not randomly selected, though. A black acquaintance of mine said he wanted to learn how to play the steel drum: "It have that white guy [New York musician Andy Narell] who comes down to beat pan. I want to learn. Is *we* instrument!" This is an especially telling comment.

As I discuss in Chapter 2, in postcolonial Trinidad the black-dominated state has worked to impose a defintion of "Trinidadian culture" in terms of "black" cultural activities like calypso and steel band, intentionally ignoring East Indian contributions to those art forms. The role of nationalist ideology in the construction of ethnicity is and ideology that is characterized by a dominant group's "eye on the future construction of putative homogeneity and its institutionalization in civil society" (Williams, 1989:439). Even though the implications of this process can only be hinted at in this context, the construction of ethnicity in the factory must be seen in relation to the discourse and forces of nationalism present in the wider society.

If individuals can adopt an outlook that makes them believe that they are "achieving" ethnicity, some feel that they must struggle against its "loss," and thus seek to shore up what they feel they have. Martha indicated that she had been reflecting on the situations of blacks in Trinidad and worldwide and that this was causing her anguish. She said that discrimination had forced blacks to abandon their culture and that she had decided to make personal statements of protest. To begin with, she tore down her poster of Jon Bon Jovi, the American heavy-metal rock star, that she kept in her bedroom. "I gettin' rid of the white boy n' go put Bob Marley instead," she said. She has also started to wear leather sandals, bought at the "Rasta Mall,"[3] and a charm around her neck—a black horn with red, yellow, and green stripes, which are Rastafarian colors. She said: "I ent have no Rastas in America [she lived in New York for six months]. It have in England. And you see more Rastas and black people wearing dashikis in the West Indies than in America. Black people in America are into this punk thing."

For Martha, people who wear dashikis and who are Rastas are "real" black people. American blacks, although still ethnically related, have been coopted by mainstream American culture. West Indian blacks are more "rootsy." However, such "rootsiness" has to be believable; it has to be legitimated, culturally, in many ways.

Perhaps the biggest fear of loss occurs among urban East Indians, even so-called "creolized" East Indians. There is concern expressed among East Indians that the Hosein celebrations are becoming too "creolized" and taking on too many attributes (drunkenness, rowdiness) of Carnival. "Hosein is like a mini-Carnival," said Rita, an EUL worker who identifies herself as "mixed." "Dem Indian people do get dressed up and ting. But dey play Indian music."

I went with Deepak, Ben, Rohan, Terry, and Carla to Hosein (sometimes called "Hosay") celebrations in St. James, a predominantly East Indian section of Port-of-Spain, where we drank rum, limed, and watched the procession and the people. Although the rest of us left at around 1 A.M., Deepak said he did not return home until 6:30 A.M., adding that, "Pretty soon Hosay going to come like Carnival." Indeed, TTT reported that the festival's organizers were issuing a plea for people to refrain from drinking and dancing because it is a serious religious occasion. These requests were largely unheeded by the revelers, half of whom were East Indian and half Creole. This indicates that some East Indians, perhaps the religious elites and others, consider "their" celebrations like Hosein and Phagwa "pure" in terms of their religious significance and of symbolizing a generic East Indian identity. This is despite the fact that blacks joined in the Hosein celebrations as drummers as early as the 1860s. Indeed, referring to the first Hosein celebrations in Trinidad, Brereton points out that "It soon lost its special religious meaning . . . and became almost entirely secular" (1979:183). However, East Indians still claim that they see their festivals threatened by a "takeover" of "black styles" (cf. Stewart 1986).

Ben, a twenty-year-old factory worker expressed the view in these terms:

> I supposed to be a Hindu and I don't even know what Phagwa is about. In this area, in Diego Martin, they don't have the facilities to teach Hindi and encourage people to go to study the religion. And you find the youths are losing it, they are losing they culture. They are exposed to other cultures and they lose interest in they own. They want to lime. That's bad. I'm not sayin' there's anything wrong with studying another man's culture, I'm just sayin' you need to know you own first.
>
> If they had the interest they wouldn't have to go to San Juan [a section of the Port-of-Spain area where East Indians are numerous] for Phagwa. They could have it here. And they would know what its about. Indians in Diego are different from in Central and South. They keep up tradition down there.
>
> I ain't against races coming together, I just sayin' you must know you own culture first. Phagwa coming like Carnival, everyone drink. It like Hosein becoming.
>
> I know people who paid money for their Carnival costumes—three hundred fifty dollars for Edmund Hart [a well-known Carnival band]—and they didn't have money for food for Wednesday [that is, Ash Wednesday, the day after Carnival]. Give Trinidadians some VAT 19 [the popular Trinidadian rum] and calypso music to fete all night and they happy. Years ago, seventy-five percent would be black. Now, fifty percent are black, twenty-five percent white, Chinese and ting, and twenty-five percent Indian. Everyone involved.

Ben's statement indicates the difference in cultural styles and stereotypes between blacks and East Indians, but it also indicates that, perhaps paradoxically, Trinidadian culture is founded on principles that are accessible to blacks and East Indians alike. It is up to them to choose "styles," which they interpret as "ethnic" that are valorized or sanctioned.

Connie, a twenty-five-year-old East Indian factory worker, was born in a Muslim family but says she converted to Catholicism after going to two Catholic schools. Although she did not go through a formal conversion ceremony, she said, "It was my choice and my parents said 'it's your life.' I found I just couldn't believe in the religion [Islam] any more." On the other hand, Carla was born Catholic (her parents converted from Hinduism to Catholicism), but her two brothers now practice Hinduism. She still participates in Hindu rites, occasionally attending Hindu "prayers," and thanksgivings. I attended a Divali ceremony at her house.

It is apparent that people practice elements of several religions, but, more important, religious practice becomes a symbol of ethnic identity, with Hinduism indicating a "*real*" Indian. There are indications, too, that religions with overt "Africanisms," like the Orisha and the Spiritual Baptists, are enjoying increases in membership (Henry 1983). Frances Henry attributes this resurgence partly to the fact that East Indians and others are joining, but she fails to emphasize strongly enough that these religions are options in which black people emphasize their "African" identity.

Ethnic Politics in the Factory

"Ethnic" behavior in the factory is obviously influenced by outside events. When the 1986 elections were drawing near, many workers' conversations focused on the likelihood of a NAR victory, about which they had strong views. Less than a week before the election, Chuck passed out PNM literature that said that the "sinister alliance" of the parties that comprised the NAR was in trouble. No East Indian read the literature, and Connie commented, "There ain't no way the PNM gettin' my vote. They could pay me a million dollars and they ain't gettin' my vote. I would take they money, but they ain't gettin' my vote."

The next day, Rohan and Winston, who are East Indian, and Martha, who is black, were discussing the election. Rohan asked Winston, "Man, what you think? The NAR is just what this country needs."

Winston: It have too much corruption in this government. Too much mismanagement. You know why? Too many niggers. I mean, listen, we been catchin' our ass for too long while these people waste our money. What about you, Martha [who was strongly pro-PNM]? You die-hard PNM. All y'all so racial.

Martha: You see? People does want to say that PNM did nothing for them. It

> have people with four kids in secondary school. It didn't have that before PNM you know.

Because ethnic voting was so entrenched, "innovators"—that is those who were not supporting the party supposedly pertaining to their "race"—were sometimes questioned. The next day, a NAR campaign car, with loudspeakers mounted on its roof, drove past the factory slowly with the music of the calypsonian Deple's "Vote Dem Out," the NAR theme song, playing loudly (see Yelvington 1987:8). Cheryl, who is black, spelled out, "N-A-R, N-A-R." And Martha replied, "NAR? Man . . ." and she steupsed. Ron, the white supervisor, added, "NAR. That's a real shit party."

> Martha: That's right.
> Rohan: [*To Cheryl*] What do you mean? You is ah NAR now? [*To no one*] What do you want when you black and stupid?
> Cheryl: [*Getting angry*] Man, what de ass you talkin' 'bout? It don't matter your color, you vote for who you feel.
> Ron: [*To Cheryl*] What's the matter with you?
> Cheryl: I just don't like it when people say nigger people don't think. They have a mind like Indian people and everyone else. If they feel that NAR is better, let them vote for they.
> Ron: Man, you sure can talk.

Rohan said that blacks usually vote for the PNM and then questioned a black who was planning to change her "natural" party affiliation. Cheryl angrily maintained that she need not be bound by past custom. This is a rather clear case of one dominant discourse on ethnicity ("nigger people don't think") being challenged by an opposing discourse.

On election day, December 15, 1986, the factory closed at noon so that the workers could vote. The Tiexieras were known to be NAR supporters, and perhaps they thought that most of the workers would vote for the NAR given that nationwide opinion polls put the NAR far ahead of the PNM. The NAR won by a landslide and there was much discussion about the election for weeks afterward in the factory and in the streets. But, in the face of these political upheavals, the workers were soon back to their rather humdrum work routines.

Ethnic politics have been extremely important and the political process continues to keep ethnic hostility entrenched. When the NAR won, many East Indians quickly voiced their hopes that they, for once, would now be able to enjoy the spoils of political patronage as blacks had done under projects targeted at them by the PNM. As Vishnu, who is Hindu, said many months after the 1986 election: "Only one of our celebrations a public holiday. That is Divali. Maybe now they'll give us more." And Cheryl made a comment that further betrayed the Trinidadian expectation that politics does bring and should bring immediate and local patronage and spoils. A roll of toilet paper is given to the female workers once a week, which they are expected to keep with them because no toilet paper is kept in the bathrooms. In the week immediately after the 1986 election two rolls were handed out to each worker (which I think was a coincidence), and when she saw this Cheryl said as a joke: "Yuh see, NAR wins and now everybody have more—even toilet paper!"

If society-wide ethnic voting further entrenches ethnic hostility, the fact that it occurs must be based on some sense of difference and a feeling that one's group's interests are inimical to the others'. This suggests that ethnicity is achieved with reference to the distribution of resources. The next section shows that the choices involved require tradeoffs.

Ethnicity and Social Resources

In the Port-of-Spain offices of the Oilfields Workers' Trade Union (OWTU) there are posters on the walls of white Trinidadian capitalists Tommy Gatcliffe and Conrad O'Brien, with captions identifying them as an "Enemy of the Working Class." This is one way in which trade unions use ethnicity in their appeals for working-class solidarity. Sometimes this is combined with other bases of social identity. A photograph in the OWTU's newspaper *Vanguard* (November 1977, p. 6) shows six black working-class women with the caption: "Some of the workers fired by the racist Unilever." Here, the union is playing on and cultivating the idea that women are the embodiment of an ethnic groups's values and to harm or defame them would indeed be a very serious affront to the entire group (more on this theme in the next chapter). If ethnicity effects the distribution of social resources, then ethnicity itself will come to be seen as a social resource. I have shown how the discourse of ethnicity helps to account for the positions of certain workers within the factory's division of labor and how Nigel Tiexiera uses ethnicity in the recruitment of workers and supervisors. Exploring the underlying meanings associated with this activity entails joining the discussion of ethnicity in Trinidad and in the general anthropological literature.

Tiexiera's actions reveal the conjunction of affect and instrumentality that characterizes ethnicity. It is possible to conclude that Tiexiera felt that whites would best protect the property of another white. The result would be to uphold the aims of the organization, and therefore Tiexiera's ends. It is also possible that he sees East Indians as more reliable and industrious than blacks, and therefore also serving his economic goals. This is evidenced by his comments on his hiring preferences reported earlier. On the one hand, it could be argued that feelings of ethnic affinity will exist only when a material advantage is realized. But this would be to ignore situations when ethnic identity claims are made and adhered to despite the possibility of real and imminent danger for doing so.

It seems the best way to typify ethnicity that takes affectivity and instrumentality into account is to speak of ethnicity in terms of fictive kinship. For, if we see ethnicity as fictive kinship (Ching 1985), then the empathy and emotion, as well as the economic rationality, that are associated with ethnic sentiments are not surprising. As Terry said, "My race is very important because its something like ah country—you would die for it. I wouldn't like to see ah white or ah Negro beating up ah Indian, if he don't deserve he cut-ass. I wouldn't like to see that." But there is still some element of choice associated with these sentiments. In Trinidadian terminology, Terry is a "dougla," his father is black and his mother is East Indian. His parents are divorced and his father lives in San Fernando. I asked him what race he considers himself: "I'm Indian. I mean, my family is all Indian, so I Indian. I consider myself Indian."

In any event, if ethnicity is properly characterized as fictive kinship we would also expect that, when challenged, members of an ethnic group would extend to each other those considerations that are normally extended to members of one's kin group. Ethnicity is intimately caught up in the distribution of resources because ideas about economics are inherently cultural. As Carla said, "I have a friend who went to the market and it have ah Negro man selling vegetables and it have ah Indian man selling vegetables. The Negro man's vegetables were better and they were cheaper; the Indian man, his own were dried up sort of. But she go to he and when I point it out to she that the other man have better, she say 'I buyin' from de Indian! You mad or what?' "

In some cases, individuals choose to interpret their ethnic identity with reference to the supposed economic "suitability" of members of their ethnic group. Conrad, the EUL supervisor, is a Muslim East Indian. He was very active in administering his mosque for several years, but now he only attends because "you have to give the younger men a chance." He goes to mosque every Friday during lunchtime: "It says that you should go forth and reap his fruits, so I go back to work. This means you should go back to work. We does work like dat."

When they reflect on how they came to work at EUL, workers express their history in similar terms. Many black and East Indian workers expressed to me that the relatively recent phenomenon of young East Indian women working in factory employment contravenes East Indian values. Lois, an East Indian, said, "Indian families would have to be in need to let their, not so much their sons, but, daughters go to work. Indians pamper they kids. Negroes, on the other hand, would encourage they kids to get a trade or job when they finish school."

If resource distribution is caught up with ethnicity, an ethnic group will be defined by itself and by "ethnic others" on how it affects such distribution among its members and the power that results. In Trinidad, these notions are directly related to how each ethnic group performs in economic situations.

Ram, an East Indian EUL supervisor, said:

> Eric Williams put water in the people's eye [fooled them]. He say "Massa Day Dead" and the black people get the wrong idea—they so stupid—and they think it OK to be lazy. They lazy man. They don't want to work. . . . You know, one reason why we catchin' we ass [i.e., struggling] now is production keeps dropping. It been going down since 1961 when he say "Massa Day Dead" . . . then they want to get rid of him but they say "Who we go put?" . . . And look at state enterprises. Indian people workin' at Caroni in the hot sun all day and get less than black people at Trintoc [the state sugar and oil enterprises, respectively]. . . . Black people and Indian people think different. They will come together when there's breeding ["miscegenation"]. But as long as you have white people, Portuguese, Indian, black, you will have difference.

This idea of economic performance and ethnicity is used when impugning the prestige of another ethnic group. As Winston said, "The most fun for me was in the Black Power revolution. I was in my college uniform, pelting stones at big glass windows and runnin' down alleys to get away. Yeah, they burned a lot of Indian businesses. But they burned everyone's business. Whoever's it was it wasn't theirs. Black people never have anything. You ever know a black man who have a business? They never have nuttin'. So it wouldn't matter what they bombed. Is only now they going into business."

Ethnicity and Gender

The Trinidadian novelist and social scientist Merle Hodge writes: "An important element of the history of male-female relations in the Caribbean has been the imposition of European standards of physical beauty—the tendency of the man to measure the desirability of women by these standards, and the corresponding struggle of black women to alter their appearance as far as possible in the direction of European requirements for beauty but of course still falling short of these requirements. A large part of male disrespect for the black woman was an expression of his dissatisfaction with her, 'inferior' as she was to accepted white ideal of womanhood" (1974:117–18).

If the black woman could not alter her appearance ("Jherri curling," a technique creating loose, wet curls in the hair, has largely taken the place of the traditional hair straighteners, although using these products is not always a sign of ethnic self-contempt) then she would, it is said, employ mating strategies to, as they say in the Caribbean, "put a little milk in her coffee." In other words, black women would try to produce a child with "lighter" skin, one with "good" (i.e., straight) hair and a "good" (i.e., thin) nose.[4]

One way to explore the apprehensions of these hegemonic images is to look at the role ethnicity plays in conceptions of female beauty. For example, consider the ways in which the ethnic identity of women has been depicted in the calypsoes. William R. Aho writes, "There is considerable opinion, both informed and otherwise, that at least there is congruence between the topics of calypsoes . . . on the one hand, and some of the social norms, values, beliefs, attitudes and behaviors of substantial numbers of Trinidadian people, on the other" (1982:77–78).

While the images of women in this Trinidadian art form have been analyzed extensively (e.g., Aho 1982; Austin 1976; Elder 1968; Rohlehr 1988, 1990; Warner 1982), of interest here are the ways in which ethnicity and ethnic conflict are expressed in these songs (cf. Deosaran 1987; Rohlehr 1985; Warner 1993). Traditionally, most of Trinidad's calypsonians have been black males. However, women and members of other ethnic groups have begun to gain prominence as calypso singers and composers (Warner 1993). "Race calypsoes," according to Gordon Rohlehr, "trade on racial stereotyping, and employ caricature and a humour based on the mockery of accent, music or gestures of the other race. They measure, or betray, the uncertainty with which the races have regarded each other; a latent atavistic mistrust, and the competition which has always been taking place against a background of chronic unemployment, poverty and dispossession on the part of the broad masses of people, and authoritarianism, patronage and manipulation on the part of those small elitist groups who control their destiny" (1985:1–2).

Elsewhere, Rohlehr shows that the calypsoes of the 1930s contained lyrics indicating positive black consciousness in the face of continued prejudice, but regarding calypsonians' views of women, "the idealized woman in calypso was usually either Caucasian or Latin, while the Black woman was presented in terms of the most negative stereotyping imaginable. . . . [However,] although white women were generally idolized by calypsonians, there existed alternative ideas about female beauty and a sense of the reality of anti-black racial prejudice" (1988:266, 273).

There is much ambiguity over the supposed characteristics of white or "high-brown" women. After the white woman, the "high-brown" woman, according to Rohlehr, was the calypsonians' "second choice." On the other hand, according to the calypsoes of the 1930s and the factory workers, the white or light-skinned woman could be finicky and demand much attention and a high style of living. Terry commented on the actions of a young "red" ("mixed") woman: "She too white in the way she move. Nobody good enough for she." By this he meant that she is snobbish because she believes her skin color, still socially valued, gives her license to be so. But, in another connection, Terry also revealed that light-skinned females are nonetheless attractive and valued: On the relative merits of Rita versus a young woman named Michelle from outside the factory, he said, "The only thing Rita has is color. But I like Michelle."

In the factory, Irene, Sybil (both dark-skinned Afro-Trinidadians), and Elaine complained that a light-skinned, mixed-race woman had won the Miss Trinidad and Tobago contest. "They would never let a darkie win," said Sybil. Yet, in November 1986, a young Trinidadian woman named Giselle LaRonde won the Miss World contest. The young women at the factory reflected the island's pride, but they chose to emphasize a particular significant factor of the event. Martha said, "How 'bout that Miss World? She the first black one. We had the first black Miss Universe [Penny Commissong in 1976] and now we have the first black Miss World." She noted that Miss USA was also black. And Sybil was likewise enthusiastic: "Ya see? The girl from Trinidad and Tobago is Miss World. And she *black*!"

Most Trinidadians would categorize LaRonde as "mixed" because she has a fair complexion, "straight" hair, and a "straight" nose. In their comments on the Miss World victory, the workers were reflecting on North American and British categorizations of "blackness" (Martha having lived in Brooklyn, New York, for six months). They were using "North Atlantic," not local, standards to make their point. By "North Atlantic" standards they shared "blackness" with Miss World. Before LaRonde's victory both had complained about prejudice against "darkies" and favoring women of LaRonde's color.

In the wake of the Black Power revolution of the early 1970s, a movement that redefined conceptions of ethnicity with an avowed "black is beautiful" perspective, there was an official government commission of inquiry into the organization of beauty contests (Trinidad and Tobago 1973). The inquiry was conducted in 1972 and the results were published in 1973. Since beauty contests of all kinds are very popular all over the Caribbean, some of the findings of this panel may illuminate this issue.

While a portion of the inquiry was devoted to investigating alleged fraud among the promoters of such contests, what interests us here is the investigation into allegations of ethnic prejudice in the recruitment of contestants and the selection of the winners. In this connection, the commission focused on the Carnival Queen show. The Junior Chamber of Commerce (Jaycees), by 1972 renamed the Junior Chamber of Port-of-Spain, took over the running of the Carnival Queen show in 1958. Previously, beauty-contest shows relating to Carnival had been set up and run by the Trinidad Publishing Company, the publisher of the *Trinidad Guardian*, which set up the Guardian Neediest Cases Fund after World War II and used the shows to raise money for charitable purposes.

The commission noted that the Jaycees' show was the greatest attraction in considering the Carnival Queen every year. "To many people, the Winner has been regarded not only as Carnival Queen of Trinidad and Tobago, but as the Beauty Queen as well" (p. 5). It also noted, "The Junior Chamber

Carnival Queen Show became more outstanding and elaborate year by year. Prizes of great value were given to the Winner and other contestants. However, as the years passed by, charges began to be levelled at the organizers of discrimination, as girls of a particular ethnic group were selected as contestants for the show. Accordingly, only such contestants could emerge as Winners or Runners-up of the Competition in accordance with the organized method of selection" (p. 1).

The president of the Junior Chamber of Port-of-Spain, Mr. Arneaud, argued that the Junior Chamber Carnival Queen Show was not a beauty contest. Arneaud said that contestants were judged on their costumes and their dressmaking. He said that as far as costumes go, the contestants were judged on the theme, impact, originality of design, ingenuity in building, ease of movement on stage, and what he called the "spirit of Carnival." The commission did not agree with this description and classified the Carnival Queen show as a beauty contest. By contrast, the commission did not classify as beauty contests the Better Village Queen Show in Tobago, in which contestants appeared in beachwear and costumes depicting village life, and the Vishva Hindu Parishad Divali Queen Competition, in which the contestants are not allowed to wear any "obscene" dress (e.g., short saris), no part of the body can be exposed except the hands, feet, and head; and the goddess Lutchmee should be portrayed by women in long saris.

The commission noted how contestants were chosen for the Carnival Queen show: "In the planning of the Junior Chamber's Queen Show evidence was adduced that members of the Committee working in various firms and organizations, primarily in Port-of-Spain, spotted girl contestants for the show. This he [Arneaud] explained was achieved through family or business connections with the girl or her relatives. He said the procedure was followed also in the selection of contestants from South Trinidad and San Fernando, before San Fernando ran their own show" (p. 5).

Arneaud said that the members of the committee were "businessmen at various levels of management" (p. 5). He was asked if he thought "girls" of "the several ethnic groups living in Trinidad and Tobago" had a chance for selection, considering the committee's method of operations. Arneaud said they did. He added that the "racial origin of the girl" was never considered, nor the "racial background" (p. 5). Arneaud stated that the Carnival Queen Contest was the Jaycees' "contribution to the National Festival, Carnival, and was a fund-raising project benefitting to the country. Further that it created an International appeal bringing several tourists into the country, with every cent going back to the country" (p. 41).

Nevertheless, the commission noted:

> There was however, an unfortunate method of selection of the contestants by the Junior Chamber in past years. The Commission was satisfied that at a

> certain period consideration was mainly given to girls of a particular ethnic background, and what is commonly called the fair-complexion girls as contestants for such shows. . . . This course of conduct as we have said, was most unfortunate in our multi-racial society where the ethnic races were mostly persons of African and Asian origin. . . . available evidence . . . from the Committee's method of selection of contestants . . . the dark-skinned girl, or purely Negro or Indian girl stood a poor chance in the past years of being sponsored in the Carnival Queen Show as a contestant. (pp. 9, 42)

Another promoter, Azad Ali, who was being investigated for his part in other beauty contests, questioned Arneaud:

> Mr. Ali: And in these 12 to 14 years, could you tell me if any black girl has ever won the competition?
>
> Mr. Arneaud: We were never concerned with this particular area. We were concerned with selecting Trinidadians.
>
> Mr. Ali: What I am asking you, is if any black girl ever won.
>
> Mr. Arneaud: We do not state what the girl's colour was. I think all the reports were in the Daily Newspapers and you can check the history if you want to. I would not like to stand and say who was black and who was white. (p. 42)

While the commission acknowledged that in years immediately prior to the inquiry the Junior Chamber had recognized the need to change the method of selecting contestants, even though "this new approach seemed to have caused financial loss to the organizers whose supporters have not shown continued interest" (p. 43), the commission underscored its suggestion that "as far as may be reasonably practicable consideration should be given to all suitable girls in Trinidad and Tobago whatever may be their racial origin" (p. 59). The report concluded by arguing that ethnic fairness was essential for an event through which the development of Trinidad and Tobago could proceed and that it was essential to project the supposed true ethnic democracy that exists there: "The Commission is of the opinion that there is no doubt that the people of Trinidad and Tobago are keenly interested in Beauty Contests and Similar Competitions. For a stage in the development of our society has been reached when it is of vital importance to this country like other developing nations, that Trinidad and Tobago should play an important part in world presentations. . . . The Beauty Contest Show is a means of projecting the image of our people and letting the rest of the world be aware of our potentials in this sphere of production, showing the multi-racial nature of our people" (p. 59).[5]

The black women in the factory are angered when this antiblack bias surfaces, especially among their family.

> Lori: My little sister say she don't like black boys, only brownskin boys. And I have a brother who say he only like brownskin girls. I say "Oh-*ho*!"
>
> Cleo: My two boys say they like *Indians*. I say "Excuse me. *Excuuuuuse me*!"

Some East Indians, too, seem to indicate that they resent a white bias. Carla said that her brother's girlfriend was "real racial," but that, "She like whites. She say, 'look at that nice white man over dere.' I say, 'I ent like whites, I ent like Negroes. I just like my own kind.' "

The ethnographic evidence presented in this chapter suggests that, for the workers, an ethnic social identity "begins" as a relatively invariant involuntary identity, but that there are certain directions in which an individual can take this identity. This, in turn, suggests that there is a "dual boundary" (Isajiw 1974) associated with ethnicity, where "internal" and "external" definitions are not necessarily conterminous. The extent to which an external identity is foisted on an individual or group depends to a large degree on the amount of power that the defining group possesses. But the "stuff" of ethnicity, what goes inside the boundaries, is also dependent on practice, especially practice that reinforces ontological security, which in turn tends to define ethnicity as fictive kinship.

That ethnicity involves "internal" and "external" definitions that are not conterminous seems to be evidenced when the data on the normative social relations of the workers is compared to the discourse of ethnicity presented here. On the one hand, female workers maintain more multiethnic social network ties than do the male workers, with younger women maintaining more multiethnic ties than any other group. On the other hand, in examining the discourse regarding ethnicity presented in this chapter, it appears that men and women of all groups hold similar ideas about each other. The discourses and ethnic stereotypes about blacks and East Indians are continually recapitulated with no clear pattern emerging as to who is doing the talking, male or female.

While it is true that two people may maintain the same kinds of relations with the same kinds of people, yet interpret those relations very differently, it is also true that the differing nature of the actual social relations and the representations of them may vary. In the factory, in this "space" between the structure of the workers' relationships and the social representations of ethnicity, there is social activity that is taking place altering the situation. The fact that the younger women maintain qualitative ties to more ethnic "others" than the older women may reflect social change as much as it reflects the differing "stages" of life, with attendant responsibilities, of the two groups of women.

The apparent contradictions between what people say and what they do points to the distinction between practiced culture and ideational culture. The apparent contradictions that characterize ethnicity in the factory are explained by data presented in subsequent chapters. However, I suggest that when a worker holds negative stereotypical views about another group while maintaining a number of important qualitative relationships with people of that group, this is not a contradiction; it reflects the difference between the individual and the group. The workers may relate to other workers from another ethnic group one-on-one but distinguish between those they relate to and other members of the group who possess the hated characteristics.

Practice theory is about adapting to constraints. The way definitions of another ethnic group are imposed has to do with the relative power of the definers and the defined. This implies that ethnicity is defined in relation to class and power. But might there be other constraints that define ethnicity? That is, might ethnicity be socially constructed with reference to class, gender, and other variables? This seems to be supported by evidence presented earlier suggesting that ethnic relations within the factory are different according to gender. However, this is to digress somewhat from my immediate task, as the conjunction of ethnicity and gender will be treated in the Conclusion. We have seen in previous chapters that ethnicity and gender are used in the composition of class—in Trinidadian history as well as in the recruitment patterns of the EUL factory. It is now time to turn to a discussion of how the experience of gender is manifested in the factory context.

Chapter 5

GENDER AT WORK

Established as an objective set of references, concepts of gender structure perception and the concrete and symbolic organization of all social life. To the extent that these references establish distributions of power (differential control over or access to material and symbolic resources), gender becomes implicated in the conception and construction of power itself.

—*Joan Wallach Scott,* Gender and the Politics of History

THE CALYPSO in Trinidad has long been a medium for political critique, pique, and satire. In 1987, during my fieldwork, sexual politics was the theme of Singing Sandra's "Die With My Dignity," which helped her win the Calypso Queen title. "Die With My Dignity" spoke to the plight of perhaps thousands of working women who faced daily sexual harassment at the workplace:

Yuh want to help to mind your family
Yuh want to help yuh man financially
But nowadays it really very hard
To get a job as a girl in Trinidad
Yuh looking now to find something to do
Yuh meet a bossman who promise to help you
But when the man lay down the condition
Is nothing else but humiliation
They want to see yuh whole anatomy
They want to see what yuh doctor never see
They want to do what yuh husband never do
Still don't know if the scamps will hire you
Well if is all this humiliation
To get ah job these days as a woman
They will keep their money
I will keep my honey
And die with my dignity
(quoted in the *Express*, February 19, 1987, p. 19)

Since that time, there has been a society-wide increase in the awareness of the problem of sexual harassment, as well as of battered women. Newspaper stories reporting sexual harassment, such as the following, became common.

There was a sexual harassment scandal at Development Finance Ltd. in 1993, where one woman's complaint was being heard in the Industrial Court. Another woman made allegations, describing her encounter with a senior official:

> He probably saw me as a kind of upstart, questioning all of his funny deals, so one day he requested that I report to his office at 1 P.M.
>
> When I got there, he asked me if I were married.
>
> I told him no.
>
> He then asked if I intended to stay single or whether I had a boyfriend abroad studying.
>
> I replied in the negative on both counts.
>
> He then asked about my plans and what do I do in the absence of a regular boyfriend.
>
> I then realised that none of that seemed to be his business and if he had no work queries that I should like to be excused.
>
> He then let me leave his office, but soon after, I was transferred to a lesser job.
>
> My new job involved nothing more than filing papers and copying documents, although I had been hired as a senior investment analyst.

Later, she said she was asked to resign and when she did not, she was fired (*TnT Mirror*, March 12, 1993, pp. 14–15).

Women also began to complain about the ways they were being depicted in the media and to link these depictions to their mistreatment. One female letter writer, who described herself as "an ardent church-goer," complained:

> Daily, we the general public, are being bombarded with advertisements and photographs in our daily Press, but more so one [*sic*] our television screens and weekly newspaper, with what I term as total disrespect for the women and young girls of our nation.
>
> It is said that these types of advertisements create higher sales of the products, but what is not said is that these advertisements also create sick minds and such wrong ideas of women in our society causing an increase in the number of rape and assault crimes now plaguing the country. (*Trinidad Guardian*, November 19, 1986, p. 8)[1]

At the same time, there developed a backlash of opinion. Conservative groups sought to blame women for what they interpreted as the breakdown of society's moral order. A *Trinidad Guardian* editorial echoed the words of Catholic archbishop Anthony Pantin and urged adults to set the tone for young people in order to have a Carnival free of vulgarity and lewdness:

> Mothers who keep telling their daughters to dress decently are seen in the most revealing outfits "wining and grining" in public on Carnival days. Is such decency only applicable outside the Carnival season?
>
> Calypsonians like to take themselves seriously as poets of the people, yet so

> many of them compose songs that consistently appeal to the lowest human instincts rather than use their wit and skill to dissect the human condition. . . .
>
> There is much to enjoy in Carnival. The calypsoes, the costuming, the infectious steelband, the street camaraderie have made our Carnival world famous and rightly so. But enjoyment must be controlled, as any form of pleasure without moral guidelines is just license.
>
> Self control is a virtue that is much is [*sic*] need in this country, and we would like to see a lot more of it exercised, day in and day out, Carnival day or any other day of the year. (*Trinidad Guardian*, February 24, 1987, p. 8)

In this editorial, as usual, women were given the task of being moral guardians.

One letter writer complained about a *Trinidad Guardian* columnist who wrote that any young woman out alone at night was almost asking for rape. She said:

> While I agree it is perhaps ill-advised for women to travel alone, are we (women) to be held responsible or even blamed for what men think or do?
>
> The fault does not rest with women who walk alone, for when viewed objectively, they are not doing anything wrong.
>
> It rests rather, in the way in which some men view this situation. . . .
>
> The [columnist's] statement indirectly justifies rape by implying that women on their own "ask for it."
>
> This damaging and ignorant assumption is, I feel, one that women can well do without. (*Trinidad Guardian*, November 19, 1986, p. 8)

Despite societal changes, the exertion of power through the idiom of sexuality, as in Sandra's calypso, is what defines gender relations in the factory. As Ann Whitehead shows in her study of an English pub, joking abuse is used by men to control women (1976:177–79). Likewise, at EUL, what I refer to as flirting has the (perhaps unintended) consequences of controlling the workers. One incident involved Lloyd, a self-described "mixed" (white and Syrian, but defined by the workers as "white") supervisor who is divorced and has several outside economic activities and a cabin cruiser moored at the Trinidad Yacht Club, and Patricia, a nineteen-year-old East Indian who at the time had been working at EUL for only about three months. Since she began to work at the factory, Lloyd's flirtation had become more and more licentious. And she often responded in kind.

On this occasion, supervisors Lloyd, Winston, Karl, Ron, Ram, and David were all liming in front of the factory at break time. As Patricia walked out of the factory to talk to other workers standing outside the front gate, Lloyd said to her, "Come here you hot bucket of food, you." Patricia only smiled and kept on walking. "She love every bone in he body," Winston said loud enough for Patricia to hear. Lloyd, grabbing his crotch, said equally loud, "There's one bone I *know* she'd love." The men chuckled.

Later, Patricia walked past the men back into the factory. After commenting to another supervisor on her propensity to wear tight jeans, Lloyd said in an audible voice as she turned the corner, "Ooh, I would love to fuck she." This is an example of *dropping words*, in which the aggressor mutters a sensitive remark, which the victim pretends not to hear, lest the accusation be legitimized.

Weeks later, Lloyd and Patricia came to Gay's wedding together. There, he asked her to go "down de islands" with him, that is, to Gaspar Grande, one of the five islands off the northwest peninsula where there is a resort hotel and where many middle-class Trinidadians maintain holiday homes. But Lloyd got drunk, and apparently they had an argument because Patricia had been dancing with one of Gay's cousins who lived in the United States and who had returned to Trinidad for the wedding. Back in the factory, Lloyd was rather tentative in his subsequent forays, and I do not believe that any sexual relationship ever developed between them.

I am not aware of any sexual activities within the factory of the kind Donald Roy (1974) documents in his study of an American factory, where male and female workers actually had sex in the basement storerooms during work hours. There are no such secluded places in the EUL factory. In fact, there were only about three cases of "dating" between workers at EUL, all involving younger workers who dated briefly. But this low number was not for the lack of trying on the part of both men and women.

Patricia was not the only worker who dealt with the sexual advances of the supervisors. Connie was the object of advances by many supervisors and, occasionally, even Nigel Tiexiera flirted with her. Johnny teased her about this, insinuating that she was the "outside woman," or mistress, of the supervisors and Tiexiera in order to further her own ends. The idea of a woman being "outside" to men in positions of power, someone who trades sex for economic goods, is entrenched in Trinidadian culture (see Miller 1994:186–88). "Hey, deputy is essential," said Sybil, referring to the lyrics of the calypsonian Penguin's song "Deputy," which won him the 1983 calypso crown. The song argues that men need a "deputy," an "outside woman." By the same token, an "outside woman" is able to manipulate the situation to her advantage. Carla supports this view: "In order to survive, women must get an outside man. That is the only way to make it. I mean, the people who work in the factories are of a lower class, according to my brother. And they got to get ah outside man. And that puts them under pressure."

Sometimes subtle talk relating to sex and sexual reproduction is used by the supervisors to embarrass the women. On one occasion Winston was upset because Dolly asked to go home early, claiming that she wasn't feeling well. Winston asked her, "Are you PMS or what?"

Dolly: What dat?
Winston: [*Rolling his eyes up*] Pre-menstrual syndrome. It when you get in a bad mood because of your periods.
Dolly: [*Smiling*] I'm always like that.

Most of the women workers feel somewhat powerless to respond in any other way. Vishnu, the toolmaker, has the reputation in the factory of constantly touching and bothering young women. One day, he leaned up against Rita and spoke to her while she was operating her machine. Afterward, she admitted that, although she did not like what Vishnu was doing, she was new at EUL and did not want to make trouble because he was like a supervisor, and she was going to have to work with him anyway.

In general, the women realize that they are in a disempowered position relative to the supervisors and, as such, are generally willing to accommodate when it means "playing along" with them by flirting and insinuating the possibility of future sexual relations in order to maintain a modicum of good workplace relations and to not jeopardize their employment. But this accommodation stops short of actual sexual relations.

On one occasion, Dolly was looking in Winston's desk for a cigarette. She looked at him and smiled, in an exaggerated way, almost to the point of fluttering her eyelashes. Without a word, he smiled and took a cigarette out of his pocket. He told me later that he knew she was being nice to him just to get a cigarette, but he just shrugged and said to me, "What you go do?"

Winston once confided in me that Antigone had asked him what he was doing for Carnival. He replied that he was going to Isla de Margarita, a free-port island off Venezuela and popular holiday resort for Trinidadians. "She said 'Can I go too?' and I said 'Are you going to sleep in the same room with me?' and she said 'Of course, why do you think I want to go.' So I keepin' this real quiet—I don't want everyone else to know." As it turned out, they never went away together. What this incident shows is the strategic use of such tactics as innuendo and flirting on the part of Antigone. It also shows that boasting by males is an essential part of the flirting.

The fact that there are hardly any instances of dating may indicate the women's view of the incompatibility of sharing a work and romantic relationship with a man. Referring to what she sees as sexual harassment by the supervisors, Maureen says that in past employment she has experienced this phenomenon: "I been through it myself. The boss may think you look attractive and he want to *fren* ["friend"; i.e., establish a romantic and sexual relationship] wid you. . . . I ain't doin' dat. I will *fren* wid you is one ting but I'm not workin' by you too."

Patterns of Flirting

As discussed in Chapter 3, the factory workers at EUL are divided into peer groups associated with age and ethnicity. In the factory, however, some of these seemingly isolated groups interact, and that interaction is regularized by flirting, which tends to include overt references to sex, obscenity, and general horseplay, as well as serious attempts designed to initiate a sexual liaison. Flirtations usually take place between supervisors and younger female workers and are usually, though not always, initiated by the supervisors. There is also considerable flirting between the young men and women, again, most of which is initiated by the men. Further, the flirting is patterned according to ethnicity: East Indian men (including the supervisors) generally flirt only with East Indian women, while the young black men tend to flirt with both black and East Indian women. The white supervisors flirt with both black and East Indian women. For their part, when the young black and East Indian women do initiate flirting, it tends to be with the young men irrespective of their ethnic group. The older workers, on the other hand, do not flirt and are not flirted with, unless they are not "respectable."

Flirting may be defined as face-to-face behavior—deeds and words—that is designed to indicate a possible sexual interest in another person. Flirting is "directed" behavior, that is, it may or may not be reciprocal. In addition, it may or may not reveal a serious interest in forming a sexual relation. The Trinidadian term for this kind of behavior is "tracking," or "making track," though these terms are usually reserved for the kind of behavior that is indicative of a serious sexual or romantic interest in another person. I refer to behavior described in the following pages as flirting in a more generic sense, even when it represents sexual harassment of the grossest kind, because it is not always clear at first glance whether the workers and managers are engaging in this behavior with the intent of initiating a sexual liaison or if they are using sexual references for purposes associated with the exercise of power. Thus, the apparent ambiguity in using this term matches the content of the behavior on the shop floor. Flirting becomes an idiom for the exercise of power between men and women, between ethnic groups, and between supervisors and workers.

The men use their mobility within the factory to play what Morris Freilich, who studied "Anamat," a village in Trinidad, calls the "sex-fame game." The essential element of this game is to "sweet-talk" a woman in order to make a sexual "conquest": "Anamatian Negroes believe that everyone has a sexual appetite the satisfaction of which is natural and pleasurable. Men whose sexual needs are almost insatiable are referred to as 'hot boys', 'sweet men', and 'wild men'; and such *real men* require sexual gratification both frequently and in great variety. Hot boys who are frequently sexually involved with many women receive the social acclaim known as 'fame', and to be a 'famous man' is the goal of almost every adult male. Men receive additional acclaim for their 'foolin' abilities—abilities to make convincing promises to women which they expect to break." Freilich quotes a peasant who says, "If you can't fool a woman you are not a famous man and the women will confuse you and get what they want" (1968:48, 49).

The emphasis on "sweet talk" is part of a pattern Roger Abrahams (1983) identifies in which Caribbean men receive status for their oratorical eloquence. The idea is to be macho, yet "soft." According to Terry, a nineteen-year-old factory worker, "A woman like a man to treat her gentle, a woman like a man to care about her. A woman like a man who attractive and who can make love good. Now ladies only lookin' for men with big body, big car, and money. I don't know why."

While there is a great deal of value put on subtle and stylized methods of flirting, some flirting is very direct and not very subtle. While he was "sweet-talking" Patricia, Robert went around behind her and pulled the back of her shirt from her jeans.

Patricia: Boy!
Robert Wha'ppen?
Patricia: Get from around here!
Robert: I'll do what de fuck I want!

Robert stormed off in anger, only to return later trying to be nice to Patricia, but she was still very anger with him.

On another occasion, Terry said to Patricia, who wanted a piece of his cake, "Give me a fuck and I'll give you a piece." Patricia, looking surprised, said with a laugh, "Come now man, don't play dat."

At another time, Paul and Johnny were "talking rude" to Lucy, Elaine, and Sybil, talking about sex. Paul said that he wanted a woman with experience to be his "teacher." He asked Lucy if she was experienced and she said, "Maybe." Wanting to know how experienced, Paul then put his thumbs and forefingers together and made the shape of a circle and said, "It big so?" referring to her vagina. Lucy, in turn, responded: "What about you—how big is you?" Paul said, "Come upstairs and I'll show yuh."

The flirting in the factory is part of a pattern of general horseplay that often has violent undertones. Overt or subverted violence pervades many male-female relations in the Caribbean, so much so that it is almost taken for granted. A 1975 *Trinidad Guardian* article quoted a doctor telling a judge casually that "the blows the victim received were not much—just like when you cuff your wife" (quoted in Aho 1982:77). Jeremy and Brian often get into mock fights, where they wrestle with each other as a sort of macho display, and then, with the workers around them laughing and commenting, proceed to tickle some of the younger women. In fact, the men often wrestle with each other in front of the female workers. Once, Vishnu lit a firecracker under Ruud. It is not clear, however, that the women are impressed. When Terry waved his nunchaku (martial-arts implements) in front of Rita, she looked angry and said, "Don't play dat stupidness, man!"

That flirting has violent undertones is further evidenced by a game that some of the younger workers play periodically called "Hits," where one raps the other person across the knuckles with the middle finger. The object of the game is to make the other person "give," or concede. One day, Rita, Jeremy, Brian, and Carole were sitting at the lunch table upstairs after finishing their lunch and started to give each other "hits." Jeremy would let Rita and Carole give him ten "hits" for each one he gave each of them. This was played out in an atmosphere of laughter, blushing, and flirting.

An essential component to flirting is bragging, when the males talk about the advances made in their direction. Once, Terry, Deepak, Deepak's cousins Richard and Sharon, and Terry's uncle Howard were liming at Terry's house. Terry was talking about how all the women in the factory were attracted to him:

Terry: I don't know what it is, I ain't that handsome, but all these girls be after me. There's Cokie [who is married] who want to give me play, Carole—now married—she want to give me play too. It have Rita, but she wid dat stupid man.

Deepak: What about Martha?

[*Laughter*]

Terry: But what, man. I friends wid she. Dat girl come lime by me here. But dat is all. She have a face like a horse.

Howard: Tie a bag over she head!

Terry: Naw, but man, dese girls at work. It have a next one, Connie. And there's Dolly.

Deepak: I hear she boyfriend beat she.

Terry: Dat good for she. She full of sheself.

The strategizing is somewhat different when the women initiate flirting. Sometimes there are "sexy" looks thrown and suggestive body language. Once, when Stephanie was about to pick up parts from a box on the floor, she said to Terry, who was standing in back of her, "Look Terry, I want to show you something," and then bent over. Terry smiled.

The younger workers in Terry's department habitually ask him in a flirting way to leave his post momentarily to fetch them boxes of parts. They call out his name in an exaggerated and whining manner. "Terrrrrrrrry." The older workers in Terry's department, though, get their own parts, except Denise, who also asks Terry to bring her parts, though not in such an exaggerated manner. Myra is scornful of the way some of the workers ask Terry to get them more parts and of the way Terry cultivates this relationship: "He have them so. I does always tell him that. They can get for theyself, if they had to. But they rely on him." Apparently, the workers are willing to feed Terry's "reputation" as long as they get something out of it.

Culture at Work: Respectability and Reputation

As discussed in Chapter 3, the older female workers at EUL are socially cut off from the younger female workers, and the young male workers tend to form separate peer groups that are differentiated by ethnicity. This division reflects the relationship between "respectability" and "reputation" and the gender relations in the factory. According to Peter J. Wilson (1969, 1971, 1973; see also Abrahams 1979), respectability is primarily the domain of women and involves the approximation of the value standards of the local elite (Segal 1993:91–93, in another context, sees respectability as "achieved whiteness"). The behavior of "respectable" women is circumscribed; they are expected to remain in the home, take care of children, remain faithful to their men, and not engage in, for example, public drinking or swearing. We might conclude, also, that respectable women are of a certain age. It is theoretically possible for young women to be respectable, but this is surely not expected of the younger EUL workers. As men became older, they, too, are expected to act respectably.

On the other hand, reputation is primarily, though not exclusively, the domain of men. Reputation is an egalitarian value system with roots in local estimations of worth. Men gain status by the number of children they father, by engaging in numerous sexual activities, by displaying a willingness to fight, and by drinking alcohol. Citing ethnographic evidence, Wilson sees these values as applying to blacks and East Indians alike.

In general, female work culture has been misunderstood because it is often hidden in women's social life at work (Creighton 1982). In the EUL factory, the discourse of the older women is one that upholds traditional notions of femininity. On Wednesdays from 10 to 11 A.M., workers regularly listen to "Family Life Forum," a popular call-in show on Radio Trinidad. The show features Dr. Springer, who receives many calls for advice on sexual matters. She also receives many calls from women complaining that they have been deserted, that they have been used for money, that they do not receive adequate financial support from their menfolk, that their men spend money on alcohol and horse racing, and that their men beat them. Many of the older women nod in assent when these claims were made. Dr. Springer often begins her advice with, "Women want this," and she often urges religious introspection. Although she decries violence toward women and urges women to have careers, she is more often the voice of "official," "respectable" values.

The older workers emphasize maintaining the proper comportment for women of their status. Daisy, forty-five, the mother of four children, says she does not like to go to parties any more: "I finish wid dat. I used to study that but that part of my life finished. Now I study Christ. You can't study both. . . . I used to wear pants. Wid me it was pants, pants, pants. Then I realize that I should be wearing dresses and now I wearing dresses. I get more respect." She said that she is concerned with the "slackness" in today's society:

> There is no discipline. Parents don't want to talk to they chirren. You know what the main problem is? TV. They show all these American programs with

> all they killing and so. So the upper class and the middle class, they go to parties and they tell they chirren, "Turn on the TV" or "Why don't you watch a video?" and the chirren don't have anybody to talk dey problems to. So they see thiefing in the programs and so they thief. They see all this set ah drugs and they do drugs. We should show more local shows. It have plenty people in Trinidad who could put on a good show. I tell my chirren that they should rule TV and not let TV rule dem. They want to buy a video. I tell them no. I would buy one if they had movies where they had meaning, like in my day. Movies like *Backstreet* and *The Ten Commandments*. But not this set of stupidness now.

These comments are indicative of a mood among some older Trinidadians, who feel that the moral order of the society is being challenged by incipient Americanization and the spread of drug abuse. Many of the poor in Trinidad see themselves as pious, the "salt of the earth," who are upholding traditional morals in the face of middle-class-led societal change. They believe that anyone can be "respectable," according to the way in which you "carry yourself" and in the social relations that you involve yourself in. Indeed, to the EUL workers, a woman's class or occupational position has little to do with her respectability. I asked one worker in her twenties if a factory job, or any other job, gave a woman "respect." She said, "That don't have anything to do with respect, you know. Respect have to do wid de way you carry youself."

In Trinidad, the old saying that you can judge people by the friends they keep is taken as truth. Therefore, to attain respectable status a person has to associate with respectable people. Respectable behavior is by definition constrained in scope, and, in practice, it follows that it is also constrained in amount. So, we can say that a criterion of respectability is that one must keep few associates, and they must be respectable.

As discussed in Chapter 3, Vera and Denise are not considered "respectable" because they associate with younger, less respectable women. As Johnny says: "Women get watch more than men. It not to say that men can't be respectable, but that women get watch for these things more than men do. A woman must act her age and be with the people her fucking age. See Vera? She don't hang wid people she age. She hang wid dem girls dere: dey cuss she and she hang wid dem." He also commented on the behavior of Patricia, who is considered to be one of the "wildest" of the younger workers, suggesting that the older, more respectable, workers would be offended by her precociousness: "Patricia have no respect. She act like she want to fuck down de place. . . . She came over to me, in front of dese big women [motioning to Cleo and April]. . . ."

Perhaps based on more than one's associations, respectable status hinges on one's own individual attributes and activities. Much has been made of the fact that Caribbean women place great value on and receive status for motherhood. While this is undoubtedly true, evidence from the factory places this observation in a different light.

Once, Cleo and some other workers were talking about how their men sometimes put pressure on them to have another child, while they were concerned with preventing pregnancy. Cleo said to me: "Boy, I had three children and I don't want more. He [her husband] say, 'Oh come on, just one more now,' and I said if I makin' it, he mindin' it." She has three children, including a thirteen-year-old son who "is a brain—he want to go to university and ting, he want to take a computer course. So I have to work."

So if children are a valued asset for women, they can also be seen as a liability for working mothers. There is a concern that people who cannot afford them should not have them, but that people who can afford the expense financially should have many more.

One day a few months after Cleo mentioned what her husband had said about wanting another child, something happened to make me believe that there is a connection between a woman's respectability and a man's reputation. Jane Tiexiera put up a typed notice several places in the factory, advising that two nurses from the Ministry of Health would be visiting the factory soon to talk about infectious diseases, and that the workers should also bring their children's immunization forms so that the nurses could see that they were in order.

When the nurses came, most of the women who had children brought their children's immunization cards, and work stopped for about fifteen minutes as they gathered around the nurses upstairs near the lunch table. The male workers were expected to continue working but, since the supervisors used the opportunity to take a break in Conrad's office, they took it easy as well. The workers used this opportunity to speak to each other about their children, and I noticed that there was some bragging going on.

The nurses said that they were from the Ministry of Health and that, as part of the United Nations' World Immunization Year, they were here to talk about the dangers of infectious diseases, like yellow fever, as well as dangerous ailments like dysentery. One said, "Now, when you go out and have your babies, you'll be sure to have them immunized before they start school." Cleo looked upset, and I asked her what was wrong. "What's wrong?" she said. "I pregnant, that what. And I sick all de time. Not another one. But if this a girl, I don't mind."

Given what she had said a few months before, the fact that Cleo was now pregnant seemed to suggest that it was important to consider the actions of men in using the respectability ethos to constrain women because her husband would increase his status, his "reputation," when she had another child.

In this connection, I asked Martha why the older workers did not go liming the way the younger ones did. She said, "See, they much older. They studyin' they kids. They don't have no time to lime and ting." But then I pointed out that although Denise had children, she still limed, Martha added, "See, she don't have no husband. The other ladies, they husbands might say 'Stay home and see about the family' and ting, so they more studyin' they family. They feel they should." Although it is almost undoubtedly the case that the women will prioritize their children's welfare over a chance to lime, this explanation provides more evidence that men enforce this value in case the women ever decide otherwise.

At work, older workers tend to talk about their families and their homes. At first glance, this may indicate that these workers are "domesticated" and accept the constraints of a "respectable" woman. But this would be to elide complex, and often paradoxical, attitudes and practices. Statements made by some of the workers suggested that the "respectability" ethos is imposed against some resistance. Cleo, on her household responsibilities, said, "I slept this weekend, but I feel like I don't sleep enough. The water truck didn't come, so I had to carry it from the river [in the dry season, her area experiences water-supply problems and the government trucks in water] . . . it had better come this week, 'cause if not . . . I have three in school and they wearin' every day, Mr. Allen [her husband] wearin' different clothes every day, and me the same here at work. Then it will all come on Saturday and I ain't able."

But the following remarks from Cleo betray the difficulties and ambiguities in the status as "respectable" woman and suggest that those so defined do not simply acquiesce to these roles:

> Some men, they only study theyselves. They selfish. You *now* make a baby for they and come out de hospital and they sayin' you should start doin' the wash. Women do give men bad habits. . . . They don't want responsibility. You make a child for they and they don't mind providing for the child. But when they see they have to take on responsibilities, they say, "You live by you and I live by me." . . . That's why I believe in a long thing. . . . My neighbor's husband does lash she. She found out he had ah outside woman, yes. So he want to be wrong and strong. But dat do affect the chirren. They see dat and they think dat's what a man supposed to do. Nah, dat ain't right. . . . You see, if they had laws in Trinidad and Tobago like they have away then they would stop that. They throw dem dat does do dat in jail one time.

She continued, "They say housewives should get paid. I think so too. Ellie [her husband] helped me cook the other day. And he wash. When he finish he lay down on de floor and hold he head and bawl. I say, 'Yuh see?' He say, 'But you ent bound to do dis, I don't ask you to.' And I say 'And if I don't do it who will?' . . . Housework is a full-time job. So is mindin' children. We should get paid."

While it may not be the primary basis upon which a woman's respectability is based, it seems that having a job is important not only for the survival of the family but for the women's self-esteem and sense of self-reliance. Women, then, believe they are also accorded prestige for activities beyond traditional mothering roles. Daisy said she would only stop working at EUL to become a social worker because of her strong religious feelings. At another time she told me that she goes several times a year to feed homeless "vagrants" in Independence Square. Other older workers agree they want to keep their jobs. Karen says: "Stay at home? No man. It makes me feel good to work. It is like an enjoyment."

I asked Cleo if she would want to stop working.

> Cleo: You kidding? I too used to the independence and having the little change to spend on things I need. . . . Workin' makes me feel good about myself. The money not enough, though.
>
> Author: But in some of the books I've read, in some of the literature on women working in factories, it says that *all* of a woman's salary goes to the household—for food and for taking care of the kids. While on the other hand, they say that the man will contribute some of his salary to the household but that he makes sure to keep some for his own recreation, for drinking and liming. What do you think about this? Do you think it's true?
>
> Cleo: Not by me! I know things hard now—he work for Customs as an "extra" and sometime he don't get a wuk—so I give a little [money] to him now and then, 'cause he get paid fortnightly. It happen by some women who allow it to go on. He does say, "I know you have a little something somewhere." I say, "Look around," knowing that he won't find it! And don't forget, it have some men who give all dey salary to de woman for she to see about everything.

The older workers feel that the horseplay of the younger workers contributes to the lack of product quality, and thus their own reputations are tarnished somewhat by working for a company that makes inferior products.

> Cleo: The tings wouldn't mash up so if dem girls and dey wouldn't skylark so much and get to some proper wuk.
>
> Karen: It have a man by me who bad-talkin' the EUL tings [products that are produced in the Downstairs Final-Assembly Department]. He bought one and it mash up two days later. He brought it back right here and spoke to the manager, and the manager say, "It not my fault." So from then, he going around to everyone and sayin', "Doh buy Tiexiera tings."

The older workers do seem proud of their work, but this does not allow them to overcome completely a negative female self-image. Walcott said: "I the only one who know how to fix rejects. I can listen to dem, test one over there and hear it bad and tell you what wrong even before I open it up. . . .

Some of dem just come to work to come to work—they ain't thinkin'. . . . I can fix the machines. One time the one over by Vera mash up and David wasn't there. I had was to go fix it and Tiexiera stood up behind me watchin' me. And he didn't say nothin'. And I fixed it, I changed the brushes." Then, she said without irony, "But it must have a man supervisor because he know how to fix the machines. When I dere for David—when he stay home—and the machine break down, I had to get Lloyd. He say he don't have time. . . . So it must have a man who can fix the machines. . . . They did ask me to be supervisor once. Tiexiera ask me. But I refuse. I can't take he set ah talk. He always gettin' on wid de supervisors. . . . But when David not here I run de line same as ever. . . . It used to have this old white feller—he retire from T&TEC [the state electric company]—he taught me how to fix the rejects. And dem always ballin' 'Walcott, Walcott, come to fix' something."

The contradictions in Walcott's comments here are striking, because she appears to be saying that she is competent enough to repair the machines, yet in the next breath she says, "it must have a man to fix the machines." This is similiar to the time I asked Daisy what she thought about women standing for election to public office. She said, "No, women shouldn't go up for election. They place is beside the man."

Despite these mitigating attitudes, among themselves the female workers place much emphasis on maternalism and reproduction, so much so that they feel that if a woman has the financial means, she should have almost as many children as possible. Cleo says, "Look at Tiexiera. Him have so much ah money and look, him have only one daughter. Jane could give he five or six more."

Lori, who was pregnant, said after a checkup, "And the nurse say, 'You want you tubes tied when you finish make it?' and I say, 'Wha? Dis my first chile!' And she say, 'Oh well, I thought that seein' times hard and . . .' and I say, 'Nah, is OK.' " She thought for a moment, and then she steupsed.

This value is so entrenched that the workers recognize it in themselves and can laugh at it. When she noticed that several women in her department were going on maternity leave soon, Cleo said laughingly, "It come like a disease. Five people get it one by one." Cleo, who was also pregnant, then became serious when she thought of EUL's maternity leave arrangements. Under Trinidad and Tobago law, maternity leave is guaranteed. According to Daly, the law states that, while on maternity leave, a female worker is entitled to full pay from a period starting six weeks before the expected delivery and ending six weeks after the birth, and the worker's entitlement to maternity leave is limited to two times in a five-year period (1982:111–13). To qualify for such benefits, the worker must be employed by a firm that has contributed to the National Insurance Scheme for ten of the thirteen weeks prior to benefit period, or have been receiving other benefits at that time.

When a batch of new workers was hired, one told me that Ruud had an informal meeting with them to explain payment procedures and payroll deductions. When he came to the deduction for the National Insurance Scheme, he said, "This is very important to pay into for when you girls get pregnant, which is like a sickness in Trinidad." The group all laughed.

Cleo and others said that the practice at EUL used to be to make these payments weekly to the worker, but that now the workers are paid only when they come back to work after the leave is finished. I was unable to verify this from the Tiexieras.

When Cleo was pregnant, she was having trouble with "morning sickness," and as a cure she started eating "salt biscuits" (saltine crackers). They were so effective that she was able to resume her normal eating habits. "My friend told me about salt biscuits," she said. "I tried dey dis weekend and I ate roti, curry chicken, curry mango—I et all." For about two months afterward she could be seen working with a piece of salt biscuit stuck on her bottom lip.

Cleo used pregnancy as a starting point to talk about women and men in general. "I can't understand they, hoppin' from one man to de other. If they read the Bible they would see that it don't say dat. I been wid my husband since I was in school. And it ain't been easy. He used to lime all de time. Oh Lawd. But I pray and I pray and little by little he changin' every day. But it not easy, yes."

She went on to say that women find it hard to get men to take care of them financially if they have had children with different men. Maureen seconds these thoughts: "Young girls just lie down, have sex, and make a baby. Then when they have three or four they realize they can't support it"—and will thus, according to Maureen, have difficulty finding a man who will want to support them and their children financially.

Cleo continued, "Sometimes it's better if they like you more than you like he. It sound bad, but you have a hold over he. Even if you have eyes for someone else, it better to stay wid de one who like you more." This, from a woman whom many of the other workers agree is one of the most respectable in the factory. These attitudes suggest that it is better to manipulate one man than several, and to do so with an air of calm and self-control. This self-control is an essential feature of respectability, but it does not equate with submission. For example, Cleo said regarding contraception: "I find men should use too. I could use for one year and you could use for one year. But no, they want you only to take [birth-control pills]. It have injection now for men." Later, she told me that she had been taking birth-control pills for two years without her husband's knowledge. When she stopped for a while, she became pregnant accidentally. She said that after the baby was born, she would probably continue this practice if her husband even hinted that he wanted another child, because she did not want one.

On another occasion, Fiona, Lori, and Cleo were having a conversation about men, having babies, sex, and preventing their younger sisters and daughters from becoming pregnant too young. Daisy said, "Chirren makin' chirren dese days."

Lori is a Seventh Day Adventist who comes from a family of fifteen children. She was lamenting the fact that her mother had her first child when she was twelve and the last when she was forty-two, and that her mother had to quit school and work when she was thirteen. Cleo, a Spiritual Baptist, said she felt that the number of children a woman has is preordained by God and that not to have one's quota would make one go crazy. In general, when a woman is pregnant (as Cleo was at the time) a man only gets in the way and is also jealous of the baby, but she thought it was a good thing that now young men were owning up to getting young women pregnant and were even helping them with shopping and other chores. Lori said that she told her younger brothers, "If dey don't want to see dey little sisters pregnant, den don't to get anybody else pregnant." She also said that her father was "one to hit my mother. But she shouldn't ah take it."

Lori and Cleo agreed that men are lecherous because many older men were seen to go after schoolgirls.

> Lori: A fourteen-year-old friend of my little sister, I over hear she say, "I ent goin' to lime tonight. I lookin' for a man to buy me a jeans for the fete tomorrow."
>
> Cleo: The young girls encourage they by doin' what the wife won't do. Like de "spit and shine" [i.e., perform oral sex].

In contrast to this explication of the ideology of respectability, the behavior of young males is characterized by an emphasis on egalitarianism and sociability among themselves and by an emphasis on sexual conquests in their dealings with females. The sociability of male peer groups is achieved through a number of idioms. The kind of sex education they receive, for example, contrasts to the above scene. Once, Deepak was talking to Rohan about sex. Rohan is a virgin and Deepak gave him the advice: "Hear now, watch some blues [pornographic movies] and you'll get experience. No, really, you'll see how it done," he said seriously. "When it you birthday, I'll carry you to '21,' " referring to a notorious bar and brothel in Port-of-Spain.

Smiling, Rohan said, "That ain't no problem."

Wilson suggests that the preferred mode of approaching women is a "tough, but sweet" attitude among men (1969, 1971, 1973). Terry personified this when he borrowed hand cream from Mary and put it on his face. "You got to keep lookin' nice if you want to get the young ladies," he said.

Another idiom seems to be rowdy behavior, especially directed at women. When asked who the least respectable people in Trinidad are, nineteen-year-old Terry said: "Youths who lime on the street are the least respected. They may soot [somewhat resembling a loud steups, generally used by men to attract the attention of a woman] a girl and she don't look they say 'I don't want a wife, I want a shit cleaner,' and they do big women that. But I classin' myself in that category too, 'cause I do that."

One of the activities that earn a man's "reputation" is fighting. In the factory, however, the women, especially the younger ones, also seem willing to engage in violence. The violence that the female workers employ is mostly symbolic, though, and it is often related to sex.

In the factory, women take opportunities to heckle men. At break time one day, Carole, Margarita, and Karen were looking out of an upstairs window when a young man got out of a delivery van and came over to urinate against the fence in front of the factory. With his trousers unzipped, he looked up to see the women looking back at him. They exploded with laughter and began heckling him as he hurriedly did up his zipper, his task not yet started. Carole yelled, "You almost get stick!" And Karen called out, "And it was almost out now!" And when he ran across the street to urinate against a building, Carole yelled, "Careful you don't lick down the wall wid dat!"

The ways in which women resist harassment and counterattack using their voices has been documented for the Caribbean. Under slavery, "resistance particularly typical of women included poisoning the master's food and the 'tongues of women'. The latter included answering back, complaining, ridicule and satire. . . . Women's dominant role in resistance based on words was reflected in the fact that female slaves were more often regarded as 'deserving' punishment than men and in the arguments against abolishing flogging, especially for women" (Besson 1993:29).

But this seems to be a general feature of women's resistance. In her study of female workers in the *maquiladoras* of the Mexico-U.S. border, Fernández-Kelly reports how women engaged in laughter and how they screamed obscenities in a teasing way to each other once they left the factory for the night:

> Individually these women bore an aura of vulnerability, even shyness. As a group they could be a formidable sight. One time an unlucky male happened to board the bus when we were already in it. His presence exacerbated the level of euphoria. He was immediately subjected to verbal attacks similar to those women sometimes experience from men. They chided and they teased him, feeling protected by anonymity and by their numerical strength. They offered kisses and asked for a smile. They exchanged laughing comments about his physical attributes and suggested a raffle to see who would keep him. To all this the man responded with silence. Curiously, he adopted the outraged and embarrassed expression that women often wear when they feel victimized by men. When he left the bus, he did so followed by the stares of whistling women. (1983:131–32)

The men in the EUL factory respond when they feel threatened. In a mild response, Winston called Carole "Nizam Mohammed—the Speaker of the House [referring to the actual Speaker of the House of Parliament at the time] That girl does talk!" Here, it is important to see that Winston was trying to control Carole's talking. In a not-so-mild response, Rohan reacted in another way to the heckling. Rohan and Sybil got into an argument. The female workers were harrassing Rohan—heckling him—but he was pretending to ignore them. Sybil called, "Hey asshole," however, and Rohan turned around and said, "Fuck you." Sybil came up to him and slapped him. He was going to hit Sybil when one of the workers grabbed him. Sybil said; "Dem [Rohan and Martha] only want to mess about when they want to. He cuss me and I lash he. It was no big ting. It might have been. . . . They expect me to lose respect? They mad or what?" But there was disagreement among the workers in the work group as to who started the quarrel. As Martha said, "She was wrong. She cuss he. He cuss she back. And she lash he. If she cuss he, why shouldn't he cuss she back?" I thought the incident might have something to do with ethnicity as Rohan is East Indian and Sybil is black. But Rohan siad, "Race have nuttin' to do wid it. Dem like to provoke me."

At another time Rita said, "I'm going to the cinema this weekend to see *Silk*. It come like *Rambo* but it starring a woman. It real sick [i.e., "cool"—fashionable or agreeable]. She shootin' up the place, she gettin' revenge. I like that. It good 'cause them kind ah pictures always starring a man."

These activities and attitudes are significant because they show how younger women, too, engage in "reputation" behavior. Sybil was very willing to "lash" Rohan in the above example so that she would not lose "respect." This kind of "respect" differs from the "respectability" of the older workers, but the incident does suggest that women as well as men compete for status. And it suggests that women as well as men seek status through behavior that has been described under the reputation and respectability banners.

Reconsidering Respectability and Reputation

Much of the evidence in this chapter challenges Wilson's conclusions on "respectability" and "reputation." Wilson's ideas have been approvingly cited and utilized (e.g., Abrahams 1979, 1983), especially those regarding the activities of Caribbean men. But Wilson has also been criticized for not taking into account power differentials and for his depictions of women that some feel obscure their activities (e.g., Austin 1983; Barrow 1976, 1988; Besson 1993; Bush 1985; Miller 1994; Mintz 1973; Moses 1977; Pyde 1990; Sutton 1974). Miller identifies an intrinsic dualism in Trinidadian culture, which he terms "transient" and "transcendent." While at first glance this may seem to replicate Wilson's distinction between "respectability" and "reputation," at several points Miller clearly diverges from Wilson, especially regarding gender (1994:259–64). In her overdue and thorough critique, Jean Besson emphasizes that women are also involved in behavior that could be classified under the "reputation" banner when they compete for status with each other and with men and when they emphasize their own autonomy and sexuality. Besson suggests that, along with characterizing women's experience as bowing to convention, we should also be sure to emphasize their participation in the Caribbean "culture of resistance" to colonial and elite authority. I want to push Besson's critique further, however, by considering the role of reputation in "enforcing" respectability. Reputation and respectability is the idiom through which men's control of women is carried out.

Women and men basically agree on what constitutes reputative and respectable behavior, and they refer to these values when reflecting upon their behavior and the behavior of others. However, they do not arrive at these judgments by simply internalizing these values. As Sutton argues, Wilson's analysis "treats power as a value in a system of meanings, not as an external reality, . . ." thus eliminating "the possibility of analyzing dynamic interaction between the external situation people find themselves in, what they think, *what they do*, and what happens to them as a result" (1974:99–100, emphasis added). In this overwhelmingly normative focus, Wilson does not answer the question of why they come to act in certain ways (beyond a normative reason) and why they hold these views. These are the questions I want to try to answer.

To answer this question it is important to look at the resources, both cultural and economic, that men and women bring to a social situation. Here, we can return to Bourdieu's notion of "symbolic capital" (1977:171–83), which represents the symbolic goods that are sought after in a given historical formation. He emphasizes that the acquisition of symbolic capital is inherently related to, and inspires, the acquisition of economic capital. Related to his analysis of symbolic capital is Bourdieu's discussion of symbolic violence as a mode of domination (1977:183–97). Relations of domination require objectification, which is made possible by the accumulation of symbolic capital. Objectification—and institutionalization—of modes of domination allow the dominant groups to dispense with strategies of actual domination and employ strategies of symbolic domination, which consume less time and effort than the former, and are therefore "cheaper." However, for symbolic violence to succeed, it must be transfigured and disguised: "In order to be socially recognized it must get itself misrecognized." It must be euphemized when more overt violence is not possible: "Gentle, hidden exploitation is the form taken by man's exploitation of man whenever overt, brutal exploitation is impossible" (1977:191, 192).

For Bourdieu, symbolic violence is "the imposition of systems of symbolism and meaning (i.e. culture) upon groups or classes in such a way that they are experienced as legitimate. This legitimacy obscures the power relations which permit that imposition to be successful. Insofar as it is accepted as legitimate, culture adds its own force to those power relations, contributing to their systematic reproduction" (Jenkins 1992:104).

Flirting in the factory can be read as symbolic violence. Flirting represents an idiom for the expression of power relations. When the male supervisors and workers flirt with the young women, the expression of their attraction has to be seen in a context of cultural expectations regarding gender and comportment as well as the formal structures of authority within the factory itself. And the flirting may indeed be experienced by the women as legitimate, in the sense that they see an aggressive sexuality as natural to masculinity (see Miller 1994:172–80). Yet the women also flirt with the men, which can be seen as attempts to define the situation to their favor, even if they lose "respect" in the process. And the women also question the legitimacy of the supervisors' flirting, which at one level is categorized and termed "sexual harassment."

So, given that symbolic violence as conceived by Bourdieu is a strategy of domination, we must also come to theoretical terms with a notion of flirting that can be seen as a mode of resistance as well as a mode of domination. I propose that we analyze flirting as "transposed violence," with symbolic violence representing one end of a continuum of possible outcomes. By "transposed" I mean a system of cultural meanings revolving around general acts, cues, stances, and symbols, where toward one side of the continuum we find ostensible meanings, and, as we move to the opposite side, there are a number of emergent meanings that become unpacked through practice. These multiple meanings are ripe for contradiction and value conflict. And they are saturated with power relations, which try to determine where and when the meanings reside. In flirting, the ostensible meaning is sexual attraction, but there are a number of emergent meanings, including conflict. This is also related to other cultural idioms, including the calypso tradition, relying as it does on double entendre and sarcasm. And violence is not only at the level of hyperbole and discourse, but pertains to real power relations, one of the fundamental principles of which is the domination over cultural meanings. Culturally acceptable and valorized practices such as flirting give way to threat and coercion, which are less acceptable and are more and more able to be resisted legitimately, judging from recent developments in the society.

The ethnographic evidence seems to support this view of flirting as transposed violence. Upholding the validity of Wilson's theory in his own account of Richland Park, St. Vincent, Abrahams writes that "it is expected of both sexes . . . that they will be *wild* in their early adulthood" (1979:451). However, if the wild young women of today become the respectable women of tomorrow, but men remain wild for a longer period, then it is possible that the wildness of the men has some part to play in this process.

Young men bring few economic resources into play in their encounters with young women, who also have few economic resources. The high general unemployment rate in the Caribbean is doubled or tripled for those under age twenty-five. With largely symbolic, reputative, public behavior—flirting, fighting, and "fathering"—the young men try to impose their definition of the situation on women. Eventually, men are able to acquire other economic-based resources that are key to converting their reputative symbolic capital into respectability. But to become respectable, they must overcome their previous reputations with respectable accomplishments. Reputation, therefore, is crucial in respectability.

Women, in contrast, have traditionally had few chances to accumulate symbolic capital except, as they become older, through respectability-enhancing activities like giving birth to children conceived in the "correct" circumstances. There is strong motivation for women to aspire to respectability because men want to engage in long-term mating relationships with and marry respectable women. Working-class Caribbean women are forced throughout their lifetimes to engage in many strategies, including respectable public behavior, to secure economic support for themselves and their children. Respectable public behavior helps ensure that this support is obtained from men. There are instances when they engage in a rather instrumental mating and domestic relationship in order to procure goods, but these kinds of relationships are usually short-term. It is in their long-term interests to be respectable because in this way they are able to convert symbolic capital into economic capital.

The situation of the EUL factory workers is further complicated. These women are engaged in steady employment, which means that they will have access to more of society's goods than their mothers were able to acquire. And this may provoke more strenuous responses on the part of males. The game of "Hits," which is always played in the factory between men and women, demonstrates the unequal power relations that underlie male-female relations.

This is not to say that older women who are ostensibly respectable do not engage in reputative behavior. They do, but in many cases not in public. Respectability is a constraining value system, and to militate against it women often clandestinely employ strategies to carve out a measure of personal freedom. The case of Cleo hiding some of her pay for her own personal use and secretly taking birth-control pills to avoid pregnancy—a pregnancy that would earn for her husband more reputation—is an example. But she does so with a public aura of respectability.

Men will often seek to gain advantage over those with less symbolic capital. For example, when Ruud playfully slapped Denise's behind, it is likely that he could not have gotten away with that with someone the workers regarded as having "respect." Reputation and respectability, then, represent men's efforts to impose a definition of the situation and women's efforts to resist it. And, of course, it reflects double standards, where men expect their "ideal woman" not to engage in such activity. Terry, who was most vocal on this subject, said, "The ideal woman has good ways, she mustn't be cursing, lying, drinking. She must be respectable in other words. She must be respectable. She must have an all right education. She don't have to be good-looking, but she don't have to be ugly neither. She have to understand people. She must have a good shape. It don't matter what she is, Indian, dougla, or Chinee. And she must be able to trust me."

In a study of male-female relations in the Caribbean, Morris Freilich and Lewis A. Coser (1972) describe the "sex-fame game" and discuss gender relations in general: "The system as a whole primarily benefits the men. We have here an almost classical case of exploitation, of asymmetrical types of relations, where benefits received by no means equal benefits conferred. Given the superior power positions of males, they manage to utilize their resources so as to shore up their positions *vis-à-vis* the women. The system does not bestow equal rewards to both sides in the sexual equation; the game is rigged in favour of the males" (p. 17).

It is clear that in an industrial setting male supervisors would have an interest in controlling female workers and encouraging docility, even if they do so unintentionally. As we have seen, the younger workers often behave in a rambunctious manner and let their horseplay take precedence over their production. The flirting relationships keep the women's sexual horseplay in check with the implied threat that if it goes too far then it will turn into actual exploitative sexual relations. It is important to note that the younger workers are targeted by the supervisors not only because they are younger and therefore possibly more attractive, and unmarried and therefore potentially "available," but also because they have less income than the older workers and therefore are possibly in need of any material goods a supervisor might be able to provide in return for a sexual liaison. So class figures in this situation. Freilich notes that lower-class women are begged for sex more often than women of higher classes, and he provides the men's reasoning: "Such lower class women will tend to have husbands who stray frequently, usually need the goods and services that an outside lover brings and generally believe that outside love affairs are all right. Lower class women who do not have these beliefs are given little sympathy concerning their economic problems" (1968:51).

In his analysis of the images of women in the calypsoes of the 1930s, Rohlehr notes how male calypsonians used their art to constrain female behavior, possibly because the calypsonians felt inadequate both sexually and in their role of provider. In general, calypsonians used acerbic lyrics in order to characterize themselves as a saga boy ["ladies' man"] while at the same time ridiculing the stupidity and gullibility of women. Several "types" of women were singled out for special treatment, one being the older woman: "If the precocious young woman was regarded with a mixture of moralizing anxiety, dread and eager anticipation of the rake on the prowl, the libidinous old woman was regarded with positive horror" (Rohlehr 1988:253; see also Rohlehr 1990). In addition, according to the calypsonians' logic, younger women are more defenseless than the older women, who sometimes fight back physically (1988:298–300).

Evidence from the factory contradicts Freilich: "Men believe that *all women*—single or married—may be begged for sex, and that *all men* may play the role of sexual beggar" (1968:49). In the factory, respectable women may not be "begged" for sex. So respectability, despite representing constraints, also provides a shield for women and a way for them to resist the exercise of male power in the factory. Even if this shield becomes a constraint. Women in the factory, therefore, are caught in a double bind. The young women are targets of aggressive men. They lose respect for flirting with the men, which in turn ensures that they will be flirted with. But, in many ways, women's initiation of flirting ensures some measure of control over the situation. The older women, deemed "respectable," do not have the sexual and authoritative energies of the men directed at them. But they pay for this by comporting themselves in a relatively reserved way. Yet, rather than directly uphold the values of colonialism, as Wilson suggests, these women may be predisposed to resist the imposition of authority. As Peter Pyde argues based on his fieldwork in Tobago, "Students of stratification, in the Caribbean specifically, have to take account of power as distributed and exercised by gender as well as by class. For example, although lower-class men may reject dominant values, this may be at the expense of women in a similar marginal economic position. Further, rejection of these values is not equivalent to resistance against the system. Women, in struggling to ensure the survival and material improvement of themselves and their children, may be greater contributors to resistance and social change" (1990:20–21).

Ethnicity and Flirting

At EUL, women of both ethnic groups initiate flirting with men of both groups, and the white supervisors flirt with both groups of young women. However, while black men flirt with black and East Indian young women, East Indian men generally only flirt with East Indian women. For the most part, it is the men who initiate flirting. When the women respond, they seem to be trying to defuse a potentially threatening situation or using their sexuality for instrumental purposes.

This pattern is related to a situation where male-dominated discourse holds that women are the "markers" of the ethnic group, that they are the "custodians" of the groups values, virtues, and culture. As Pat Caplan writes, "Numerous examples show that it is particularly the bodies of women which are made to serve as social symbols. . . . Women, and particularly their sexuality, serve as important boundary markers . . . women represent the privacy of the group" (1987:14–15).

Women are made by men to be "markers" of the group, where, in protecting the "purity" of women, men protect the "purity" of the group. This is seen, for example, in the enforced isolation of white women in slave societies from Cuba (see Martínez-Alier 1989 [1974]) to the U.S. South. In his classic discussion of southern social psychology, W. J. Cash points to the "Cult of Southern Womanhood," where the white woman became "the mystic symbol of its nationality in the face of the foe" and "her identification [was caught up] with the very notion of the South itself" (1941:86, 116).

The Southern "rape complex" existed not because of any real threat of sexual attack on white women by black men. It arose from the need to justify violence against blacks and "the fact that this Southern woman's place in the Southern mind proceeded primarily from the natural tendency of the great basic pattern of pride in superiority of race to center upon her as the perpetrator of that superiority in legitimate line, and attached itself precisely, and before everything else, to her enormous remoteness from the males of the inferior group, to the absolute taboo on any sexual approach to her by the Negro" (1941:116).

If women are made to be the definers of group identity, then, from the point of view of ethnicity, men have a further reason for emphasizing and enforcing respectability: The respectability of the group's women is intimately caught up in, and defines, the status-honor of the group itself. Men seek to enforce conformity to this norm by imposing sanctions designed to ensure respectable behavior and by imposing sanctions on exogamy. Some succeed more than others.

Among the factory workers, there was a general feeling that interethnic mating relationships were difficult to maintain in the face of societal pressure and that they involved social and physical violence. Carla said:

> I ain't racial but I would never marry a Negro man. I have friends that have married them and is nothing but trouble. Is *licks* [meaning "blows received"]. They come home and don't respect the wife. They beat she, they bring another woman inside the house.
>
> My sister is married to a Negro man in England, and she say, "Never marry a Negro." Indian men respect they women—I'm not saying all, the majority.
>
> My fiancé is real racial. He don't like Negores at all. That's what I don't like about him.
>
> It just much easier with ah Indian. My sister and my niece were walking in Town and this Indian man jump up and say, "You get a real niggerman to make that chile" and she feel real bad. She do try to fit in. She Jherri curl she hair, but it don't work. She don't fit in wid the friends he keep.

> See, if you get married to a Negro man and he cut you ass [beat you up] you ent get no help from your mother, because it come like she warn you. But if you marry ah Indian man and he carry on you mother will help you. It come like it your fault if you marry a Negro. But it's vice versa. I was on Henry Street and this Indian woman and black man was walkin' together and these Negro girls walkin' behind dem givin' de gurl one set o' horrors, sayin', "Eh, you like black ting or what?" and ting.

While there are few overall instances of interethnic long-term mating or marrige, as reported in Chapter 2, there seems to be more reluctance to intermarry on the part of East Indians than on the part of blacks, which Miller relates to East Indians' projects of transcendence through descent continuity (1994:198–200). The subject of sexual relations and marriage between a black man and an East Indian woman is a "constant refrain" (1994:200) in discussions of ethnicity in Trinidad.

Regarding the image of East Indian women in calypsoes, Rohlehr writes that "many calypsoes in which such women appear are really not about the women at all, but about masked inter-racial confict." These calypsoes, then, were about ethnic stereotyping: "The stereotype of the Indians was that of a people who wanted to preserve ethnic purity, and were totally against its violation, particularly via the marriage or sexual cohabitation of Indian woman and Creole man" (Rohlehr 1988:275, 277).

In his biographical sketch of Dum-Dum, a black pimp, Lieber writes that many of Dum-Dum's prostitutes were "young East Indian women who left their villages as a result of some transgression or disagreement followed by ostracism (typically becoming pregnant by a non-Indian male)" (1981:45). In addition, Mohammed writes that even the term "creolization" has particularly pejorative connotations along these lines: "It is a particularly daring, even offensive word to use in reference to Indian women in Trinidad for it was used popularly to refer to those women who mixed or consorted with people of African descent, especially men" (1988a:381).

Further, if the unmarried woman and her family lose prestige, the loss is even worse if there is a chance that the woman will develop relations with black men: "Apart from being an economic liability, it was feared that she would lose her virginity or become pregnant before she could be married, or worse yet, consort with the dreaded polluted race of Black men—bringing utter shame and disgrace on the family" (1988a:386).

Indian men are seen as using violence to circumscribe the activities of East Indian females who mate with non-Indian men: "This violence is not always manifested physically but can take the form of vicious, degrading or obscene insults slung at Indian women *who choose to be friendly with men outside of their ethnic group*" (1988a:395, emphasis added).

It is not only East Indian women who are prohibited from a relationship with blacks. The following newspaper article, entitled "Suicide after Relatives

Object to Inter-Racial Love," while reporting a true incident, plays on the stereotype of East Indians getting *tabanka* [a depressed state resulting from unrequited love; see Sampath 1993:248] and committing suicide by drinking an insecticide:

> Villagers of Picton Settlement, San Fernando, are still talking about the shock suicide of a 20-year-old villager.
>
> Dead is Christopher Rampersad, who committed suicide by drinking the insecticide Gramoxone.
>
> Rampersad died at the San Fernando General Hospital last Sunday evening.
>
> According to reports, Rampersad, who comes from a staunch Hindu family, was dating a young woman of African descent.
>
> "His relatives never approved of the relationship and they ordered him to forget about the girl," a neighbor told *TnT Mirror*.
>
> He, however, ignored the demand and continued the relationship with his loved one much to the annoyance of his relatives.
>
> After a heated argument with certain relatives last Thursday, Rampersad reportedly left home to stay with another relative.
>
> Shortly after, he took a bottle of Gramoxone and drank some of the poisonous substance. (*TnT Mirror*, March 12, 1993, p. 3)

These general society-wide feelings are substantiated by opinion research that reveals, among other things, that blacks have more objections to blacks marrying other blacks than blacks marrying East Indians, more than half of East Indians surveyed had definite objections to East Indians marrying blacks, and all groups were generally favorable to members of their own group marrying whites (see Table 25). The survey research reported in Table 25 was undertaken in 1976. In a 1987 survey, respondents were asked the same

TABLE 25
Workers' Attitudes About Ethnic Intermarriage, 1979

Question: Do you have any objections toward people of your race marrying a(n) . . .

Ethnicity of Respondent	*African?*	*Indian?*	*European?*	*Mixed?*
African				
Objections	13%	7%	11%	8%
No Objections	87	93	89	92
Indian				
Objections	53	10	28	28
No Objections	47	90	72	72
Mixed				
Objections	2	4	4	4
No Objections	98	96	96	96

Source: Adapted from Ryan, Greene, and Harewood 1979:63, tables 2.41, 2.42, and 2.43.

question. While at this time only 31 percent of East Indians were reported to have objections to blacks marrying whites, a fact that Miller attributes to the "sensitivity of the community in response to accusations of racism and knowing the now-appropriate answer to a formal survey" (1994:163), the survey-taker concluded that "not much had changed in this particular area" between 1976 and 1987 (Ryan 1988b:227).

The flirting relationships in the factory can be related to historical patterns of mating in Trinidad. The flirting between supervisors and line workers tends to reproduce a system whereby white men had sexual access to black and East Indian women under slavery and indenture. In addition, the flirting patterns demonstrate cultural biases[2] and economic structure. To get at the underlying meanings of these practices, the symbolic capital argument is useful when we relate flirting to mating. Urging that we extend the concept of economic calculation to the pursuit of symbolic capital, Bourdieu suggests that mating strategies are one way a group can improve its symbolic capital, accumulating symbolic profits, as it were, by acquiring powerful affines. This, in turn, elevates the group's standing in the eyes of others, and such a relatively high standing not only enables the group to acquire even more powerful affines, but "defines the group's capacity to preserve its land and honour, and *in particular the honour of its women* (i.e. the capital of material and economic strength which can actually be mobilized for market transactions, contests of honour, or work on the land)" (Bourdieu 1977:181, emphasis added).

Women, it seems, become integral to a group's strategies of pursuing a symbolic capital. Ethnicity receives its power from kinship-like metaphors and is often expressed in kinship-like terms. In the kinds of situations we see in the factory context the force of such social ideologies are driven home. Gender generally becomes important for ethnicity when we consider the importance of women for the so-called private sphere, the area associated with the microprocesses of "inner" ethnicity formation.

If a group's females were regarded by the men as the receptacles of that group's values and virtues, then "violating" those females through sexual "conquest" would, by implication, defile that group and violate the group's prestige and honor. Black men understand these attitudes on the part of East Indians. By flirting with East Indians, black men may feel that they are able simultaneously to lower the esteem of the East Indian group while possibly improving, according to them, their own symbolic capital given the society's pervasive (at times) anti-black bias.

According to the attitudes of the East Indian man, on the other hand, they would lose symbolic capital if they flirt with black women because to mate with blacks would depreciate the capital of East Indians without having a detrimental effect on black esteem. Rohan said to Deepak, who was flirting with two East Indian women who were working on the night shift, "Man, why do you get all hot over every Indian girl you see?" Deepak laughed. Terry, who sometimes refers to himself as a dougla and at other times as Indian, said, "When I get married, I want ah *Indian* girl."

That East Indian men lose more symbolic capital than they gain by mating with black women may reflect not only the aesthetic bias constituted by hegemonic cultural processes but the differing family structures of blacks and East Indians, although it seems clear that these traditional patterns are breaking down somewhat. The East Indian family may be described as "patriarchal" (Angrosino 1976), and, thus, the symbolic capital accrues to the father and other senior males in terms of mating strategies. On the other hand, while historical evidence shows that the black family should never have been characaterized as "matriarchal" (Higman 1975; Mohammed 1988b), it may be correct to say that the situation there is more ambiguous in terms of who gains in symbolic capital in a sometimes "female-headed" system. Black men, then, may be relatively freer to mate with women from other groups and, at least, they would not lose symbolic capital.

For East Indian men, the greater emphasis on the ethnicity of the mate relates to the historical shortage of females, as discussed in Chapter 2, and the fact that black women are regarded as more "independent" (Bolles and D'Amico-Samuels 1989:175–76) and thus potentially threatening to male control within the family. These tendencies, according to the workers, are evident to black men. As Carla (who is East Indian) said, "You kidding? A black man would love to marry ah Indian woman. She will cook for he and keep he house clean and look after the chirren. A black woman, he couldn't keep she at home."

Wilson sees respectability and reputation as crosscutting ethnicity and applying to blacks and East Indians equally. But there are some EUL workers, both black and East Indian, who feel that East Indians are more respectable than blacks. Terry, speaking to what he saw as the major differences between blacks and East Indians, said, "Indians is the most highly respectable people. If you watchin' ah Indian movie they never kiss on the screen. Ah *real* Hindu, you won't see they holding hands in the streets. For a Negro, you might see all sorts ah ting. In Carnival you might see Indian man and woman wining on each other—that necessary—but a *real* Hindu and a *real* Indian? That don't enter they head. Negroes are respectable and do good things, but Indians most respectable."

Terry's remarks about East Indians being the most respectable people in Trinidad require some explanation. At one level, he seems to be upholding the honor of his own ethnic group. But there are other aspects as well. It seems that, in his mind, there is a difference between activities that are respectable and not respectable, and people who are respectable and not respectable. In such a highly individualized society, which nonetheless adheres to certain group stereotypes, respectability is there for the individual to achieve. It is just that, for Terry, East Indians by and large engage in respectable activities while most blacks do not. It is not that blacks cannot achieve respectable status. It is just that relatively few actually do, according to Terry. This is consistent with Wilson's thesis on one level—that the ethos of respectability and reputation cut across ethnic groups—but Terry's remarks point to the possibility of status differentials between groups on the basis of respectability. That is, while blacks and East Indians share ideas about what respectability and reputation constitute, only East Indians are really respectable in practice.

Terry's opinion might be based somewhat on the belief that East Indian men are able to "control" East Indian women more effectively than black men are able to control black women. Historically, East Indian women initially enjoyed considerable independence on the sugar estates. Later, however, toward the end of the indenture system, estate owners encouraged marital stability in order to reproduce their labor supply. Additionally, there was the move from estate residence to village residence, which entailed attempts to re-create the North Indian joint family (Poynting 1987:232–34). Working-class East Indian women then concentrated their economic efforts on family farms in rural areas and therefore became less economically independent. Economic marginalization and dependency on the male wage and economic decision-making combined to provide East Indian males with the ability to wield physical and cultural violence and effectively constrain East Indian women.

Black men are regarded by some Trinidadians, and regard themselves, as being more "masculine" than East Indian men. Therefore, if one gains status by being a "sweet man" or "hot boy" then this entails a willingness to seduce and subjugate women from other groups, and, in some cases, the more such exotic "conquests," the more status achieved. While this argument may not explain why East Indian men do not also engage in this activity, the perception that black men are more masculine may suggest why East Indian females flirt with black males as much as they do with East Indian males. The point is that flirting is one way of affecting a transfer of power. As Frances Henry and Pamela Wilson note, the exploitative nature of Caribbean male-female relationships has "necessitated [women's] employment of certain manipulative techniques and rationalizations in order to attain, or convince themselves they have attained, it would seem, the kind of relationships which they desire" (1975:178).

The idea of pressure and resistance in this dynamic process is crucial. Flirting in the factory—and elsewhere in Caribbean society—is one way men control women.[3] Flirting by the supervisors further ensconces their positions of authority and thus diminishes the younger women's statuses as workers. This tends to support the owners' strategies of hiring these relatively vulnerable workers. Flirting by the younger male workers is no less harmful, because it further objectifies them as sexually available and subordinate. Here the young men unwittingly uphold the aims of capital. Older, "respectable" women do not face such objectification, because their respectability acts as a shield. Given that respectability entails "traditional" female stances, however, respectability can insure objectification and subjugation by different means. Flirting is socially misrecognized violence, involving such "niceties" as sweet talk and begging, but often the undertone of this transposed violence leads to actual violence. And flirting and heckling, on the other hand, are patterns of behavior in which women attempt to mitigate and resist men's control.

Chapter 6

CLASS AT WORK

Despite the considerable theoretical sophistication of many studies of resistance and their contribution to the widening of our definition of the political, it seems to me that because they are ultimately more concerned with finding resistors and explaining resistance than with examining power, they do not explore as fully as they might the implications of the forms of resistance they locate. In some of my own earlier work, as in that of others, there is perhaps a tendency to romanticize resistance, to read all forms of resistance as signs of the ineffectiveness of systems of power and the resilience and creativity of the human spirit in its refusal to be dominated. By reading resistance in this way, we collapse distinctions between forms of resistance and foreclose certain questions about the workings of power.

—*Lila Abu-Lughod, "The Romance of Resistance: Tracing Transformations of Power Through Bedouin Women"*

RECENT TRENDS in history and anthropology have explored the themes of power and, especially, the resistance to it. Studies of social, political, and economic resistance—which has been defined in various ways—proliferated in the bleak political times of the 1980s. But, like the "goods" produced by much industry, it is not at all clear how much use notions of resistance are to those of us encountering situations in our research where real power is being wielded.

It is not at all clear whether the fairly recently returned-to Gramscian notions of hegemony can do justice to the complexity of lived experiences of those whose lives we study. Gramscian notions of hegemony tend to be characterized especially among contemporary interpreters like Raymond Williams, by those looking for resistance in a way that treats power as a monolithic force, thus relegating resistance to the same status: a monolithical effort to ward off the effects of the (external) exercise of power. James Scott's book *Weapons of the Weak* (1985) is an example of this tendency. As Lila Abu-Lughod (1990) and others have pointed out, work such as Scott's generally does not take into account contextuality, and thus any existence of contradictions and ironies in the resistance of disempowered groups is elided.

What domain could be more rife with contradictions and ironies and the workings of power and resistance than the workplace, where ethnicity, class, and gender identities become part of the "contested terrain?" That, for example, gender itself is an index of and vehicle for power is apparent from the evidence present, which contradicts any claims that class position on its own provides the sole and primary basis for power. Gender, then, along with class and other forms of social identity like ethnicity, is a means, a resource, of empowerment. And this is especially relevant in the context of gender relations, where the idiom of sexuality is salient (see Chapter 5).

With these remarks in mind, I want to compare the evidence I present with two other recent anthropological studies of women in factory work: Ong's 1987 book *Spirits of Resistance and Capitalist Discipline*, a study of women factory workers in Malaysia, and Kondo's 1990 book *Crafting Selves: Power, Gender, and Discourses of Identity in a Japanese Factory*, a study of a small confectionery factory in suburban Tokyo. My remarks below do not do justice to these rich studies, which show the nuanced ways in which women factory workers both resist power and exercise power in their own right. I begin this chapter with reference to these works to situate my own discussion of class in the EUL factory and, in so doing, draw on them for comparison.

Ong considers the roles of the state, the family, and the (many Japanese- and American-owned) corporations in the insertion of female workers in foreign-owned factories, the factories themselves representing the increasing insertion of Malaysia into the world economic system. Ong constructs an argument about how this develops culturally, with special attention paid to gender relations within the family before the advent of industrialization and the nature of gender relations in the transitional phase. Not surprisingly, she finds that industrialization causes "dislocation" from "traditional" patterns and that women's sexuality is a target of social control.

When women entered into the work force, the state-owned media focused attention on their "Westernization"—the proclivity to wear Western clothes, to shop for consumer goods, and to supposedly become sexually active and even "promiscuous." In response, Muslim clerics and others referring to Islam critiqued the factory women for this behavior. The Islamic fundamentalist *dakwah* movement defined "proper" Islamic behavior in opposition to Western culture. Women were encouraged to veil themselves, refrain from drinking alcohol, observe the segregation of the sexes, and engage in Koranic studies. Ong mentions that,

> Although few, if any, of the Malay factory women (as compared to office workers) donned Arabic robes in voluntary *purdah*, the *dakwah* movement has struck a responsive chord in many young women who wished to be recognized as morally upright Muslims engaged in honest hard work (*kerja halal*). They saw in Islamic resurgence an assertion of pride in Malay-Muslim culture and an affirmation of its fundamental values in opposition to foreign consumer culture. For instance, the widespread influence of foreign advertising and the promotion of beauty contests in American electronics companies have promoted Western images of feminine passivity and consumption. . . . Assailed by contradictory, unflattering representations of themselves, factory women often

> sought in Islam guidance [and] self-regulation to comply with work discipline and to inculcate an ascetic attitude towards life. (1987:185)

Ong makes this point in passing because one of her main points is to show how manifestations of spirit possession in the factories are actually demonstrations of resistance against work conditions. These bouts of possession occur when one or more women suddenly become hysterical, claiming to see spirits. Often, this leads to hysteria in others. Sometimes, women have to be sedated with drugs and sent home from work for a few days. Women who experience this more than twice are fired. On occasion, whole factories have to be closed for days and exorcism rights performed by religious specialists.

In viewing this hysteria as resistance—which I think is innovative and insightful on Ong's part—there is the possibility of forgotten, unintended consequences. While the bouts of spirit possession may earn the women "space" in the short-term, in the long-term it may reinforce ideas that women are not "in control"—of their sexual desires or whatever—and thus they require controlling. And, it may be that "conformity" to Islamic cultural forms may be a more profound way to resist. As Ong herself writes: "In Telok, culturally-specific forms of protest and retaliation in the corporate arena were directed ultimately not at 'capital' but at the transgression of local boundaries governing proper human relations and moral justice" (1987:202).

Ensuring proper "respect" in their treatment by men could have its emancipatory consequences. But this view is precluded from Ong's analysis because she sees it as "conforming" to Islam, thus implying that Western culture does in fact offer more emancipatory opportunities for women. It may be that this "conformity" is really resistance to "open" Western culture. After all, her whole book is devoted to demonstrating the control that the advent of Western capitalism entails. To be fair, the historical context of Ong's study is one of emerging capitalism, thus capitalism and its attendant social relationships and culture have not yet "replaced" (not that it ever really or completely does) "cultural" relationships. It is therefore not surprising that resistance should occur in this way.

The factory in Kondo's study features the relations between a number of male artisans who are full-time workers and defined as skilled, and a number of part-time female workers, defined as unskilled. Kondo analyzes the Japanese notion of *uchi no kaisha*, "the company as family," to trace the contradictions of resistance: Workers invoke this idiom subversively, but in so doing legitimate the established order. The owner periodically becomes angry with the workers and reinforces his authority as owner. However, he unwittingly provides the workers with materials for their critiques. So the owner might use *uchi no kaisha* to characterize company benefits like group holidays as gifts, but the workers would say that such "gifts" are owed to them as family members, and thus not gifts at all. When the owner talks about economic rationality, the workers use *uchi no kaisha* to critique him for not being familial enough.

The male workers criticize the company at one level, but at another take pride in belonging to *uchi no kaisha* as testament to their masculinity and skill, earned through hard work as an apprentice, which has taught them self-sufficiency. The hierarchy in the factory is based on gender, "skill," and employee status. The males often downplay the contribution of the females by pointing to their other obligations, for example, their kin-based family, not just their company family, and by overtly referring to their nonartisanal status.

For their part, the women scorn their male coworkers—some of whom are thirty years younger than the women—by impugning their lack of maturity. The women feel that the men want the women to provide assistance in doing their jobs—an especially damning critique, the women charge, given the males' denigration of the women's work.

The woman act as companions and maternal figures for the younger male artisans, often cooking for them. Motherhood is especially valued among the workers and relationships between men and their mothers is seen to be especially important. Mother-son incest, Kondo reports, is the source of some cultural preoccupation in Japan. The factory women often act as surrogate mothers, eroticized or not. Women are constructed as emotional workers and care givers, and this sets them apart from "the central story of maturity through apprenticeship and masculine toughness and skill" (1990:295). At the same time, it gives women some position of power over man. One who caters to the selfish whims of another (the *amayakasu* position) is culturally superordinate.

Further, as in the EUL factory, in the Satō factory there is an abundance of sexual banter by men directed at the women. This reinforces for men a sense of masculinity as embodied in the sexual appropriation of women, who, in turn, are expected to be receptive audiences. This activity inevitably facilitates women's subordination. Yet, without this gendered "other," masculinity could not be constructed. Kondo adds, "Women, in enacting their genders and in being crafted by men as the receptive audience, the eroticized mother, and the undifferentiated erotic object, are marginalized and poignantly, paradoxically marginalize themselves from the central narrative of masculine work identity. Yet in so doing they also make themselves virtually indispensable to the felicitous recital of the narrative. And through marshalling these ideologies and enacting them positively, they can also create a sense of self-fulfillment and power" (1990:298).

In both cases cited above, the terms of power, resistance, and class practice are both connected to the wider culture and are a function of the structural arrangements of factory work under capitalism. The terms of power and resistance—and, for that matter, class practice—in the EUL factory differ somewhat from the contexts Ong and Kondo describe it. In Trinidad, for example, there is no such cultural notion as *uchi no kaisha*, which is not surprising given the history of an ethnic division of labor. While there are significant friendship ties among workers, and many bring family matters to the workplace for their birthday parties and other such events, there is no notion of "company as family." There is no such notion cultivated by Tiexiera, either, as a strategy of domination. Further, many of the divisions among the EUL workers have to do with their kin-based family and their obligations outside the workplace. Nonetheless, Tiexiera's behavior often resembles that of the owner of the Japanese factory and when this happens, there is a reaction against such an overt use of power. But there is no completely unified "voice," partially because of the workers' differences in age and partially because of their differences in ethnicity.

Female sexuality is more assertive in the EUL factory than in the factories in Malaysia and Japan. Women in the EUL factory are more "interventive" in their uses of sexuality as a form of reacting to and resisting male power. There is irony in this, however. To the extent that sexuality continues to be a primary idiom of resistance, men will use it in their continued attempts to control women.

As we shall see, the evidence from the EUL factory also contrasts with descriptions of other Caribbean settings. For example, in contrast to Helen I. Safa's (1990) study of factory women in the Dominican Republic and Puerto Rico, it is the younger workers in the EUL factory that exhibit an emerging class consciousness, which is evidenced by their somewhat greater willingness to take group action against the owners. This could be, on one hand, the result of their being more subject to the pressure attendant to the flirtations of the supervisors than the older "respectable" workers as well as, on the other hand, the result of their position as supplemental wage earners and care givers in their own household without the full household responsibilities of the older women.

Kondo offers a more complex notion of resistance than Ong. However, while she argues that "there is no utopian place beyond power" (1990:225), it seems in her account that there is no power outside the "discourse" and the "narrative" in the Satō factory. In this sense, Ong's book provides more of a sense of the "real-life" consequences for the wielding of power and the resistance to it.

At the same time, there are some general similarities between the EUL factory and the Malaysian and Japanese settings. In the passages cited above regarding women's use of Islamic norms in Malaysia and women's use of identities that emphasize traditional care-giving duties in Japan, one sees women utilizing the very cultural forms that ensure their subordination in order to resist. In other words, it is a case of necessity being made into a virtue. Yet these acts of resistance are almost unnoticed and therefore underanalyzed by the authors.

Abu-Lughod suggests that "we use resistance as a *diagnostic* of power." Inverting Foucault's assertion that "where there is power there is resistance" (1978:95–96), she argues " 'where there is resistance, there is power,' which is both less problematic and potentially more fruitful for ethnographic analysis because it enables us to move away from abstract theories of power toward methodological strategies for the study of power in particular situations" (1990:42). This perspective allows us to see the nuanced ways in which power is historically and culturally variable through an examination of the workings of resistance. Indeed, this perspective allows us to see that there are different levels of power operating in one single context. This reaffirms that power is not external to social relations and that everyone "has" power, a realization that should not foreclose investigation—or, even worse, make us adopt the politically conservative viewpoint that the relatively disempowered can "make it" if they really want—but to begin thinking about how we can develop a theory of social resources with emancipatory potential.

Turning the Screws

The EUL owners refer to the country's financial situation to justify their attempts at controlling the work force. Jane Tiexiera said that during the oil boom there was a tremendous rate of employee turnover at the factory. However, she added, during the Recession the work force seems much more stable. She agreed, though, that the workers "have it rough" during these recessionary times. But she didn't associate their "having it rough" with the wages paid by EUL. She referred to "external" causes and she said that if there was another devaluation of the TT dollar she feared there would be social violence akin to the Black Power demonstrations of the early 1970s.

But the workers know these circumstances better than anyone. Rohan said, "You see in Town? In Town it be hard to get a job. People does keep they jobs now." They argue that the employment situation in the Recession pales to the oil-boom days of only a few years earlier, and dictates that the owners can apply more "pressure" and that the employees must take it. As Maureen put it, "It not easy now. Before, no one would take what de man sayin', how he carryin' on. You would leave work here today and find ah next job tomorrow. But no more."

The evidence shows some of the consequences of the class practice that is employed by the owners and, at times, by the managers over the workers. At times the consequences are intended, at times they are not. The owners maintain a superior position over the workers by their access to capital (of all kinds), their ability to control the production process generally, and, in extreme circumstances, by demanding performance even to the point of breaking the country's labor laws regarding overtime payments. Control over the production process is effected by a number of exclusionary and inclusionary practices, which are "cultural" yet nonetheless an instrinsic part of capitalist class practice in the factory.

For example, there is a clear division of labor according to gender and ethnicity. Black and East Indian women are hired as workers, with younger ones being preferred. Younger women are presumed to be still living with older kin and thus immune from the responsibility of a man and children. While they are valued because it is assumed that they will be able to devote all their attention to their work—and not to, for example, miss work because of their children—at the same time they can be paid much less than older women because it is rationalized that they have less responsibilities.

Control over the production process is effected, at one level, by Tiexiera's position regarding the industrialization policies of the state. Besides the formal advantage this provides him—in terms of access to subsidized facilities, credit, tax concessions, and technical assistance, for example—I also suspect that the export performance of his factory as well as his contributions to the NAR party have earned him an informal advantage as well, given how patronage works in formal policies in Trinidad. The EUL factory is not likely to be the target of investigations into illegal labor practices, for instance.

More directly, control over the production process relies on men's control over women in relatively hidden ways as well as in very overt ways. An example of a relatively hidden way is how women's space within the factory is clearly defined and constrained. Women are confined to jobs where they are sedentary and required to perform repeated monotonous tasks. The supervisors and the male workers, by contrast, are given jobs that allow for and even require movement within the factory. These activities reinforce women's subordination. More overt ways that women's productive activities in the factory are controlled include an aggressive sexuality on the part of the male workers and supervisors (see Chapter 5). Whereas these effects may not be intended on the part of the men, they have consequences for class practice nonetheless.

Many of the attempts to control production in the factory are carried out, as it were, by the supervisors. The supervisors are generally invested with superior symbolic capital over the workers in terms of ethnicity, class, and gender. But their class position remains, in some ways, an intermediate one. Although their economic capital is by no means sufficient to afford them more than working-class membership, and despite being white in a postcolonial society that still values "whiteness," they are susceptible to Tiexiera's exclusionary practices, leading them to practice a combination of closure strategies. They practice strategies designed to usurp some of Tiexiera's power over them, while employing a means to this end—that of exclusionary closure with regard to the workers. The workers do not react passively to such exercises of power. Later in this chapter we will discuss some of their strategies of resistance and the degree of success they are able to achieve.

Despite their efforts, it seems the supervisors are barely able to keep the line workers in check, especially the younger ones. There is, however, a different atmosphere when Tiexiera comes on to the adjacent factory floor. The skylarking stops. All pretence of not working hard is forgotten and the supervisors and the workers alike put their heads down and concentrate on their work: Tiexiera has a reputation for having a terrible temper and often the supervisors are buffed up in front of the workers for not being in proper "control" of their workers. He stands in front of work benches observing, often barking out orders, and asking, rhetorically, "What's the holdup?"

On a few occasions during my fieldwork I observed Tiexiera catch a worker idling and suspend them right then and there. On some occasions, temporary workers were fired on the spot. Once, Tiexiera went to the Motor-Assembly Department and found out who had been late for work. He sent home five workers without pay. That day he seemed in a particularly bad mood, and during his rounds Winston paused only long enough to tell me, "There's pressure in this factory, pressure like fuck." Tiexiera snapped at Deepak, saying, "What do you have, a union or something? The way you're carrying on and laughing."

Then, Tiexiera wheeled around and yelled at Melvin for "talking back to him." However, Melvin did not appear to say anything. Later, Melvin calmly said, "He frustrated. That's the wrong strategy for gettin' on with the people you work with. You don't talk to them so."

I talked to Tiexiera briefly that day, asking him what he thought the problems were. He replied, "Problems. People. People not knowing what they supposed to do."

On another occasion, Johnny was standing around with some doubles and gave one to Brian. Tiexiera caught Johnny and asked him, in a loud voice, "Are you on break?" When Johnny replied, "No," Tiexiera responded, "Then what the fuck are you doing here?" Johnny then went back to his machine. Tiexiera went over to David and asked if Johnny had his permission to be away from his machine. When he replied that he did not, Tiexiera told Johnny to go home. Elaine said, "Johnny was skylarking wid dem over dere by the container. We saw Tiexiera come out and he talk rough to Johnny and the next thing we know he walk by the gate and clock he card." It must be pointed out here that the abrupt and summary way in which Tiexiera dealt with Johnny by sending him home was compounded by the words with which Tiexiera chose to address Johnny. In Trinidad, when profanity is being used in such a situation as a means of emphasis, the recipient takes great offense, even if the profanity was not strictly directed at them in the form of an insult. A few days later, while relating his version of the incident, Johnny asked, "And did you see the way he cuss me?"

A few moments after Johnny was sent home, Melvin explained what he saw as the reasons for Tiexiera's management techniques: "If a man payin' another man a fair salary, he can talk to him fair. But if he payin' next to nuttin', he got to tell him to do this n' dat and yell at he." In other words, Melvin was saying that workers would be willing to put forth more effort if they were better paid and that Tiexiera's demeanor was a function of the low wages he paid. Still later he told me, "Don't forget to put this in you book: The employees give it their *best* and the bosses don't appreciate it."

These kinds of activities are only effective when used in concert with other, more systematic, strategies to control the work force. For example, it is a policy to pay extra TT$20 a week to workers who are on time for work for at least four out of five days. One week after he opened his paycheck and found that he did not get the $20, Terry complained to Candace. She replied, "These are Mr. Tiexiera's rules." Knowing that he had nothing to stand on, Terry abruptly went back upstairs.

This policy is backed up by sanctions. Ruud takes the time cards out of the rack of workers who are more than fifteen minutes late. As he was doing this once, Lisa came up and asked for her card. He refused, saying, "We don't want to hear any problems from home." But Brian was also late, and he got his card back. Brian, as was discussed in Chapter 3, is paid much more than the female workers. Furthermore, the Tiexieras like him and consider him a dependable and valuable worker who fulfills a specialized function. Billy, an office worker and cousin of Jane Tiexiera, told Brian, "If anytime you have problems, come to me." And at the Christmas party, Jane Tiexiera gave Brian a kiss on the cheek. He was the only worker so "recognized."

Everywhere in the factory there are reminders to the workers of their vulnerability. The following notice appeared on the bulletin board:

> You say you love me but sometimes you don't show it. In the beginning you couldn't do enough for me. Now you seem to take me for granted. . . . Some days I even wonder if I mean anything at all to you.
>
> Maybe when I'm gone, you'll appreciate me and all the things I do for you. I'm responsible for getting the food on your table, for your clean shirt, for the welfare of your children . . . a thousand and one things you want and need. Why if it weren't for me you wouldn't have anything.
>
> I've kept quiet and waited to see how long it would take for you to realize how much you really need me.
>
> Cherish me . . . take care of me and I'll continue to take good care of you.
>
> Who am I? I am your job.

Tiexiera, who posted the notice, is constantly telling the workers that they must keep up production because EUL is in a precarious position and in danger of going out of business. However, during my fieldwork, EUL was presented with an international award for product quality for Third World manufacturers. When the workers read about this in the newspaper, they were angered because it reinforced their beliefs that they were grossly underpaid and that the firm was, in fact, very successful. Cleo said, "There he go, winnin' ah award again and he sayin' he ain't makin' no money. . . . They won't have no party for we. Only a party for the big boys in the big house wherever he live. . . . The man makin' all that money and think we see any?"

When there are market fluctuations in the demand for EUL items there are related fluctuations in the demand for EUL workers. During the months leading up to Christmas, the factory is very busy because of increasing orders. Beginning in September, temporary workers are hired for a night shift that works from 4 P.M. until 11 P.M. These workers are hired with the understanding that they are temporary and are laid off when the factory closes down for two weeks over the Christmas holidays. A few workers, however, are asked to stay on to work permanently.

Another management technique during this time of the year is to provide opportunities for overtime to the regular workers. Sometimes the opportunity for overtime is presented as optional and sometimes heavy moral suasion is used by supervisors. At other times, when the need arises, supervisors cajole the workers to work a few hours overtime at the end of their shifts. But this does not happen very often, since it makes economic sense for the owners to hire new workers for the night shift because they are paid less than veteran workers.

At first, the permanent workers were paid "time and a half" for overtime and many took the opportunity to make the extra money. However, one day Candace informed a group of workers that, in the future, permanent workers on overtime would be paid only at their regular rate. In addition, permanent workers were to be allowed only two days of overtime a week. The owners soon changed the wage rates again. The very next day a paper was passed around that the workers were required to read and sign. The note reminded them that their regular working hours were 8 A.M. to 4:30 P.M., Monday through Friday, and it indicated that they were to receive overtime pay only after forty hours. However, henceforth, their overtime rate would be the same rate that was paid to the night shift, that is, TT$2.75 per hour. The note also admonished them that on Fridays they should return to work after receiving their pay and not take time to settle debts and make their *sou-sou* payments. (*Sou-sou* is based on a West African rotating credit system. Each member of the group contributes a fixed amount each week, and one member gets to keep the whole amount—i.e., gets his or her "hand" on a rotating basis.) Finally, the workers were warned not to punch out another worker's time card and that the security guard would be doing spot checks of their bags while they worked.

(Although temporary workers seem to be reducing the wages of permanent workers, the latter do not show hostility toward the former. They do not, therefore, try to effect class closure against them. In some cases, this may be due to the fact that many of the temporary workers were introduced to the factory by their friends or kin who are permanent workers. The owners benefit by this situation because their "reserve army" of workers are brought into the production process, trained and ready to take a permanent job should a permanent worker be dismissed.)

Workers are often forced to work several hours past 4:30 P.M. when an emergency arises. In such a situation, the workers are paid at a number of different rates, as we have seen. "Time and a half" for any work over forty hours a week is mandated by Trinidad and Tobago law. EUL's practice of overtime pay is clearly illegal, as is forced overtime.

This situation is mitigated somewhat by the benefits that accrue to employees. One extra way for male workers to earn money is to unload container trailers when they arrive. It is essential that this task is performed quickly because the company is charged extra by the transport company if the container remains on the factory premises for more than the stipulated amount of time. Consequently, the containers are unloaded the day they come in, after factory working hours. The workers are paid a flat rate of TT$30 for this task. In addition, Ramgoolie, one of the security guards, cuts the grass in the front of the factory for TT$50. He does this approximately every two weeks in the rainy season, and less frequently at other times.

On the other hand, there are occasions when the workers are sent home when parts run out before new supplies arrive. There are several reasons for these shortages: shipping problems, mistakes by office workers, or the supervisors forget to reorder supplies. In every case, though, the workers are made to suffer. They usually lose a whole day's pay as a result. They are extremely upset when this occurs, arguing that they lose money through no fault of their own. But there is little they can do.

When the owners and managers cannot convince—through carrot-and-stick means—enough workers to work overtime at the end of their shifts, they often resort to demanding the workers work for up to four hours on Saturdays. This usually occurs only in extreme cases when a large order is in need of immediate filling. After incidents like the one reported at the beginning of Chapter 1, workers began to be paid for Saturday work at their regular hourly rate, even though this would put them over forty hours a week and legally require overtime compensation. Later, as mentioned, this was further reduced. While most workers agree that they need the money—few describe it as "extra money"—they are also very reluctant to work on Saturday because, being responsible for their men, children, and, often, other kin, they feel they have concerns that take precedence over the chance to earn more cash. For example, many workers say that they do most of their shopping for groceries and other goods on Saturday mornings. Indeed, on Saturday mornings Port-of-Spain is jammed with shoppers crowding into its department stores, boutiques, and fabric stores. On many a Saturday morning I encountered EUL workers shopping in Town. Many were buying fabric in order to make garments to sell (see below for a discussion of the EUL workers' informal labor-market participation).

On one Saturday when I observed factory work, the workers upstairs worked in a rather relaxed atmosphere. There was no office staff and Tiexiera was not on the premises. The radio was playing louder than normal and Margarita was even wearing curlers in her hair. Myra was late because "I had to do my wuk first—cooking, cleaning, washing." Cleo was late as well, and she said that she will work late until Christmas because she needed the money. "I was late 'cause I had to cook. I only hope I can keep up. God does love how we get on."

Denise and Mary were the only ones absent. Filling in upstairs were some workers from the downstairs departments, including Martha, Elaine, and Connie. In what seemed like an attempt to win favor with the workers, Winston said, "Those who ent come, if I report they, they get suspended. Denise, whoever." However, by the way he posed his remarks, he seemed to be suggesting that he was not going to use his authority to punish workers and would instead show leniency. This may have been a tactic to make the workers, and especially Denise, feel they owed him something.

In Chapter 3 I referred to the upstairs-downstairs division among the workers. There, we saw that the majority of women's friendship relationships are with fellow workers who work on the same floor. When Winston announced to the workers in his department that they would have to work on Saturday, many downstairs workers professed disbelief when they heard that the upstairs workers were balking. The upstairs-downstairs dichotomy was invoked. Fiona said: "Dem upstairs ent like we downstairs . . . the majority are Seventh Day Adventists and dem don't like to work on Saturday. I been working here coming up on six years. Me don't have a family. When David ask us to wuk on Saturday, we does wuk. Dem upstairs, dem don't like to wuk on Saturday, Dem have to see about dey family and ting."

However, the downstairs workers have to see about their families as well. Fiona herself has three children. Here, it seems, she is referring to "husbands" who may need "taking care of" and who will object to their womenfolk working in the factory on Saturday. There are practically no significant differences between the upstairs and downstairs workers in terms of their domestic situations, and none of the upstairs workers are Seventh Day Adventists.

Winston offered his view of the upstairs-downstairs division: "Downstairs, they have better relations with their supervisors; they never get sent home, so there's no problem to work on Saturday. Up here, they been sent home so they have this thing. . . . Tiexiera makes the shit and he wants me to clean it up. They [the workers] think its my fault. Fuck them."

After work one day, there was a heated conversation in a taxi as Cleo and Lori were angry that Winston had asked them to work late in order to make parts for the products that his department produces. When they refused, he said "Oh come now, how can you do David like that?" In the taxi, Lori recounted this and said, "What? David do we worse!" They were angry that there were receiving overtime pay at a rate lower than their normal rate, and they were angry that some of the workers stayed behind to work, thus underming any form of collective protest. Cleo said: "If we all stick together, we will get change. But them don't want to listen to that."

Some of the workers who worked overtime said that it was easy for Cleo and Lori to refuse because they had husbands who were contributing to the household income. Lori said, "It have some who say dey don't have husband and so they got to work. . . . I tell her 'But, eh-eh, who is dat man who meet you every day outside de factory? What is dat, a manicou [an animal similar to an opossum]?' . . . So I have a husband. But if I workin' I ain't makin' enough to even pay my fares."

Others, too, had reason to withhold their labor. Brian asked Denise if she was going to work overtime, pointing out that it was, after all, a chance to earn more money.

> Brian: So you workin' at night?
> Denise: No.
> Brian: But money important.
> Denise: That's right. Money *is* important. Tiexiera got to realize that. So is time.

She said she was thinking about spending time with her two children. She went on, saying that the chance to work overtime is not offered out of goodwill, but in order to meet a contingency situation, and that workers were still vulnerable to being sent home: "Winston tryin' to hustle up work for us, but he don't give a damn about we. As soon as they bidness fix, we done sent home."

The workers know all too well that their wage-earning position is precarious and that unforeseen events can leave their lives changed, even if apparently in minor ways.

One night the factory was robbed. Workers had knocked a large hole in one of the walls so that a huge machine could be moved in, and before the cinder blocks were replaced, a plastic tarpaulin covered the hole. Thieves apparently entered through this hole and used tools and blowtorches from the factory to break open the office safe. They escaped with a large amount of cash, which was in the safe for the payroll (Tiexiera would not tell me how much), and a security guard from another factory caught them dividing up the money. They escaped with the cash but left behind company checks. Mohun, the security guard, was unaware that anything happened.

The workers mused that the construction workers hired to build an addition to the factory were the culprits, because some of the construction workers apparently told some of the factory workers how Tiexiera originally told them he would pay them fortnightly, and then monthly. After the month was up the workers supposedly were still not paid. They allegedly threatened Tiexiera and said they would "damage" him. As evidence, the factory workers pointed to the pickaxes and sledgehammers that the thieves left behind.

> Daisy: He want too much money too fast. See what he get.
> Johnny: It hard to feel sorry for he. I mean to say, he don't feel sorry for he workers who gettin' this little salary, he don't feel sorry for dem out dere [*pointing to the construction workers*].

The upshot was that Tiexiera fired the security guards—even those who were not working that night—and replaced them with uniformed guards from a security firm. It was also decided that the workers would henceforth be paid by check. Work would now cease on Friday at 4 P.M. The workers were required to sign their time cards on Friday and then receive a receipt from Candace. They then had to travel to the Republic Bank in Four Roads, wait in line, present the receipt to a teller, sign another slip of paper, and then receive their money.

This new routine threatened to disrupt the sou-sou payments and payments to those who had given credit for food sold in the factory. Below I indicate the economic importance of the sou-sou and the internal economy. This new arrangement threatened to make the repayment of credit inconvenient, if not impossible. In the first week, Karen said, "they thinkin' about endin' the sou-sou. We don't know what Tiexiera doin', the way he gettin' on. He fire Ramgoolie just so—we could be next." Ramgoolie, who was not even working on the night of the robbery, had been working at EUL for ten years. But the workers started going to the bank en masse, and the sou-sou and credit payments were collected outside the bank after checks were cashed.

Just when the employees' collective grumblings about these events became louder, the owners offered a "carrot" of sorts. A notice went up that read "in the national interest [and] to revitalize management/employee relations," an Employee of the Month contest would start based on attendance and punctuality, work attitude, appearance, and cleanliness in the work area. No prize was announced. The workers, however, were skeptical and treated the announcement with sardonic humor. I left my fieldwork in the factory before the award was given out and have no idea what happened.

Acts of Resistance

In the factory, one of the norms is not to be seen working hard. At first glance, this seems to support the Carnival mentality thesis. Sometimes it seems that the workers work hard at not working hard. But beneath this surface are strategies of active resistance, such as the break-time ritual. At 10 A.M. the buzzer rings for a fifteen minute coffee break. Workers take the time to visit friends in other departments, get a drink from the water fountain upstairs, or takes a walk and stand outside the front of the factory. However, machine-paced workers in the Plastics Department have to keep on working because the supervisors maintain that the machines cannot be turned off for such a short time. These workers also take turns going to lunch. When the bell rings to signal the end of the break, the workers are very slow at returning to work and only do so at the prodding of the supervisors. There is also a conspiracy to cease working—for all intents and purposes—at around 4 P.M. every day, even though work officially stops at 4:30 P.M.

One day at about 4 P.M., Cheryl and Carla were standing upstairs. Jeremy came from downstairs, and when he saw them he said, "Hey, Ron lookin' for ya."

> Cheryl: I don't care. For de money I work for? Nah. I stoppin' at four on de dot. Why shouldn't we work to suit? Let we work out we own system of work. With de money he payin', I can hardly get milk for my child. Nah man.
>
> Carla: She right. I ain't workin' past four. Not for this money.
>
> Cheryl: You know how much a tin of Klim [a popular brand of powdered milk] is? You know how much for nappies [diapers]?

These actions also reveal a lack of incentive for the workers. Therefore, they see these strategies as justified. Martha said: "You should be *kicksin' off* [i.e., enjoying yourself] at work because you spend most of you time there. . . . I take sick days when I does feel like it. But you entitled. . . . We'd be makin' the same amount if productivity increases."

Since there is always the danger that Tiexiera will walk out of the office door, the workers take considerable risks when they are idling and kicksin' off. Because of what appears to be deliberate understaffing, the line supervisors always work on the assembly line and thus cannot always keep a watchful eye over the workers. At around 4 P.M. the supervisors often go and lime in the stores office, which is on the factory floor. The workers then relax and begin to slow up production considerably or stop altogether. I do not believe this is deliberate and premeditated collusion between the supervisors and the workers against the owners. Despite their role, the supervisors also do not always identify with the aims of the owners.

However, the company tries to impose limits on what the workers can get away with. After a certain point, the workers are in danger of losing their jobs. Elaine and Sybil went to Tobago on the ferryboat for a long weekend. There was a public holiday one Friday, and they left on Wednesday night, missing work on Thursday claiming to be ill, and planned to return to work on time the following Monday. However, they did not arrive back at the factory until the following Thursday. When they came, the guard would not let them in because he had instructions from Tiexiera to send them straight to Candace. Candace sent for Ron, their supervisor, and after a discussion Elaine was suspended without pay for two weeks and Sybil was fired outright. Sybil told the workers, who were on break outside the factory, about the meeting: "I was going to tell them another ting, but I decided to tell dem de truth because I was with Elaine. We couldn't get ah tickets. It was all book up. So she [Candace] ask Ron and he say 'Do what is according to policy'—he didn't try to help we. She say, 'Why didn't you let us know? Why didn't you call?' Well, we was to come back Monday so we didn't see any reason for tellin' them. And we couldn't find a phone directory and where we was it ain't have no phone. . . . I will get a next work. I have a connection at Rossi [a garment factory] and I have a next connection at this factory higher up makin' wall plaques."

The other workers were disappointed and sympathized with them, but after they left some of their closest friends criticized what they saw as their irresponsibility. Irene said:

> Sybil was warned about five times by Candace. That is why she wasn't made permanent. They withheld the letter makin' her permanent for another month because she always stayin' home and always late. What was she thinkin' about? She have to help her mother—her elder sister ain't workin', the brother ain't workin', and she have a little sister. And they renovatin' the house. In these times she is actin' crazy. . . . Elaine have it easier. She permanent and she brother workin' and she the youngest. The old people have a saying 'Your friends can carry you but they can't bring you back.' Sybil mother check for a job for she at Rossi. It payin' $138 after tax but the supervisor real hoggish and Sybil say you can't talk and they real miserable. So I guess she have to try there now.

But others had no sympathy. Martha added, "Sheer slackness."

The example of Elaine and Sybil may, at first, seem to indicate that the workers do not care about their jobs or, worse, that they do not even think about them. This is not true, however, as problems at work are major conversation topics for the workers even when they are not in the factory. I once ran into Martha in my neighborhood after work one day and she began to discuss the various goings on and characters at the factory. I asked her why she always talked about work and she replied, "Work must enter the conversation. It is the most important thing in we life. You work more than you sleep." However, seen another way, the skylarking is some evidence that the workers are engaging in a strategy of resistance, with the object being to selectively withdraw their labor.

One example of the withdrawal of labor is illustrative. Workers in the Downstairs Final-Assembly Department, where nearly all the workers are under twenty-five years of age, have a daily quota of 200 products. At the end of the week, supervisors are given a computer readout by Tiexiera that indicates the quota for the upcoming week. Except for the three months leading up to Christmas, this number is relatively stable. The workers say they do not feel they are able to make 200 and, instead, set the quota among themselves at 150. And this is how much they actually make. The workers keep a close count on the number produced and, usually, they nearly reach their target at about 4 P.M. Between 4 and 4:30, which is when work ends, about three more items are produced. They reason, correctly I think, that if Tiexiera knew they were capable of making 200, he would set the quota at 225. Instead, through their collective action, they are able to alter the formal production schedule. When they see someone apparently working hard, the usual verbal barb is, "Tiexiera you[r] father, or what?"

One day, when Jeremy was sent to work on this department's production line to replace an absent worker, the line made 200 finished products and the female workers were angry with him. Irene said afterward, "It not worth it because of the money, really." In other words, there was no use in increasing production because pay would still be as meager as before.

There are other methods of dealing with management techniques. Often, for example, workers on good terms help one another by switching jobs and diverting themselves from their own jobs to help workers behind in their production. In addition, some workers steal items, piece by piece, and assemble them at home. Theft is a form of resistance for the workers, who justify their actions with reference to the low wages and onerous working conditions at EUL. Some even make a business of it by selling the assembled product to friends. There is considerable risk, however, because the security guard at the front gate requires everyone to open their bags and parcels.

Once Tiexiera called several workers into the office and told them that three products were stolen from the factory and that he would give a $500 reward to anyone who turned in the guilty party. Deepak said, "If I know who it is, I ain't tellin' him. He don't pay us enough. I feel good for whoever thief de ting."

The Unionization Attempt

Lori echoed the thoughts of many workers when she spoke about the hiring and firing processes at EUL, saying that the owners use the Recession as an excuse to fire workers, especially those believed to be advocating the establishment of a union in the factory. I asked her about the pay reduction:

"They said it was so they wouldn't have to retrench, [but] last year they retrenched twenty-two workers. But its just ah excuse. When everywhere else says 'We're retrenching,' they retrench here. When they say 'We givin' pay cut,' they use it as an excuse here to give pay cuts. There was talk about gettin' a union here but those who did talk get retrenched. So we have to keep quiet."

Cleo told me that people wanting to start a trade union "open they mouts too much" and were subsequently retrenched, allegedly because a worker "*carried news*" to (informed) Tiexiera in return for some reward. "But they come like cowards now," she said. As a consequence, I began to investigate the allegation that some three years before my fieldwork workers had tried to obtain union representation. Trade unions have been very successful at certain points in Trinidadian history and during the oil boom some were able to secure huge increases in the pay packets of their members. But, despite some notable exceptions—like the OWTU's Daisy Crick, a legendary figure who was prominent in the 1937 disturbances and for thirty years thereafter—women have not been able to become involved in union organizing. As Thelma Henderson writes: "Generally, women have not been very active in the trade union movement. Although they make up a sizable percentage of the national work force and are generally underpaid and more exploited than the working men (60¢ to the $1.00 a man gets) they are still yet considerably inactive in their unions. The women's auxiliaries in the unions are anything but active and investigation showed that in the ranks of the more progressive trade unions, the male workers are actually the ones pushing for discussion within the women's arm of the union" (Henderson 1973:64).

Research on attitudes toward unions and the place of unions in determining economic and political life in Trinidad and Tobago is equivocal. The Ryan, Greene, and Harewood study (1979) indicates that men seem to have slightly less confidence in the political capacity of labor union leaders than do women (see Table 26). More men than women felt that union leaders

TABLE 26
Workers' Attitudes About the Political Capacity of Union Leaders

Question: Should workers elect their own trade union leaders to represent them in Parliament?

Reply	*Males*	*Females*
Yes	27%	20%
No	51	38
Undecided	22	42

Source: Ryan, Greene, and Harewood 1979:85, table 3.33.

should be elected to Parliament, but also, more men than women felt that they should not be elected to Parliament.

Slightly more men than women were recorded as favoring state involvement in the commanding heights of the economy (see Table 27). Ryan, Greene, and Harewood relate this to the fact that 48 percent of women said that anything the government runs is run badly, whereas 32 percent of men felt this way.

These researchers point out that there was "no overwhelming rejection of the idea of greater government ownership of business. However, it would be inaccurate to say that there was overwhelming support for the idea" (1979:136). What is clearer, though, is that unions and worker participation in business is favored as one goes down the class scale (see Table 28).

Even though the workers at EUL are not unionized, as part of my research I had several conversations with male and female union officials about the situation of female workers. These officials all commented on what they saw

TABLE 27
Workers' Attitudes About Government Ownership

QUESTION: Should the government own most of the banks, large businesses, and estates in Trinidad and Tobago?

Reply	*Male*	*Female*
Yes	41%	36%
No	34	27
Don't know	25	37

SOURCE: Ryan, Greene, and Harewood 1979:86, table 3.34.

TABLE 28
Workers' Views on Participation, by Level of Occupation, 1979

QUESTION: Should workers have a significant say in running businesses?

	Occupation/Occupational Level of Respondent				
Reply	Level I[a]	Level II[b]	Level III[c]	Housewife	Unemployed
Yes	23%	42%	62%	33%	41%
No	58	36	19	25	20
Don't know/uncertain	19	22	19	41	39

SOURCE: Adapted from Ryan, Greene, and Harewood 1979:136, table 6.9.
[a]Manager, professional, farmer.
[b]White-collar worker, teacher, technician.
[c]Agricultural worker, laborer, domestic.

as women's reluctance to become involved in higher-level union activities and general lack of interest in trade unions. One female official of the Transport and Industrial Workers Union (TIWU) told me of the unwillingness of "reactionary male comrades," as she termed them, to incorporate women into the power structure. She told me that female members are harassed by their husbands and boyfriends, who are reluctant to allow them to attend meetings, which are held at night. On occasion, meetings are disrupted by men demanding that their womenfolk return home.

In a recent seminar document, OWTU official Cecil Paul addresses the problem, but I doubt that his explanations would be acceptable to female unionists, because he seems to forget about the power differential between men and women, almost to the point of "blaming the victim":

> what we have not had is women coming forward on a consistent manner as men, developing at the same level as men, participating to the same degree as men, aspiring to the leadership posts in the Union as men. . . . Despite the fact, that when struggle erupts with the Union where women are involved, we see the women playing the leading role, being in the most cases more defiant, more aggressive and better able to sustain a struggle than the men. . . . But once that struggle ends, the women go back into a shell. . . .
>
> Women have a lesser degree of understanding of the Union and consequently, have a lower level of working class consciousness than men. At present the average working class woman is at a disadvantage in terms of attaining an equal status with men because they are not equipped with a proper understanding of their capacity and the importance of their role. . . .
>
> What is the Future Role of our Women in the Trade Union Movement? First of all, I am contending that there must not be a separate Women's Group in the Union. I am contending Comrades, that women must develop alongside the men and must be involved together with the men. . . . Your task as participants in this Seminar is to throw off your Inferiority Complex, develop your consciousness through the Education bodies of the Union and through participation in the Union. You must demand equality of treatment at Union forums and functions. You must not allow the male members to have you serve food and drinks at functions. Only to be present to dress up the place and to provide a good sight with your beauty and sexy looks. I am not saying you must not look sexy and beautiful. That is good, but that must not be the reason for your presence. In addition to your beauty and looks and your companionship to the men, you must be equal participants and must have equal status with the men. You must struggle for this and must encourage other women to struggle for this achievement, just as the Working Class are our own Liberators. So also the Working Class Woman is her own Liberator. And you have a Democratic Institution—the Trade Union—to achieve that equality, which the Capitalist Society deny [*sic*] you. (Paul 1985:3–4)

Evidence suggests that when they are officially represented by unions, women's interests are not generally vigorously defended by the union. In 1979, the Trinidad and Tobago government investigated the garment industry, resulting in the Pounder Report (Trinidad and Tobago 1979). It is amazing the extent to which the report neglects the fact that the workers are female and that this has any significance for the poor wages and poor working conditions found in the industry. Indeed, to read the report one would never know that the bulk of the employees within the industry are female at all. Still, the report can provide us with some insight on the plight of female workers in Trinidadian manufacturing.

The commission investigating the industry took testimony from thirty-three garment workers. Their main complaints were about the poor physical working conditions and the propensity for management to deviate from union production agreements, especially by arbitrarily increasing the number of pieces the workers were required to stitch in order to qualify for the incentive rate of pay. Further, they complained about the poor wages in general, with one woman stating that, after paying transportation costs, she was left with $14 at the end of the week (Trinidad and Tobago 1979:67). An industrial-safety officer from the Factory Inspectorate Division corroborated the claims of poor physical facilities within the factories by pointing to the poor ventilation and lighting found in almost all garment factories. In one particular factory, the outside temperature was 90 degrees Fahrenheit, while the temperature in the working area was from 95 to 98 degrees. It is no wonder that Matthew Gonzales, the president of the Garment Manufacturers Association, commenting on his own factory, "spoke of workers's absentee-ism, as well as the distinct tendency of workers to waste time on the job. He referred to many workers in his factory preferring to take all of their sick leave rather than to earn double pay for the period of sick leave, for which they are eligible under the agreement. He saw this as indicative of a mental attitude to work and thought that improved conditions in factories would make little difference in workers' performance. He felt the same way about profit-sharing schemes" (Trinidad and Tobago 1979:71).

The commission concluded that, while unions had succeeded in increasing wages, they had not improved working conditions, and that improvement in the physical conditions alone would not increase production. The commission felt that incentive systems that did not provide workers with significant additional earnings were sure to breed frustration and worker discontent. The commission recommended that these problems be rectified within the existing labor-relations framework. The only recommendation that was apparently designed to help female workers in particular was one that suggested the construction of day-care centers near garment factories, with the cost to be shared by the government and the manufacturers (Trinidad and Tobago 1979:80). The commission had no power to enforce its proposals, however, and it seems little was done in the way of improvements since then.

Similar to the onerous conditions suffered by the garment workers is the lot of the domestic workers. Mohammed (1987:13) cites a Housewives Association of Trinidad and Tobago (HATT) survey done in 1975 that provides important information on the working conditions of "domestics," which are one of the largest categories of female workers. The HATT study found that over 40 percent worked more than eight hours a day, with 32 percent of workers surveyed working six and a half to seven days a week, and a further 29 percent working five and a half to six days a week. At the time of the survey, the average weekly wage was $15, with maternity leave or other benefits basically dependent on the generosity of the employer. The problem is that, under the 1972 Industrial Relations Act (IRA), household workers are not covered. In 1980, the Minimum Wages Board did stipulate that household attendants were to be paid at least $55 a week in 1980 and $70 a week in 1981 for a forty-four-hour week spread over six days. And household workers are now represented by a union, led by Clotil Walcott. But they are not guaranteed the same benefits as other service workers, such as maternity leave, extended vacation leave for long service, and a cost-of-living allowance (Walcott 1987).[1]

In the EUL factory, the story was recounted that twenty of the workers, mostly over twenty-five years of age, planned to obtain union recognition for the work force. A few went to a union office in Laventille to discuss the procedure. According to Trinidad and Tobago law, union recognition is mandatory after a vote among the work force yields a simple majority in favor of recognition, but unions are not permitted to initiate or instigate this vote. However, word leaked to Tiexiera and all the workers were "retrenched," that is, told that they had to leave because of the firm's financial difficulty. As it happened, the only retrenched workers were those involved in the plot. Later, rumor had it that one of the workers was paid by Tiexiera for the information, but I could not confirm this.

Cleo was involved in the effort and was fired, but a year later she was the only one asked to return, although it is not clear just why. She said that she undertook various part-time jobs for more than a year before EUL called her back. She received the following letter:

> May 3, 1983
> Dear: Cleo Allen
>
> As you are no doubt aware EUL has built its production and sales around the International Export Markets. The year 1983 has proved so far to be the worst year ever for exporters. We have lost the following markets:
>
> Jamaica
> Venezuela
> Columbia [*sic*]
> Equador [*sic*]
> Nigeria
> Costa Rica
>
> These markets have been closed to us either thru [*sic*] import restrictions or the inability of the Central Banks in those countries to pay their bills. Other

potential markets like the U.S., Canada, Europe and Puerto Rico are highly competitive and are still facing a recession.

Because of falling sales and therefore production, we have no alternative but to retrench some production employees.

By way of this letter, I hearby advise you of your immediate retrenchment. Enclosed is your cheque including one weeks [*sic*] notice. Severance pay at the rate of 1 week per year for service of one to two years and two weeks [*sic*] pay for service in excess of three years [apparently the country's severance pay formula at the time]. Any accrued vacation pay has also been included.

I assure [*sic*] that this decision has indeed been difficult for me and if in the future the economic climate improves we will reconsider your employment.

Yours truly,
Essential Utensils Ltd.
N. Tiexiera
Managing Director

Attached was the following accounting of Cleo's wages and severance pay, which shows that she was suspended before she received this letter:

Pay for week ending May 4, 1983	–0– suspended
One week's notice	190.00
Vacation pay 4 days	152.00
No. of years service 5.1	
Severance pay at 10.2 weeks	1938.00
Total	2280.00
Less N.I.S.	<5.75>
Less owning on account	–0–
Nett [*sic*] total	2274.25

During my fieldwork, workers certainly complained about their conditions, especially forced overtime and low wages, but they were reluctant to publicly advocate bringing in a union. In part, this reluctance may have been the result of antiunion propaganda where, during the Recession, the gains of the oil boom have been represented to the general public as a cause of financial woes, as we saw in Chapter 2.

It is apparent that Tiexiera's actions accomplished what they intended; during my fieldwork EUL workers were reluctant to consider another union attempt. According to Connie, "People in here are scared. They need to stick together to make things better. But you see in here? If you talk about bringing in a union it will get carried back to Nigel and you will be out the gate. That is the hold that Nigel has over us. I could be talking to the people I lime with about bringing in a union and somehow it will get back. I don't understand it, because it will be helping them."

Is Tiexiera's fear of unionization legitimate? Maybe so: As I discuss in Chapter 3, the wages paid by EUL rank with the lowest rates paid in industrial production. Presumably, a union would increase the workers' share. He always maintained that if a union did manage to get recognition, he would close up the factory.

Evidence shows that the country's business elite in recent years has not suffered overall compared to the working population, who have achieved only minor gains. Ralph Henry (1988a:482–86) suggests that the "pushfulness" of the active trade-union movement and the redistributive efforts of the PNM government had the effect of enhancing wider income distribution among workers, or at least arresting the rate of decline against industry's profits. But (Table 29) during the oil boom from 1974 to 1981 labor's share (compensation of employees) was still exceeded by profit incomes (operating surplus).

In his study of Caribbean labor relations, Zin Henry writes that the struggle for union recognition, a conflict-ridden process, initiates a "pathological trend" that pervades labor-management relations after the recognition process has been completed. In order to obstruct the process, "One or more of a number of techniques may be encouraged; employees who are identified as persons responsible for the advent of a particular union may be dismissed for good cause or otherwise; but more frequently Caribbean employers resort to evasive and delaying tactics designed to frustrate and procrastinate claims for recognition" (1972:95). Tiexiera apparently chose the route of eliminating those responsible for the plan to bring in a union, which is illegal as Trinidad and Tobago law supports union recognition.

As mentioned in Chapter 2, the 1972 IRA replaced the 1965 Industrial Stabilisation Act (ISA). Both of these laws were seen as antiunion and antilabor by union leaders because they curbed the right to strike and

TABLE 29
Cost Components of Gross Domestic Product, Percentage Distribution, Trinidad and Tobago, 1966–1985 (current prices)

Year	*Compensation of Employees*	*Operating Surplus*	*Year*	*Compensation of Employees*	*Operating Surplus*
1966	52.2	33.1	1976	40.4	50.4
1967	51.0	33.2	1977	40.7	49.1
1968	47.7	38.2	1978	45.2	46.9
1969	49.9	35.8	1979	44.8	50.9
1970	51.5	33.9	1980	40.8	57.4
1971	55.2	29.5	1981	46.5	51.1
1972	54.7	27.7	1982	55.3	43.2
1973	50.8	35.5	1983	57.7	38.9
1974	37.1	54.2	1984	57.8[a]	35.6
1975	37.0	55.2	1985	60.5[a]	31.8

SOURCE: Henry 1988a:485, table 3.
[a]Provisional.

limited other labor activities (Parris 1976). However, the problem of union recognition, not adequately remedied by the ISA, is one of the principle concerns of the IRA. The IRA mandates that recognition for a union with more than 50 percent of the workers within a bargaining unit as members is automatic, and that, after such recognition, the employer is bound to enter negotiations with the union in good faith. The IRA also established a tribunal called the Registration Recognition and Certification Board to deal with recognition issues. When a union wants to be recognized by an employer, it no longer approaches the employer, as under the ISA, but addresses its claim to the board, which deals with the claim (Okpaluba 1975:57–60).

The IRA has built-in protections against employee victimization, and it is a summary offense for an employer to victimize an employee for being a union member or for being absent from work because of union activities. In addition, the employer is prevented from stipulating as a condition of employment that the worker shall not join a union, nor can the worker be forced to resign from a union. An employer can be convicted under this law and be fined or imprisoned, and the courts can order that the employee be paid back wages and be reinstated. The employer can, of course, claim that the worker was fired without such intent, but the law puts the burden of proof on the employer (Okpaluba 1975:67–68).

It appears, then, that Tiexiera was acting illegally when he dismissed the workers and that they would have been on solid legal ground in initiating legal proceedings against him. But there are several obstacles in the way of nonunionized workers in such situations. The IRA stipulates that individual workers cannot initiate litigation before the Industrial Court. A worker's union must take his or her case to the Industrial Court, and, if not a member of a union, he or she must find a union, become a member in good standing, and have that union take the fight to the Industrial Court. It is difficult to believe why any union would be interested in spending its resources fighting on behalf of unemployed workers, who probably do not have the money to pay union dues, when the outcome is far from certain. It is a difficult position for workers indeed: What appeared to be a gamble for Tiexiera in flouting the law was really a calculated move designed to eradicate the immediate problem and to issue a warning to the remaining workers.

These events traumatized the EUL workers and made them reluctant to take further concrete actions to become represented by a union. However, they still were interested in improving their lot. Norma, for example, said that, although she would like a union, she is mindful of Tiexiera's way of dealing with the threat in the past and of the contemporary business environment, in which unions are frequently blamed in the media for instigating the financial crisis: "It ain't time now. If a union come, I be glad but I won't worry myself or say anything. But now that business pushin' unions down, it ain't time. Before, yes, when unions used to be able to do good."

Workers referred to conditions in the factory when outside events paralleled their own situation. Talking about the mistreatment of undocumented Mexican workers by California agribusinesses, Carla said, "To think that human beings could be treated in such a way. I'm sure that if Tiexiera has he way he would do the same."

Val is rumored to be the one who informed Tiexiera about those involved in the previous unionization attempt. Some workers said she was made an unofficial supervisor and given added responsibilities for a time after the incident, but that those privileges were soon taken away. I could never get her to talk to me on the subject. Once, on maternity leave, she came back to the factory to visit. She was talking to a group of workers at break time when Carla called out to her, "What the baby name, Nigel?" referring to Tiexiera's first name. The workers—and Val herself—laughed at this bit of *picong* [teasing banter].

Of the prospect of a union and of workers' options, Martha, twenty-one, said, "It [the union] is supposed to make things better. He [Tiexiera] say if we bring in a union he closing the company. Who get hurt more, we or him? Him. We could scatter around Trinidad and get jobs. This he only source of income." It is hard to imagine an older worker with children and a male partner seriously considering that they could "scatter around Trinidad and get jobs." However, the fact that Cleo joined in the attempt to obtain union representation shows that even some older workers are willing to take such steps. But they have reason to be cautious, especially during the Recession, when many of their menfolk are being retrenched.

The Supervisors: Caught in the Middle?

In attempting to bring the workers under their control, supervisors alternate between the "tough" and the "nice" approach. Once, Ron angrily told Irene that she was not working fast enough and sent her for a week to Ruud's department, where the tasks are machine regulated, as a punishment. Irene said, "It was revenge. He get vex and he send me by Ruud 'cause Ruud don't make joke. You workin' there and you can't get up to go to the bathroom, you can't go for water, because you can't leave the machine. It was revenge." After she worked there for a week and came back to her department, she said, "Ron like to play around. He nice-nice all the time and say he on your side, but when you don't do what he want he get vex and he get nasty."

Hilda told me about her previous job and about how the supervisors were relatively lax at EUL: "At the other wuk, the boss was always looking so we could only talk when he wasn't there. There was more hustling on that job [because it was piecework]. Here I've noticed that the supervisors don't care if we talk while we work. I find here so slack. That why I does do my work without talking." Rita, with feigned disbelief, said, "What?" Hilda responded, "You find I does talk a lot?" "Yes," Rita replied.

On occasion, supervisors give the workers friendly *fatigue* (teasing and ridicule) after Tiexiera upbraided them. Once, Tiexiera went upstairs and caught Rohan and Deepak talking. Tiexiera said, "What's going on here? Are you having a meeting or what?" He ordered Deepak to go downstairs. "You," he said to Rohan, "what are you doing?" Rohan told him what he was supposed to be doing and went back to his task. Later, Ron came upstairs and joked with Rohan: "You chairing a meeting? The man tell me you chairing a meeting." All the workers within earshot laughed.

Ron explained that the supervisors are hamstrung by Tiexiera, saying that things were different in the north of England, where he lived and worked for years: "Tiexiera say 'Fire them' but if you do it, it another story. In England, you would go to the personnel department and they would investigate their record and take the necessary action. Here, it a different story. I might make the recommendation and he might say another thing and make we look foolish."

The actions of the supervisors are considered crucial by management for production and product quality. Craig is the quality-control engineer. From Northern Ireland, he is a former Labour Party councilor of a London borough. He said, "The operators are good. They are, often times, just ignorant. By that I mean they just don't know what to do. But when they're told the proper way to do things, they do a good job." He then emphasized that it was up to the supervisors to make sure that they were given the proper instruction.

The supervisors are not immune from being forced to work overtime and from Tiexiera's wrath in general. Karl said, "My ulcers are acting up. But he [Tiexiera] don't give a fuck about your health. Only 'How much production Karl?' That's all he care about."

According to Ron, "We have no union so we have no unity. And we workin' for a dictator. Five years is no time as far as the payin' off goes in this economy. . . . What he do with supervisors is apply the pressure until they quit on they own and he don't have to pay them off." Ron has been at EUL for five years, and when he speaks about "payin' off" he is referring to the mandatory severance pay that employers must provide when workers are fired or retrenched. Because of the Recession, Ron felt that it would be imprudent to do anything but go along with Tiexiera.

However, Tiexiera tends to relent after pushing them to a certain point because he feels that they are more likely to take retributive action than are the female workers. It is clear, however, that one avenue of such action—the country's Industrial Court—would be a difficult one to travel, given that they are not already members of a union.

One Friday afternoon close to the time to stop work, Tiexiera told Ron that he had to work that night supervising the night shift. Tiexiera and the usually quiet Ron then got into a heated argument, which culminated with Tiexiera telling Ron not to come back if he did not work that night, Ron saying that he was going to punch in like usual at 8 A.M. on Monday, and Tiexiera shouting, as Ron walked away, "Don't bother to take me to the Court. Because I have money and I have power."

Ron was back at work on the Monday. He and Tiexiera had struck a compromise after Tiexiera had come back and asked Ron to work overtime two nights a week. But Ron and the other supervisors are still not paid overtime rates, a fact which obviously displeased Ron: "The labor unions work to get proper conditions in this country and now we go back to the 1920s. We're working under 1920s conditions here." (It was not until the late 1930s that the labor movement in Trinidad was firmly established, beginning with the strikes and riots of 1937.)

One lunchtime, at the rum shop near the factory, Ron and Karl were complaining about conditions in the factory and about Tiexiera. Although lunch break officially ended at 12:30, it was now 12:50, and they carried on drinking beer and talking:

> Karl: I only wish things turn around for him [Tiexiera].
>
> Ron: Like it was in the oil boom—which was just five years ago. He have it good right now.
>
> Karl: He say "Recession" and we have to listen.
>
> Ron: He can get on like he does because of the Recession. 'Cause *he* has the advantage on us. But if it change, *we* will be able to tell him to fuck off.
>
> Karl: We could say "You want 200? You gettin' 25. And don't forget you have to pay me my salary." Now he say he want 200 and we say, "Yes sir."
>
> Ron: A union will have to come in here. He 'fraid unions boy. About two years ago he fire ah girl. She had written "Love to All" or some stupid shit on ah piece of paper. He said it could have something to do with unions. The wife said that too. So she was fired. . . . But the unions fucked up. They had their chance a few years ago in the oil boom. But all they cared about was money. That's all they went for. They couldn't get together. If they would ah planned . . . but they stupid. They could ah been dictatin' to business all now. . . . He is supposed to be a big man. I seen bigger than he.

At least one worker agreed with Ron's last statement. After Tiexiera buffed up the supervisors one Friday while the workers were leaving, Jeremy said, "You think he could get away with dat in de North [North America]? Somebody would ah *pass he out* [assassinate him]." And when Irene overheard Tiexiera talking rough to Ron, urging him to be more cognizant of the need for production, she said, "Imagine talking to a big man like Ron, who is older than Tiexiera, like that. He must think we're children. You just don't talk to older people like that."

If Tiexiera intends to play them off against each other, his plans sometimes succeed. There is a sign in Conrad's office, a favorite liming place for supervisors and for some of the members of his staff: "If you have *nothing* to do, don't do it *here*. N. Tiexiera."

I assumed that Tiexiera had posted the note, but when I asked Conrad about it, he told me that he had posted it. "I didn't want they [other supervisors, workers] to lime in here 'cause I get the blame if Mr. Tiexiera catch us," he said.

Karl complained to Ruud about having to work overtime. Although Ruud had his title of factory manager taken away by Tiexiera as a reprimand for falling production, he is still regarded as in charge of supervisors. To Karl's complaints, Ruud said, "It's his company. He can do what he wants." Afterward, Ron said, "Ruud is like a snake. You have to watch what you say to him because he may tell you one thing, be one way, and then go back and tell [Tiexiera]."

The other supervisors feel that Ruud does this in order to ingratiate himself with Tiexiera in an attempt to get his old title back. Shortly after this incident, Tiexiera was out on the factory floor. He started to loudly upbraid Ron, and then turned to Lisa and said, "Shut up. You are always complaining. *You* don't tell *me* how to run my factory. *I* tell *you* how it's run!"

Although Tiexiera may have hired white and East Indian male supervisors because he thought they would in some way be more protective of his assets and because he thinks social distance is essential for effective supervision, supervisors do not completely support the company. Once, when Winston and I went to a rum shop near the factory, he sat down, faced the factory, and before taking his first drink said, "I now sit here and see what I'm looking at? I'm looking at *jail*." On another occasion, Karl showed me several diplomas he had earned from technical schools in the United States for courses in repairing adding machines and cash registers. "Look, I've got all these, and I'm stuck with their shit."

The Informal Economy

With their labor—indeed, their identities—being commodified in the factory labor process, the workers respond to exploitation by and through activities outside the formal worker-owner relationship of the factory. Given their relative lack of power and economic resources, the workers are involved in a number of informal economic activities. This includes formal labor-market participation and a complex web of mutual assistance that bears economic benefits while not explicitly producing economic goods. While these activities do provide economic benefits for the workers, they also, unintentionally, serve to subsidize the formal economy and the owners of the EUL factory.

Obviously, it is in the employers' interest to effect measures that put downward pressure on wages, even though it is equally as obvious that not all intentional actions of this type have the desired results. In general, the strategies of employers are mitigated by pressure exerted by unions and by other circumstances, such as social-security payments. However, as we have seen, the EUL owners are able to restrict the workers' access to the benefits of unionization. In addition, there is good reason to believe that these very support networks and secondary occupations play a part in the impoverishment of these workers over the long-term.

The urban workers contribute to their own low wages by subsidizing the reproduction of that labor, once it has been commodified (Portes and Walton 1981: chap. 3). The level of wages paid by employers and demanded by organized workers is related to the costs of subsistence. The employers have the interest and ability to lower these reproduction costs, but could not do so if the means of consumption for urban workers were restricted to commodities obtained in the formal market. Costs for formal-market goods and services in the Third World are similar to those in metropolitan centers. Yet, labor is renumerated at a much lower rate. Therefore, the reduction in the cost of reproduction must occur through extra-market means. Typically, for the urban proletariat, these means include entering the informal sector, secondary employment, and cultivating support networks. For their part, the employers also seek access to reserve labor supplies and hire people outside of the formal market for temporary and semiskilled tasks, or what they perceive and value as semiskilled (e.g., the role of gender in the market for domestic workers). Goods and services can be bought on the informal market cheaper because the activities there usually depend on unpaid family labor or on "cheap" labor generally, as when the workers make pillows and stuffed animals. The availability of goods and services on the informal market tend to keep down the wages on the formal market, and thus increase the rate of the extraction of surplus value in the formal sector.

The kinds of resources exchanged along the lines of support networks are crucial in this process: "By facilitating subsistence production and other informal activities, networks lower costs of reproduction relative to what they would be in a fully monetized market economy. Thus, mechanisms of survival—signalling the rationality of workers under the scarcity conditions of peripheral cities—ultimately benefit capitalist firms that appropriate them in the form of lower wages" (Portes and Walton 1981:91).

Although the EUL factory workers represent only one small part of the urban proletariat in Trinidad, we can hypothesize that they are caught up in the larger processes of class formation. Alejandro Portes and John Walton (1981:105) state that cheap informal goods and services directly subsidize the middle classes, but that evidence for this is scarce. But when we think of evidence provided above, this view can be supported. Examples would be when Tiexiera hires workers to unload container trailers for "extra" pay and when the supervisor Conrad hires the workers Jeremy and Robert to help him do construction work on his house. Here, Conrad is appropriating the labor of others. This shows how it is difficult to place him directly with workers in terms of class.

The evidence presented here differs from many other studies of the informal sector in that it shows the cultural bases for such activity and demonstrates that, as in the formal sector, all individuals do not share the same burdens when it comes to informal-sector activity. Lambros Comitas (1973) has pointed out the prevalence of occupational multiplicity in the rural Caribbean, but I see this pattern as applying fairly generally to the working class. Supervisors included, many have supplementary ways of earning money: growing and selling fruits and vegetables, dressmaking, minding children, making stuffed animals, installing car stereos, and catering fetes and weddings. And in the factory's informal internal economy, affective network ties—such as those that allow access to credit—are important. In fact, the entrepreneurs would not do very well at all if they did not cultivate these relationships.

The internal economy at EUL was almost identical to the pattern Sonia Cuales writes of in her study of female workers in a factory in Curaçao (1980:81–83). It is "informal" in the sense that it operates outside the bounds of the country's legal economic framework of taxation and employee benefits, but it is not "informal" in the sense of being loosely structured and without its own set of rules.

Brian is training to be a Spiritual Baptist pastor and he sells sweet bread, *aloo* (potato) pies, and soft drinks at the factory. His godmother makes the bread, he makes the pies, and he gives her some of the profits. He is part of the fairly extensive internal informal economy. One worker quipped, "Carolina [his godmother] should be working here 'cause how much a ting Brian does sell for her here."

Myra is Brian's friendly competition. She bakes and sells bread and cake. She reports profits of around TT$40 a week. Denise roasts peanuts, bags them, and brings them to work to sell. Tia's aunt, who works in a garment factory in the same estate, often goes to Isla de Margarita, a free-port island off Venezuela, and brings back clothing that Tia sells in the factory. Trinidadians are known for their preference for foreign goods, and the items usually attract attention. However, when their quality is judged as poor, the customers charge that the aunt is merely supplying goods that are produced in the factory where she works. All entrepreneurs grant credit to other workers and usually there is a scramble to collect what is owed after pay packets are passed out on Friday.

When asked about the types of jobs they would like, almost all of the workers indicate that they would like to open up their own businesses. Cheryl said, "I quittin' just now. The work gettin' too hard and the pay not enough.

I takin' sewing lessons at night and I want to open a boutique." She then produced her sewing class notebook, which contained drawings of dresses, blouses, and other items of clothing.

The links between the workers who sell goods in the factory are important. Brian acts as Denise's "agent," accepting money for the peanuts she sells when she is not present and marking down the amount in a book. Later, he gives her the money he collected.

Even those with outside occupations rely on others for assistance in some way, and it might or might not be with a fellow EUL worker. Chuck, Jeremy, and Robert work for Conrad on the weekends, helping him build an addition to his house. Johnny, on the other hand, sold his car in order to buy a taxi. But because he does not have all the money yet, he drives his cousin's taxi on the weekends and makes between TT$170 and $200 for both days, which he splits with his cousin. On Saturdays and Sundays he works from 7 A.M. to 6:30 P.M. He said, "I does real hustle, man. It tough all over. I feel the whole world have it tough in this time we are going through. I have ah aunt in England and is real thunder for she. She want to come back. I have a next set of relatives in the States. Same for they. And I have one in Paris, she a model. It not so bad for she because she a model. And she marry a white man."

Also important are the sou-sous that exist within the factory. The sou-sou organizations in the factory are for TT$10, $20, $50 and $100 per week. The captains are the people who run the sou-sou, and in Trinidad they are almost always women. Women, it was explained to me, could be trusted with money, whereas men could not. "Men ain't interested in dat," said Carole, "women know how to deal wid money, they know how to economize."

At 4 P.M. on Fridays the workers crowd around the stores office, where the personnel manager distributes pay packets. In the past, workers have been reminded to return to work after receiving their pay, but the verbal and written reminders have always been ignored. At this time, large and small amounts of money change hands as the workers settle their accounts for food purchased during the week from Myra, Brian, and Denise. In addition, the sou-sou captains take their deposits. The sou-sou captains change occasionally. The sou-sou dissolves once all members have received their "hands" and new captain emerges to "throw" another sou-sou. The sou-sou captains are always older women, but there is no group that is excluded from membership because of department affiliation, age, ethnicity, or gender. However, the older women seem to make up the bulk of the members. Some are involved in more than one sou-sou at a time.

For workers, a sou-sou can provide them with the capital necessary for establishing a secondary occupation or a way of earning additional income. Walcott told me, "I love sewing. I bought a machine with a sou-sou. I got a thousand-something, and I bought a machine for fifteen hundred dollars. A

Brother with twenty-three stitches. It have this guy who work T&TEC. He give me cushions to fix and to make. Ten dollars for a small, fifteen dollars for a large. I must be made four hundred dollars for de Christmas. And see, dat from a sou-sou." Walcott was also taking courses in catering and cake icing at the Diego Martin Community Centre. He said, "Some of dem don't want to take courses. And they gettin' dem free from the government. They say they don't have the time. You have to make de time."

Many workers prefer to have their money in the sou-sou rather than the bank because it forces them to save. As Irene said: "Sou-sou is a good thing. Where, if you had the money in the bank, you might say 'I'll put some in next week instead,' but you never do and you end up not saving. But when others depend on you, you have to put that money in every week." One worker explained that the sou-sou is more convenient and even safer than a bank: "By the time you get paid at four-thirty and get transport and stand in line, the bank close. . . . You see, in these times banks always get rip off. And even though the government has to give the people they money back 'cause they insured, people still be scared. That's why I like sou-sou better."

It is assumed that the construction and maintenance of support networks and other "survival strategies" is imperative for the working classes in Trinidad (for Jamaica, see Bolles 1985). This is especially so in that Trinidadians have recently seen prices on basic food items shoot up rapidly. In the context of a worsening financial picture, the workers have to look for additional means of support, in order to "mek do."

They will use the resources at their disposal—such as power, influence, or the willingness to reciprocate—to acquire the goods and services they need. This kind of activity has been recognized historically by Trinidadians and it is valued by Trinidadian culture. There are two snackettes at the front of the industrial estate. Once, when there was a shortage of food items like cheese, potatoes, and onions, one snackette nevertheless had cheese and onions. I asked the owner how he obtained them, and he answered, "*connec*" (that is, "connections"), which usually refers to a favor from a well-placed friend. But accepting these favors requires a willingness to reciprocate in the future.

The economic role of the networks that the women workers maintain have been recognized by marketing experts. A 1986 report entitled "How Are the Women in Our Market Coping with the Recession[?]" concluded that women shoppers were relying more on newspaper advertisements that announce sales items, but that this was still second to the information provided by a circle of friends. It also concluded that brand-name items were becoming important when performance was key, otherwise price was the overriding consideration, with shoppers becoming more discerning and discriminating about which items to buy at which stores (Market Facts and Opinions, Ltd. 1986).

We can get a rough idea of the financial constraints faced by urban

Trinidadians in Table 30, which calculates a cost-of-living index for expatriates living in certain countries based on the price of a range of goods and services typically used by expatriate families, and expressing that cost as a percentage of a range of comparable costs of the items in London. The index does not include house prices. The spending patterns of expatriates will not always be representative of those of the wider population, perhaps especially so in the Third World. But still, the table shows that the cost of living for expatriates living in Port-of-Spain at the time of my fieldwork was near that of London, and ranked higher than New York City. And, of course, Trinidadian salaries are a fraction of what they are in those places.

In general, the workers' support networks mirror their workplace friendship ties. Older women are connected to older women. Younger women are connected to other younger women. The young men are connected to other young men, but mainly confined to their own ethnic group. The fact that fellow workers are important in the support networks of female workers takes on added significance because of the possibility that the kinds of relationships

TABLE 30
Cost of Living in Selected Cities, 1988

City	*Cost of Living Index*	*Inflation (%)*	*Exchange Rate (£1)*
Tokyo	163.9	1.2	234.25
Oslo	128.6	7.0	11.78
Helsinki	123.6	4.1	7.52
Zurich	123.4	1.7	2.58
Tripoli	115.8	9.0	0.52
Baghdad	110.1	13.0	0.58
Amsterdam	100.8	0.5	3.51
London	100.0	3.3	1.00
Madrid	96.6	4.3	208.40
Nassau	93.5	6.3	1.89
Los Angeles	92.3	3.9	1.89
Port-of-Spain	91.0	12.1	6.77
New York	90.6	3.9	1.89
Toronto	85.7	4.0	2.33
Sydney	83.8	7.1	2.54
Jakarta	80.9	14.5	3,121.41
Lisbon	79.7	8.9	255.70
Manila	72.8	5.0	39.10
Colombo (Sri Lanka)	70.1	10.2	59.00
Kingston (Jamaica)	69.6	7.5	10.13
La Paz (Bolivia)	66.0	11.0	4.23
Mbabana (Swaziland)	63.0	13.3	3.99

SOURCE: Compiled from the *Financial Times*, August 3, 1988, p. 8.
NOTE: Based on prices in London, April 1988.

developed at work are essential not only for economic survival, but emotional health as well. The data also show the importance of class, as there are very few cross-class support relationships among the workers.

Ethnicity, Class, Gender, and Support Networks

It has been said that many women in the Third World work "triple shifts," that is, formal wage employment, household duties, and informal-sector employment (Ward 1990). Given the importance of support networks, it seems possible to conceive of women working a "fourth shift" (Yelvington 1991c). I do not want to give the impression that support networks are enjoyed only by women and that men are totally cut off from social support. However, if male support networks are characterized as "sociable," whereas female support networks are characterized as intimate (cf. Vaux 1985), we can probably assume, given the variables of ethnicity and class, that the content of male relationships and the content of male networks will be different from the content of female relationships and networks.

I would like to examine the apparent differing relationships between men and women. Goods and services are exchanged across ethnic lines much more among the women than among the men. Many of the factory workers feel that women have more and better interethnic relationships with women than men have with men of other ethnic groups. Winston said, "There's some instinct in women" that makes them get along with other ethnic groups. Denise, who is black, said: "I *wouldn't like to think so*, but it have some who move racial in the factory. You see, Indians started this racial thing in Trinidad. They have something naturally racial in them. Negroes, or black people as we say now, try to get on—they ain't racial—but when the Indians and they start, Negroes gonna get that way too."

When I questioned Denise about whether she thought women of different groups get along better than men, she said, "You see a Indian man will work-work while the Negro man will sit down and say 'Nah, I takin' it easy now.' So this start the trouble. But with women, we don't see so much a difference. . . . I think we help each other out more." She seems to suggest that economic conditions influence the relationships between ethnic groups, and that an essential quality of masculinity is competition for economic resources. Obviously, women compete as well, with each other and with men, but this evidence suggests that there exists a different quality to interethnic female relationships.

Carla told me how she once had her taxi fare paid by a black woman when Carla had nothing less than a $20 bill and the taxi driver did not want to make change. "This Negro lady paid my fare [$2] and said 'That's all right darliing.' I was surprised . . . because it don't happen down here [in the suburban areas, as opposed to the country] and because she was a Negro."

Even when people are expressing racist views, it seems that they hold that the women of the opposing group are somewhat different than the men. A sixty-two-year-old black electrician, the cousin of the factory worker Daisy, said: "Wherever you go in the world that have East Indians, they take their racial thing with them. If only East Indian men would be more cooperative . . . they women are different, they are more cooperative. . . . I don't know what it is the world have against the Negroes."

On one hand, the situation with the males can be related to the social construction of masculinity, which emphasizes a certain independence and even a competitive ethic. On the other hand, the evidence of females forming multiethnic support networks and peer groups is counterintuitive because of the discourse that holds that women are the receptacles and embodiment of a particular group's values. Therefore, we would expect the ethnic boundary to be patrolled by women with greater vigilance. However, a close reading of some literary and anthropological works on Trinidad reveals evidence to support my findings. This seems another area where the novelist's art can lend some insight.

An example from Trinidadian fiction is Samuel Selvon's classic *A Brighter Sun* (1979 [1952]).Tiger and Urmilla are a young East Indian couple who live in humble surroundings in 1940s Barataria next to Rita and Joe, a slightly older Creole couple. In the following scene. Tiger has invited two white American soldiers he works with home for dinner and orders Urmilla to spare no expense in preparing the food and drinks to impress the guests. Urmilla looks to Rita for assistance:

> Urmilla hardly slept for thinking of what she was going to do. She got up determined and went to Rita.
> "Girl, I in big trouble. Big, big trouble. If you know what Tiger go and do! He go and invite two Americans he does work with to come for Indian food tonight!"
> "Is wat happen to him at all? He crack? He is ah damn fool in truth. He bringing wite people to eat in dat hut? Tiger must be really going out of he head, yes. Gul, yuh making joke!"
> "Man, Rita, I tell you is true! My head hot! I don't know what to do."
> "Well, yes," Rita mused, "Ah did know he chupid, but not so chupid! Well, all you have to do is yuh best, gul."
> "Rita, you have to help me, girl."
> "But sure, man. What yuh want me to do?"
> "You have to lend me plenty thing. I want glass. Plate, Cup. Spoon. Knife. Fork. Tablecloth—"
> "Take ease, keep cool! Between de two ah we we go fix up everyting good. Don't look so frighten. Why de hell yuh fraid Tiger so? Allyuh Indian people have some funny ways, *oui*."
> "Girl, me and Tiger not like you and Joe. It different with we. If Tiger not pleased this evening, I sure he go beat me and kick me up. You don't know

> how funny he is these days. Last night he using one set of big words, I can't understand him at all."
> "Well, look, Ah don't like how yuh getting so upset dese days, especially as de baby coming. You don't worry bout nutting, Ah go help yuh to do everyting."
> On Rita's dumbwaiter were cutlery and glasses and a lot of table necessities which she only used at Christmas time. She cast a glance at them.
> "Ah don't know why Ah doing dis," she grumbled. "Tiger is ah damn fool, and Joe tell me to keep from interfering in allyuh business. Allyuh not even creole like we. It look like if Ah always doing something for you all. Ah always helping allyuh out ah something."
> Urmilla didn't know what to say.
>
> Rita said, "Well, don't stand up dere like ah statue! Yuh ain't have nutting else to do?"
> "I have to go and buy clothes for me and Chandra."
> "Well, wat de hell yuh waiting for? Gone nar, yuh know how de morning does fly. By de time yuh come back Ah have everyting clean and wash, ready for yuh."
> "I don't know what to tell you—"
> "Gone nar! Make haste and come back!" (pp. 161–62)

Evidence to support my arguments is also found in the ethnographic record. In his anthropological study of Lacotan village in south Trinidad, John O. Stewart discusses the "informal" economic exchanges—that is, those not involving cash—across households, reporting that exchanges are "easier" among members of the same ethnic group and almost nonexistent between blacks and East Indians (1973:157–65). However, in the midst of this discussion, he describes a black woman, Florence, who reacts negatively to the avaricious East Indian sterotype as seen in her male neighbor. Nevertheless, her most intimate drinking partners are two East Indian women who, she says, would be there with assistance at any time when needed. Stewart, though, gives no explanation for this.

The workers stress that in order to succeed in Trinidad one must have and use connections. But the workers also stress that one must maintain one's independence. Women can and do form multiethnic support networks because notions of femininity—nurturing, caring—paradoxically do not conflict with such activity. But perhaps more important, given their economic position and familial responsibility, they need to utilize and mobilize a range of goods, services, and other resources, and this may be done more effectively if such activity is not confined to those of one ethnic group. Given their usually stronger economic and social position, men may not form cooperative networks because they have less of a need to.

Further, this might make more sense when seen in the light of gender ideology. Masculinity—which "reputation" sets out to construct—emphasizes competition, aloofness, and independence. As Victor Seidler writes, "It is the nature of this displacement from emotional lives and needs for dependency which has so deeply formed masculine sexuality. Often it is closeness and intimacy which are feared; men experience any compromise of their independence, defined as self-sufficiency, as a threat to their very sense of male identity. Femininity, on the other hand, emphasizes the nurturing, caring and sharing that would lend itself to cross-ethnic cooperation. Although women may be imbued by men with exemplifying the 'group's' values, and although women may approvingly recapitulate conflictatory ethnic discourse, they may also simultaneously practice cooperation on another level" (1987:97–98).[2]

Theorizing Class in Trinidad

The ethnography suggests that a conventional Marxist approach to class is inadequate, but that an approach that emphasizes the "cultural" aspects of class along with the economic ones, and the intersections between them, is more useful. In the case of Trinidadian society generally and the EUL factory particularly, what I have called embodied social capital, in its articulation with other forms of capital, (i.e., economic, cultural, social, and symbolic, as defined in Chapter 1), plays a central role in the processes of class formation. However, in taking a "practice approach," we cannot stop with an identification of the intersecting forms of an individual's or a group's capital. Using the "lens" of closure, we must look at the struggles over the convertability of capital (e.g., social into economic) and at the efforts to legitimize various configurations of capital.

It is best to see class practice in the factory as the interplay between individuals employing differing modes of closure. However, those who are able to exercise exclusionary activities are in a better position to dictate the outcome of any class conflict. Further, the interplay in the factory has to be seen within the context of country's economic situation, both its effects on the national population and as a result of Trinidad's insection into the world economy.

What the ethnographic description of this chapter describes, then, are examples of closure in action. Beginning from the recruitment patterns of the factory workers discussed earlier, the EUL owners affect various strategies to restrict the workers' access to the rewards of the organization and to trade-union membership, which is the workers' lawful right in Trinidad. On the other hand, the workers employ various strategies of usurpation within the narrow constraints within which they operate. The supervisors are caught in the middle, as it were, excluded by the owners, while employing exclusionary practices against the workers. While there are perhaps three basic modes of closure in the factory—those employed by the owners, the managers, and the workers—this does not mean that these modes of closure correspond ipso facto to three distinct classes. These closure practices are complex ensembles of behavior and consciousness that relate to and comprise the culture of class in Trinidad. Parkin's model cannot wholly account for their practices and therefore should be modified. In modifying Marx and Parkin, the theory I set out here helps us envisage the complex and intersecting cultural processes known as class.

To reiterate, Murphy has carefully scrutinized Parkin's closure theory and suggested important alterations, which seem to be supported by the ethnographic evidence here. Parkin suggests that there are two opposing modes of closure, usurpation (closure in a upward direction) and exclusion (closure in a downward direction). Parkin sees these two modes as polar opposites. Murphy, however, argues that usurpation should not be seen as the opposite of exclusion, but rather as a subtype of it (1986:30–32). This is because excluded groups, in reacting to pressure from above, use downward exclusion against even less powerful groups as an indirect mode of usurpation. This has affinities with Parkin's concept of dual closure, with the difference being that dual closure occurs when an excluded group reacts to downward pressure by excluding even less powerful groups without taking away any advantages of the more powerful group. Indirect usurpation occurs when the advantages of a higher group are curtailed by means of the exclusion of lower groups.

The EUL factory owner, Tiexiera, continually threatens to close the factory down, a practice which, in Parkin's sense, is exclusionary. The Pounder Report noted this propensity in regard to garment manufacturers:

> The Commission believes that garment manufacturers can, if they wish, frustrate the operation of union agreements, as well as they entry of unions into their factory. This is so, we think, because of the fact that the majority of garment factories are family-owned, and in the extreme situation the owners can close down their factories. The Commission is informed that there have been a few instances where factories have been closed down and re-opened subsequently, because of what appeared to be resistance to the Union which represented the workers in those factories. The Commission holds the view that measures ought to be taken to protect the worker from arbitrary closure of a factory by its management. (Trinidad and Tobago 1979:79)

The case of the supervisors, with their incongruent amounts of capital (symbolic versus economic, for example), seems to offer an example of indirect usurpation, even if the activities that limit some of Tiexiera's advantages are largely unintended. On one hand, the supervisors seek to exclude the workers: As Winston said, "We can't have they think they are like us." On the other hand, failure in preventing the workers from skylarking limits production and cuts into Tiexiera's profits, even though this is not the stated aim of the supervisors.

The workers seem to demonstrate dual closure. There are significant differences among female workers on the basis of age and domestic responsibilities. Older workers are quick to criticize the younger workers for their behavior in the factory, which they attribute to their lack of household responsibilities. In some cases this is well-founded. However, this closure is based on symbolic capital and status. The older workers do not have the power to restrict access to the factory's rewards and opportunity.

The job means different things for different workers. The older women must support not only themselves but their children on their factory earnings. Although many of the younger workers also have children, most live at home in their mother's household. There, in many cases, they are at least partially supported by their mother's income and any additional wage earners in the home. This arrangement cushions the economic blows. Yet the women are well aware of their lack of options. Further, the support networks that all the workers cultivate are embedded in their relations with fellow workers. While ensuring familial survival strategies, in most cases, the presence of these networks may further tie the workers to the EUL factory. To leave EUL would be to leave important sources of emotional and material support.

Maureen said the reason why women were employed at EUL rather than men was that "Men wouldn't take the pay we get here. Women take it 'cause it's all they can get." She said she knows male construction workers who are jobless who "would rather look after they garden" until they get a construction job than work at EUL. This is because they see the work and pay as not befitting a man. And Carla said, "I tell you why its only women that work here. The money. You wouldn't get no men—with families to support—workin' here." Martha added, "No one would work here if they had to support a family. That's why they only employ teenagers."

Carla said that the rough treatment meted out by Tiexiera was not because of racial antipathy but simply because he could get away with it: "Tiexiera not racial. He know he have the advantage on the girls because they don't have a union. He can tell they to work late because we have no one to speak for us. It have older workers than me sitting back and taking what they get. So we have no union. If someone stand up to him he say, 'If you don't like it, leave.' "

There is, then, an emergent working-class consciousness as conventionally defined among the workers. Based on her studies of working-class women in Puerto Rico, Helen I. Safa argues that labor-force participation is not a sufficient condition for the development of class consciousness among women because they suffer from sexual as well as class exploitation. She defines class consciousness "as a cumulative process by which women, (1) recognize that they are exploited and oppressed, (2) recognize the source of their exploitation and oppression, and (3) are willing and able to organize and mobilize in their own class interests" (1975:379).

Class consciousness among workers in the EUL factory is manifested in discourse. For example, Tiexiera's nickname (behind his back, of course) is "Bourgs," short for "Bourgeois." When Tiexiera comes out onto the floor, workers may warn each other with "Look now, the Bourgs comin'." But the workers are not at all clear about the significance of the nickname. Martha said, "I heard Ben call he that, but I don't know what it means." When I asked Ben about this, he said that other workers were calling Tiexiera "Bourgs" before he started working there three years before my fieldwork.

There are obstacles to any collective action on the part of the workers in response to the exercise of authority. Besides the upstairs-downstairs division, there are workers who feel that they have to offer their labor, no matter what the terms, because of their household situation. In addition, and related to this, one has also to consider the aspects of age, authority, "respectability," and even ability. Cleo said, "They using the excuse that work tough to get to push down the wages. He sendin' people home right and left. And who do he get to work and for how long? In this case cheap becomes dear. Dem new workers don't have the experience and don't know how to look for the little extra things that we do."

It could be that the "respect" they feel they deserve and receive in the "outside" world is mitigated by the factory situation where, for example, it is possible that a twenty-one-year-old worker who has been working for four years would earn more than a forty-year-old worker who has been an EUL employee for only two. As Martha, who is twenty-one, said, "I don't want to work here for long. There are people who work here nine years and ting. I been workin' here a year and I get treated the same way."

To give their claims legitimacy, workers apparently must have had certain life experiences, especially bearing children, as indicated by Val's successful rebuff of Carla (see Chapter 1). Those without "responsibilities" could not possibly know what it is to be in a position of being forced to meet familial obligations. As a result of all this, much of the resistance seems to take insidious and less dramatic forms.

There exists, then, a classic Catch-22 situation regarding trade-union recognition at EUL. On one hand, younger workers, who want a union, are not taken seriously by the older female workers, because the younger ones, in general, do not have the status associated with being a mother and a wife. "If I went to talk to they, think they take me on? I is just come here. They don't respect me," said Martha. On the other hand, the older workers—those with "responsibilities"—are apparently reluctant to agitate for a union in the factory, because they feel they have much more to lose if Tiexiera dismisses those involved in agitation. He has shown himself capable of such action in the past. However, as the unionization attempt shows, the older workers will struggle to get union recognition—under certain conditions. One of those conditions, however, appears to be that their authority not be challenged by younger females.

Moreover, this situation must be related to the wider social structure and the failures of the unions themselves. As Walcott, thirty-six, said, "I ain't lucky wid a union. Dey ain't for de worker. The bosses take they out to lunch and bribe them. I seen it happen at Kirpalani's. Tiexiera can't do me nothin'. As you see, he never say nothin' to me 'cause I always doin' my work. . . . Tiexiera may be a bit racial, but he don't say nothin' to me."

By saying that Tiexiera gets "racial" when he sees workers slacking off, Walcott seems to be implying that she understands Tiexiera to use his "racialism" to get workers to work, that the vehemence with which he upbraids the workers is based on racist attitudes. This relates to the ethnic closure that Tiexiera and the workers practice. As discussed in previous chapters, ethnicity (and gender) figure prominently in Tiexiera's recruitment practices, white and East Indian male supervisors are chosen because they are thought to uphold the aims of the organization (Chapter 3). Furthermore, the workers hold ethnic stereotypes relating to the supposed economic performance and capabilities of different ethnic groups (Chapter 4). This orientation is important in understanding the problems faced by those who would attempt to unite black and East Indian workers in the wider society. The historical practice by the powerful groups of playing one group off against the other can partially explain the disunity between blacks and East Indians as workers.

The ethnic stereotypes regarding economic performance are a form of symbolic closure that helps to restrict access to goods in the wider society. However, at EUL, the line workers never make direct reference to the ethnicity of fellow workers when considering the advantages and disadvantages of trying to bring in a union. This is because they do not have the power to restrict access to the factory's goods by anything more than symbolic ethnic closure as they are not employed in positions of power or authority. Further, both East Indian and black workers make statements for and against the union. When Val rebuffed Carla for trying to bring in a union, she did so on the basis of Carla not being old enough to have the experience and "responsibilities" of motherhood. Val could have made explicit reference to ethnicity, but she did not. But, as the evidence in Chapter 4 suggests, the line workers engage in ethnic "closure" against one another, especially on a more symbolic level.

Tiexiera contravenes the union recognition law and threatens to close the factory if a union is brought in, but he does not come under official scrutiny because he is a powerful man in Trinidad. One reason is that EUL is one of the few factories that export and therefore earn foreign exchange (although it is not at all clear how much of this foreign exchange is used in the business and how much is put to personal use), and it is in the government's interest to keep the company happy and operating. So it is not surprising that EUL receives inducements other than the (fairly usual) extension of import tax holidays and import licenses by the IDC. In the face of competition in 1986, EUL was able to get the exclusive license to import the necessary parts in order to begin the production of a new item, and an addition to the factory was being built to put this item into production.

And finally, it appears that Tiexiera's position of privilege was further solidified with the coming to power of the NAR. He was a vocal supporter of middle-class Alliance for National Reconstruction in the 1981 elections and a staunch—if less visible—supporter of the NAR during the 1986 campaign. Further, he was personally close to several officials in the party. One can expect that Trinidad's traditional avenues of patronage operated in this case.

The power that the Tiexieras wield, however, does not fully account for the workers' practices. There is reason to believe that the face-to-face activities of the male supervisors, male line workers, and the female line workers may preclude any such "identification" as workers. As discussed in Chapter 5, the supervisors and the male workers engage in flirting relationships with the workers, which may serve to alienate the female workers and further entrench sociocultural divisions among them.

In all, I believe the historical and ethnographic evidence supports my assertions for an approach to class that is cultural, and that emphasizes the intersection of "subjective" and "objective" criteria not only in the process of exploitation but in the larger processes of class formation, class practice, and class conflict. Further, the theory of class that I am advocating also considers the role of activities, stances, ideologies, and practices that constitute power—a process in which the workers' forms of capital are utilized in their strategies of resistance (and hopefully ascendance). Taking a cue from Abu-Lughod and analyzing resistance as an index of the relationships of power, I want to call on the work of Michel de Certeau (1984) to propose a way of conceptualizing resistance that does not "romanticize" it but instead captures the vagaries of grossly unequal power relationships.

To capture both the ambiguities and devastating terror of colonial power, at least two other scholars of the Caribbean, the literary critic Richard D. E. Burton (1993a, 1993b) and the historical sociologist O. Nigel Bolland (1992), have utilized the work of de Certeau. To conceive of how the weak are able to resist the strong by using the forms foisted upon them, de Certeau differentiates between a "strategy" and a "tactic," where

> a *strategy* [is] the calculation (or manipulation) of power relationships that becomes possible as soon as a subject with will and power . . . can be isolated. It postulates a *place* that can be determined as its *own* and serve as the base from which relations with an *exteriority* composed of targets or threats . . . can be managed. As in management, every "strategic" rationalization seeks first of

> all to distinguish its "own" place, that is, the place of its own power and will, from an "environment." . . . A *tactic* is a calculated action determined by the absence of a proper locus. No delimitation of an exteriority, then, provides it with the condition necessary for autonomy. The space of a tactic is the space of the other. This it must play on and with a terrain imposed on it and organized by the law of a foreign power. It does not have the means to *keep to itself*, at a distance, in a position of withdrawal, foresight, and self-collection. . . . In short, a tactic is an art of the weak. (1984:35–37).[3]

This conceptualization touches on the intricacies revealed in the ethnography. When the young women in the factory resist the aggressive sexuality of the male supervisors, for instance, they do so by making use of their (imposed) identities as sexual objects. When black workers resist the (imposed) industrial regime in the factory by apparently not working hard and by organized "go-slows," they make use of dominant cultural images of blacks as poor workers. In these cases, a tactic is all that could be managed on the part of the workers. Even the attempt at unionization, which, it could be argued, would have created "space" for the workers and altered the balance of power somewhat, was a tactic in that the workers were operating on "a terrain imposed . . . and organized by the law of a foreign power."

Yet, to go beyond de Certeau, the function of tactics such as these may ultimately be to further the interests of the powerful groups. This is because the very operation of these tactics—predicated as they often are on the subordinate groups assuming negative cultural depictions—serves to reinforce subordination in a cultural sense. In the short-term, tactics do indeed yield results for the "tacticians." However, given the nature of the overarching power relationships, the utilization of these tactics provide a basis of further attempts to subordinate the subordinate in the long run. This is the operation of a historical dialectic.

When a slave assumed the "Quashie" personality and feigned ignorance in the presence of his master, this tactic of resistance may have achieved the slave's short-term ends, but it did so at a cost. The "Quashie" personality became a focus for white fear and loathing and became a justification for continued subordination. When the older women in the factory preclude the sexual advances of male supervisors and workers they do so by erecting an aura of "respectability." However, "respectability" in this sense entails an emphasis on traditional female roles and values and ensures not only the continuation of patriarchal gender relations. It also ensures a kind of self-censorship that ultimately pays dividends for the factory owners. "Respectable" women, with children to care for, do not want to take the chance of being fired and thus not being able to care for their children properly and losing their "respectability." In this light, the dakwah movement among women factory workers in Malaysia described by Ong, which emphasizes a rather passive female identity, and the subordinate role of women in the central narrative of masculine work identity in the Japanese factory described by Kondo can be characterized as tactics of resistance that, ultimately, contribute to the further subordination of these groups as well.

Analyzing resistance in the factory and the role it plays in class practice is crucial for understanding how class works in general. Analyzing resistance in situations of hegemonic power in terms of tactics has, in my view, more general applications as well. If class is conceptualized as intersecting forms of capital (symbolic, social, cultural, and economic) and closure is conceived as playing the central role in the struggles over the convertability of capital, then resistance-as-tactic becomes one main way for the relatively powerless to both block the strategies of capital conversion on the part of dominant groups and to convert and expand their own capital. Even if this process of making a virtue out of necessity tends in most cases to further subordinate the disempowered, this dialectical process is empirically documentable and in no way is a foregone conclusion.

CONCLUSION

The whole of anything is never told: you can only take what groups together.
—Henry James

THIS HISTORICAL and ethnographic study of the workplace raises a number of theoretical issues relating to contemporary anthropology's focus on identities—be they related to ethnicity, gender, nationalism, place, or religion—and the relationship of identities to arrangements of power. In his book *Big Structures, Large Processes, Huge Comparisons*, Charles Tilly seeks to dismiss the "pernicious postulates" of social theory—one being that mental events cause social behavior. He argues against seeing the mind as an entity that internalizes society's teachings and then directs behavior, and against seeing mental events as the prime ties of individuals to societies. He urges "Rather than individual orientations, social ties. Rather than social atoms, social networks. . . . What we normally experience as sameness ultimately depends on the reckoning of relationships. Al remains Al the son of Bill, the lover of Cathy, the father of Dorothy, the employer of Ed." This is true because the obverse is true: "The ability to simulate or reconstruct such relationships, in fact, allows imposture: By falsely claiming the same set of relationships, one organism can assume the identity of another" (1984:27).

Yet, it is not enough to say that these identities have a form and structure, as well as a logic, that pertains to the form and structure of social relationships. People are socially defined in relation to their ethnic, class, and gender identities. By "defined" I mean not only through the behavior of members of their society and their "inner" self-definition, but in structural ways as well. Individual social relationships are structurally ordered but not structurally determined. Social relationships are thus hierarchically ordered, as are identities. The "stuff" of one's social identity depends on the nature of those relationships. We are, then, socially "positioned" according to certain criteria, with "positioning" involving what Giddens, in another connection, has described as "the specification of a definite 'identity' within a network of social relations, that identity, however, being a 'category' to which a particular range of normative sanctions is relevant" (1984:83).

Social identities will tend to be enduring because the effects of initial enculturation on personality and the social relations that they are predicated upon will remain enduring as long as the "practice" that makes them so continues to be the precondition for their very existence and structure. But stating that social relationships are structured and enduring does not commit us to the position of orthodox reproduction theory (e.g., Bourdieu 1977; Giddens 1984). The practice theory of social identity advanced in this book holds that a person is born into a society that precedes them, and a system of social identities, of which ethnicity, class, and gender are particularly salient because they enable and restrict access to power and privilege. There is a "dual boundary" of social identity, where the inner portion of the boundary has to do with conceptions of the self, by the self, and the outer portion is the identity that is ascribed by the cultural setting, by others. This boundary is characterized by tension and even violence, and by a constant struggle both to circumscribe and define and to change these definitions or keep them as they are, depending on the position of power in a particular circumstance.[1]

When I say that the social identity of an individual reflects his or her attempts to fit into the collective representations of their society, I am implying that social identity depends on the manipulation of social relationships. In any given society, subordinate gender identity in a particular situation (usually female) may try to redefine its relations and thus its identity. In any given society, an ethnic group that is dominant in certain situations may work very hard to maintain the status quo in its identity by seeking to ensure that its internal and external social relations remain the same. Social identities can be precarious and often are subject to debate and wrangling. They therefore must be reinvented, a process that works best when it is legitimated by the "invention of tradition" (cf. Hobsbawm and Ranger 1983; Sollors 1989). This kind of historical and cultural dynamic cannot be fully accounted for by the general models provided by such thinkers as Bourdieu and Giddens.

The notion that power is somehow involved in the construction, consecration, and contestation of identities offers up further problems. What is the relationship between power and culture? To what extent do dominant material relationships completely determine power? To what extent do dominant material relationships make dominant ideological relationships?

Seeking to answer these and similar questions, anthropologists have turned to literary critics (e.g., Williams 1977) and philosophers (e.g., Gramsci 1971) for the concept of hegemony.[2] Yet while anthropologists have articulately elucidated what is meant by hegemony, or the ways in which we intend to use or apply the concept, we have in general been unwilling or unable to explain hegemony and the bases upon which hegemonic relationships exist. In this book, I have endeavored to show that the concept of hegemony is useful because it defines a state of dominant cultural and material power arrangements. At the same time I have endeavored to explain that the means by which an individual or a group establishes the ability to depict and subject—and resist such depictions and subjections—is a complexity derived function of their ability to control the production process.

The relative ability to control the production process determines, though not in a straightforward way, relations of power, which I have defined as a determined causal property. It also provides resources, entities that are hierarchically distributed and become the media through which power is exercised. In the EUL factory, power is relational in that the exercise of power by an individual depends on the exercise of power by others. Power is structural in the sense that power flows through hierarchical, relatively enduring structures that stand partially independent of everyday social activity. Power is the effects of people occupying positions in the social structure. In the factory, power is also definitional in that it is involved in determining who the workers, managers, and owners are, what they will produce, and when they will produce it. Power is historical, and it is also cultural. That is, power in the factory receives its particular configuration from the particularities of the situation, and it is experienced and felt through real individuals in the real world and not in some abstract sense.

Ethnicity, Class, and Gender

Not long ago there was a backlash against what was defined as white, Western, middle-class feminism. This backlash was based on the charge that it did not incorporate the experiences nor perspectives of "women of color" into its theorization and advocacy. Feminist scholars are now striving to create a richer view of women by formulating theories that take ethnicity and class as well as gender into account. Yet, new problems arise with a view that constructs and privileges women's supposed common biologically based experiences while trying to reconcile this view with a realization of the influence of ethnicity, class, and other variables. As Patricia Zavella observes, "On the one hand, proponents wish to recognize women's many voices, that women from diverse class, ethnic, or racial groups have very different perspectives on so-called universal feminine experiences. On the other hand, simply recognizing the richness of diversity leads to an atheoretical pluralism." She goes on to suggest:

> We need to research women's and men's lives in ways that identify the sources of diversity without resorting to the mechanistic conclusion that class, race, or gender alone gives rise to difference. . . . I suggest we must begin our analysis with the historically specific structural conditions constraining women's experiences. We can then link these conditions to the varieties of ways in which women respond to and construct cultural representations of their experiences. This suggestion helps us to avoid the problematic assumption of much recent feminist scholarship: beginning with historical material conditions rather than with "experience" embeds "women's diversity" as a theoretical a priori and

> frees us from the artificial task of deriving diversity from prior commonality. (1991:313)

However, a number of earlier, pioneering studies that sought to theorize the relationships between ethnicity, class, and gender were hampered precisely by not adopting the perspective offered by Zavella. There have been three tendencies among these theorists, which in my view, are flawed. The first approach I call *additive*. In this approach, ethnicity, class, and gender are heaped upon each other and are seen to affect social life in successive waves. For example, while pointing to Caribbean women's oppression in a searching, comparative article, Gloria I. Joseph writes: "Among the Caribbean women there is a recognizable force growing in awareness of consciousness. These Caribbean women know that they are grossly exploited because of their sex. However, their job categories are inextricably bound to their belonging to the exploited, poor, oppressed, working class. Being nonwhite is practically endemic to being exploited in the Caribbean, and so race and class are tightly woven. Their sexual identification adds the final strike" (1980:158–59).

According to Joseph, Caribbean women are exploited because of their "sex." They are (tautologically) in working-class job categories because of they belong to the "exploited poor, oppressed, working class." And "being nonwhite is practically endemic to being exploited," but we are not sure just how. It is almost as if Joseph is explicitly saying Caribbean women are exploited by reference to their "sex," then by reference to their "class," and then by reference to their "race." But there is no attempt to theorize the interconnections between these phenomena. And this is especially important when we are discussing exploitation, which by definition entails an economic component (even if the exploitation occurs by market as well as nonmarket means, as in the EUL factory).

Closely related to this approach is one that considers ethnicity, class, and gender as *separate but coequal* variables. This approach acknowledges that each of these phenomena affect the other. But their relations are conceived of as being external. Ethnicity is seen to exist separate from class, which in turn is separate from gender (gender, of course, is also distinct from ethnicity in this view). Ethnicity, class, and gender are seen to be socially and culturally constructed, but each on its own terms. Further, each phenomenon is given equal weight in determining the outcome of social action. So we are left in an "ethnicity affects class, which affects gender, which affects ethnicity, and so on" theoretical quagmire.

In their important book *Race, Gender, and Work: A Multicultural Economic History of Women in the United States*, economists Teresa L. Amott and Julie A. Matthaei seem to grasp the issue correctly:

> Race-ethnicity, gender, and class are interconnected, interdetermining historical processes, rather than separate systems. This is true in two senses. . . .

> First, it is often difficult to determine whether an economic practice constitutes class, race, or gender oppression: for example, slavery in the U.S. South was at the same time a system of class oppression (of slaves by owners) and of racial-ethnic oppression (of Africans by Europeans). Second, a person does not experience these different processes of domination and subordination independently of one another; in philosopher Elizabeth Spelman's metaphor, gender, race-ethnicity, and class are not separate "pop-beads" on a necklace of identity. Hence, there is no generic gender oppressions which is experienced by all women regardless of their race-ethnicity or class. (1991:13)

Elsewhere, however, they reveal that they are relying on a conceptual framework that merely identifies separate but coequal variables. Existing separately of each other, there is no sense of the phenomena combining to form a new kind of identity or a new form of domination. They remain related, but we are not sure just how. For example: "The essentially economic nature of real racial-ethnic oppression in the United States makes it difficult to isolate whether peoples of color were subordinated in the emerging U.S. economy because of race-ethnicity *or* their economic class. . . . Race-ethnicity and class intertwined in the patterns of displacement from land, genocide, forced labor, and recruitment from the seventeenth through the twentieth centuries. While it is impossible, in our minds, to determine which came first in these instances—race-ethnicity or class—it is clear that they were intertwined and inseparable" (1991:19, emphasis added).

The third flawed approach is one that seeks to identify a *basic* phenomenon that ultimately determines the other two. This approach is itself divided into two perspectives, both of which are sometimes adopted by the same researcher. One perspective is to hold, for heuristic purposes, one phenomena constant and use it as a "lens" to identify and describe one or both of the others. For example, André Béteille uses gender to compare caste and race (1990; see also Currie 1992), and Pratiba Parmar, who has studied ethnic minority and immigrant women in Britain, writes that "Women are defined differently according to their 'race' " (1982:258). The other perspective is to theorize that one or more phenomena are actually more salient than the other or others in determining social action. In this approach, there is no consensus as to which is ultimately determining. Some theorists argue that two are determining (though usually not specifying their interrelationship) at the expense of another one. For example, Rosina Wiltshire-Brodber argues that "race and class . . . have traditionally ordered Caribbean dominance systems and have therefore superseded gender as the principle organizing forces for resistance and change" (1988:142).

For most theorists, however, one of these phenomena determines in the last instance the nature of the other two: Either ethnicity, class, or gender is more efficacious and enduring. For example, in her fine, detailed social history of women workers in Durham, North Carolina, Dolores E. Janiewski concludes, "Rather than accepting racial and sexual hierarchies as natural or God-ordained, women and men must recognize them as flawed social conditions that can be changed." However, on the same page she states that her history shows that "Black and white women—'sisters under their skins'—never fully realized their kinship in a society where skin color blinded them to their common interests" (1985:178), implying that their real, basic common interests were of gender (after all, they are *really* sisters) and that skin color (and presumably class) was thus epiphenomenal.

Similarly, in her classic study *Marriage, Class, and Colour in Nineteenth-Century Cuba*, Verena Martínez-Alier (now Stolcke) analyzes the complex interplay of ethnicity, class, and gender with extraordinary skill. Yet, she argues that ethnicity and gender are merely symbols of an individual's class position: "in nineteenth-century Cuba it was not physical appearance as such that caused prejudice and discrimination, but what physical appearance stood for, i.e. and individual's occupational role in an economic system based on the exploitation of one group by another." Cuba was not unique in this sense: "In the United States, for example, the 'visibility' of racial distinctions—a legacy from slavery—endows race with a degree of autonomy as a source of discrimination that obscures class as its ultimate root," and the ethnically homogeneous Mediterranean peasant communities and multiracial nineteenth-century Cuba share features that show "that ultimately race relations are class relations" (1989 [1974]: 5, xviii, 124).

Strategies of ethnic discrimination and sexual exploitation become integral in the class struggle: "Hence, if social position is seen as expressing genetic endowment, then for those claiming social preeminence, class endogamy and the use of women's reproductive capacity in the interest of social purity continue to be crucial to ensure this preeminence" (1989 [1974]: xviii). Ethnic and gender identities, then, serve to legitimate and naturalize a social order based on (prior, more powerful) class inequalities. As she writes elsewhere,

> Sex no less than 'race' differences have been and continue to be ideologically marked as socially significant biological 'facts' in class society as a way of naturalizing and thereby perpetuating class and, in a related way, gender inequality. In other words, social and gender inequalities are construed and legitimized by rooting them in the assumed biological 'facts' of race and sex differences. The decisive characteristic of class society, as it were, its ideological 'underpinning', in this respect is a widespread tendency to naturalize social inequality. The naturalization of social inequality constitutes, in effect, a fundamental ideological procedure in class society to overcome the contradictions inherent in it. (Stolcke 1993:30)

I am sympathetic to this approach because it represents an attempt to theorize the precise ways in which one phenomenon is affected by and determined by the others. However, Deborah Posel's criticism of the "either-or" approach to ethnicity and class in South African historiography is fitting here. She writes,

> "Class" and "race" are presumed to be analytically independent categories, ranked hierarchically and invariably, *with "class" as the more fundamental variable, accounting for the development and functions of racial policies.* The very terms in which the "race-class" debate is set up thus preclude a different mode of inquiry, oriented by a different question, which does not seek a uniform ranking of one variable over another, but rather their concrete interrelationships, in ways in which racial cleavages and practices themselves structure class relations. This would make the concept of "race" analytically inseparable from our understanding and very conceptualisation of existing class relations in any particular conjuncture. (1983:52, emphasis added)

In contrast, a good example of an approach that considers ethnicity, class, and gender in their complex interaction is Beverly Jones's historical study of female workers in the North Carolina tobacco industry from the 1920s to the 1940s. She shows how the divisions along ethnic, class, and gender lines coalesce, but she does not reduce these phenomena to each other:

> The factory policies of hiring, wages, working conditions, and spatial segregation, inherently reinforced by racism, the "cult of true white womanhood," and the inadvertent effect of New Deal governmental measures, all came together to touch the lives of black women tobacco workers, with sex, race and class exploitation. These practices further dissipated any possible gender bonds between black women and white women workers. As a race, black female tobacco workers were confined to unhealthy segregated areas either in separate buildings or on separate floors. As a working class, they were paid inadequate wages. As a sex they were relegated to the worst, lowest paid, black women's jobs. (1987:329)

Our efforts, then, should be, as Karen Brodkin Sacks writes, "to comprehend class, race, and gender oppression as parts of a unitary system, as opposed to analyses that envision capitalism and patriarchy as separate systems" (1989:545).

Capitalism, Production, and Power

The three approaches criticized above, while distinct, share at least two common characteristics. One is that each seeks to state in "once and for all" blanket terms the nature of the relationships between ethnicity, class, and gender. If it is really women's biology or the class structure of capitalism that is essential, these approaches, for all their best intentions, wrench their case studies from their contexts and thus arrive at an ahistorical position. The identities of ethnicity, class, and gender are linked in specific ways under specific conditions. The "conditions" (that is, history) have to become part of our theoretical explanations (see Mohammed 1993).

The second characteristic shared by the three approaches is that each considers ethnicity, class, and gender as "external" to the others. Now, I do not want to suggest that these phenomena can be reduced to each other, or that we can replace any one of them with any other as units of analysis. As the factory study suggests, ethnicity, class, and gender are "internally" related in the construction of each of these aspects of identity. Therefore, a critique invoking, for example, the notion of "false consciousness" with reference to gender or ethnicity obscuring the "reality" of the class experience actually has things reversed: Any understanding of class separate from ethnic and gender differences is "false."

In the factory, ethnicity, class, and gender are "united" and forged in a labor process particular to a particular kind of capitalism. As we have seen, the labor process recruits and sorts out different kinds of labor. Class relations are composed of ethnic and gender relations. That is, class—as a conjunction of the forms of capital achieved through closure—is defined to varying degrees by the way in which ethnicity and gender are used in the recruitment to it. This is of course not to say that gender and ethnicity are *prior* to class (logically or historically) or not to say that class does not inform the substance of gender and ethnic identity. This is also not to say that class fractions are totally distinct and bounded ethnic-based or gender-based entities. Thus, ethnicity and gender become invested with unequal status, it is not part of their definition. To argue against this would be to argue for inherent qualities in a certain gender identity or ethnic identity and not to see how they are constructed with regard to material processes. Class, by contrast, is by definition a relational property (as are ethnicity and gender), but one that implies material distribution inequalities. Given the historical record and what the ethnography shows, access to resources in Trinidad (and elsewhere) is achieved through exploitative relationships beyond the point of production. If all of this is so, then class practice—the means that people are able to acquire scarce social and economic resources, and the means that others prevent them from doing so—must be fundamentally different from the orthodox Marxian (and commonsense) view that defines class merely as an individual's relation to the means of production.

Despite emerging anthropological (crosscultural) perspectives on capitalisms, this view of capitalism is anathema to many theorists who conceive of capitalism as tearing asunder the "qualitative" social relationships characteristic of precapitalist systems. This view is held in common by "modernization" theorists as well as neo-Marxists—two traditions hardly compatible in any other respect. For example, writing on the "sex-fame" game and exploitative male-female relationships in Trinidad, Freilich and Coser remark, "When the forces of industrialization or urbanization begin seriously to impinge on the system, the male-female relationship will emerge as one of the weakest links in the structure. Here, as elsewhere, exploitative relationships will be resisted, and strains toward complete reciprocity will emerge in full force once traditional impediments to equalization have begun to crumble" (1972:18). This is curiously similar to some neo-Marxist approaches. For example, Wolf writes, "Capitalist formations peel the individual out of encompassing ascriptive bodies and install people as separate actors, free to exchange, truck, or barter in the market, as well as in other provinces of life" (1990:593).[3]

However, conventional conceptions of capitalism cannot account for processes, as evident in the EUL factory, where qualitative relationships and identities are used and produced and become integral to the very functioning of capitalist practice. As Connell suggests, we need to see capitalism "as a system for the concentration and regulation of profits extracted by a number of qualitatively different mechanisms of exploitation, rather than the basically homogeneous structure implied by the concept of a 'mode of production' " (Connell 1987:104).

Fortunately, we have comparative empirical data to support this assertion. For example, in studies of women's work in Moroccan industry, Susan Joekes (1982, 1985) has argued convincingly against the "deskilling" hypothesis as applied to female labor. Deskilling refers to the unskilled, low-paid, repetitive jobs created with the advent of technological change, which reduces the wage bill. The argument also implies that employers actively seek to bring in these technologies because of this advantage and others, and that all this translates into their demand for specifically female labor to fill the growing numbers of these new jobs. As Joekes points out, however, this cannot explain why some industries are "feminized" and others are not, and it cannot explain why unskilled male workers are not favored. The emphasis on women's lower level of skill is incomplete: Women are primarily distinguished in the labor market by their relative cheapness as a source of labor, and not as a reflection of their relative lack of education (indeed, in the case of Trinidad, many women even better equipped educationally than men): "If it is a fact that women can be paid less than men, then by the same token women will be placed in jobs with a low grade rating" (Joekes 1985:189). The implication is that the skill-labeling of the job performed is determined more by the sex of the worker than by the nature of the task.

John Humphrey's (1985, 1987) studies of women in Brazilian industry suggest this. Humphrey argues against the "dual market" theory of female labor, which holds that women are excluded from the productivity-enhancing jobs that would enable them to increase their wages and, hence, their status. As he points out, this view assumes that the market operates "impersonally." He argues, "the supposedly objective economic laws of market competition work through and within gendered structures. The market does not value male and female labour independently of gender" (1985:189).

More specifically, the factory study shows that the power the owners of the EUL factory enjoy is to invent labor by commodifying laborers, through a process that, in turn, constructs identities such as ethnicity, class, and gender. In this sense, this book is part of an older anthropological project that is concerned with the ways in which noneconomic forces impinge on emerging class systems (e.g., Epstein 1958). My aim has been to extend that project.

The EUL owners are thus able to exploit the workers not only through the extraction of surplus value but, relatedly, they are able to exploit the workers beyond the point of production by nonmarket means. By bringing them into the market and making them salient there, identities become commodified and are given value. In this process, individuals come to possess capital (economic and noneconomic). Power becomes determined by the levels and kinds of capital individuals possess. The levels and kinds of capital, and the evaluations of them, in turn, is a result of the wielding of power. Power is exercised through the resources of capital.

In the ethnography, evidence for this view has come not only from an examination of the practices of the EUL owners and supervisors but, perhaps more effectively, from an examination of the varying acts of resistance practiced by the workers. As Abu-Lughod (1990) suggests, the existence of acts of resistance does not so much demonstrate the fragility and ineffectiveness of hegemony as its existence and efficacy. In the factory, given the superior overall power wielded by the owners, the workers are generally forced into tactical resistance where strategic resistance is not possible (de Certeau 1984). Often, these tactics buy time and space for the workers on one level but serve to reinforce and legitimize their subordination on another level. This occurs when the workers resist management-imposed production quotas by not working at full capacity. This may serve to reinforce, in the owners' eyes, notions of the Carnival mentality and its relationship to ethnic identity. This also occurs when women identify themselves through the idiom of respectability. This may prove to be a shield for resisting sexual harassment, but the other side of the coin is that it reinforces traditional notions of feminity. These notions of femininity are used by the owners to justify placing the women in "women's jobs" and paying them "women's wages." Further, notions of femininity are used in trying to lower the subsistence wage. Women (and men) resist by entering the informal economy and by establishing informal support networks. While these activities provide necessary resources in the context of poverty and scarcity, they ultimately subsidize the capitalists by relieving them of some of the responsibility for the reproduction of the workers' labor. The fits and starts of domination and resistance show that, instead of a social order that is automatically reproduced under its own weight—a process that we as anthropologists often take for granted—hegemonic social relations and the identities they create and imply are the result of real people making real history under historical conditions of enablement and constraint.

Appendix: The EUL Supervisors and Line Workers

The Floor Supervisors

Name	*Sex*	*Age*	*Ethnicity*	*Religion*	*Department*
David	M	35	White	Catholic	Motor-Assembly
Winston	M	30	East Indian	Presbyterian	Upstairs Final-Assembly I
Ron	M	40	White/Chinese	Catholic	Downstairs Final-Assembly/ Upstairs Final-Assembly II
Lloyd	M	41	White/Syrian	Catholic	Machinery
Ruud	M	51	White	Catholic	Plastics
Karl	M	45	White	Anglican	Motor-Testing
Conrad	M	37	East Indian	Muslim	Storeroom
Ram	M	36	East Indian	Hindu	Primary-Assembly

The Line Workers

Name	*Sex*	*Age*	*Ethnicity*	*Religion*	*Occupation*
			MOTOR-ASSEMBLY DEPARTMENT		
Johnny	M	20	Black	Catholic	Machine operator/loader
Vera	F	45	Black	Baptist	Machine operator
Lori	F	25	Black	Seventh Day Adventist	Machine operator
Sheena	F	39	Black	Anglican	Machine operator
Walcott	F	36	Black	Catholic	Tester
Marina	F	22	Black	Catholic	Machine operator
Cleo	F	36	Black	Spiritual Baptist	Machine operator
Karen	F	40	Black	Spiritual Baptist	Machine operator
Gloria	F	38	Black	Catholic	Machine operator
Indira	F	44	East Indian	Hindu	Machine operator
Sonia	F	19	Black	Catholic	Machine operator
Fiona	F	26	Black	Anglican	Machine operator

(Continued on next page)

The Line Workers (Continued)

Name	*Sex*	*Age*	*Ethnicity*	*Religion*	*Occupation*
Rachel	F	39	Black	Catholic	Machine operator
Helen	F	42	Black	Catholic	Machine operator
Val	F	29	Black	Spiritual Baptist	Machine operator
Nicole	F	25	East Indian	Catholic	Machine operator
			UPSTAIRS FINAL-ASSEMBLY I DEPARTMENT		
Terry	M	19	East Indian	Catholic	Packer
Rita	F	19	Mixed	Catholic	Machine operator
Carole	F	19	Black	Catholic	Machine operator
Mary	F	42	Black	Pentacostal	Machine operator
Susan	F	24	Black	Catholic	Machine operator
Cokie	F	20	Black	Catholic	Assembler
Dolly	F	21	East Indian	Hindu	Assembler
Tanya	F	33	East Indian	Presbyterian	Machine operator
May	F	46	Black	Anglican	Machine operator
Margarita	F	37	Black	Jehovah's Witness	Machine operator
April	F	22	Black	Catholic	Machine operator
Stephanie	F	25	East Indian	Catholic	Assembler
Myra	F	33	Black	Spiritual Baptist	Tester
Denise	F	35	Black	Anglican	Assembler
			DOWNSTAIRS FINAL-ASSEMBLY DEPARTMENT		
Martha	F	21	Black	Catholic	Gluer
Connie	F	25	East Indian	Catholic	Assembler/Tester
Sybil	F	20	Black	Catholic	Solderer
Jenny	F	27	East Indian	Hindu	Assembler
Elaine	F	20	Black	Anglican	Solderer
Lisette	F	21	Black	Anglican	Packer
Irene	F	24	Black	Catholic	Solderer
Imogene	F	19	Black	Catholic	Assembler
Art	M	19	Black	Catholic	Packer
Gay	F	19	East Indian	Catholic	Solderer
Rohan	M	19	East Indian	Muslim	Tester
Geneveve	F	23	East Indian	Catholic	Assembler
Patricia	F	19	East Indian	Catholic	Assembler
			MACHINERY DEPARTMENT		
Daisy	F	45	Black	Spiritual Baptist	Machine operator
Antigone	F	25	Black	Spiritual Baptist	Machine operator
Chuck	M	21	Black	Spiritual Baptist	Machine operator/loader

(Continued)

The Line Workers (Continued)

Name	*Sex*	*Age*	*Ethnicity*	*Religion*	*Occupation*
			PLASTICS DEPARTMENT		
Deepak	M	21	East Indian	Hindu	Mechanic/machine operator
Gail	F	25	Black	Catholic	Machine operator
Monique	F	28	Black	Seventh Day Adventist	Machine operator
Faith	F	21	Mixed	Catholic	Machine operator
			MOTOR-TESTING DEPARTMENT		
Norma	F	38	East Indian	Catholic	Machine operator
Anneka	F	21	Black	Spiritual Baptist	Machine operator
Roxanne	F	23	East Indian	Hindu	Machine operator
Tia	F	38	Black	Spiritual Baptist	Machine operator
			STOREROOM		
Robert	M	19	Black	Catholic	Stores attendant
Brian	M	21	Black	Spiritual Baptist	Stores attendant
			PRIMARY-ASSEMBLY DEPARTMENT		
Melvina	F	39	Black	Anglican	Machine operator
Joan	F	36	Black	Catholic	Machine operator
			UPSTAIRS FINAL-ASSEMBLY II DEPARTMENT		
Cheryl	F	21	Black	Spiritual Baptist	Machine operator
Carla	F	24	East Indian	Catholic	Assembler
Jeremy	M	19	Black	Catholic	Loader/packer
			TOOL-MAKING AND REPAIR DEPARTMENT		
Vishnu	M	35	East Indian	Hindu	Toolmaker
Ben	M	20	East Indian	Hindu	Assistant toolmaker

Notes

INTRODUCTION

1. In many ways, then, this book unites the traditional concerns of Caribbean anthropology. Anthropological approaches to Trinidadian society have tended to be from two paradigms: the study of ethnicity, class, and cultural differences, and the study of family life, from which we can extrapolate some information on gender relations. The interest in the ethnic diversity has made Trinidad a veritable social-science laboratory for more than forty years.

2. For a similar formulation, consider Bourdieu's notion of *habitus*: "The structures constitutive of a particular type of environment (e.g. the material conditions of existence characteristic of a class condition) produce *habitus*, systems of durable, transposable *dispositions*, structured structures predisposed to function as structuring structures, that is, as principles of the generation and structuring of practices and representations which can be objectively 'regulated' and 'regular' without in any way being the product of obedience to rules, objectively adapted to their goals without presupposing a conscious aiming at ends or an express mastery of the operations necessary to obtain them and, being all this, collectively orchestrated without being the product of the orchestrating action of a conductor" (1977:72).

3. *Lime* is a Trinidadian word that can be used as a noun or verb and denotes a popular uninstitutional institution in Trinidad. To *lime* is to pass the time with others doing not much of anything except engaging in conversation. One *limes* or is *liming*. One goes to a beach *lime*. Some people are known as "real *limers*" (see, for example, Eriksen 1990).

CHAPTER 1

1. At the same time as elaborating a theory of subjection, Foucault tends to accord to power the capacity of intentionality. As Wartenberg explains, "He tends to *subjectify* power, to treat it as an agent capable of having its own aims, strategies, and the like" (1990:138).

2. This is where "practice" approaches to ethnicity (e.g., Bentley 1987; Vertovec 1992), in their current form or with modifications (cf. Yelvington 1991a; Bentley 1991), are useful. In one recent "practice" approach to ethnicity, Bentley extrapolates from Bourdieu (1977) and argues that ethnicity involves "consciousness of affinities

of interest and experience [that] embodies subliminal awareness of objective commonalities in practice" (1987:27). Bentley argues that the inculcation of the habitus involves the practical mastery of classificatory schemes (which does not mean that symbolic systems are necessarily grasped) and that differences in habitus can account for conflict, both being relevant for ethnic identity formation. Here, I think he is right. However, as I point out elsewhere (Yelvington 1991a), what Bentley's approach cannot account for is a situation in which two individuals live side by side, exploit the environment in the same manner, adopt similar patterns of dress and speech—in short, share the same culture and habitus—and yet still come to identify themselves, and become identified by others, as possessing different ethnic identities. By tying ethnicity to the habitus Bentley also cannot account for instances when two groups in different contexts, each presumably possessing a distinct habitus, identify with each other and claim a common ethnic identity.

3. But the role of biology in behavior and being is a topic of debate within not only the cultures anthropologists describe but in the culture of Western social science itself. The biologists Lynda I. Birke and Gail Vines (1987) acknowledge that the "biologism" versus "social construction" debate, (i.e., "nature versus nurture") in its approaches to gender, is deep and wide. When this divide has been bridged in the form of "interactive" approaches, that is, ones that take into account biology and social environment, they have been flawed, Birke and Vines argue, in two major ways. One interactive approach can be termed "additive." This approach sees biology's role as a limited one in gender formation, perhaps to a certain age in the individual, usually in early childhood, whereupon socialization then takes over. The other flawed interactive approach is the "unfolding" one. This approach sees biology and social and environmental factors as unfolding toward a certain end, the form an entity takes or its behavior, where the individual becomes a passive product of past interaction, not actively engaged in this process. Instead of conceptualizing a separation between "biological" and "social," Birke and Vines see gender as a transformative process whereby behavior, the end product of interaction, is itself part of the process of interaction. The implications of this view are that a person's sense of gender identity is variable throughout life, and that, if biological and social interaction shapes the social environment, "genderised behaviour is relational, depending upon its social context and social effects, rather than being an intrinsic property of the individual" (1987:564).

This means that gender must be conceived of as a particular social identity constructed through a process of social interaction with, and interpretations of, one's biology. Gender identity, then, incorporates individuals' experiences of biological processes, some of which are apparent to them. This experience arises from a social environment, which is a political one, where gender is constructed and evaluated, and where individuals "make sense" of their experience of their biology through the mediation of culture.

In an article entitled "Theorising Gender," Connell criticizes "sex role theory" and "categorical" approaches to gender. Role theory is seen to be both static and voluntaristic in that it emphasizes the stereotypical normative expectations of behavior, while assuming that people choose to maintain existing customs. Further, he argues, "role theory cannot grasp social change as history, that is, as transformation generated in the interplay of social practice and social structure. . . . Sex role theory has no way of grasping change as a dialectic arising within gender relations themselves" (1985:263).

Sex-role theory, then, has no conceptual room for dynamic change and power relations. Power analysis, by contrast, is the starting point for categorical theory. However, the problem here is "In much of this theorising the categories of 'women' and 'men' are taken as being in no need of further examination or finer differentiation. Theory operates with the categories as given; it does not concern itself with how they come to be what they are" (1985:264).

Additionally, there is a tendency to presume that the categories are biological in origin and that they determine the experiences of all women and all men and account for the power that they are able to wield. Categorical theory, therefore, has ultimately to fall back on biological determinism. To overcome these limited and limiting theories, Connell proposes an approach in line with the practice approach articulated in this book. A practice approach to gender is one that recognizes that structure is a precondition for social interaction, and that status differentials are implicated in all interactions. But this approach also pays attention to the ways in which people shape their social relations by practice within and through these structures.

4. "Decommodification" is conceived of here as a general process, not necessarily entailing the creation of family nor implying that the creation of family always entails a decommodification process.

CHAPTER 2

1. This is true of controversies such as whether the plantation slave was a proletarian or not (Mintz 1978) or whether rural dwellers on the island of Nevis are really peasants or proletarians (Frucht 1968). Such theoretical issues based on the Caribbean's specific and unique historical context make it even more compelling to situate the focus of the ethnography into wider social forms.

2. Some of the many books published on Trinidadian history are: Brereton 1979, 1981; Brereton and Dookeran 1982; Carmichael 1961; John 1988; LaGuerre 1985; Malik 1971; Millette 1970; Newson 1976; Niehoff and Niehoff 1960; Oxaal 1968; Ramdin 1982; Singh 1988; Trotman 1986; Vertovec 1992; Warner-Lewis 1991; Williams 1964; Wood 1968; and Yelvington 1993a. In addition, there have been numerous important doctoral dissertations on a number of themes in Trinidadian history.

The islands of Trinidad and Tobago were united administratively in 1889, and, since independence from Britain in 1962, have formed the modern state of Trinidad and Tobago. The following historical discussion is limited to Trinidad, however, because the two islands have developed in very distinct directions.

3. The emerging literature on the history of women in Trinidad includes Brereton 1988; Harry 1993; Mohammed 1993; and Reddock 1984, 1985a, 1985b, 1986, 1988, 1989, 1990, 1993, 1994.

4. It is unfortunate that some social scientists continue to rely on a number of flawed and biased studies arising from this era. See Yelvington 1992.

5. This came to be the source of another Trinidadian ethnic stereotype. East

Indians were seen to go into fits of jealousy, using the "coolie" weapon, the cutlass (Brereton 1974:20).

6. The origins and content of colonial "ethnic" terminology is complex indeed (see Brereton 1993; Kahn 1993; and Segal 1993). Here, my use of "ethnic" terms derives from their usages in the contemporary Trinidadian "culture of ethnicity" (cf. Alexander 1977), which is transmitted through the idiom of "race," where "races" were seen to be "pure" in their ancestral homelands and, in some cases, "mixed" only once they got to Trinidad (see Segal 1993). However, I can only touch upon the history and significance of these terms here.

The term "white" refers to those seen to be of wholly European descent, while terms like "Trinidad white" and "pass as white" indicate an individual who is seen as being of not wholly European ancestry, so that in Trinidad they may be taken for "white" because of class position, behavior, or "culture," but would not be so classified in other countries. The term "colored" (also referred to as "brown," "mixed," or "red") refers to those individuals seen to be offspring of black-white sexual unions. Originating in the context of slavery (see Alexander 1984 for more on their "origin myth"), this group has traditionally distanced itself from the black masses while suffering prejudice at the hands of whites. The term "black" is generally used interchangeably with "Negro" in Trinidad, referring to Trinidadians deemed to be wholly or mostly of African descent. In Trinidad, the term "Creole" has traditionally referred to those of European, African, and Euro-African ancestry. Thus, Creole generally does not refer to other ethnic groups, such as "East Indians," "Chinese," "Portuguese," and "Syrian/Lebanese." Creole is also used to modify various local "white" groups such as the French Creoles, the group who saw themselves as Trinidad's aristocrats, often in "cultural" opposition to British merchants and colonial officials. "East Indian" refers to the descendants of Hindu and Muslim indentured workers from India. While "East" is used as a modifier to differentiate East Indians from the indigenous groups encountered by European explorers and colonists, this group is also referred to as "Indian" in contemporary Trinidad. The term "Chinese" refers to the descendants of indentured laborers from China. It also often refers to those individuals seen as having been "mixed" with Chinese and non-Chinese ancestors so that in their appearance they are seen to retain "Chinese features." The term "Portuguese" refers to the descendants of indentured workers from Madeira. The term "Syrian/Lebanese" refers to the descendants of immigrants from the Middle East who came in the first part of the twentieth century. There are also other terms for "mixed" ethnic identities, such as "*dougla*," an individual taken to be the offspring of an African-East Indian union, and "Spanish," said to be a descendant of peon laborers from Venezuelan and African ancestors.

7. The large number of studies of ethnic politics in Trinidad include: Bahadoorsingh 1968; Clarke 1991; Eriksen 1993; LaGuerre 1982; Malik 1971; Oxaal 1968, 1971; Premdas 1993; Ryan 1972, 1989, 1990; and Yelvington 1987, 1991b.

8. It is not just "ethnic" politicians who purvey these notions. Sociologists and anthropologists studying Trinidad have tended to operate with Morton Klass's (1961) notions of East Indian "cultural persistence," and cite evidence that is supposed to indicate how they have tended to cling tenaciously to their "traditional" cultural practices (see Vertovec 1991). Wiliams took issue, albeit obliquely, with Klass's

findings: "A foreign student, with all the impetuosity of youth rushing in where angels fear to tread, may talk glibly of an Indian village in Trinidad not being West Indian, and predict that Indians will never be assimilated. It is certain, however, that he did not have to paint his white face black or brown to ascertain this, as a compatriot of his had to do in respect of his native country. The fact of the matter is, however, that in Trinidad the Negro, the Indian, French and Spaniard, English and Portuguese, Syrian and Lebanese, Chinese and Jew, all have messed out of the same pot, all are victims of the same subordination, all have been tarred with the same brush of political inferiority. Divergent customs and antipathetic attitudes have all been submerged in the common subordinate status of colonialism" (1964:278).

9. In an oft-quoted remark, Williams wrote as the country came into independence: "Together the various groups in Trinidad and Tobago have suffered, together that have aspired, together they have achieved. Only together can they succeed." He added, "And only together can they build a society, can they build a nation, can they build a homeland. There can be no Mother India for those whose ancestors came from India. . . . There can be no Mother Africa for those of African origin, and the Trinidad and Tobago society is living a lie and heading for trouble if it seeks to create the impression or to allow others to act under the delusion that Trinidad and Tobago is an African society. There can be no Mother England and no dual loyalties; no person can be allowed to get the best of both worlds, and to enjoy the privileges of citizenship in Trinidad and Tobago whilst expecting to retain United Kingdom citizenship. There can be no Mother China, even if one could agree as to which China is the Mother; and there can be no Mother Syria or no Mother Lebanon. A nation, like an individual, can have only one Mother. The only Mother we recognise is Mother Trinidad and Tobago, and Mother cannot discriminate between her children. All must be equal in her eyes" (1964:279).

10. There have been a number of recent studies of manufacturing in Trinidad and Tobago, comparing the country's performance with the other economies in the region, including: Crichton and Farrell 1988; Long 1986; Thoumi 1989; Schoepfle and Pérez-López 1989; and Turner 1982.

11. Perhaps the "Budget of Sacrifices" was, ironically, overly optimistic. Shortly before the budget speech, OPEC announced production quotas designed to drive the worldwide price of oil up to around U.S.$18 per barrel. This price underpinned the budget revenue estimates, and it seems that Robinson's planners assumed that this would remain stable. But there have traditionally been difficulties among OPEC members in keeping to agreed production quotas. Indeed, in June 1988, Saudi Arabia began to sell its crude for U.S.$13.40 a barrel, and this move was seen by oil analysts as one that would push world-market prices to around the U.S.$13 a barrel mark (*Times* [London], June 27, 1988, p.25). It was clear that revenue would fall far short of government estimates.

12. While there was a general increase in the standard of living as a result of the oil boom, there remain significant levels of extreme poverty. For example gastroenteritis, a condition that is common to the Third World, still plagues Trinidad and Tobago. Margaret Hector, Parliamentary Secretary in the Ministry of Health, Welfare, and the Status of Women, said that in 1976 the number of deaths at Port-of-Spain General Hospital due to gastro-enteritis was 137, with a case fatality rate of 6.7

percent. Enteritis and other similar diseases accounted for 25.9 percent of all deaths of children under one year in 1978. However, by 1984, there were 16 deaths with a case fatality rate of 0.9 percent. A similar decline was recorded at the San Fernando Hospital. She noted that these rates were even lower over the previous two years and attributed the decline in mortality to the establishment of oral rehydration units, improved sanitation and public education. But she added that gastro enteritis was still a major cause of morbidity with 24,642 cases reported in 1985 and 20,425 in 1986 (*Trinidad Guardian*, Feb. 24, 1987, p. 3).

13. The Carnival-mentality idea is used when purveying racism: "Yes, this would be a great country," a middle-aged male East Indian taxi driver told me one Saturday morning, "if it weren't for the Negro people." Speculating on the impending 1986 election, he continued, "They don't know what it is to work hard. They lazy. If this government [PNM] gets in again, there will be a revolution in this country. And it will be the Negro people who fight. That 'cause they gettin' the most pressure because they don't want to work. The whites, Syrians, Chinese, or Indians won't be affected, because they does know how to work and put money away. Take me. This morning I went to feed the chickens and goats and cows I do keep and then I came to work. You wouldn't see Negro people doing dat."

14. Moreover, CBI countries may be adversely affected by the free trade zone between the United States, Canada, and Mexico created by the North American Free Trade Agreement (see Consejo de Desarrollo Estratégico para Puerto Rico, 1991; Lewis 1991).

CHAPTER 3

1. In her study of Jamaican female industrial workers, A. Lynn Bolles describes the effects of the post-oil-crisis economic depression and the IMF prescriptions on "screwdriver" manufacturing. This seems analogous to the present situation in Trinidad: "The depression cut deeply into domestic sales because of higher consumer prices. Devaluation raised costs (in local currency) of imported components—the essence of the screwdriver operation. Paying for and buying imported materials became more and more difficult and high interest rates raised bank loans beyond the reach of most manufacturers" (1983:143). Thus, "When the necessary foreign exchange to procure these essential resources is lacking, then production slows down or ceases, and workers suffer accordingly" (1983:154–55).

2. A *gayap* is an event that usually occurs in rural areas. It is when a person wants some work performed, usually the building of a house. That person buys the materials and the rest of the community works all day to complete the task. The workers are not paid but it is expected that they will be provided with food and alcoholic beverages. Today, Trinidadians seem to feel that the days of the gayap and cooperation from neighbors are over.

3. "You from Penal or what?" is a put-down that is used by urban non-Indians and Indians alike to point out words or actions of an individual that reflect the antiquated, backward ways associated with rural Indian village life (and rural "Indianess"), in contrast to "town" (and, thus, "sophisticated" and "Creole") ways. Penal is a village in southern Trinidad.

4. A *steups* is when someone sucks their teeth loudly in disapproval. "It come like

sayin' 'Kiss my ass,' " explained Terry. This is called *churi* in Surinam and *chups* in other parts of the Caribbean.

5. Another example of factory social relations being put into action for a specific purpose was when Terry decided to hold a party at his home. He asked only the men—Johnny, Chuck, Jeremy, Deepak, Brian, and me—to contribute $10 each to help him "keep" his party. I asked Terry why he only asked the men and he indicated that it is almost taken for granted that the men are going to be the ones doing most of the drinking and that they should, in effect, subsidize women's attendance at a party.

CHAPTER 4

1. Regarding job satisfaction, Button says, "The frequently cited variables in Trinidad of race, religion and national origin were found to be of no measurable explanatory significance at all" (1981:168). In Camejo's study of workers' attitudes in Trinidad, there was no difference attributed to ethnicity regarding rules of work, promotions and means of promotion, approval of supervisors, attitude toward friendship groups, and instrumental attitudes toward work (1978:347–68). Camejo did, however, note differences regarding supervisor authority—more East Indians than blacks felt the supervisor was "right"—and identification with the firm—more East Indians than blacks felt the firm was a satisfactory place to work.

2. Compare Martha's comments to Naipaul's observations: "For all the complaints about white and whitish staff in the banks, there is a strong feeling among Negroes that black people, even when they can be trusted, don't know how to handle money. In money matters generally there is almost a superstition among both Indians and Negroes about the unreliability of their own race; there is scarcely a Trinidadian who has not at one time felt or said, 'I don't have any luck with my race.' It is an aspect of the multi-racial society to which sociologists pay little attention" (Naipaul 1981 [1962]:80).

3. The "Rasta Mall" is a group of wooden shops on Frederick Street in the main downtown Port-of-Spain shopping district that have many Rastafarians as proprietors. It was created by Eric Williams as a response to the Black Power calls for "people's capitalism."

4. In *Black Skin, White Masks,* Frantz Fanon writes, "I begin to suffer from not being a white man to the degree that the white man imposes discrimination on me, makes me a colonized native, robs me of all worth, all individuality, tells me that I am a parasite on the world, that I must bring myself as quickly as possible into step with the white world. . . . *Then I will quite simply try to make myself white*: that is, I will compel the white man to acknowledge that I am human" (1967:98, emphasis added).

5. In a corruption scandal that became public in 1987, it was alleged that officials of the Tesoro Petroleum Corporation of the United States bribed Trinidad and Tobago officials in order to form a joint-venture oil company. During the negotiations to set up the company, a move that turned out to be very successful for Tesoro, it was alleged that Tesoro provided Finance Minister George Chambers, who later became prime minister, with a prostitute. An article in the March 12, 1987, *Wall Street Journal* stated, "Finance ministers prefer blondes." According to the article, Cham-

bers apparently had requested a blond prostitute as part of his bribe (*Trinidad Guardian*, March 14, 1987, pp. 1, 4).

CHAPTER 5

1. One journalist, Ronald John, complained in an article entitled "Calypsonians must tell the truth about our women." He wrote in part: "The most popular kaisos heard every year are those that celebrate the sexual exploits of men, mainly during the Carnival season. Another kind is the kaiso that make women the butt of rude or insulting jokes. All of them fit into one category, casting women in an ungracious light.

"Now while these smut, or to use the contemporary 'jam and wine,' tunes are strictly male compositions, make no mistake about it, in spite of the vulgarity they contain, many women applaud them.

"This writer is not suggesting that a banner proposing a moral code for kaisonians be put up. As in other areas of the creative arts, poetic licence [*sic*] should be guarded like this Republic's constitution.

"At the same time kaisonians should be honest when projecting the image or role models of our mothers, wives, sisters and daughters to the world.

"And yet, kaisonians have been true when dealing with other concerns. I always praise them for their social commentary and humour, because unlike in other countries where the mood of the populace are [*sic*] felt on the University campus, as in China recently, it's different.

"Here we depend, not on the students at UWI, but on people like Black Stalin, Chalkdust, and Brother Valentino for feedback on national issues."

John took on the veteran calypsonian Roaring Lion, "this grandfather of the art form," who recorded the "classic" calypso "Ugly Woman," which was composed in 1933 and was featured in the film *Happy Go Lucky* in 1942 (Rohlehr 1987:17):

> If you want to be happy and live a king life
> Never make a pretty woman your wife
> All you have to do is just what I say
> And you will be happy, merry and gay

The article continues: "Lion concluded that it was 'from a logical point of view' that a man should resist marrying a woman prettier than him. Everlasting happiness was with the alleged ugly woman. . . . But Lion's view was based on a chauvinistic distortion of women. Although not a vulgar tune, 'Ugly woman' insults all women.

"To be frank, the jamette [prostitute or woman of 'loose morals'] woman of the past, the winer girl of today, the heart breaker, and the alleged ugly woman all exist then as they do now. But they never were a reflection of our women. . . .

"But now it's reconstruction time, and the truth is that the ungracious kaiso woman is antiquated. Now is the time for kaisonians to create female images that tell the truth about our women.

"This country is a maternal country. Every man, from Prime Minister down to commoner has been shaped by the enduring mother, who in most instances nursed them together with six others, father or no father.

"Every man knows about the resourceful mother who spun miracles out of thin air. Every man knows of the loyal wife, lover, or friend" (*Trinidad Guardian*, January 28, 1987, p. 17).

A week after John's article appeared, the Roaring Lion (Raphael de Leon) replied that he was merely telling the truth, as all calypsonians did. He claimed that the following lyrics based on a true story:

> Bad woman oh oh oh
> Bad woman ah ah ah
> Bad woman make good man
> Sleep in a old bread van

The Lion explained: "It all happened on Prince Street on the premises of M. I. Baking Company. A man who was said to be madly in love with a woman of easy virtue discovered that she was having a fling with another man who in fact was her 'do-do-man' [her sweetheart].

"Naturally the man was offended and showed it, but when he returned the night to her he found that he was locked out.

"He was a stranger to Town, or so it was said, so he went and slept for many knights [*sic*] in an 'old bread van' in the bakershop yard.

"It was brought to light by the very woman who knew he was sleeping there, and made a scandal with him one Saturday night."

About his "Ugly Woman," Lion explained: "In the first place, I said nothing about everlasting happiness with an ugly woman. I said from a logical point of view, that is a reasonable point of view, always marry a woman uglier.

"Certainly Mr. John is living in a fool's paradise, not to be able to see the logic of my song.

"For daily, what I have expressed herein is taking place not only in Trinidad, but around the world. I wonder if Mr. John is aware of some of the proverbs of this country that are attributed to women as being the authors.

"Here is one: 'Pretty women—bad habits.' " Here is another: " 'The redder the woman—dirtier her habits.' "

"Calypsonians did not coin these proverbs; . . . they simply used them when it suited their purpose.

"Now what is wrong with these sayings; surely no one would expect them to be applied generally, but undoubtedly, they are statements of facts, and it is only one who is very inexperienced who would doubt the truth of these sayings.

"The calypsonian, apart from imaginary subjects, bases his songs on realities, the facts of life, however distasteful they might be. And, he ridicules or praises anyone, man or woman, who deserves such treatment. Note the following:

> "Men are always arguing stupidness,
> Saying woman is that, and woman is this;
> (Repeat)
> How the devil they expect the woman to be good
> When they don't treat the woman as they really should,
> And they walk around Trinidad,
> Telling everybody how the women bad.

"Tell me, Mr. John, isn't this also true?

"What do you think?" (*Trinidad Guardian*, February 4, 1987, pp. 19, 24).

2. Although the reasons for black–East Indian animosity are complex, each group's prejudices do seem to have a different tenor and tone. Besides the general and pervasive antiblack bias arising out of the colonial period, according to John Gaffar LaGuerre, "blackness" also took on pejorative connotations for East Indians who reinterpreted it in terms of the black Hindu demon Rawan, a sexual interloper (1974:50–51). Blacks, for their part, originally regarded the East Indian indentures as "strikebreakers" who served to lower wages, and regarded their non-Western customs as barbaric. In many cases, the men at EUL seem to reject "blackness" in females—which may underscore Terry's comments above about Martha's desirability—and show a bias for white or "high brown" (sometimes called "red" or "fair-skinned") women.

3. For a somewhat contrasting situation among women workers in Barbados, see Freeman 1993b.

CHAPTER 6

1. More insight can be gained into the working conditions of female factory workers in the Caribbean when we compare the above observations with Kelly's (1986) study of female St. Lucian workers, where the average pay was EC$60 (US$22.50) per week. There, the women cited piece work, lack of company uniforms, poor transportation, health problems due to working with hazardous materials and poor pay as chief complaints.

2. Seidler, citing Chodorow (1978), continues, "Nancy Chodorow in her book *The Reproduction of Mothering* has challenged the tacit assumption which renders male identity as the norm, in an attempt to attribute differences between the sexes not to anatomy but rather to the fact that women, universally, are largely responsible for early child care. This gives girls more continuous experience of relationships, since they do not have to separate themselves from their mothers to achieve their sense of sexual identity. As a result 'feminine personality comes to define itself in relation and connection to other people more than masculine personality does' (Chodorow 1978:43–44). . . . Girls emerge with a stronger basis for experiencing another's needs or feelings as their own. So it is that girls emerge from this period with a basis of 'empathy' built into their primary definition of self in a way that boys do not. . . . It can make it difficult for men to support others, since they readily assume they should be able to pull themselves together as an act of will" (Seidler 1987:97–98).

3. Although, in general, Bourdieu's theories tend to be weighted toward stasis (cf. Gell 1985; Gose 1988), there does seem to be room for agency on the part of actors who are "trapped" in disadvantaged categorical identities: "Social categories disadvantaged by the symbolic order, such as women and the young, cannot but recognize the legitimacy of the dominant classification in the very fact that their only chance of neutralizing those of its effects most contrary to their own interests lies in submitting to them in order to make use of them (in accordance with the logic of the *èminence grise*)" (Bourdieu 1977:165–66).

CONCLUSION

1. For example, although Epstein is concerned to look at ethnicity in its personal identity manifestations, he proposes a duality that broaches the instrumental-primordial gap: "I have been suggesting then that 'tribalism' on the Copperbelt has to be

looked at in two aspects: one, socio-centrically or 'objectively', as a system of social categories; and two, egocentrically or 'subjectively'. It is this second aspect one has in mind when one speaks of ethnic identity. . . . When, for example, a man like Mulenga thinks of himself his self-image is primarily that of an educated African of the 'middle-class'; when he refers to others, however, he is likely to resort to stereotypy, reflecting the 'external' system of tribal categories. Similarly, despite his own self-image, Mulenga may appear to others as 'a man who hates all Lozi'. Here, that is to say, his Bemba identity is 'imposed' upon him as it were from the outside; it does not coincide with his own perception of self" (1978:38–39; see also, Epstein 1958). Epstein suggests that the link between the two concepts is dependent upon varying historical situations, and further suggests that ethnic identity is characterized by the friction between internal and external processes.

2. See also Brow (1988) and Woost (1993) for their attempts to define hegemony as a useful and useable anthropological concept.

3. For a "Maussian" history, with similar conclusions, see Carrier 1992.

References

Abdulah, Norma. 1988. "Structure of the Population: Demographic Developments in the Independence Years." In Selwyn Ryan, ed., *Trinidad and Tobago: The Independence Experience 1962–1987*, pp. 437–69. St. Augustine: Institute of Social and Economic Research, University of the West Indies.

Abraham-van der Mark, Eve E. 1983. "The Impact of Industrialization on Women: A Caribbean Case." In June Nash and María Patricia Fernández-Kelly, eds., *Women, Men, and the International Division of Labor*, pp. 374–86. Albany: State University of New York Press.

Abrahams, Roger D. 1979. "Reputation vs. Respectability: A Review of Peter J. Wilson's Concept." *Revista/Review Interamericana* 9, no. 3:448–53.

———. 1983. *The Man-of-Words in the West Indies*. Baltimore: Johns Hopkins University Press.

Abu-Lughod, Lila. 1990. "The Romance of Resistance: Tracing Transformations of Power Through Bedouin Women." *American Ethnologist* 17, no. 1:41–55.

Adams, Richard N. 1970. *Crucifixion by Power: Essays in the National Social Structure of Guatemala, 1944–1966*. Austin: University of Texas Press.

———. 1975. *Energy and Structure: A Theory of Social Power*. Austin: University of Texas Press.

Aho, William R. 1982. "Sex Conflict in Trinidad Calypsoes, 1969–1979." *Revista/Review Interamericana* 11, no. 1:76–81.

Alexander, Jack. 1977. "The Culture of Race in Middle-Class Kingston, Jamaica." *American Ethnologist* 4, no. 3:413–35.

———. 1984. "Love, Race, Slavery, and Sexuality in Jamaican Images of the Family." In Raymond T. Smith, ed., *Kinship Ideology and Practice in Latin America*, pp. 147–80. Chapel Hill: University of North Carolina Press.

Amott, Teresa L., and Julie A. Matthaei. 1991. *Race, Gender, and Work: A Multicultural Economic History of Women in the United States*. Boston: South End Press.

Angrosino, Michael V. 1976. "Sexual Politics in the East Indian Family in Trinidad." *Caribbean Studies* 16, no. 1:44–66.

Anthias, Floya, and Nira Yuval-Davis. 1983. "Contextualizing Feminism—Gender, Ethnic, and Class Divisions." *Feminist Review* 15:62–75.

Anthony, Michael. 1983. *Port-of-Spain in a World at War, 1939–1945*. Port-of-Spain: Ministry of Sports, Culture, and Youth Affairs.

Archer, John, and Barbara B. Lloyd. 1985. *Sex and Gender.* New York: Cambridge University Press.

Archer, Margaret S. 1982. "Morphogenesis Versus Structuration." *British Journal of Sociology* 33, no. 4:453–80.

———. 1985. "The Myth of Cultural Integration." *British Journal of Sociology* 36, no. 3:333–53.

———. 1988. *Culture and Agency: The Place of Culture in Social Theory.* Cambridge: Cambridge University Press.

Austin, Diane J. 1983. "Culture and Ideology in the English-Speaking Caribbean: A View from Jamaica." *American Ethnologist* 10, no. 2:232–40.

Austin, Roy L. 1976. "Understanding Calypso Content: A Critique and an Alternative Explanation." *Caribbean Quarterly* 22, nos. 2 and 3:74–83.

Bahadoorsingh, Krishna. 1968. *Trinidad Electoral Politics: The Persistence of the Race Factor.* New York: Oxford University Press.

Baksh, Ishmael J. 1978. "Stereotypes of Negroes and East Indians in Trinidad: A Re-Examination." *Caribbean Quarterly* 25, nos. 1 and 2:52–71.

Barrow, Christine. 1976. "Reputation and Ranking in a Barbadian Locality." *Social and Economic Studies* 25, no. 2:106–21.

———. 1988. "Anthropology, The Family, and Women in the Caribbean." In Patricia Mohammed and Catherine Shepherd, eds., *Gender in Caribbean Development*, pp. 156–69. St. Augustine: Institute of Social and Economic Research, University of the West Indies.

Basdeo, Sahadeo. 1985. *Labour Organisation and Labour Reform in Trinidad, 1919–1939.* St. Augustine: Institute of Social and Economic Research, University of the West Indies.

Bennett, Herman L. 1989. "The Challenge to the Post-Colonial State: A Case Study of the February Revolution in Trinidad." In Franklin W. Knight and Colin A. Palmer, eds., *The Modern Caribbean*, pp. 129–46. Chapel Hill: University of North Carolina Press.

Bennett, Karl. 1987. "The Caribbean Basin Initiative and Its Implications for CARICOM Exports." *Social and Economic Studies* 36, no. 2:21–40.

Bentley, G. Carter. 1987. "Ethnicity and Practice." *Comparative Studies in Society and History* 29, no. 1:24–55.

———. 1991. "Response to Yelvington." *Comparative Studies in Society and History* 33, no. 1:169–75.

Besson, Jean. 1993. "Reputation and Respectability Reconsidered: A New Perspective on Afro-Caribbean Peasant Women." In Janet H. Momsen, ed., *Women and Change in the Caribbean*, pp. 15–37. Bloomington: Indiana University Press.

Béteille, André. 1990. "Race, Caste, and Gender." *Man* 25, no. 3:489–504.

Bhaskar, Roy. 1983. "Beef, Structure, and Place: Notes from a Critical Naturalist Perspective." *Journal for the Theory of Social Behaviour* 13, no. 1:81–95.

Birke, Lynda I., and Gail Vines. 1987. "Beyond Nature Versus Nurture: Process and Biology in the Development of Gender." *Women's Studies International Forum* 10, no. 6:555–70.

Boissiere, Ralph de. 1956. *Rum and Coca-Cola.* Melbourne: Australasian Book Society.

Bolland, O. Nigel. 1992. "Creolization and Creole Societies: A Cultural Nationalism View of Caribbean Social History." In Alistair Hennessy, ed., *Intellectuals in the Twentieth-Century Caribbean*. Volume I, *Spectre of the New Class: The Commonwealth Caribbean*, pp. 50–79. London: Macmillan.

Bolles, A. Lynn. 1983. "Kitchens Hit by Priorities: Employed Working-Class Jamaican Women Confront the IMF." In June Nash and María Patricia Fernández-Kelly, eds., *Women, Men, and the International Division of Labor*, pp. 138–60. Albany: State University of New York Press.

———. 1985. "Economic Crisis and Female-Headed Households in Urban Jamaica." In June Nash and Helen I. Safa, eds., *Women and Change in Latin America*, pp. 65–83. New York: Bergin and Garvey.

Bolles, A. Lynn, and Deborah D'Amico-Samuels. 1989. "Anthropological Scholarship on Gender in the English-Speaking Caribbean." In Sandra Morgen, ed., *Gender and Anthropology*, pp. 171–88. Washington, D.C.: American Anthropological Association.

Boodhoo, Kenneth I., ed. 1986. *Eric Williams, the Man and the Leader*. Lanham, Md.: University Press of America.

Bookman, Ann. 1988. "Unionization in an Electronics Factory: The Interplay of Gender, Ethnicity, and Class." In Ann Bookman and Sandra Morgen, eds., *Women and the Politics of Empowerment*, pp. 159–79. Philadelphia: Temple University Press.

Bourdieu, Pierre. 1977. *Outline of a Theory of Practice*. Translated by Richard Nice. Cambridge: Cambridge University Press.

———. 1984. *Distinction*. Translated by Richard Nice. Cambridge, Mass.: Harvard University Press.

———. 1986 [1983]. "The Forms of Capital." In John G. Richardson, ed., *Handbook of Theory and Research for the Sociology of Education*, pp. 241–58. Westport, Conn.: Greenwood Press.

———. 1991. *Language and Symbolic Power*. Edited by J. B. Thompson. Cambridge: Polity Press.

Braithwaite, Lloyd. 1975 [1953]. *Social Stratification in Trinidad*. Mona: Institute of Social and Economic Research, University of the West Indies.

Brereton, Bridget. 1974. "The Foundations of Prejudice: Indians and Africans in Nineteenth-Century Trinidad." *Caribbean Issues* 1, no. 1:15–28.

———. 1979. *Race Relations in Colonial Trinidad, 1870–1900*. Cambridge: Cambridge University Press.

———. 1981. *A History of Modern Trinidad 1783–1962*. London: Heinemann.

———. 1988. "General Problems and Issues in Studying the History of Women." In Patricia Mohammed and Catherine Shepherd, eds., *Gender in Caribbean Development*, pp. 123–41. St. Augustine: Institute of Social and Economic Research, University of the West Indies.

———. 1993. "Social Organisation and Class, Racial, and Cultural Conflict in Nineteenth-Century Trinidad." In Kevin A. Yelvington, ed., *Trinidad Ethnicity*, pp. 33–55. Knoxville: University of Tennessee Press.

Brereton, Bridget, and Winston Dookeran, eds. 1982. *East Indians in the Caribbean: Colonialism and the Struggle for Identity*. New York: Krauss International Publications.

Brow, James. 1988. "In Pursuit of Hegemony: Representations of Authority and Justice in a Sri Lankan Village." *American Ethnologist* 15, no. 2:311–27.

Burton, Richard D. E. 1993a. "*Debrouya pa Peche*; or, *Il y a Toujours Moyen de Moyenner*: Patterns of Opposition in the Fiction of Patrick Chamoiseau." *Callaloo* 16, no. 2:466–81.

———. 1993b. "*Ki Mon Nou Ye?* The Idea of Difference in Contemporary French West Indian Thought." *Nieuwe West-Indische Gids* 67, nos. 1 and 2:5–32.

Bush, Barbara J. 1985. "Towards Emancipation: Slave Women and Resistance to Coercive Labour Regimes in the British West Indian Colonies, 1790–1838." In David Richardson, ed., *Abolition and Its Aftermath: The Historical Context, 1790–1916*, pp. 27–54. London: Frank Cass.

Button, Kenneth R. 1981. "Development and Work Attitudes: Attitudes Toward Work Among Trinidadian Industrial Workers." Ph.D. dissertation. Fletcher School of Law and Diplomacy, Tufts University.

Camejo, Acton. 1971. "Racial Discrimination in Employment in the Private Sector in Trinidad and Tobago: A Study of the Business Elite and the Social Structure." *Social and Economic Studies* 20, no. 3:294–318.

———. 1978. "Industrialization, Labour Utilization, and Commitment in Manufacturing in Organizations in Trinidad and Tobago." Ph.D. dissertation. University of the West Indies, St. Augustine.

Caplan, Pat. 1987. "Introduction." In Pat Caplan, ed., *The Cultural Construction of Sexuality*, pp. 1–30. London: Tavistock.

Caribbean Conference of Churches. 1986. *A Social Survey of the Poverty Situation in Trinidad*. Port-of-Spain: Caribbean Conference of Churches.

Carmichael, Gertrude. 1961. *The History of the West Indian Islands of Trinidad and Tobago, 1498–1900*. London: Alvin Redman.

Carrier, James G. 1992. "Emerging Alienation in Production: A Maussian History." *Man* 27, no. 3:539–58.

Carrington, Edwin. 1971. "Industrialization in Trinidad and Tobago since 1950." In Norman Girvan and Owen Jefferson, eds., *Readings in the Political Economy of the Caribbean*, pp. 143–50. Mona: New World Group.

Cash, W. J. 1941. *The Mind of the South*. New York: Alfred A. Knopf.

Cavendish, Ruth. 1982. *Women on the Line*. London: Routledge and Kegan Paul.

Centre for Ethnic Studies. 1993. *Employment Practices in the Public and Private Sectors in Trinidad and Tobago*. 2 vols. St. Augustine: Centre for Ethnic Studies, University of the West Indies.

Certeau, Michel de. 1984. *The Practice of Everyday Life*. Berkeley: University of California Press.

Ching, Annette M. T. 1985. "Ethnicity Reconsidered, with Reference to Sugar and Society in Trinidad." D.Phil. thesis. University of Sussex.

Chodorow, Nancy. 1978. *The Reproduction of Mothering*. Berkeley: University of California Press.

Clarke, Colin G. 1971. "Residential Segregation and Intermarriage in San Fernando, Trinidad." *Geographical Review* 61, no. 2:198–218.

———. 1986. *East Indians in a West Indian Town: San Fernando, Trinidad, 1930–1970*. London: Allen and Unwin.

———. 1991. "Society and Electoral Politics in Trinidad and Tobago." In Colin G. Clarke, ed., *Society and Politics in the Caribbean*, pp. 47–77. New York: St. Martin's Press.

———. 1993. "Spatial Pattern and Social Interaction among Creoles and Indians in Trinidad and Tobago." In Kevin A. Yelvington, ed., *Trinidad Ethnicity*, pp. 116–35. Knoxville: University of Tennessee Press.

Cohen, G. A. 1979. "The Labor Theory of Value and the Concept of Exploitation." *Philosophy and Public Affairs* 8, no. 4:338–60.

———. 1983. "More on Exploitation and the Labour Theory of Value." *Inquiry* 26, no. 3:309–31.

Comitas, Lambros. 1973. "Occupational Multiplicity in Rural Jamaica." In Lambros Comitas and David Lowenthal, eds., *Work and Family Life: West Indian Perspectives*, pp. 156–73. Garden City, N.Y.: Anchor.

Connell, R. W. 1983. *Which Way Is Up?* Sydney: George Allen and Unwin.

———. 1985. "Theorising Gender." *Sociology* 19, no. 2:260–72.

———. 1987. *Gender and Power*. Cambridge: Polity.

Consejo de Desarrollo Estratégico para Puerto Rico. 1991. *Impacto económico sobre Puerto Rico del acuerdo libre comercio entre Estados Unidos, Canadá y México*. San Juan: Oficina del Gobernador.

Conway, Dennis. 1989. "Trinidad and Tobago." In Robert B. Potter, ed., *Urbanization, Planning, and Development in the Caribbean*, pp. 49–76. London: Mansell.

Conzen, Kathleen Neils. 1989. "Ethnicity as Festive Culture: Nineteenth-Century German America on Parade." In Werner Sollors, ed., *The Invention of Ethnicity*, pp. 44–76. New York: Oxford University Press.

Coombs-Montrose, Donna. N.d. "Women and the Explosive Eighties: A Contribution to the Debate on the Historical Role of Women in Trinidad and Tobago." Mimeo. Port-of-Spain: Oilfields Workers' Trade Union.

Cowan, Jane K. 1990. *Dance and the Body Politic in Northern Greece*. Princeton: Princeton University Press.

Craig, Susan, 1974. "Community Development in Trinidad and Tobago, 1943–1973: From Welfare to Patronage." Working Paper No. 4. Institute for Social and Economic Research, University of the West Indies, Mona.

———. 1985. "Political Patronage and Community Resistance: Village Councils in Trinidad and Tobago." In P. I. Gomes, ed., *Rural Development in the Caribbean*, pp. 173–93. New York: St. Martin's Press.

Craton, Michael. 1982. *Testing the Chains*. Ithaca: Cornell University Press.

Creighton, Hannah. 1982. "Tied by Double Apron Strings: Female Work Culture and Organization in a Restaurant." *Insurgent Sociologist* 11, no. 3:59–64.

Crichton, Nigel, and Terrence W. Farrell. 1988. "Market Structure and Concentration in the Manufacturing Sector in Trinidad and Tobago." *Social and Economic Studies* 37, no. 3:151–92.

Cuales, Sonia. 1980. "Women, Reproduction, and Foreign Capital in Curaçao." *Caraïbisch Forum* 1, no. 2:75–86.

Currie, Kate. 1992. "The Indian Stratification Debate: A Discursive Exposition of Problems and Issues in the Analysis of Class, Caste, and Gender." *Dialectical Anthropology* 17, no. 2:115–39.

Daly, Stephanie. 1982. *The Developing Legal Status of Women in Trinidad and Tobago*. Port-of-Spain: The National Commission on the Status of Women.

Deosaran, Ramesh. 1987. "The 'Caribbean Man': A Study of the Psychology of

Perception and the Media." In David Dabydeen and Brinsley Samaroo, eds., *India in the Caribbean*, pp. 81–117. London: Hansib/University of Warwick.

Dookeran, Winston. 1985. "East Indians and the Economy of Trinidad and Tobago." In John G. LaGuerre, ed., *Calcutta to Caroni*, 2d ed., pp. 63–73. St. Augustine: Extra-Mural Unit, University of the West Indies.

Douglass, Lisa. 1992. *The Power of Sentiment: Love, Hierarchy, and the Jamaican Family Elite.* Boulder: Westview Press.

Durant-González, Victoria. 1976. "Role and Status of Rural Jamaican Women: Higglering and Mothering." Ph.D. dissertation. University of California, Berkeley.

———. 1983. "Female Factory Workers: Attitudes and Reality." *Concerning Women in Development*, pp. 1–6. Cave Hill: Women in Development Unit, Extra-Mural Department, University of the West Indies, April.

———. 1987. "Women are Better Suited." In Women's International Resource Exchange, *Women in the Rebel Tradition: The English-Speaking Caribbean*, pp. 8–9. New York: Women's International Resource Exchange.

Duveen, Gerard, and Barbara B. Lloyd. 1986. "The Significance of Social Identities." *British Journal of Social Psychology* 25, no. 3:219–30.

Economist Intelligence Unit. 1987–88. *Country Profile: Trinidad and Tobago*. London: Economist Intelligence Unit.

Elder, J. D. 1968. "The Male/Female Conflict in Calypso." *Caribbean Quarterly* 14, no. 3:23–41.

Elson, Diane, and Ruth Pearson. 1980. "The Latest Phase of the Internationalisation of Capital and Its Implications for Women in the Third World." IDS Discussion Paper No. 150. Institute of Development Studies, University of Sussex.

———. 1984. "The Subordination of Women and the Internationalisation of Factory Production." In Kate Young, Carol Wolkowitz, and Roslyn McCullagh, eds., *Of Marriage and the Market*, 2d ed., pp. 18–40. London: Routledge and Kegan Paul.

Employers' Consultative Association. 1987. "Summary of Wages, Salaries, and Fringe Benefits for Selected Weekly Rated Workers in the Manufacturing Industry." Mimeo. Employers' Consultative Association, Port-of-Spain.

Epstein, A. L. 1958. *Politics in an Urban African Community*. Manchester: Manchester University Press.

———. 1978. *Ethos and Identity*. London: Tavistock.

Erikson, Erik H. 1964. *Childhood and Society*. 2d ed. New York: Norton.

Eriksen, Thomas Hylland. 1990. "Liming in Trinidad: The Art of Doing Nothing." *Folk* 32:23–43.

———. 1993. "Formal and Informal Nationalism." *Ethnic and Racial Studies* 16, no. 1:1–25.

Fanon, Frantz. 1967. *Black Skin, White Masks*. New York: Grove Press.

Farrell, Trevor M. A. 1978. "The Unemployment Crisis in Trinidad and Tobago." *Social and Economic Studies* 27, no. 2:117–52.

———. 1980. "The Measurement of Unemployment in Trinidad and Tobago: Are the Official Figures Wrong?" *Social and Economic Studies* 29, nos. 2 and 3:35–51.

Fernández-Kelly, María Patricia. 1983. *For We Are Sold, I and My People*. Albany: State University of New York Press.

Fjellman, Stephen M. 1992. *Vinyl Leaves: Walt Disney World and America*. Boulder: Westview Press.

Fogelson, Raymond D., and Richard N. Adams, eds. 1977. *The Anthropology of Power: Ethnographic Studies from Asia, Oceania, and the New World*. New York: Academic Press.

Foster-Carter, Aidan. 1978. "The Modes of Production Controversy." *New Left Review* 107:47–77.

Foucault, Michel. 1978. *History of Sexuality*. Vol. 1. New York: Random House.

———. 1979. *Discipline and Punish*. Translated by Alan Sheridan. New York: Random House.

———. 1982. "The Subject and Power." In Hubert J. Dreyfus and Paul Rabinow, eds., *Michel Foucault: Beyond Structuralism and Hermeneutics*, pp. 208–26. Brighton: Harvester Press.

Freeman, Carla S. 1993a. "High Tech and High Heels in the Global Economy: The Off-Shore Information Industry in Barbados." Ph.D. dissertation. Temple University.

———. 1993b. "Designing Women: Corporate Discipline in Barbados's Off-Shore Pink-Collar Sector." *Cultural Anthropology* 8, no. 2:169–86.

Freilich, Morris. 1968. "Sex, Secrets, and Systems." In Stanford N. Gerber, ed., *The Family in the Caribbean*, pp. 47–62. Rio Piedras: Institute of Caribbean Studies, University of Puerto Rico.

Freilich, Morris, and Lewis A. Coser. 1972. "Structured Imbalances of Gratification: The Case of the Caribbean Mating System." *British Journal of Sociology* 23, no. 1:1–19.

Frucht, Richard. 1968. "A Caribbean Social Type: Neither 'Peasant' nor 'Proletarian.' " *Social and Economic Studies* 16, no. 3:295–300.

Gell, Alfred,. 1985. "How to Read a Map: Remarks on the Practical Logic of Navigation." *Man* 20, no. 2:222–41.

Giddens, Anthony. 1979. *Central Problems in Social Theory*. London: Macmillan.

———. 1982. *Profiles and Critiques in Social Theory*. London: Macmillan

———. 1984. *The Constitution of Society*. Cambridge: Polity.

Gintis, Herbert, and Samuel Bowles. 1981. "Structure and Practice in the Labor Theory of Value." *Review of Radical Political Economics* 12, no. 4:1–26.

Goodenough, Stephanie. 1978. "Race, Status, and Ecology in Port-of-Spain, Trinidad." In Colin G. Clarke, ed., *Caribbean Social Relations*, pp. 17–45. Monograph Series no. 8. Liverpool: Centre for Latin-American Studies, University of Liverpool.

Gose, Peter. 1988. "Labor and the Materiality of the Sign: Beyond Dualist Theories of Culture." *Dialectical Anthropology* 13, no. 2:90–124.

Gramsci, Antonio. 1971. *Selections from the Prison Notebooks of Antonio Gramsci*. New York: International Publishers.

Grenier, Guillermo J. 1988. *Inhuman Relations: Quality Circles and Anti-Unionism in American Industry*. Philadelphia: Temple University Press.

Griffith, David C. 1987. "Nonmarket Labor Processes in an Advanced Capitalist Economy." *American Anthropologist* 89, no. 4:838–52.

Haraksingh, Kusha. 1988. "Sugar, Labour, and Livelihood in Trinidad, 1940–1970." *Social and Economic Studies* 37, nos. 1 and 2:271–91.

Harewood, Jack. 1963. "Employment in Trinidad and Tobago." *Research Papers No. 1*. Port-of-Spain: Central Statistical Office, Government Printing.

———. 1971. "Racial Discrimination in Employment in Trinidad and Tobago." *Social and Economic Studies* 20, no. 3:267–93.
———. 1975. *The Population of Trinidad and Tobago.* United Nations series. Paris: C.I.C.R.E.D.
Harewood, Jack, and Norma Abdulah. 1972. *What Our Women Know, Think, and Do about Birth Control.* St. Augustine: Institute of Social and Economic Research, University of the West Indies.
Harewood, Jack, and Ralph Henry. 1985. *Inequality in a Post-Colonial Society: Trinidad and Tobago.* St. Augustine: Institute of Social and Economic Research, University of the West Indies.
Harry, Indra S. 1993. "Women in Agriculture in Trinidad: An Overview." In Janet H. Momsen, ed., *Women and Change in the Caribbrean*, pp. 205–18. Bloomington: Indiana University Press.
Harvey, David. 1989. *The Condition of Postmodernity.* Oxford: Basil Blackwell.
Henderson, Thelma. 1973. "The Role of Women in Politics in Trinidad and Tobago: 1925–1972." Caribbean Studies thesis. University of the West Indies, St. Augustine.
Henry, Frances. 1983. "Religion and Ideology in Trinidad: The Resurgence of the Shango Religion." *Caribbean Quarterly* 29, nos. 3 and 4:63–69.
Henry, Frances, and Pamela Wilson. 1975. "The Status of Women in the Caribbean: An Overview of Their Social, Economic, and Sexual Roles." *Social and Economic Studies* 24, no. 2:165–98.
Henry, Ralph M. 1988a. "The State and Income Distribution in an Independent Trinidad and Tobago." In Selwyn Ryan, ed., *Trinidad and Tobago: The Independence Experience 1962–1987*, pp. 471–93. St. Augustine: Institute of Social and Economic Research, University of the West Indies.
———. 1988b. "Jobs, Gender, and Development Strategy in the Commonwealth Caribbean." In Patricia Mohammed and Catherine Shepherd, eds., *Gender in Caribbean Development*, pp. 183–205. St. Augustine: Institute of Social and Economic Research, University of the West Indies.
———. 1989. "Inequalities in Plural Societies: An Exploration." *Social and Economic Studies* 38, no. 2:69–110.
———. 1993. "Notes on the Evolution of Inequality in Trinidad and Tobago." In Kevin A. Yelvington, ed., *Trinidad Ethnicity*, pp. 56–80. Knoxville: University of Tennessee Press.
Henry, Zin. 1972. *Labour Relations and Industrial Conflict in Commonwealth Caribbean Countries.* Port-of-Spain: Columbus Publishers.
Higman, Barry W. 1975. "The Slave Family and Household in the British West Indies, 1800–1834." *Journal of Interdisciplinary History* 6, no. 2:261–87.
———. 1979. "African and Creole Slave Family Patterns in Trinidad." In Margaret E. Crahan and Franklin W. Knight, eds., *Africa and the Caribbean: Legacies of a Link*, pp. 41–64. Baltimore: Johns Hopkins University Press.
———. 1984. *Slave Populations of the British Caribbean, 1807–1834.* Baltimore: Johns Hopkins University Press.
Hintzen, Percy C. 1985. "Ethnicity, Class, and Internal Capital Penetration." *Social and Economic Studies* 34, no. 3:107–63.

———. 1989. *The Costs of Regime Survival: Racial Mobilization, Elite Domination, and Control of the State in Guyana and Trinidad.* Cambridge: Cambridge University Press.

Hobsbawm, Eric. 1983. "Introduction: Inventing Traditions." In Eric Hobsbawm and Terence Ranger, eds., *The Invention of Tradition,* pp. 1–14. Cambridge: Cambridge University Press.

Hobsbawm, Eric, and Terence Ranger, eds., 1983. *The Invention of Tradition.* Cambridge: Cambridge University Press.

Hodge, Merle. 1974. "The Shadow of the Whip: A Comment on Male-Female Relations in the Caribbean." In Orde Coombs, ed., *Is Massa Day Dead?* pp. 111–18. Garden City, N.Y.: Anchor.

Holmstrom, Nancy. 1983. "Marx and Cohen on Exploitation and the Labor Theory of Value." *Inquiry* 26, no. 3:287–307.

Homans, George. 1951. *The Human Group.* London: Routledge and Kegan Paul.

Humphrey, John. 1985. "Gender, Pay, and Skill: Manual Workers in Brazilian Industry." In Haleh Afshar, ed., *Women, Work, and Ideology in the Third World,* pp. 214–31. London: Tavistock.

———. 1987. *Gender and Work in the Third World.* London: Tavistock.

Hyacinth, H. 1979. "Changes in the Status of Women, 1900–1977." Mimeo (restricted circulation). Central Statistical Office, Port-of-Spain.

Isaac, Jeffrey C. 1987. *Power and Marxist Theory: A Realist View.* Ithaca: Cornell University Press.

Isajiw, Wsevolod W. 1974. "Definitions of Ethnicity." *Ethnicity* 1, no. 2:111–24.

Jain, Ravindra K. 1986. "Freedom Denied? Indian Women and Indentureship." *Economic and Political Weekly* 21:316.

James, C. L. R. 1971 [1936]. *Minty Alley.* London: New Beacon Books.

Janiewski, Dolores E. 1985. *Sisterhood Denied: Race, Gender, and Class in a New South Community.* Philadelphia: Temple University Press.

Jenkins, Richard. 1992. *Pierre Bourdieu.* London: Routledge.

Joekes, Susan P. 1982. "Female-Led Industrialisation: Women's Jobs in Third World Export Manufacturing: The Case of the Moroccan Clothing Industry." Research Report No. 15. Institute for Development Studies, University of Sussex.

———. 1985. "Working for Lipstick? Male and Female Labour in the Clothing Industry in Morocco." In Haleh Afshar, ed., *Women, Work, and Ideology in the Third World,* pp. 183–213. London: Tavistock.

John, A. Meredith. 1988. *The Plantation Slaves of Trinidad, 1783–1816: A Mathematical and Demographic Inquiry.* Cambridge: Cambridge University Press.

Jones, Beverly W. 1987. "Race, Sex, and Class: Black Female Tobacco Workers in Durham, North Carolina, 1920–1940, and the Development of Female Consciousness." In Mary Jo Deegan and Michael Hill, eds., *Women and Symbolic Interaction,* pp. 323–32. Boston: Allen and Unwin.

Joseph, Gloria I. 1980. "Caribbean Women: The Impact of Race, Sex, and Class." In Beverly Lindsay, ed., *Comparative Perspectives of Third World Women: The Impact of Race, Sex, and Class,* pp. 143–61. New York: Praeger.

Katzin, Margaret. 1959. "The Jamaican Country Higgler," *Social and Economic Studies* 8, no. 4:421–40.

———. 1960. "The Business of Higglering in Jamaica." *Social and Economic Studies* 9, no. 3:297–331.
Kelly, Dierdre. 1986. "St. Lucia's Electronics Factory Workers: Key Components in an Export-Oriented Industrialization Strategy." *World Development* 14, no. 7:828–38.
———. 1987. "Hard Work, Hard Choices: A Survey of Women in St. Lucia's Export-Oriented Electronics Factories." Occasional Paper No. 20. Institute of Social and Economic Research, University of the West Indies, Cave Hill.
Kelly, John D. 1990. "Discourse about Sexuality and the End of Indenture in Fiji: the Making of Counter-Hegemonic Discourse." *History and Anthropology* 5, no. 1:19–61.
———. 1992. "Fiji Indians and 'Commoditization of Labor.' " *American Ethnologist* 19, no. 1:97–120.
Khan, Aisha. 1993. "What Is 'a Spanish'? Ambiguity and 'Mixed' Ethnicity in Trinidad." In Kevin A. Yelvington, ed., *Trinidad Ethnicity*, pp. 180–207. Knoxville: University of Tennessee Press.
———. 1994. "Homeland, Motherland: Authenticity, Legitimacy, and Ideologies of Place Among Muslims in Trinidad." In Peter van der Veer, ed., *Nation and Migration: The Politics of Space in the South Asian Diaspora*, pp. 93–131. Philadelphia: University of Pennsylvania Press.
Kiple, Kenneth. 1984. *The Caribbean Slave: A Biological History*. New York: Cambridge University Press.
Klass, Morton. 1961. *East Indians in Trinidad*. New York: Columbia University Press.
Knight, Franklin W. 1978. *The Caribbean: The Genesis of a Fragmented Nationalism*. New York: Oxford University Press.
Kondo, Dorinne K. 1990. *Crafting Selves: Power, Gender, and Discourses of Identity in a Japanese Workplace*. Chicago: University of Chicago Press.
Krips, Henry. 1990. "Power and Resistance." *Philosophy of the Social Sciences* 20, no. 2:170–82.
LaGuerre, John G. 1974. "Afro-Indian Relations in Trinidad and Tobago." *Caribbean Issues* 1, no. 1:49–61.
———. 1982. *The Politics of Communalism*. 2d ed. Port-of-Spain: Pan-Caribbean Publications.
———, ed. 1985. *Calcutta to Caroni*. 2d ed. St. Augustine: Extra-Mural Unit, University of the West Indies.
Lamming, George. 1985. "The Role of the Intellectual in the Caribbean." *Cimarrón* 1, no. 1:11–22.
Lamphere, Louise. 1987. *From Working Daughters to Working Mothers*. Ithaca: Cornell University Press.
Lewis, David E. 1991. "The North American Free Trade Agreement (NAFTA) and Its Impact on the Caribbean Basin Economies." *Caribbean Studies* 24, nos. 3 and 4:99–116.
Lewis, Gordon K. 1968. *The Growth of the Modern West Indies*. New York: Monthly Review Press.
———. 1985. "The Contemporary Caribbean: A General Overview." In Sidney W.

Mintz and Sally Price, eds., *Caribbean Contours*, pp. 219–50. Baltimore: Johns Hopkins University Press.

Lewis, W. Arthur. 1950. "The Industrialisation of the British West Indies." *Caribbean Economic Review* 2, no. 1:1–61.

Lieber, Michael. 1981. *Street Scenes: Afro-American Culture in Urban Trinidad.* Cambridge: Mass.: Schenkman.

Lincoln, James R., and Jon Miller. 1979. "Work and Friendship Ties in Organizations: A Comparative Analysis of Relational Networks." *Administrative Science Quarterly* 24:181–99.

LiPuma, Edward, and Sarah Keene Meltzoff. 1989. "Toward a Theory of Culture and Class: An Iberian Example." *American Ethnologist* 16, no. 2:313–34.

London, Clement B. G. 1991. *On Wings of Change: Self-Portrait of a Developing Caribbean Country, Trinidad-Tobago.* Wellesley, Mass.: Calaloux Publications.

Long, Frank. 1986. "Employment Effects of Multinational Enterprises in Export Processing Zones in the Caribbean." Working Paper No. 42. Multinational Enterprises Programme, International Labour Office, Geneva.

Lovelace, Earl. 1979. *The Dragon Can't Dance.* London: Longman.

Lukes, Steven. 1973. *Emile Durkheim: His Life and Work.* London: Allen Lane.

———. 1974. *Power: A Radical View.* London: Macmillan.

Mackenzie, Gavin. 1980. Review of *Marxism and Class Theory: A Bourgeois Critique*, by Frank Parkin. *British Journal of Sociology* 31, no. 4:582–84.

Magid, Alvin. 1988. *Urban Nationalism: A Study of Political Development in Trinidad.* Gainesville: University Presses of Florida.

Maingot, Anthony P. 1983. "Caribbean Studies as Area Studies: Past Performances and Recent Stirrings." *Caribbean Educational Bulletin* 10, no. 1:1–14.

Malik, Yogendra K. 1971. *East Indians in Trinidad.* New York: Oxford University Press.

Mangru, Basdeo. 1987. "The Sex Ratio Disparity and its Consequences under the Indenture in British Guiana." In David Dabydeen and Brinsley Samaroo, eds., *India in the Caribbean*, pp. 211–30. London: Hansib/University of Warwick.

Market Facts and Opinions, Ltd. 1986. "How Are the Women in Our Market Coping with the Recession[?]" Report by Market Facts and Opinoins, Ltd., Port-of-Spain. October.

Martínez-Alier, Verena. 1989 [1974]. *Marriage, Class, and Colour in Nineteenth-Century Cuba: A Study of Racial Attitudes and Sexual Values in a Slave Society.* Ann Arbor: University of Michigan Press.

Marx, Karl. 1961 [1844]. *The Economic and Philosophical Manuscripts of 1844.* Translated by T. B. Bottomore. In Erich Fromm, *Marx's Concept of Man*, pp. 87–196. New York: Frederick Ungar.

———. 1967 [1867]. *Capital.* Vol. I. New York: International Publishers.

———. 1976 [1867]. *Capital.* Vol. I. New York: Vintage Books.

Massiah, Joycelin. 1986. "Work in the Lives of Caribbean Women." *Social and Economic Studies* 35, no. 2:177–239.

Mathurin, Lucille. 1974. "A Historical Study of Women in Jamaica from 1655 to 1844." Ph.D. dissertation. University of the West Indies, Mona.

Mendes, Alfred H. 1984 [1935]. *Black Fauns.* London: New Beacon Books.

Mendes, John. 1986. *Cote ce Cote la: Trinidad and Tobago Dictionary*. Arima, Trinidad: John Mendes.

Merrill, Michael. 1978–1979. "Raymond Williams and the Theory of English Marxism." *Radical History Review* 19:9–31.

McGregor, Douglas. 1960. *The Human Side of Enterprise*. New York: McGraw-Hill.

McKay, Lesley, 1993. "Women's Contribution to Tourism in Negril, Jamaica." In Janet H. Momsen, ed., *Women and Change in the Caribbean*, pp. 278–86. Bloomington: Indiana University Press.

Miller, Daniel. 1991. "Absolute Freedom in Trinidad," *Man* 26, no. 2:323–41.

———. 1992. "The Young and the Restless in Trinidad: A Case of the Local and the Global in Mass Consumption." In R. Silverstone and E. Hirsch, eds., *Consuming Technologies*, pp. 163–82. London: Routledge.

———. 1993. "Christmas Against Materialism in Trinidad." In Daniel Miller, ed., *Unwrapping Christmas*, pp. 134–53. Oxford: Oxford University Press.

———. 1994. *Modernity: An Ethnographic Approach: Dualism and Mass Consumption in Trinidad*. Oxford: Berg.

Millette, James. 1970. *The Genesis of Crown Colony Government: Trinidad, 1783–1810*. Cuerpe, Trinidad: Moko.

Mintz, Sidney W. 1971. "Men, Women, and Trade." *Comparative Studies in Society and History* 13, no. 3:247–69.

———. 1973. "Introduction." In Peter J. Wilson, *Crab Antics*. New Haven: Yale University Press.

———. 1977. "The So-Called World System: Local Initiative and Local Response." *Dialectical Anthropology* 2, no. 2:253–70.

———. 1978. "Was the Plantation Slave a Proletarian?" *Review* 2, no. 1:81–98.

———. 1987. "Labor and Ethnicity: The Caribbean Conjuncture." In Richard Tardanico, ed., *Crises in the Caribbean Basin*, pp. 47–57. Beverly Hills: Sage.

———. 1989 [1974]. *Caribbean Transformations*. New York: Columbia University Press.

Mittelholzer, Edgar. 1974 [1950]. *A Morning at the Office*. London: Heinemann.

Mohammed, Patricia. 1987. "Domestic Workers in the Caribbean." In Women's International Resource Exchange, *Women in the Rebel Tradition: The English-Speaking Caribbean*, pp. 12–15. New York: Women's International Resource Exchange.

———. 1988a. "The 'Creolization' of Indian Women in Trinidad." In Selwyn Ryan, ed., *Trinidad and Tobago: The Independence Experience 1962–1987*, pp. 381–97. St. Augustine: Institute of Social and Economic Research, University of the West Indies.

———. 1988b. "The Caribbean Family Revisited." In Patricia Mohammed and Catherine Shepherd, eds., *Gender in Caribbean Development*, pp. 170–82. St. Augustine: Institute of Social and Economic Research, Univeresity of the West Indies.

———. 1989. "Women's Responses in the Seventies and Eighties in Trinidad: A Country Report." *Caribbean Quarterly* 35, nos. 1 and 2:36–45.

———. 1993. "Structures of Experience: Gender, Ethnicity, and Class in the Lives of Two East Indian Women." In Kevin A. Yelvington, ed., *Trinidad Ethnicity*, pp. 208–34. Knoxville: University of Tennessee Press.

Moses, Yolanda T. 1977. "Female Status, the Family, and Male Dominance in a West Indian Community." *Signs* 3, no. 1:142–53.
Munasinghe, Viranjini. 1992. "Renovating National Identity: The East Indian Struggle in Trinidad." Paper presented to the 91st Annual Meetings of the American Anthropological Association, San Francisco. December 2–6.
Murphy, Raymond. 1986. "Weberian Closure Theory: A Contribution to the Ongoing Assessment." *British Journal of Sociology* 37, no. 1:21–41.
Naipaul, V. S. 1981 [1962]. *The Middle Passage*. New York: Vintage Books.
Newson, Linda. 1976. *Aboriginal and Spanish Colonial Trinidad*. New York: Academic Press.
Nicholls, David G. 1971. "East Indians and Black Power in Trinidad." *Race* 12, no. 4:283–326.
Niehoff, Arthur, and Juanita Niehoff. 1960. *East Indians in the West Indies*. Milwaukee: Milwaukee Public Museum.
Nunes, Frederick E. 1987. "Culture, Motivation, and Organizational Performance." *Asset* 5, no. 2:3–16.
Okpaluba, Chuks. 1975. *Statutory Regulation of Collective Bargaining*. Mona: Institute of Social and Economic Research, University of the West Indies.
Ong, Aiwha. 1987. *Spirits of Resistance and Capitalist Discipline: Factory Women in Malaysia*. Albany: State University of New York Press.
———. 1991. "The Gender and Labor Politics of Postmodernity." *Annual Review of Anthropology* 20:279–309.
Ortner, Sherry B. 1984. "Theory in Anthropology Since the Sixties." *Comparative Studies in Society and History* 26, no. 1:126–66.
Ortner, Sherry B., and Harriet Whitehead. 1981. "Introduction: Accounting for Sexual Meanings." In Sherry B. Ortner and Harriet Whitehead, eds., *Sexual Meanings: The Cultural Construction of Gender and Sexuality*, pp. 1–27. New York: Cambridge University Press.
Oxaal, Ivar. 1968. *Black Intellectuals Come to Power*. Cambridge, Mass.: Schenkman.
———. 1971. *Race and Revolutionary Consciousness*. Cambridge, Mass.: Schenkman.
Parkin, Frank. 1979. *Marxism and Class Theory: A Bourgeois Critique*. London: Tavistock.
Parmar, Pratiba. 1982. "Gender, Race, and Class: Asian Women in Resistance." In Centre for Contemporary Cultural Studies, University of Birmingham, *The Empire Strikes Back*, pp. 237–75. London: Hutchinson.
Parris, Carl. 1976. "Capital or Labour? The Decision to Introduce the Industrial Stabilisation Act in Trinidad and Tobago, March 1965." Working Paper No. 8. Institute of Social and Economic Research, Univerity of the West Indies, Mona.
———. 1983. "Reasource Ownership and the Prospects for Democracy: The Case of Trinidad and Tobago." In Paget Henry and Carl Stone, eds., *The Newer Caribbean*, pp. 313–26. Philadelphia: Institute for the Study of Human Issues.
———. 1985. "Power and Privilege in Trinidad and Tobago." *Social and Economic Studies* 34, no. 2:97–109.
Patterson, Orlando. 1967. *The Sociology of Slavery*. London: MacGibbon and Key.

Paul, Cecil. 1985. "The Past, Present, and Future Role of Women in the Trade Union Movement in Trinidad and Tobago." Paper presented to the Women's Seminar of the Oilfields Workers' Trade Union, Port-of-Spain. May 11.

Payne, Anthony. 1980. *The Politics of the Caribbean Community, 1961–79: Regional Integration Among New States*. New York: St. Martin's Press.

Pearson, Ruth. 1993. "Gender and New Technology in the Caribbean: New Work for Women?" In Janet H. Momsen, ed., *Women and Change in the Caribbean*, pp. 287–95. Bloomington: Indiana University Press.

Polanyi, Karl. 1957 [1944]. *The Great Transformation: The Political and Economic Origin of Our Time*. Boston: Beacon Books.

Pollert, Anna. 1981. *Girls, Wives, Factory Lives*. London: Macmillan.

Portes, Alejandro, and John Walton. 1981. *Labor, Class, and the International System*. New York: Academic Press.

Posel, Deborah. 1983. "Rethinking the 'Race-Class Debate' in South African Historiography." *Social Dynamics* 9, no. 1:50–66.

Poynting, Jeremy. 1987. "East Indian Women in the Caribbean: Experience and Voice." In David Dabydeen and Brinsley Samaroo, eds., *India in the Caribbean*, pp. 231–63. London: Hansib/University of Warwick.

Powell, Dorian L. 1976. "Female Labour Force Participation and Fertility: An Exploratory Study of Jamaican Women." *Social and Economic Studies* 25, no. 3:234–58.

Premdas, Ralph. 1993. "Ethnic Conflict in Trinidad and Tobago: Domination and Reconciliation." In Kevin A. Yelvington, ed., *Trinidad Ethnicity*, pp. 136–60. Knoxville: University of Tennessee Press.

Premdas, Ralph, and Eric St. Cyr, eds. 1991. *Sir Arthur Lewis: An Economic and Political Portrait*. Mona: Regional Programme of Monetary Studies, Institute of Social and Economic Research, University of the West Indies.

Pyde, Peter. 1990. "Gender and Crab Antics in Tobago: Using Wilson's Reputation and Respectability." Paper presented to the 89th Annual Meetings of the American Anthropological Association, New Orleans. November 28–December 2.

Ramdin, Ron. 1982. *From Chattel Slave to Wage Earner: A History of Trade Unionism in Trinidad and Tobago*. London: Martin, Brian, and O'Keefe.

Ramesar, Marianne D. 1976. "Pattern of Regional Settlement and Economic Activity by Immigrant Groups in Trinidad, 1851–1900." *Social and Economic Studies* 25, no. 3:187–215.

Ramsaran, Ramesh, 1992. "Growth, Employment, and the Standard of Living in Selected Commonwealth Caribbean Countries." *Caribbean Studies* 25, nos. 1 and 2: 103–22.

Rampersad, Frank. [1963?]. *Growth and Structural Change in the Economy of Trinidad and Tobago, 1951–1961*. Mona: Institute of Social and Economic Research, University of the West Indies.

Reddock, Rhoda E. 1984. "Women, Labour, and Struggle in 20th Century Trinidad and Tobago: 1898–1960." Ph.D. dissertation. University of Amsterdam.

———. 1985a. "Women and Slavery in the Caribbean: A Feminist Perspective." *Latin American Perspectives* 12, no. 1:63–80.

———. 1985b. "Freedom Denied: Indian Women and Indentureship in Trinidad and Tobago, 1845–1917." *Economic and Political Weekly* 20:79–87.

———. 1986. "Indian Women and Indentureship in Trinidad and Tobago, 1845–1917: Freedom Denied." *Caribbean Quarterly* 32, nos. 3 and 4:27–49.

———. 1988. "Women and the Slave Plantation Economy in the Caribbean." In S. Jay Kleinberg, ed., *Retrieving Women's History*, pp. 105–32. Oxford: Berg/UNESCO.

———. 1989. "Historical and Contemporary Perspectives: The Case of Trinidad and Tobago." In Keith Hart, ed., *Women and the Sexual Division of Labour in the Caribbean*, pp. 47–65. Mona: Consortium Graduate School of Social Sciences, University of the West Indies.

———. 1990. "Women and Garment Production in Trinidad and Tobago, 1900–1960." *Social and Economic Studies* 39, no. 1:89–125.

———. 1991. "Social Mobility in Trinidad and Tobago, 1960–1980." In Selwyn Ryan, ed., *Social and Occupational Stratification in Contemporary Trinidad and Tobago*, pp. 210–33. St. Augustine: Institute of Social and Economic Research, University of the West Indies.

———. 1993. "Transformation in the Needle Trades: Women in Garment and Textile Production in Early Twentieth Century Trinidad and Tobago." In Janet H. Momsen, ed., *Women and Change in the Caribbean*, pp. 249–62. Bloomington: Indiana University Press.

———. 1994. *Women, Labour, and Politics in Trinidad and Tobago: A History*. London: Zed Books.

Rigby, Peter. 1992. *Cattle, Capitalism, and Class: Ilparakuyo Maasai Transformations*. Philadelphia: Temple University Press.

Robben, Antonius C. G. M. 1989. *Sons of the Sea Goddess: Economic Practice and Discursive Conflict in Brazil*. New York: Columbia University Press.

Roberts, George W. 1952. "A Life Table for a West Indian Slave Population." *Population Studies* 5, no. 3:238–43.

Roberts, George W., and Lloyd Braithwaite. 1967. "Mating Among East Indian and Non-Indian Women in Trinidad." *Research Papers*, pp. 148–85. Port-of-Spain: Central Statistical Office.

Rohlehr, Gordon. 1985. " 'Man Talking to Man': Calypso and Social Confrontation in Trinidad, 1970 to 1984." *Caribbean Quarterly* 31, no. 2:1–13.

———. 1987. "Fantasy Life of the Calypsonian." *Trinidad and Tobago Review*, June, pp. 17–18.

———. 1988. "Images of Men and Women in the 1930s Calypsoes: The Sociology of Food Acquisition in the Context of Survivalism." In Patricia Mohammed and Catherine Shepherd, eds., *Gender in Caribbean Development*, pp. 232–306. St. Augustine: Institute of Social and Economic Research, University of the West Indies.

———. 1990. *Calypso and Society in Pre-Independence Trinidad*. Port-of-Spain: Gordon Rohlehr.

Roseberry, William. 1988. "Political Economy." *Annual Review of Anthropology* 17:161–85.

———. 1989. *Anthropologies and Histories*. New Brunswick: Rutgers University Press.

Roy, Donald. 1974. "Sex in the Factory: Informal Heterosexual Relationships between Supervisors and Work Groups." In Clifton Bryant, ed., *Deviant Behavior*, pp. 44–66. Chicago: Rand McNally.

Ryan, Selwyn. 1972. *Race and Nationalism in Trinidad and Tobago*. Toronto: University of Toronto Press.

———. 1981. "The Church that Williams Built: Electoral Possibilities in Trinidad and Tobago." *Caribbean Review* 10, no. 2:12–13, 45–46.

———. 1982. "The Role of Management in Productivity." In Trinidad and Tobago, *National Consultation on Productivity Report*, pp. 41–46. Port-of-Spain: Ministry of Labour, Social Security, and Cooperatives.

———. 1988a. "Political Change and Economic Reconstruction in Trinidad and Tobago." *Caribbean Affairs* 1, no. 1:126–60.

———. 1988b. "Popular Attitudes Towards Independence, Race Relations, and the People's National Movement." In Selwyn Ryan, ed., *Trinidad and Tobago: The Independence Experience 1962–1987*, pp. 217–28. St. Augustine: Institute of Social and Economic Research, University of the West Indies.

———. 1989. *Revolution and Reaction: Parties and Politics in Trinidad and Tobago, 1970–1981*. St. Augustine: Institute of Social and Economic Research, University of the West Indies.

———. 1990. *The Disillusioned Electorate: The Politics of Succession in Trinidad and Tobago*. Port-of-Spain: Imprint Caribbean.

———. 1991a. "Social Stratification in Trinidad and Tobago: Lloyd Braithwaite Revisited." In Selwyn Ryan, ed., *Social and Occupational Stratification in Contemporary Trinidad and Tobago*, pp. 58–79. St. Augustine: Institute of Social and Economic Research, University of the West Indies.

———. 1991b. *The Muslimeen Grab for Power: Race, Religion, and Revolution in Trinidad and Tobago*. Port-of-Spain: Imprint.

Ryan, Selwyn, Eddie Greene, and Jack Harewood. 1979. *The Confused Electorate: A Study of Political Attitudes and Opinions in Trinidad and Tobago*. St. Augustine: Institute of Social and Economic Research, University of the West Indies.

Sacks, Karen Brodkin. 1989. "Toward a Unified Theory of Class, Race, and Gender." *American Ethnologist* 16, no. 3:534–50.

Safa, Helen I. 1975. "Class Consciousness Among Working Class Women in Latin America: A Case Study of Puerto Rico." *Politics and Society*, 5, no. 3:377–94.

———. 1981. "Runaway Shops and Female Employment: The Search for Cheap Labor." *Signs* 7, no. 2:418–34.

———. 1983. "The CBI and Women Workers." In *Concerning Women in Development*, pp. 1–6. Extra-Mural Department, University of the West Indies, Cave Hill. September.

———. 1986. "Economic Autonomy and Sexual Equality in Caribbean Society." *Social and Economic Studies* 35, no. 3:1–21.

———. 1990. "Women and Industrialisation in the Caribbean." In Sharon Stichter and Jane L. Parpart, eds., *Women, Employment, and the Family in the International Division of Labour*, pp. 72–97. Philadelphia: Temple University Press.

———. 1995. *The Myth of the Male Breadwinner: Women and Industrialization in the Caribbean*. Boulder: Westview Press.

Samaroo, Brinsley. 1987. "Two Abolitions: African Slavery and East Indian Inden-

tureship." In David Dabydeen and Brinsley Samaroo, eds., *India in the Caribbean*, pp. 25–41. London: Hansib/University of Warwick.
Sampath, Niels M. 1993. "An Evaluation of the 'Creolisation' of Trinidad East Indian Adolescent Masculinity." In Kevin A. Yelvington, ed., *Trinidad Ethnicity*, pp. 235–53. Knoxville: University of Tennessee Press.
Sander, Reinhard W., ed. 1978. *From Trinidad: An Anthology of Early West Indian Writing*. New York: Africana.
———. 1988. *The Trinidad Awakening: West Indian Literature of the Nineteen-Thirties*. Westport, Conn.: Greenwood Press.
Sandoval, José Miguel. 1983. "State Capitalism in a Petroleum-Based Economy: The Case of Trinidad and Tobago." In Fitzroy Ambursley and Robin Cohen, eds., *Crisis in the Caribbean*, pp. 247–68. New York: Monthly Review Press.
Schoepfle, Gregory K., and Jorge F. Pérez-López. 1989. "Export Assembly Operations in Mexico and the Caribbean." *Journal of Interamerican Studies and World Affairs* 31, no. 4:131–61.
Scott, James C. 1985. *Weapons of the Weak: Everyday Forms of Peasant Resistance*. New Haven: Yale University Press.
Scott, Joan. 1988. *Gender and the Politics of History*. New York: Columbia University Press.
———. 1992. "Multiculturalism and the Politics of Identity." *October* 61:12–19.
Sebastien, Raphael. 1978. "The Development of Capitalism in Trinidad, 1845–1917." Ph.D. dissertation. Howard University.
Seers, Dudley. 1964. "Mechanism of an Open Petroleum Economy." *Social and Economic Studies* 13, no. 2:233–42.
Segal, Daniel A. 1987. "Nationalism in a Colonial State: A Study of Trinidad and Tobago." Ph.D. dissertation. University of Chicago.
———. 1993. " 'Race' and 'Colour' in Pre-Independence Trinidad and Tobago." In Kevin A. Yelvington, ed., *Trinidad Ethnicity*, pp. 81–115. Knoxville: University of Tennessee Press.
Seidler, Victor J. 1987. "Reason, Desire, and Male Sexuality." In Pat Caplan, ed., *The Cultural Construction of Sexuality*, pp. 82–112. London: Tavistock.
Selvon, Samuel. 1979 [1952]. *A Brighter Sun*. London: Longman.
Senior, Olive. 1991. *Working Miracles: Women's Lives in the English-Speaking Caribbean*. Bloomington: Indiana University Press.
Sheridan, Richard B. 1985. *Doctors and Slaves: A Medical and Demographic History of Slavery in the British West Indies, 1680–1834*. Cambridge: Cambridge University Press.
Simmel, Georg. 1978. *The Philosophy of Money*. Boston: Routledge and Kegan Paul.
Simpson, Joy M. 1973. *A Demographic Analysis of Internal Migration in Trinidad and Tobago*. Mona: Institute of Social and Economic Research, University of the West Indies.
Singh, Kelvin. 1985. "Indians and the Larger Society." In John G. LaGuerre, ed., *Calcutta to Caroni*, 2d ed., pp. 33–60. St. Augustine: Extra-Mural Unit, University of the West Indies.
———. 1988. *The Bloodstained Tombs: The Muharram Massacre in Trinidad, 1884*. London: Macmillan.

Smith, M. G. 1962. *Kinship and Community in Carriacou*. New Haven: Yale University Press.
Sollors, Werner, ed. 1989. *The Invention of Ethnicity*. New York: Oxford University Press.
Solomos, John. 1986. "Varieties of Marxist Conceptions of 'Race', Class, and the State: A Critical Analysis." In John Rex and David Mason, eds., *Theories of Race and Ethnic Relations*, pp. 84–109. Cambridge: Cambridge University Press.
Stepick, Alex III. 1992. "The Refugees Nobody Wants: Haitians in Miami." In Guillermo J. Grenier and Alex Stepick III eds., *Miami Now! Immigration, Ethnicity, and Social Change*, pp. 57–82. Gainesville: University Press of Florida.
Stewart, John O. 1973. "Coolie and Creole: Differential Adaptations in a Neo-Plantation Village—Trinidad, West Indies." Ph.D. dissertation. University of California, Los Angeles.
———. 1986. "Patronage and Control in the Trinidad Carnival." In Victor W. Turner and Edward M. Bruner, eds., *The Anthropology of Experience*, pp. 289–315. Urbana: University of Illinois Press.
Stichter, Sharon, 1990. "Women, Employment, and the Family: Current Debates." In Sharon Stichter and Jane L. Parpart, eds., *Women, Employment, and the Family in the International Division of Labour*, pp. 11–71. Philadelphia: Temple University Press.
Stoffle, Richard W. 1977. "Industrial Impact on Family Formation in Barbados, West Indies." *Ethnology* 16, no. 3:253–67.
Stolcke, Verena. 1993. "Is Sex to Gender as Race is to Ethnicity?" In Teresa del Valle, ed., *Gendered Anthropology*, pp. 17–37. London: Routledge.
Sutton, Constance R. 1974. "Cultural Duality in the Caribbean." Review of *Crab Antics* by Peter J. Wilson. *Caribbean Studies* 14, no. 2:96–101.
Sutton, Constance R., and Susan Makiesky-Barrow. 1977. "Social Inequality and Sexual Status in Barbados." In Alice Schlegel, ed., *Sexual Stratification: A Cross-Cultural View*, pp. 292–326. New York: Columbia University Press.
Sutton, Paul. 1983. "Black Power in Trinidad and Tobago: The 'Crisis' of 1970." *Journal of Commonwealth and Comparative Politics* 21, no. 2:115–32.
———. 1984. "Trinidad and Tobago: Oil Capitalism and the 'Presidential Power' of Eric Williams." In Anthony Payne and Paul Sutton, eds., *Dependency Under Challenge: The Political Economy of the Commonwealth Caribbean*, pp. 43–76. Manchester: Manchester University Press.
Thomas, Nicholas. 1989. *Out of Time*. Cambridge: Cambridge University Press.
———. 1992. "The Inversion of Tradition." *American Ethnologist* 19, no. 2:213–32.
Thomas, Roy, ed. 1987. *The Trinidad Labour Riots of 1937: Perspectives Fifty Years Later*. St. Augustine: Extra-Mural Studies Unit, University of the West Indies.
Thoumi, Francisco E. 1989. "Thwarted Comparative Advantage, Economic Policy, and Industrialization in the Dominican Republic and Trinidad and Tobago." *Journal of Interamerican Studies and World Affairs* 31, nos. 1 and 2:147–68.
Tilly, Charles. 1984. *Big Structures, Large Processes, Huge Comparisons*. New York: Russell Sage Foundation.
Trinidad and Tobago. 1959. *Report on the Manpower Situation in Trinidad and Tobago*. No. 1, March. Port-of-Spain: Government Printing.

———. 1972. *Continuous Sample Survey of Population Bulletin*. Vol. 1, no. 12. Port-of-Spain: Government Printing.

———. 1973. "Report of the Commission of Enquiry into the Miss Trinidad and Tobago Beauty Contest 1971, and the Organization of Such Contests and Competitions in Trinidad and Tobago." Report presented to the Acting Governor-General Sir Arthur H. McShine.

———. 1976. *Report of the National Commission on the Status of Women*. Port-of-Spain: National Commission on the Status of Women.

———. 1979. *Report of the Commission of Enquiry into all Aspects of the Garment Industry in Trinidad and Tobago*. Port-of-Spain: Government Printing.

———. 1980. *Population and Housing Census 1980*. Port-of-Spain: Government Printing.

———. 1987a. *Annual Statistical Digest 1985*. Port-of-Spain: Central Statistical Office.

———. 1987b. *Economic Indicators: Oct.–Dec. 1986*. Port-of-Spain: Central Statistical Office.

———. 1987c. *Review of the Economy 1986*. Port-of-Spain: Central Statistical Office.

———. 1987d. *Budget Speech 1987*. Port-of-Spain: House of Representatives.

Trotman, David V. 1986. *Crime in Trinidad*. Knoxville: University of Tennessee Press.

Turner, Terisa, 1982. "Multinational Enterprises and Employment in the Caribbean with Special Reference to Trinidad and Tobago." Working Paper No. 20. Multinational Enterprises Programme, International Labour Office, Geneva.

Vaux, Alan. 1985. "Variations in Social Support Associated with Gender, Ethnicity, and Age." *Journal of Social Issues* 41, no. 1:89–110.

Verteuil, Anthony de. 1987. *A History of Diego Martin, 1784–1884*. Port-of-Spain: Paria.

Vertovec, Steven. 1991. "East Indians and Anthropologists: A Critical Review." *Social and Economic Studies* 40, no. 1:133–69.

———. 1992. *Hindu Trinidad: Religion, Ethnicity, and Socio-Economic Change*. London: Macmillan.

Wade, Peter. 1993. " 'Race,' Nature, and Culture." *Man* 28, no. 1:17–34.

Wajcman, Judy. 1983. *Women in Control: Dilemmas of a Workers Co-Operative*. Milton Keynes: Open University Press.

Walcott, Clotil. 1987. "Domestic Workers' Rights." In Women's International Resource Exchange, *Women in the Rebel Tradition: The English-Speaking Caribbean*, pp. 16–17. New York: Women's International Resource Exchange.

Ward, Kathryn. 1990. "Introduction and Overview." In Kathryn Ward, ed., *Women Workers and Global Restructuring*, pp. 1–22. Ithaca: ILR Press.

Warner, Keith Q. 1982. *Kaiso! The Trinidad Calypso*. Washington, D.C.: Three Continents Press.

———. 1993. "Ethnicity and the Contemporary Calypso." In Kevin A. Yelvington, ed., *Trinidad Ethnicity*, pp. 275–91. Knoxville: University of Tennessee Press.

Warner-Lewis, Maureen. 1991. *Guinea's Other Suns: The African Dynamic in Trinidad Culture*. Dover, Mass.: Majority Press.

Warren, Kay B., and Susan C. Bourque. 1991. "Women, Technology, and International Development Ideologies." In Micaela di Leonardo, ed., *Gender at the Crossroads of Knowledge: Feminist Anthropology in the Postmodern Era*, pp. 278–311. Berkeley: University of California Press.

Warren, Paul. 1993. "Why Marxists Should Still Be Interested in Exploitation." In Milton Fisk, ed., pp. 192–204. Atlantic Highlands, N.J.: *Justice*, Humanities Press.

Wartenberg, Thomas E. 1985. "Marx and the Social Constitution of Value." *Philosophical Forum* 16, no. 4: 249–73.

———. 1990. *The Forms of Power: From Domination to Transformation*. Philadelphia: Temple University Press.

Weber, Max. 1968. *Economy and Society*. Edited by Guenther Roth and Claus Wittich. New York: Bedminster.

Weismantel, M. J. 1988. *Food, Gender, and Poverty in the Ecuadorian Andes*. Philadelphia: University of Pennsylvania Press.

Westwood, Sallie. 1984. *All Day, Every Day: Factory and Family in the Making of Women's Lives*. London: Pluto Press.

Whitehead, Ann. 1976. "Sexual Antagonism in Herefordshire." In Diana Leonard Barker and Sheila Allen, eds., *Dependence and Exploitation in Work and Marriage*, pp. 169–203. London: Longman.

———. 1979. "Some Preliminary Notes on the Subordination of Women." *IDS Bulletin* 10, no. 3:10–13.

Williams, Brackette F. 1989. "A Class Act: Anthropology and the Race to Nation across Ethnic Terrain." *Annual Review of Anthropology* 18:401–44.

———. 1990. "Nationalism, Traditionalism, and the Problem of Cultural Inauthenticity." In Richard Fox, ed., *Nationalist Ideologies and the Production of National Cultures*, pp. 112–29. Washington, D.C.: American Anthropological Association.

———. 1991. *Stains on My Name, War in My Veins: Guyana and the Politics of Cultural Struggle*. Durham: Duke University Press.

Williams, Eric E. 1961. *Massa Day Done: A Masterpiece of Political and Sociological Analysis*. Port-of-Spain: PNM Publishing.

———. 1964. *History of the People of Trinidad and Tobago*. London: Andre Deutsch.

Williams, Gwendoline A. 1987. "Management and Development in the Business/Industrial Environment of Trinidad and Tobago: A Focus on Major Socio-Cultural Issues." *Asset* 5, no. 2:17–33.

Williams, Raymond. 1977. *Marxism and Literature*. London: Oxford University Press.

Willis, Paul. 1981 [1977]. *Learning to Labor: How Working Class Kids Get Working Class Jobs*. New York: Columbia University Press.

Wilson, Peter J. 1969. "Reputation and Respectability: A Suggestion for Caribbean Ethnography." *Man* 4, no. 1:70–84.

———. 1971. "Caribbean Crews: Peer Groups and Male Society." *Caribbean Studies* 10, no. 4:18–34.

———. 1973. *Crab Antics*. New Haven: Yale University Press.

Wiltshire-Brodber, Rosina. 1988. "Gender, Race, and Class in the Caribbean." In Patricia Mohammed and Catherine Shepherd, eds., *Gender in Caribbean Development*, pp. 142–55. St. Augustine: Institute of Social and Economic Research, University of the West Indies.

Wolf, Eric R. 1990. "Distinguished Lecture: Facing Power—Old Insights, New Questions." *American Anthropologist* 92, no. 3:586–96.
Wood, Donald. 1968. *Trinidad in Transition*. London: Oxford University Press.
Woost, Michael D. 1993. "Nationalizing the Local Past in Sri Lanka: Histories of Nation and Development in a Sinhalese Village." *American Ethnologist* 20, no. 3:502–21.
World Fertility Survey. 1981. *Trinidad and Tobago Fertility Survey 1977*. Port-of-Spain: Central Statistical Office.
Yelvington, Kevin A. 1985. "The Context of Acculturation: Occupational Diversification and Cultural Change in Trinidad and Tobago." M.A. thesis. Florida International University.
———. 1987. "Vote Dem Out: The Demise of the PNM in Trinidad and Tobago." *Caribbean Review* 14, no. 4:8–33.
———. 1990a. "Ethnicity, Class, and Gender at Work in a Trinidadian Factory." D.Phil. thesis. University of Sussex.
———. 1990b. "Gender, Ethnicity, and the Labor Process in a Trinidadian Factory." Discussion Paper No. 9. Center for Labor Research and Studies, Florida International University, Miami.
———. 1991a. "Ethnicity as Practice? A Comment on Bentley." *Comparative Studies in Society and History* 33, no. 1:158–68.
———. 1991b. "Trinidad and Tobago, 1988–1989." In James A. Malloy and Eduardo A. Gamarra, eds., *Latin American and Caribbean Contemporary Record*, vol. 8, pp. B459–77. New York: Holmes and Meier.
———. 1991c. "A Fourth Shift? Making '*Connec*' and Keeping Support Among Female Factory Workers in Trinidad." Paper presented to the 13th Annual Meetings of the Southern Regional Science Association, Miami. April 12.
———. 1992. Review of *Working Miracles: Women's Lives in the English-Speaking Caribbean* by Olive Senior. *Hispanic American Historical Review* 72, no. 4:616–18.
———, ed. 1993a. *Trinidad Ethnicity*. Knoxville: University of Tennessee Press.
———. 1993b. "Introduction: Trinidad Ethnicity." In Kevin A. Yelvington, ed., *Trinidad Ethnicity*, pp. 1–32. Knoxville: University of Tennessee Press.
———. 1993c. "Gender and Ethnicity at Work in a Trinidadian Factory." In Janet H. Momsen, ed., *Women and Change in the Caribbean*, pp. 263–77. Bloomington: Indiana University Press.
———. 1993d. "Ethnicity at Work in Trinidad." In Ralph Premdas, ed., *The Enigma of Ethnicity: An Analysis of Race in the Caribbean and the World*, pp. 99–122. St. Augustine: School of Continuing Studies, University of the West Indies.
Zavella, Patricia. 1988. "The Politics of Race and Gender: Organizing Chicana Cannery Workers in Northern California." In Ann Bookman and Sandra Morgen, eds., *Women and the Politics of Empowerment*, pp. 202–24. Philadelphia: Temple University Press.
———. 1991. "*Mujeres* in Factories: Race and Class Perspectives on Women, Work, and Family." In Micaela di Leonardo, ed., *Gender at the Crossroads of Knowledge: Feminist Anthropology in the Postmodern Era*, pp. 312–36. Berkeley: University of California Press.

Index